USDA

United States
Department of
Agriculture

Forest Service

Pacific Northwest
Research Station

General Technical
Report
PNW-GTR-610
September 2004

Methods for Integrated Modeling of Landscape Change:

Interior Northwest Landscape Analysis System

INLAS
Integrated Multiple
Management Objectives

INLAS Project
USDA FS PNW Research Station

Technical Editors

Jane L. Hayes is a research biological scientist, and **Alan A. Ager** is an operations research analyst, Forestry and Range Sciences Laboratory, 1401 Gekeler Lane, La Grande, OR 97850; and **R. James Barbour** is a research forest products technologist, Forestry Sciences Laboratory, P.O. Box 3890, Portland OR 97208-3890

Contributing Authors

Alan A. Ager is an operations research analyst, U.S. Department of Agriculture, Forest Service, Pacific Northwest Research Station, Forestry and Range Sciences Laboratory, 1401 Gekeler Lane, La Grande, OR 97850.
aager@fs.fed.us

Marti Aitken is a resource information manager, U.S. Department of Agriculture, Forest Service, Pacific Northwest Research Station, Forestry and Range Sciences Laboratory, 1401 Gekeler Lane, La Grande, OR 97850.
mtaiken@fs.fed.us

R. James Barbour is a research forest products technologist, U.S. Department of Agriculture, Forest Service, Pacific Northwest Research Station, Forestry Sciences Laboratory, 620 SW Main, Suite 400, Portland, OR 97205.
jbarbour01@fs.fed.us

Pete Bettinger is an associate professor, Daniel B. Warnell School of Forest Resources, University of Georgia, Athens, GA 30602.
pbettinger@smokey.forestry.uga.edu

Roger N. Clark is a research social scientist, U.S. Department of Agriculture, Forest Service, Pacific Northwest Research Station, Pacific Wildland Fire Sciences Laboratory, 400 N 34th Street, Suite 201, Seattle, WA 98103.
rnclark@fs.fed.us

Mark A. Finney is a research forester, U.S. Department of Agriculture, Forest Service, Rocky Mountain Research Station, Fire Sciences Laboratory, P.O. Box 8089, Missoula, MT 59807.
mfinney@fs.fed.us

David Graetz is a Ph.D. candidate, Department of Forest Resources, Oregon State University, Corvallis, OR 97331.

Jane L. Hayes is a research biological scientist, U.S. Department of Agriculture, Forest Service, Pacific Northwest Research Station, Forestry and Range Sciences Laboratory, 1401 Gekeler Lane, La Grande, OR 97850.
jlhayes@fs.fed.us

Miles Hemstrom is a research ecologist, U.S. Department of Agriculture, Forest Service, Pacific Northwest Research Station, Forestry Sciences Laboratory, 620 SW Main, Suite 400, Portland, OR 97205.
mhemstrom@fs.fed.us

Philip J. Howell is a fisheries biologist, U.S. Department of Agriculture, Forest Service, Pacific Northwest Region. Howell is located at the Forestry and Range Sciences Laboratory, 1401 Gekeler Lane, La Grande, OR 97850.
phowell@fs.fed.us

Bruce Johnson is a fish and wildlife biologist, Oregon Department of Fish and Wildlife, 1401 Gekeler Lane, La Grande, OR 97850.
johnsonbd@eou.edu

Jeffrey Kline is a research forester, U.S. Department of Agriculture, Forest Service, Pacific Northwest Research Station, Forestry Sciences Laboratory, 3200 SW Jefferson Way, Corvallis, OR 97331.
jkline@fs.fed.us

Gary J. Lettman is a principal forest economist, Oregon Department of Forestry, 2600 State Street, Salem, OR 97310.
glettman@odf.state.or.us

Douglas Maguire is an associate professor of silviculture, Department of Forest Science, Oregon State University, Corvallis, OR 97331.
Doug.Maguire@orst.edu

Robert Riggs is a research wildlife biologist, Boise Building Solutions, Northeast Oregon/Idaho Region, 1917 Jackson Street, La Grande, OR 97850.
RobertRiggs@BoiseBuilding.com

Craig L. Schmitt is a plant pathologist, U.S. Department of Agriculture, Forest Service, Blue Mountains Pest Management Service Center, 1401 Gekeler Lane, La Grande, OR 97850.
clschmitt@fs.fed.us

John Sessions is a university distinguished professor and Stewart Professor of forest engineering, Department of Forest Engineering, Oregon State University, Corvallis, OR 97331.
john.sessions@orst.edu

Ryan Singleton is a research forester, Department of Forest Science, Oregon State University, Corvallis, OR 97331.
Ryan.Singleton@orst.edu

Lowell H. Suring is a wildlife ecologist, U.S. Department of Agriculture, Forest Service, Terrestrial Wildlife Unit, Forestry Sciences Laboratory, 316 E Myrtle Street, Boise, ID 83702.
lsuring@fs.fed.us

Martin Vavra is a research range scientist, U.S. Department of Agriculture, Forest Service, Pacific Northwest Research Station, Forestry and Range Sciences Laboratory, 1401 Gekeler Lane, La Grande, OR 97850.
mvavra@fs.fed.us

Barbara C. Wales is a wildlife biologist, U.S. Department of Agriculture, Forest Service, Pacific Northwest Research Station, Forestry and Range Sciences Laboratory, 1401 Gekeler Lane, La Grande, OR 97850.
bwales@fs.fed.us

Michael J. Wisdom is a research wildlife biologist, U.S. Department of Agriculture, Forest Service, Pacific Northwest Research Station, Forest Service, Forestry and Range Sciences Laboratory, 1401 Gekeler Lane, La Grande, OR 97850.
mwisdom@fs.fed.us

Steven M. Wondzell is a research aquatic ecologist, U.S. Department of Agriculture, Forest Service, Pacific Northwest Research Station, Forestry Sciences Laboratory, 3625 93rd Ave., Olympia, WA 98512.
swondzell@fs.fed.us

Methods for Integrated Modeling of Landscape Change:

Interior Northwest Landscape Analysis System

Jane L. Hayes, Alan A. Ager, and R. James Barbour

Technical Editors

U.S. Department of Agriculture, Forest Service
Pacific Northwest Research Station
Portland, Oregon
General Technical Report PNW-GTR-610
September 2004

Abstract

Hayes, Jane L.; Ager, Alan. A.; Barbour, R. James, tech. eds. 2004. Methods for integrated modeling of landscape change: Interior Northwest Landscape Analysis System. Gen. Tech. Rep. PNW-GTR-610. Portland, OR: U.S. Department of Agriculture, Forest Service, Pacific Northwest Research Station. 218 p.

The Interior Northwest Landscape Analysis System (INLAS) links a number of resource, disturbance, and landscape simulations models to examine the interactions of vegetative succession, management, and disturbance with policy goals. The effects of natural disturbance like wildfire, herbivory, forest insects and diseases, as well as specific management actions are included. The outputs from simulations illustrate potential changes in aquatic conditions and terrestrial habitat, potential for wood utilization, and socioeconomic opportunities. The 14 chapters of this document outline the current state of knowledge in each of the areas covered by the INLAS project and describe the objectives and organization of the project. The project explores ways to integrate the effects of natural disturbances and management into planning and policy analyses; illustrate potential conflicts among current policies, natural distrubances, and management activities; and explore the policy, economics, and ecological constraints associated with the application of effective fuel treatments on midscale landscapes in the interior Northwest.

Keywords: Forest simulation analysis, midscale, vegetation succession, disturbance, management.

Preface

The concept of a process for evaluating policy direction and management options for subbasin-size landscapes in the interior West evolved from the Pacific Northwest Research Station's Research Initiative for Improving Forest Ecosystem Health and Productivity in Eastern Oregon and Washington. The Interior Northwest Landscape Analysis System (INLAS) project was initiated to explore this concept and began with meetings of resource managers and scientists from various disciplines and institutions. This group suggested ways to build an integrated set of tools and methods for addressing resource management questions on large, multiowner landscapes. The papers in this volume are the outcome of these meetings and document our initial approach to developing an integrated landscape analysis framework. Collectively, the papers illustrate the diversity of methods for modeling different resources and reflect the inherent complexity of linking models to create a functional framework for integrated resource analysis. We are still a long way from a perfect tool, the linkages among the chapters are not always apparent, and integration issues have not been consistently addressed. We cannot yet address the interrelationships between many key natural and anthropomorphic processes on large landscapes. We also found that integration forced scientists to generalize relationships and to summarize detailed research findings in order to incorporate their disciplines at the landscape scale of the INLAS framework. With a growing interest in integrated natural resource modeling, we concluded that, despite the fact that we have not solved all the problems associated with integrating information from different scientific disciplines, creating this document will provide a valuable resource for future researchers who want to understand how groups of scientists organize themselves for a project like INLAS. There are few examples of case studies of similar work in other regions, and to our knowledge, none that document such early stages of these projects' organization. The reader can learn from both the continuity and lack thereof among the chapters, and perhaps use this publication to learn new ways to deal with the dilemma of how to hybridize long-term research lineages into coherent ways of thinking about integrated natural resource management.

Acknowledgments

We thank the many disciplinary experts who reviewed the individual chapters. We appreciate the thoughtful reviews of the entire document provided by W. Connelly, T.M. Quigley, and T. Spies. Thanks also to Judy Mikowski for assistance with formatting the entire document. For their continued invaluable input throughout the INLAS project, we thank Kurt Wiedenmann and personnel from the La Grande Ranger District. We are also grateful for the many contributions of Bob Rainville to this project.

Contents

Chapter 1: A Framework for the Development and Application of INLAS: the Interior Northwest Landscape Analysis System

R. James Barbour, Alan A. Ager, and Jane L. Hayes[1]

Abstract

The Interior Northwest Landscape Analysis System is a partnership among researchers and natural resource managers from both the public and private sectors. The project is an effort to increase our understanding of the role of vegetative succession, natural disturbance, and management actions at the watershed scale. The effort will advance the development and application of integrated landscape-level planning tools (models, methods, and information) that use consistent assumptions and common data. Focusing on the subbasin (landscape units of about 202 300 ha) and smaller scales, we will demonstrate the use of existing and new landscape simulation tools to project future succession, disturbance, and management under various policy scenarios. These scenarios will compare different approaches to achieving short- and long-term ecosystem goals and the effects of regulatory constraints, ownership patterns, and limited budgets. Of specific interest is the measurement of the long-term cumulative effects of fuels management and other treatments on key resources. The project is using a 178 000 ha watershed in northeast Oregon to prototype modeling tools and methods. The results of landscape simulations will help to inform the debate over sustainability of forest, range, and aquatic ecosystems in the intermountain West.

Keywords: Forest simulation analysis, midscale, vegetative succession, disturbance, management.

[1] **R. James Barbour** is a research forest products techno ogist U S Department of Agricu ture Forest Service Pacific Northwest Research Station Forestry Sciences Laboratory 620 SW Main Suite 400 Port and OR 97205 **Alan A. Ager** is an operations research ana yst and **Jane L. Hayes** is a research bio ogica scientist U S Department of Agricu ture Forest Service Pacific Northwest Research Station Forestry and Range Sciences Laboratory 1401 Geke er Lane La Grande OR 97850

Introduction

Despite a decade of scientific assessments throughout the interior Pacific Northwest (e.g., Caraher et al. 1992, Everett et al. 1994, Gast et al. 1991, Quigley et al. 1996) and elsewhere (e.g., FEMAT 1993, Johnson 1996), the debate continues over management of forested and range lands, and aquatic systems. It is clear from these and other analyses that decades of human activities to reduce the risk of unwanted disturbances like wildfires and to extract goods and services have led to substantial changes in forest conditions and productivity. It is also evident that there is no simple remedy given landownership patterns, ecosystem-level management objectives, existing landscape conditions, and the complex array of state and federal regulatory constraints (e.g., Clean Water Act 1977, Endangered Species Act [ESA] 1973, National Environmental Policy Act 1969, National Forest Management Act 1976). Large areas of forest land in the intermountain West remain in conditions lending themselves to uncharacteristically large and severe wildfires and insect or disease outbreaks (Ottmar and Sandberg 2001). The problems are compounded by finite budgets and changing economic conditions and social concerns that can contribute to constraints on land managers (Quigley et al. 2001).

With the continued dispersal of human populations into areas that were once considered "wild," the problem of how to manage for natural disturbance over large areas while not impinging on human populations or negatively affecting the conservation of rare or valuable resources becomes increasingly complex. Much of the debate over how to manage federal lands is focused on the tradeoffs among active management to produce goods and services, moderate wildfire and other natural disturbances, and the long-term preservation of federally protected plant and animal species. A relevant policy question is whether short-term goals intended to protect aquatic and terrestrial habitat for species listed under the 1973 ESA might impede forest management activities that are necessary to improve the long-term sustainability of these species. In the Blue Mountains of northeast Oregon, management direction for resource protection and other amenities may prevent treatment of the majority of fuel-laden stands (Wilson et al., n.d.). Market conditions and operational costs further reduce the extent to which management can be applied to reduce risk from natural disturbances (Barbour et al., in press).

One thing that is clear from these debates is that society as a whole does not share a common strategic vision of future forested landscapes. A blueprint for restoring and maintaining these landscapes is needed that considers the combined effects of forest succession, disturbance, and management (Quigley et al. 2001). Many questions remain concerning efficient and cost-effective scheduling and spatial distribution of management activities, such as prescribed fire, thinning, and selective harvesting, on large landscapes to achieve specified goals over the long run (Finney Chapter 9). Further, we do not understand the long-term compatibilities among commodity production, recreational use, fire risks, fuel treatments, cumulative effects of management activities on key resources, and fish and wildlife habitat goals. Some hypothesize that restricting active management will eventually lead to large natural disturbances that will negate the net effect of protective resource policies. Others feel that management itself poses the greatest threat to sensitive resources. Unfortunately, the debate has been fed, in part, from conflicting projections of potential outcomes. Decisionmakers need unbiased and consistent information about the likely outcomes of different policies or management practices as they evaluate options.

Landscape simulation tools can aid in the development of strategic visions for managing forested and range lands by providing a means to project long-term changes from succession, management, and disturbance (e.g., Bettinger et al. Chapter 4, Johnson et al. 1998, Keane et al. 1996, Mladenoff and Baker 1999, Spies et al. 2002). Understanding how landscapes respond over time to perturbations is key to the development of effective forest policy (Turner et al. 2002). Landscape simulation tools also can aid in the growing need to integrate social concerns with tradeoff analyses of natural resource values (Vogt et al. 2002) and provide a framework to build consistent modeling approaches across resource disciplines. Although a number of recent efforts have applied forest landscape simulation modules to analyze policy issues at broad scales (e.g., Johnson et al. 1998, Keane et al. 1996, Spies et al. 2002), there has been little operational use of these tools to examine management issues at the watershed or subbasin scale. In addition, previous work has largely been concerned with modeling of forest vegetation, with relatively little attention to the problem of modeling nonforest conditions and social values.

The overall goal of the Interior Northwest Landscape Analysis System (INLAS) project is to advance the development and application of integrated landscape models and apply these tools to examine the effects of forest management on long-term trajectories of forest, range, and aquatic conditions at the subbasin and smaller scales. A primary focus of this work will be to apply simulation methods to measure the relative effects of forest succession, disturbance, and management on multiple-resource goals (fig. 1).

Decisionmakers can apply the techniques developed in this project to measure the response of large landscapes to different management scenarios ranging from active to passive, while accounting for expected levels of natural disturbance (Quigley et al. 2001). They also can help landowners, managers, and regulatory agencies integrate new scientific information into biological assessments, watershed analyses, subbasin reviews, and forest management plans. The landscape simulation methods that are advanced by this project will also have utility in a wide range of ecological research, especially that pertaining to disturbance processes and their effects on landscape pattern.

The combined development and application of landscape simulation methods will focus on a set of research objectives that will be addressed on a prototype analysis area. These are:

1. Evaluate the combined effects of management, natural disturbance, and succession on current and future resource conditions. The current set of regulations and management directions for individual species and habitats may not allow achievement of long-term, landscape-level ecosystem goals to both manage fuels and protect resources. We will examine possible conflicts created by existing policy and management directions between short-term management for site-specific conditions and the long-term potential for episodic and chronic disturbances to degrade those conditions. We will create a baseline scenario against which we can compare alternative policy and management options. This baseline scenario will follow current guidelines and forest plans. We will then contrast potential outcomes from this scenario with two opposing scenarios: (1) **passive**, i.e., custodial management and (2) **active**, i.e., management actions aimed at accelerated achievement of goals. Each scenario will examine a range of approaches that might be followed by different owners.

2. Develop new knowledge about how to reduce resource impacts by arranging spatial schedules of treatments to manage disturbance. We will use an adaptive approach to apply information developed during early analyses to design spatially explicit schedules of treatments that reduce both immediate adverse effects on desirable site-specific conditions and long-term risks from stochastic disturbances. This work will illustrate ways to make the most of spatial and temporal variation in terrestrial and aquatic conditions to reduce adverse long-term cumulative effects on sensitive resources by taking selective management actions, such as reducing fuel loads.

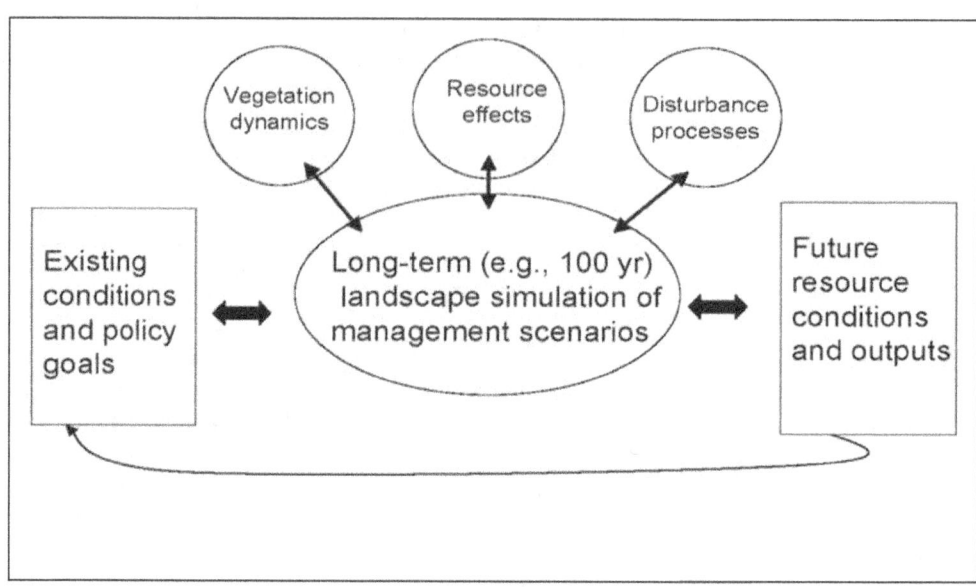

Figure 1   Interior Northwest Landscape Analysis System conceptual framework

3. Identify the policy, sociocultural, economic, and ecological constraints associated with the application of active or idealized spatially explicit schedules of fuel treatments. Spatial arrangement of fuel treatments on large landscapes can have an important effect on wildfire spread rates (Finney 1998, 2001). Idealized spatial and temporal distributions of fuels management treatments that attempt to minimize wildfire risk may, however, violate constraints imposed by other objectives or policies. Our analysis will identify policy, sociocultural, economic, and resource constraints that might prevent implementation of otherwise theoretically optimal treatment patterns (e.g., Finney 1998).

4. Develop methods to help managers identify problematic watersheds. The difficulty of achieving management objectives in individual watersheds differs considerably owing to particular combinations of physiography, vegetation, social values, economics, and management strategies. Our methods integrate finer resolution variables (e.g., stand density, fire hazard, wildlife habitat, economics, and management restrictions) to help to identify subwatersheds where actions might enhance specific goals or where current policies intended to mitigate risks and effects of unpredicted disturbances might be ineffective over the long term.

5. Examine the long-term consequences and socioeconomic feasibility of density management objectives at the watershed scale. Current assessments by the USDA Forest Service reveal large areas of dense stands that exceed desired stocking levels (Wilson et al., n.d.). What are the most economically efficient ways of altering these conditions, and maintaining stands at desired stocking levels? What are the implications and conflicts associated with achieving these objectives in terms of other resource values? Can we effectively integrate socioeconomic considerations into analyses of subwatershed-scale risk factors that measure deviations from desired stocking? Will the net effects of some management activities result in more long-term stocking problems than they solve? Long-term simulation of forest management will be used to address these and related questions.

Research Approach

The INLAS is building on two alternative methods to create a framework for modeling landscape change. First, a state and transition approach (see Hemstrom et al. Chapter 2) is being used to build a relatively coarse simulation system that integrates conifer succession and disturbance, forest management, fluvial processes, invasive plants, and herbivory. State and transition modeling uses a relatively coarse stratification of landscape conditions into **states** and simulates changes in landscape condition over time by using **transition probabilities** (Hemstrom et al. Chapter 2). These state and transition models evolved from successional studies in ecology and have recently found their way into forest planning and landscape assessment (Hann et al. 1997). Some of the advantages of this system are that software is well developed (Kurz et al. 2000), and data needed to run the model are available. The disadvantage of these methods is that they do not consider tree list type data or other detailed information about vegetative conditions (Hemstrom et al. Chapter 2).

The second approach uses the extension of tree-level growth models (e.g., Forest Vegetation Simulator [FVS], Stage 1973; ORGANON, Hann et al. 1995) to simulate landscapes as an assemblage of individual stands, polygons, or pixels (Ager Chapter 3, Bettinger et al. Chapter 4). This stand-level simulation approach has been the focus of considerable work over the past 10 to 15 years, and many improvements have been made to consider stand contagion, optimization, wildlife, spatial spread of insect epidemics, and consideration of nontimber values, as well as interfaces to the stand simulators to simplify the process of organizing stands for simulation (reviewed in Ager Chapter 3). We are exploring several stand-level simulation approaches, ranging from simple systems that use FVS and FVS postprocessors to model each stand in a landscape (Ager Chapter 3) to systems based on the Simulation and Analysis of Forests with Episodic Disturbance (SafeD) model (Graetz 2000) that can perform spatial optimization and incorporate natural disturbances (Bettinger et al. Chapter 4). Like the state and transition approach, there is a growing interest in this type of modeling for both research and operational applications. Stand-level landscape simulation models are well suited to problems where a relatively high degree of biological and spatial resolution is required. This includes studies where tree-level parameters like size and species are needed, and where management choices are tailored to stand metrics.

By applying both models, we will demonstrate tradeoffs between the two modeling approaches and their relative merits at different biological and spatial scales (fig. 2). For instance, state and transition models are relatively easy to build for large areas because they represent landscapes as a discrete and finite number of states and transitions. They also can be applied to a wide range of problems where process models or data are not available. A state and transition approach may be the most viable approach to building an integrated landscape simulation system. By comparison, stand-level process models require fine-scale quantitative data on stand conditions and can provide detailed data on stand characteristics through time, which are needed for many assessment and planning projects.

By using the two modeling frameworks described above, we will explore how to integrate other important ecosystem components (fig. 1). Each of the ecosystem components represents a model (or models) that is integrated into the framework and takes information from and feeds information to the vegetation simulator. Output from these resource effects models alters vegetative conditions or constrains management or succession and changes the resource outputs available from the landscape.

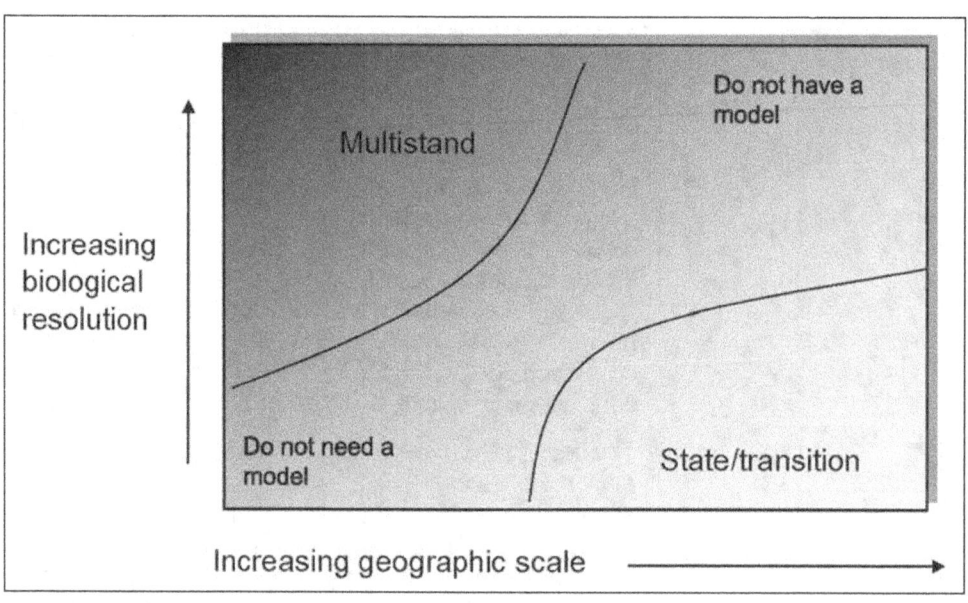

Figure 2 Comparison of a mu tistand versus state/transition mode ing approach for forest andscape simu ation in terms of bio ogica and geographic sca e

Descriptions of the status or state of the art of modeling efforts in each of the areas, along with research needs, are provided in the subsequent chapters of this volume. Wales and Suring (Chapter 5) identify methods to describe and evaluate habitat abundance, quality, and distribution across space and time to help managers and policymakers understand how successional processes, natural disturbance, and management actions influence terrestrial habitats. Wondzell and Howell (Chapter 6) review alternative modeling approaches for assessing conditions and prioritizing the restoration of aquatic habitat in the context of biophysical characteristics of streams and watersheds and landscape processes. Chronic disturbance by domestic and wild ungulates is known to significantly affect ecosystem patterns, but as Vavra et al. (Chapter 7) describe, there is a need to develop models that can project the effects of ungulate herbivory at multiple scales. By contrast, episodic disturbances such as insect and disease outbreaks or wildfire have been the subjects of intensive modeling efforts. Ager et al. (Chapter 8) review the quantitative methods for modeling mortality caused by insects and disease and describe the major gaps in this area. Finney (Chapter 9) describes the state of the art and research needs in integrating wildfire into landscape planning models. Lettman and Kline (Chapter 10) examine approaches to evaluate economic impacts of current and alternative management scenarios, and public values and attitudes toward forests. The impacts of human population growth, diversification, movement, and accompanying land use change are important factors in forest management as the wildland/urban interface expands. Clark (Chapter 11) describes approaches for identifying and evaluating the values and places that are important to people. Kline (Chapter 12) describes modeling and analyses of residential and other development scenarios that can contribute to anticipating where land use change is likely to occur. Barbour et al. (Chapter 13) describe techniques for displaying the ecological and economic costs and benefits of timber removal or gathering nontimber forest products.

The specifics of how these individual components might be refined and integrated are part of the major developmental challenges of the INLAS project. Some aspects of integration are covered in the chapters that follow in this volume, whereas others will be developed as the project evolves.

Project Area

Lying within the Upper Grande Ronde watershed, a 4th-hydrologic unit code (HUC4) subbasin, the INLAS project area comprises four HUC5 units occupying about 178 000 ha of mixed forest and rangelands on the eastern flank of the Blue Mountains southwest of La Grande, Oregon (fig. 3). The La Grande Ranger District of the Wallowa-Whitman National Forest administers about 123 000 of these ha (fig. 4). Most of the remaining land is nonindustrial private (about 55 000 ha). Smaller areas are owned by the Confederated Tribes of the Umatilla (about 13 800 ha), Boise Cascade (about 5000 ha), and the state of Oregon (about 810 ha). Numerous residences exist on nonindustrial private lands around the town of Starkey. The topography is highly varied and complex, with deeply dissected drainages feeding into the Grande Ronde River as it runs north through the center of the subbasin (fig. 5). Elevations range from 820 to over 2130 m. Vegetation ranges from xeric, bunchgrass communities at the lower, north end of the project area, to mixed conifer and subalpine fir (*Abies lasiocarpa* (Hook.) Nutt.) on the eastern flanks of the Elkhorn Mountains. Fuel loadings are highly heterogeneous across the project area, and a number of large wildfires have occurred over the last 10 years, burning about 8100 ha. Two additional large wildfires burned as much as 24 300 ha on lands immediately adjacent to the Upper Grande Ronde subbasin and project area. An outbreak of spruce budworm (*Choristoneura occidentalis*) occurred throughout the 1980s causing extensive Douglas-fir (*Pseudotsuga menziesii* (Mirb.) Franco) and grand fir (*Abies grandis* (Dougl. ex D. Don) Lindl.) mortality throughout the Blue Mountains including the Upper Grande Ronde subbasin. Outbreaks of bark beetles (*Dendroctonus* spp.) have also occurred in and adjacent to the project area.

Forest Service lands are managed with emphases ranging from scenic areas to commodity production. The Starkey Experimental Forest and Range (about 8900 ha) is located in the project area on the southwestern portion of the subbasin and includes research facilities of the Starkey Project (Rowland et al. 1997, Vavra et al. 2002). The Upper Grande Ronde subbasin contains habitat for three federally threatened species, the Canada lynx (*Lynx canadensis*), the gray wolf (*Canis lupus*), and the bald eagle (*Haliaeetus leucocephalus*). About 40 additional terrestrial vertebrates of conservation concern identified by Wisdom et al. (2000) are likely to occur in the Upper Grande Ronde subbasin. This area may provide habitat for several of the 15 insect species currently listed as threatened, endangered, or sensitive in east-side forests (LaBonte et al. 2001). The project area includes potential habitat for three federally listed threatened and one candidate plant species (USF&WS 2002). An additional eight plant species, currently designated as sensitive by the USDA, Forest Service, Pacific Northwest Region, have been documented in the INLAS project area. The Grande Ronde River and its tributaries also contain habitat for federally threatened chinook salmon (*Oncorhynchus tshwaytscha* (Walbaum)), bull trout (*Salvelinus fontinalis*), and steelhead (*Salvelinus confluentus*). For more detailed information about this area, an extensive bibliography of reports and published literature is provided in the final chapter of this volume (Aitken and Ager Chapter 14). *Text continues on page 11*

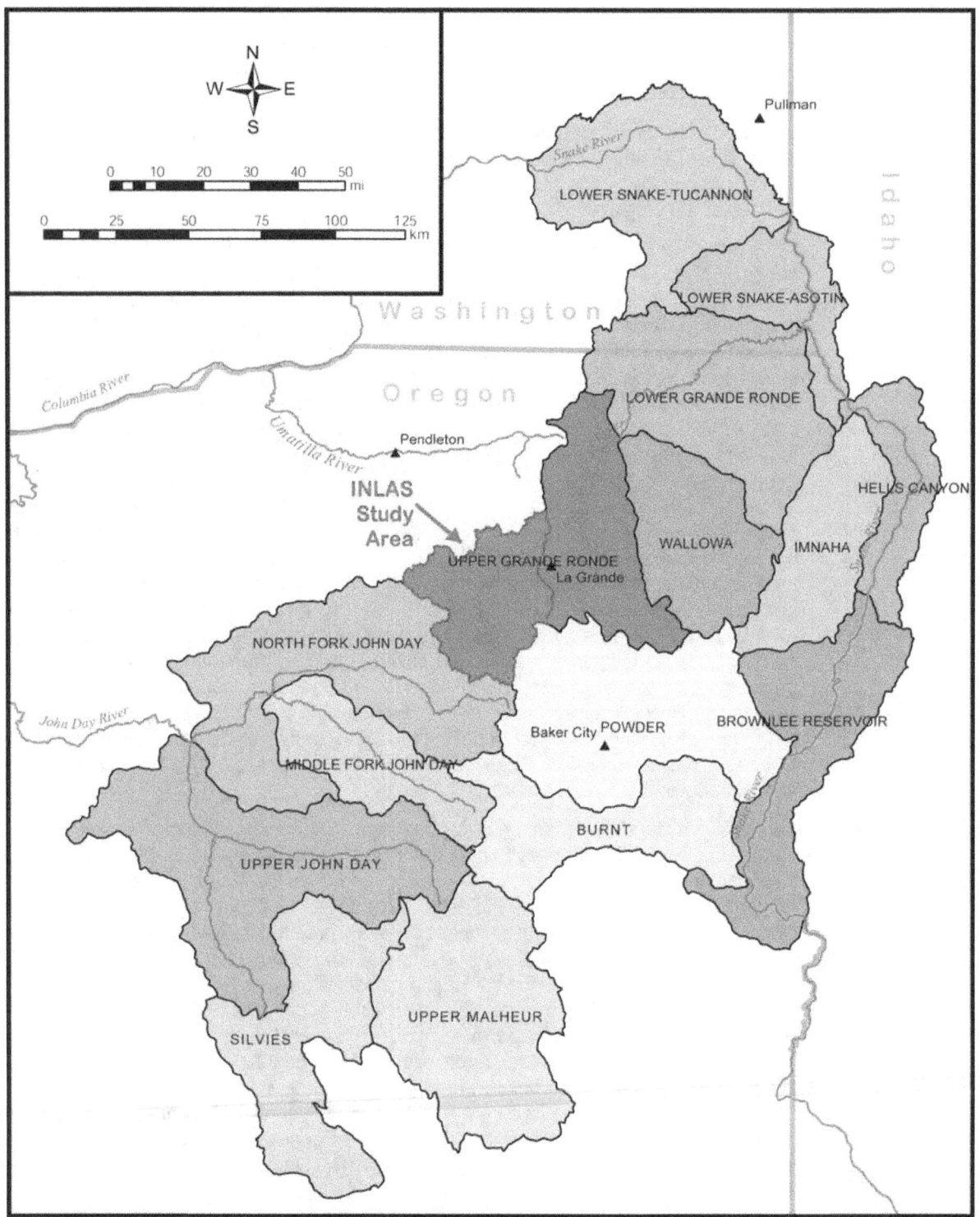

Figure 3   Location of Interior Northwest Landscape Analysis System project area within the Blue Mountains ecoregion (in 4th-hydrologic unit codes)

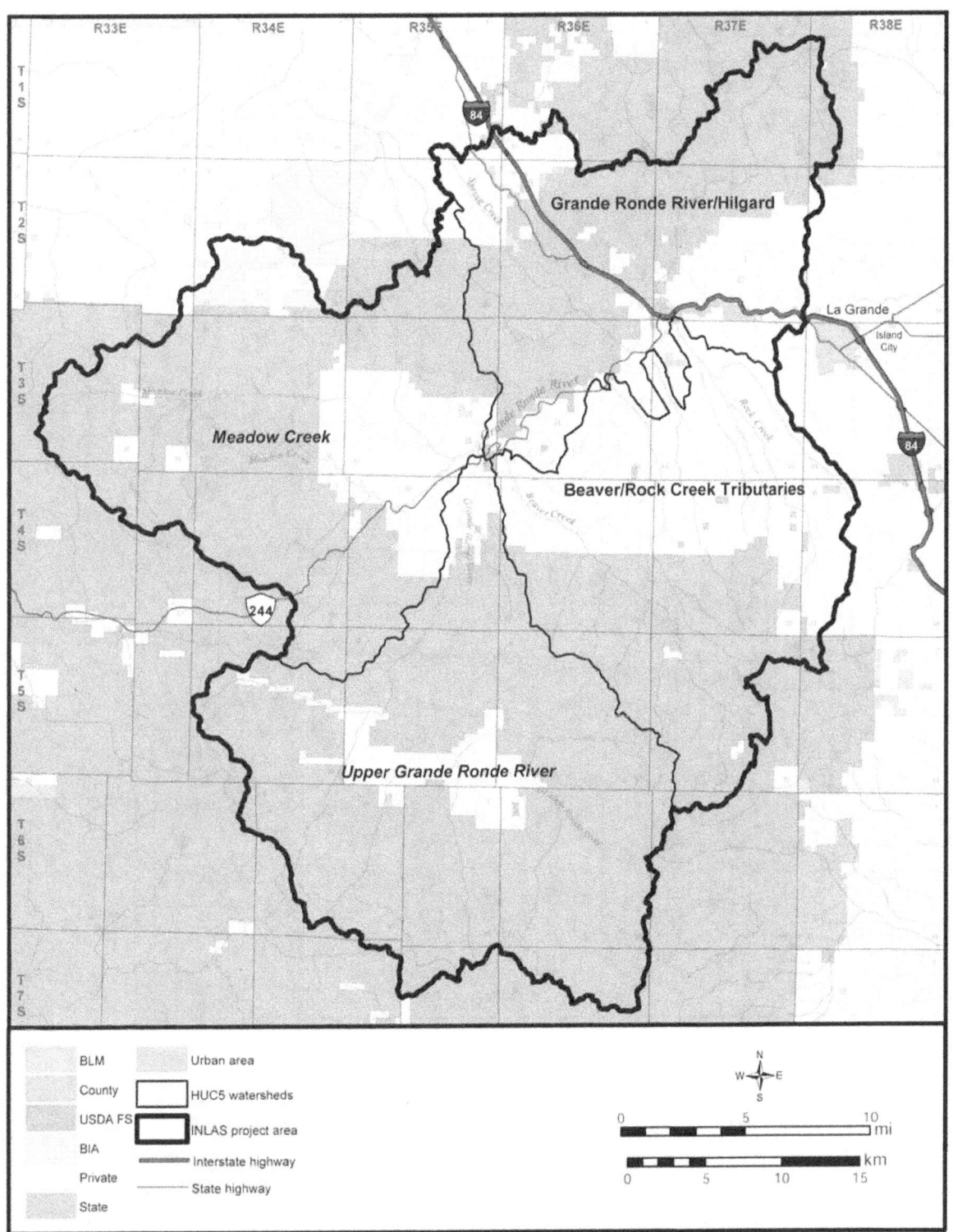

Figure 4   Ownership in Interior Northwest Landscape Analysis System project area

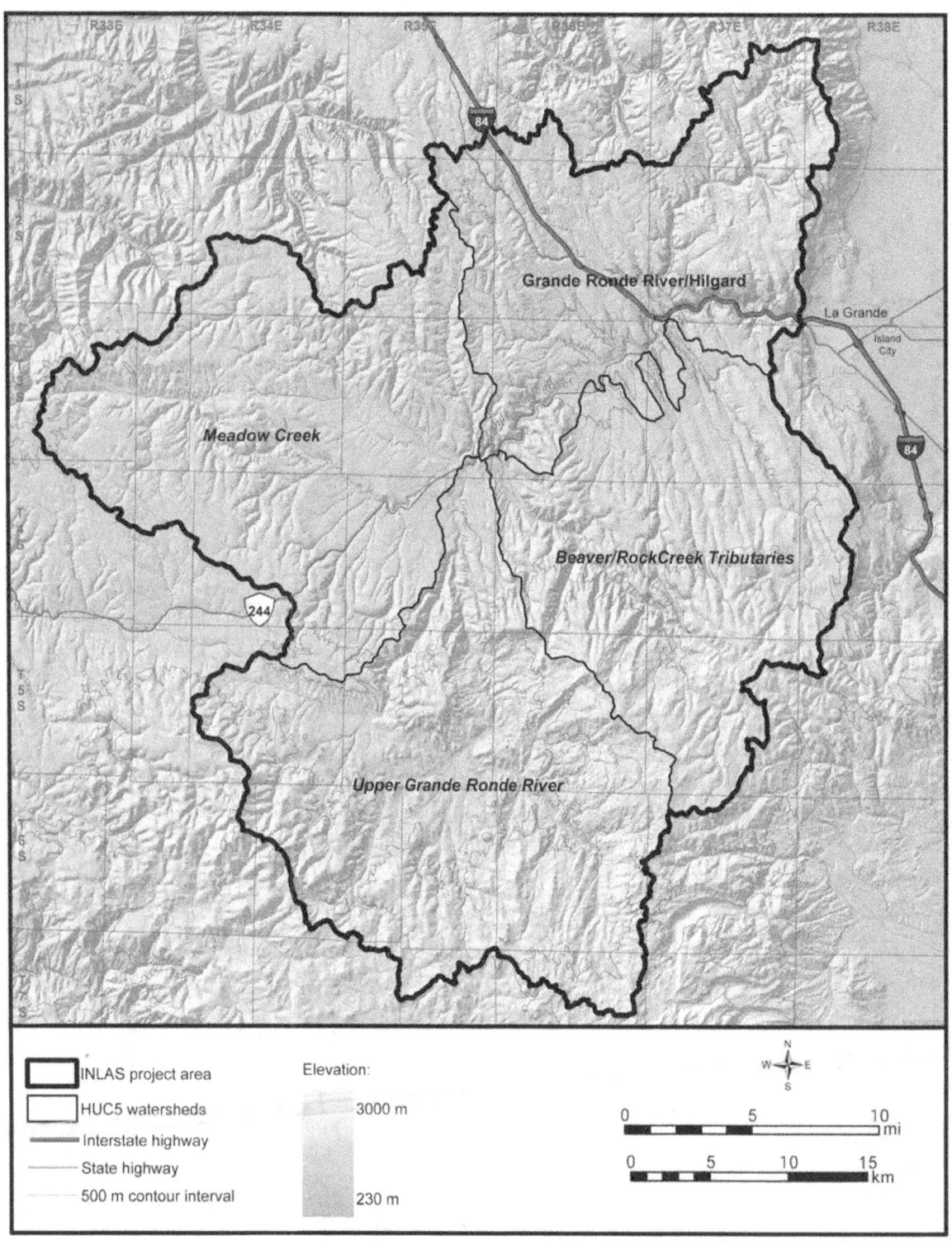

Figure 5   Topography of Interior Northwest Landscape Analysis System project area

Audience and Products

Although the direct application of analyses from the prototype area is limited in geographic scope, the lessons learned while conducting these analyses will find use in the much broader policy arena. The product mix from the INLAS project will include methodologies, new scientific knowledge, and much information germane to current policy debates over sustainability and conservation of natural resources. Analyses will clarify many socioeconomic and ecological interactions for which we have a poor understanding. This will help scientists identify the most productive areas for future research.

We anticipate that methods we develop for the Upper Grande Ronde prototype area will have applicability to other areas. Some of the methods we develop at the subbasin scale can be "scaled up" to larger areas, e.g., analysis of lynx habitat, or applied on a large number of other subbasins across the Blue Mountains to answer midscale questions. In addition, by developing methods at the midscale, we hope to better understand the larger scale issues and develop ways to use our methods and results at both larger (e.g., forest or regional planning) and smaller scales, (e.g., watershed assessments and project plans). We are working closely with the regional planning staff members to ensure the products produced by INLAS are useful and fit into the planning process. We are also working with the La Grande Ranger District on a relatively small (about 2400 ha) wildland/urban interface fuels-reduction project to prototype some of the analysis tools.

The users of the products developed during this project include those involved in, or interested in the outcome of, watershed assessments, forest planning, and policy analysis. A major drawback of previous landscape modeling efforts is that the data requirements and intricacies of the modeling process rendered existing systems unworkable to most prospective users. Many of our methods and processes are built on existing data, tools, and software to make them more readily adaptable by managers who may already be familiar with the underlying programs. Where new design and development are needed, we plan to work with developers to facilitate the incorporation of our prototype software into preferred systems.

Some of the anticipated outcomes from the INLAS project include:

- Developing methods to perform analyses at the interface of policy, management, and science that rely on a consistent set of assumptions and common data.

- Providing information from landscape analyses to local and state political leaders, government and private resource managers, scientists, and policymakers.

- Demonstrating the breadth of management options to policymakers, resource managers, researchers, and the public.

- Facilitating discussions about realistic balances among goals among managers, policymakers who represent different landowners, and the public.

- Illustrating how actions by nonfederal owners might influence the capability of meeting different policy objectives on federally managed land and vice versa.

- Gaining insights into the influence of scale in determining the importance of management actions within different ownership patterns.

- Identifying specific knowledge gaps in ecological research, management science, and resource planning analysis.

The development and application of different aspects of the work are described in the chapters that follow. Each of these component efforts will produce methods and tools that not only contribute to accomplishing the specific goals of the INLAS project but also can operate outside of the INLAS simulation framework. The integrative products resulting from interactions among sets of two or more components of the framework will help to highlight how different resource values complement or conflict with one another.

English Equivalent

When you know:	Multiply by:	To get:
Hectares (ha)	2.47	Acres (ac)
Meters (m)	3.28	Feet (ft)

Literature Cited

Ager, A.A. 2004. Application of the Forest Vegetation Simulator and related tools for integrated modeling of forest landscapes. In: Hayes, J.L.; Ager, A.A.; Barbour, R.J., tech. eds. Methods for integrating modeling of landscape change: Interior Northwest Landscape Analysis System. Gen. Tech. Rep. PNW-GTR-610. Portland, OR: U.S. Department of Agriculture, Forest Service, Pacific Northwest Research Station: 33-40. Chapter 3.

Ager, A.A.; Hayes, J.L.; Schmitt, C.L. 2004. Simulating mortality from forest insects and diseases. In: Hayes, J.L.; Ager, A.A.; Barbour, R.J., tech. eds. Methods for integrating modeling of landscape change: Interior Northwest Landscape Analysis System. Gen. Tech. Rep. PNW-GTR-610. Portland, OR: U.S. Department of Agriculture, Forest Service, Pacific Northwest Research Station: 104-116. Chapter 8.

Aitken, M.; Ager, A.A. 2004. Bibliography. In: Hayes, J.L.; Ager, A.A.; Barbour, R.J., tech. eds. Methods for integrating modeling of landscape change: Interior Northwest Landscape Analysis System. Gen. Tech. Rep. PNW-GTR-610. Portland, OR: U.S. Department of Agriculture, Forest Service, Pacific Northwest Research Station: 171-218. Chapter 14.

Barbour, R.J.; Fight, R.D.; Christensen, G.A.; Pinjuv, G.L.; Nagubadi, V. 2004. Thinning and prescribed fire and projected trends in wood product potential, financial return, and fire hazard in Montana. Gen. Tech. Rep. PNW-GTR-606. Portland, OR: U.S. Department of Agriculture, Forest Service, Pacific Northwest Research Station. 78 p.

Barbour, R.J.; Maguire, D.; Singleton, R. 2004. Evaluating forest products as part of landscape planning. In: Hayes, J.L.; Ager, A.A.; Barbour, R.J., tech. eds. Methods for integrating modeling of landscape change: Interior Northwest Landscape Analysis System. Gen. Tech. Rep. PNW-GTR-610. Portland, OR: U.S. Department of Agriculture, Forest Service, Pacific Northwest Research Station: 161-170. Chapter 13.

Bettinger, P.; Graetz, D.; Ager, A.A.; Sessions, J. 2004. The SafeD forest landscape planning model. In: Hayes, J.L.; Ager, A.A.; Barbour, R.J., tech. eds. Methods for integrating modeling of landscape change: Interior Northwest Landscape Analysis System. Gen. Tech. Rep. PNW-GTR-610. Portland, OR: U.S. Department of Agriculture, Forest Service, Pacific Northwest Research Station: 41-63. Chapter 4.

Caraher, D.L.; Henshaw, J.; Hall, F. [et al.], [panel members]. 1992. Restoring ecosystems in the Blue Mountains: a report to the Regional Forester and forest supervisors of the Blue Mountains forests; final report. Portland, OR: U.S. Department of Agriculture, Forest Service, Pacific Northwest Region. 14 p. [plus appendices].

Clark, R.N. 2004. Conflicts and opportunities in natural resource management: concepts, tools, and information for assessing values and places important to people. In: Hayes, J.L.; Ager, A.A.; Barbour, R.J., tech. eds. Methods for integrating modeling of landscape change: Interior Northwest Landscape Analysis System. Gen. Tech. Rep. PNW-GTR-610. Portland, OR: U.S. Department of Agriculture, Forest Service, Pacific Northwest Research Station: 137-152. Chapter 11.

Clean Water Act of 1977; 33 U.S.C. s/s 1251 et seq.

Endangered Species Act of 1973 [ESA]; 16 U.S.C. 1531-1536, 1538-1540.

Everett, R.L.; Hessburg, P.F.; Jensen, M.E.; Bormann, B.T. 1994. Eastside forest ecosystem health assessment, executive summary. Gen. Tech. Rep. PNW-GTR-317. Portland, OR: U.S. Department of Agriculture, Forest Service, Pacific Northwest Research Station. 61 p. Vol. 1. (Everett, R.L., assessment team leader, Eastside forest ecosystem health assessment).

Finney, M.A. 1998. FARSITE: fire area simulator—model development and evaluation. Res. Pap. RMRS-RP-4. Fort Collins, CO: U.S. Department of Agriculture, Forest Service, Rocky Mountain Research Station. 47 p.

Finney, M.A. 2001. Design of regular landscape fuel treatment patterns for modifying fire growth and behavior. Forest Science. 47: 219-228.

Finney, M.A. 2004. Landscape fire simulation and fuel treatment optimization. In: Hayes, J.L.; Ager, A.A.; Barbour, R.J., tech. eds. Methods for integrating modeling of landscape change: Interior Northwest Landscape Analysis System. Gen. Tech. Rep. PNW-GTR-610. Portland, OR: U.S. Department of Agriculture, Forest Service, Pacific Northwest Research Station: 117-131. Chapter 9.

Forest Ecosystem Management Assessment Team [FEMAT]. 1993. Forest ecosystem management: an ecological, economic, and social assessment. Portland, OR: U.S. Department of Agriculture; U.S. Department of the Interior [et al.]. [Irregular pagination].

Gast, W.R., Jr.; Scott, D.W.; Schmitt, C. [et al.]. 1991. Blue Mountains forest health report: new perspectives in forest health. Portland, OR: U.S. Department of Agriculture, Forest Service, Malheur, Umatilla, and Wallowa-Whitman National Forests. [Irregular pagination].

Graetz, D. 2000. The SafeD model: incorporating episodic disturbances and heuristic programming into forest management planning for the Applegate River watershed, southwestern Oregon. Corvallis, OR: College of Forest Resources, Oregon State University. 127 p. M.S. thesis.

Hann, D.W.; Hester, A.S.; Olsen, C.L. 1995. ORGANON user's manual: edition 5.0. Corvallis, OR: Department of Forest Resources, Oregon State University. 127 p.

Hann, W.J.; Jones, J.L.; Karl, M.G. [et al.]. 1997. Landscape dynamics in the basin. In: Quigley, T.M.; Arbelbide, S.J., eds. An assessment of ecosystem components in the interior Columbia basin and portions of the Klamath and Great Basins. Gen. Tech. Rep. PNW-GTR-405. Portland, OR: U.S. Department of Agriculture, Forest Service, Pacific Northwest Research Station: 337-1077. Vol. 2. (Quigley, T.M., ed.; Interior Columbia Basin Ecosystem Management Project: scientific assessment).

Hemstrom, M.; Ager, A.A.; Vavra, M. [et al.]. 2004. A state and transition approach for integrating landscape models. In: Hayes, J.L.; Ager, A.A.; Barbour, R.J., tech. eds. Methods for integrating modeling of landscape change: Interior Northwest Landscape Analysis System. Gen. Tech. Rep. PNW-GTR-610. Portland, OR: U.S. Department of Agriculture, Forest Service, Pacific Northwest Research Station: 17-32. Chapter 2.

Johnson, K.N. 1996. Bioregional assessments in the Pacific Northwest—past, present, and future. In: Kohm, K.; Franklin, J., eds. Forestry for the 21st century. Washington, DC: Island Press: 397-409.

Johnson, K.N.; Sessions, J.; Franklin, J.; Gabriel, J. 1998. Integrating wildfire into strategic planning for Sierra Nevada forests. Journal of Forestry. 96(1): 42-49.

Keane, R.E.; Long, D.G.; Menakis, J.P. [et al.]. 1996. Simulating coarse scale vegetation dynamics using the Columbia River basin succession model—CRBSUM. Gen. Tech. Rep. INT-GTR-340. Ogden, UT: U.S. Department of Agriculture, Forest Service, Intermountain Research Station. 50 p.

Kline, J. 2004. Analysis and modeling of forest land development at the forest/urban interface. In: Hayes, J.L.; Ager, A.A.; Barbour, R.J., tech. eds. Methods for integrating modeling of landscape change: Interior Northwest Landscape Analysis System. Gen. Tech. Rep. PNW-GTR-610. Portland, OR: U.S. Department of Agriculture, Forest Service, Pacific Northwest Research Station: 153-160. Chapter 12.

Kurz, W.A.; Beukema, S.J.; Klenner, W. [et al.]. 2000. TELSA: the tool for exploratory landscape scenario analysis. Computers and Electronics in Agriculture. 27: 227-242.

LaBonte, J.R.; Scott, D.W.; McIver, J.; Hayes, J.L. 2001. Threatened, endangered, and sensitive insects in eastern Oregon and Washington forests and adjacent lands. Northwest Science. 75(Spec. issue): 185-198.

Lettman, G.J.; Kline, J.D. 2004. Connection to local communities. In: Hayes, J.L.; Ager, A.A.; Barbour, R.J., tech. eds. Methods for integrating modeling of landscape change: Interior Northwest Landscape Analysis System. Gen. Tech. Rep. PNW-GTR-610. Portland, OR: U.S. Department of Agriculture, Forest Service, Pacific Northwest Research Station: 132-136. Chapter 10.

Mladenoff, D.; Baker, W.L. 1999. Development of forest and landscape modeling approaches. In: Mladenoff, D.; Baker, B.L., eds. Spatial modeling of forest landscape change: approaches and applications. Cambridge, United Kingdom: Cambridge University Press: 1-13.

National Environmental Policy Act of 1969 [NEPA]; 42 U.S.C. 4321 et seq.

National Forest Management Act of 1976 [NFMA]; Act of October 22, 1976; 16 U.S.C. 1600.

Ottmar, R.D.; Sandberg, D.V. 2001. Wildland fire in eastern Oregon and Washington. Northwest Science. 75(Spec. issue): 46-54.

Quigley, T.M.; Hayes, J.L.; Starr, G.L. [et al.]. 2001. Improving forest health and productivity in eastern Oregon and Washington and adjacent lands. Northwest Science. 75(Spec. issue): 234-251.

Quigley, T.M.; Haynes, R.W.; Graham, R.T., tech. eds. 1996. Integrated scientific assessment for ecosystem management in the interior Columbia basin and portions of the Klamath and Great Basins. Gen. Tech. Rep. PNW-GTR-382. Portland, OR: U.S. Department of Agriculture, Forest Service, Pacific Northwest Research Station. 303 p. (Quigley, T.M., ed.; Interior Columbia Basin Ecosystem Management Project: scientific assessment).

Rowland, M.M.; Bryant, L.D.; Johnson, B.K. [et al.]. 1997. The Starkey project: history, facilities, and data collection methods for ungulate research. Gen. Tech. Rep. PNW-GTR-396. Portland, OR: U.S. Department of Agriculture, Forest Service, Pacific Northwest Research Station. 62 p.

Spies, T.; Reeves, G.; Burnett, K.M. [et al.]. 2002. Assessing the ecological consequences of forest policies in a multi-ownership province in Oregon. In: Liu, J.; Taylor, W.W., eds. Integrating landscape ecology into natural resource management. Cambridge, United Kingdom: Cambridge Press: 177-207.

Stage, A.R. 1973. Prognosis model for stand development. Res. Pap. RP-INT-137. Ogden, UT: U.S. Department of Agriculture, Forest Service, Intermountain Research Station. 32 p.

Turner, M.; Crow T.R.; Liu, J. [et al.]. 2002. Bridging the gap between landscape ecology and natural resource management. In: Liu, J.; Taylor, W.W., eds. Integrating landscape ecology into natural resource management. Cambridge, United Kingdom: Cambridge Press: 433-460.

U.S. Fish and Wildlife Service [USF&WS]. 2002. Species list No. 1-4-02-SP-912, File No. 118.0000 of September 2002. (Letter to Forest Supervisor listing species of concern for the La Grande Ranger District, Wallowa-Whitman National Forest). On file with: La Grande Ranger District, 3502 Hwy 30, La Grande, OR 97850.

Vavra, M.; Ager, A.A.; Johnson, B. [et al.]. 2004. Modeling the effects of large herbivores. In: Hayes, J.L.; Ager, A.A.; Barbour, R.J., tech. eds. Methods for integrating modeling of landscape change: Interior Northwest Landscape Analysis System. Gen. Tech. Rep. PNW-GTR-610. Portland, OR: U.S. Department of Agriculture, Forest Service, Pacific Northwest Research Station: 82-103. Chapter 7.

Vavra, M.; Wisdom, W.; Kie, J. 2002. Ecology effects of ungulate team problem analysis, managing disturbance regimes program. Team problem analysis. On file with: Pacific Northwest Research Station, 1401 Gekeler Lane, La Grande, OR 97850.

Vogt, K.; Grove, M.; Asbjornsen, H. [et al.]. 2002. Linking ecological and social scales for natural resource management. In: Liu, J.; Taylor, W.W., eds. Integrating landscape ecology into natural resource management. Cambridge, United Kingdom: Cambridge Press: 143-175.

Wales, B.C.; Suring, L. 2004. Assessment techniques for terrestrial vertebrates of conservation concern. In: Hayes, J.L.; Ager, A.A.; Barbour, R.J., tech. eds. Methods for integrating modeling of landscape change: Interior Northwest Landscape Analysis System. Gen. Tech. Rep. PNW-GTR-610. Portland, OR: U.S. Department of Agriculture, Forest Service, Pacific Northwest Research Station: 64-72. Chapter 5.

Wilson, D.; Maguire, D.; Barbour, J. [N.d.]. Assessment of the small-diameter timber harvest from restoration treatments in densely-stocked stands on national forests in eastern Oregon. Western Journal of Applied Forestry.

Wisdom, M.J.; Holthausen, R.S.; Wales, B.C. [et al.]. 2000. Source habitats for terrestrial vertebrates of focus in the interior Columbia basin: broad-scale trends and management implications. Gen. Tech. Rep. PNW-GTR-485. Portland, OR: U.S. Department of Agriculture, Forest Service, Pacific Northwest Research Station. 1119 p. 3 vol.

Wondzell, S.; Howell, P. 2004. Developing a decision support model for assessing condition and prioritizing the restoration of aquatic habitat in the interior Columbia Basin. In: Hayes, J.L.; Ager, A.A.; Barbour, R.J., tech. eds. Methods for integrating modeling of landscape change: Interior Northwest Landscape Analysis System. Gen. Tech. Rep. PNW-GTR-610. Portland, OR: U.S. Department of Agriculture, Forest Service, Pacific Northwest Research Station: 73-81. Chapter 6.

Chapter 2: A State and Transition Approach for Integrating Landscape Models

Miles Hemstrom, Alan A. Ager, Martin Vavra, Barbara C. Wales, and Michael J. Wisdom[1]

Abstract

We will use state and transition modeling (STM) to project landscape dynamics in a portion of the Upper Grande Ronde subbasin, northeastern Oregon. The Interior Northwest Landscape Analysis System effort will develop both process-based models and STM to represent vegetation, disturbance, and management interactions across large landscapes. State and transition models are useful for integrating disturbances, management activities, and vegetation growth and development across large, variable landscapes, but are not currently useful for finding optimal solutions to meet landscape management objectives. Process-based models are useful for detailed modeling of vegetation changes and optimization but can be difficult to develop and parameterize across many disturbances and highly variable vegetation conditions. We discuss advantages and limitations of STM in the context of integrated scientific analysis and land management planning at subbasin and broader scales. We provide an example of how such models might be used to project the integrated effects of vegetation management, fire, invasive plants, ungulate herbivory, and other disturbances on vegetation across a large landscape in northeastern Oregon. We suggest enhancements of existing STMs that will use process-based models to calibrate states and transitions.

Keywords: Landscape simulation, northeastern Oregon, landscape ecology.

[1] **Miles Hemstrom** is a research ecologist U S Department of Agriculture Forest Service Pacific Northwest Research Station Forestry Sciences Laboratory 620 SW Main Suite 400 Portland OR 97205 **Alan A. Ager** is an operations research analyst **Martin Vavra** is a research range scientist **Barbara C. Wales** is a wildife biologist and **Michael J. Wisdom** is a research wildife biologist U S Department of Agriculture Forest Service Pacific Northwest Research Station Forestry and Range Sciences Laboratory 1401 Gekeler Lane La Grande OR 97850

Introduction

Landscape simulation models have been widely applied to address research and land management policy questions in the Western United States and elsewhere (Bettinger et al. 1997, 1998; Graetz 2000; Hann et al. 1997; Mladenoff and He 1999; USDA and USDI 2000). Advances in modeling techniques, computer technology, and geographic information systems (GIS) have made it possible to model large landscapes at increasingly finer scales of spatial and temporal resolution. However, natural resource planning models used in the past focused primarily on conifer succession and management while representing other key ecosystem elements as byproducts (e.g., Alig et al. 2000, Johnson et al. 1986). Although progress has been made in the formulation of multiobjective goals in landscape simulations (e.g., Sessions et al. 1999, Wedin 1999), there remain many challenges to building landscape planning models that include all the important disturbance processes that influence landscape change. Previous efforts have often not included widespread, chronic disturbances (e.g., ungulate herbivory) or have focused on selected environments (e.g., forests) rather than entire landscapes. Of particular interest in the Interior Northwest Landscape Analysis System (INLAS) context are the net, synergistic effects of various disturbances (e.g., fire, invasive plants, large herbivores, and hydrologic processes as they affect geomorphology and associated riparian habitat) across a large landscape that includes a variety of environments. Integrating these kinds of disturbances is exceedingly complex in models that treat vegetation and disturbance on continuous scales.

An alternative approach is to represent the effects of these disturbances in discrete form in state and transition modeling (STM). In parallel with Simulation and analysis of forests with episodic Disturbances (SafeD) developments for INLAS (Bettinger et al. Chapter 4), we will use STM for multiresource integration in a landscape planning model. The broad goal of this work is to develop prototype disturbance models in a STM framework that integrates major environments, vegetation types, ownerships, and disturbances across a large and diverse landscape. This effort will use the Vegetation Development Dynamics Tool (VDDT; Beukema and Kurz 1995) and the associated Tool for Exploratory Landscape Scenario Analysis (TELSA; Kurz et al. 2000), which have many features that make them well suited for developing and testing new approaches to landscape simulation. Ultimately, this work will lead to more refined, integrated approaches to understanding the interplay of disturbances and vegetation across large, variable landscapes. We also will examine the potentially complementary linkage of STM with more detailed, continuous simulations from SafeD. Our expectation is that detailed simulations from SafeD can be used to calibrate states and transitions while STM can examine landscape-wide interactions of vegetation types and disturbances that cannot readily be included in SafeD.

State and Transition Models

State and transition models treat vegetation composition and structure as "states," connected by transitions that indicate vegetation development over time and disturbance (fig. 6). This STM approach builds from transition matrix models that represent vegetation development as a set of transition probabilities among various vegetation conditions (e.g., Cattelino et al. 1979, Hann et al. 1997, Horn 1975, Laycock 1991, Noble and Slatyer 1980) (figs. 7 and 8). Vegetation states change over time barring management activities or disturbances. For example, grass/forb-closed herblands become shrub/tree regeneration-open midheight shrubs after 15 years. State change along the successional, time-dependent path is deterministic and, without disturbance or management, all the vegetation would ultimately accumulate in one long-term stable state. However, disturbance or management activities can change the course of vegetative development

Text continues on page 22

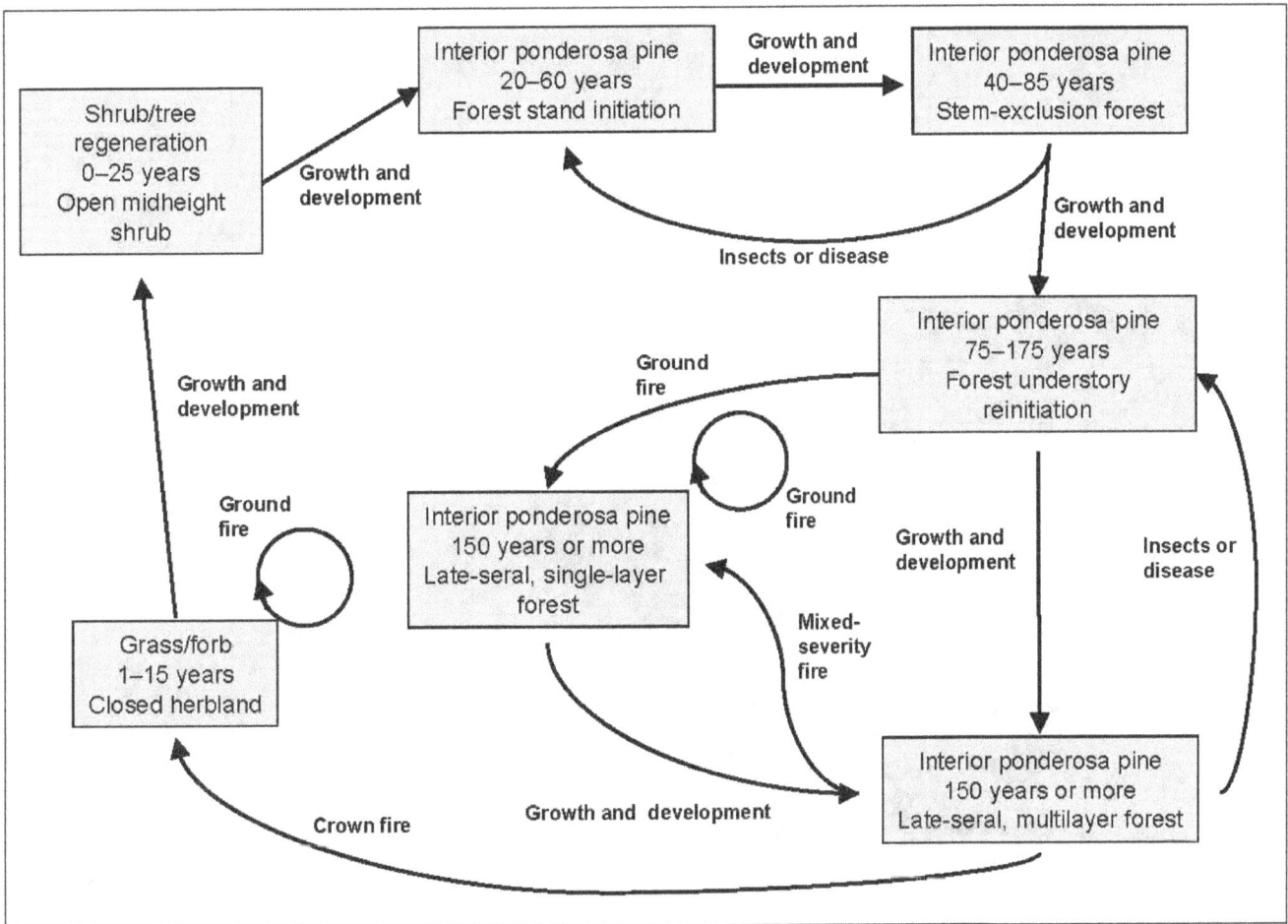

Figure 6   Example of simplified state and transition model for dry forests in the Interior Northwest Landscape Analysis System study area northeastern Oregon

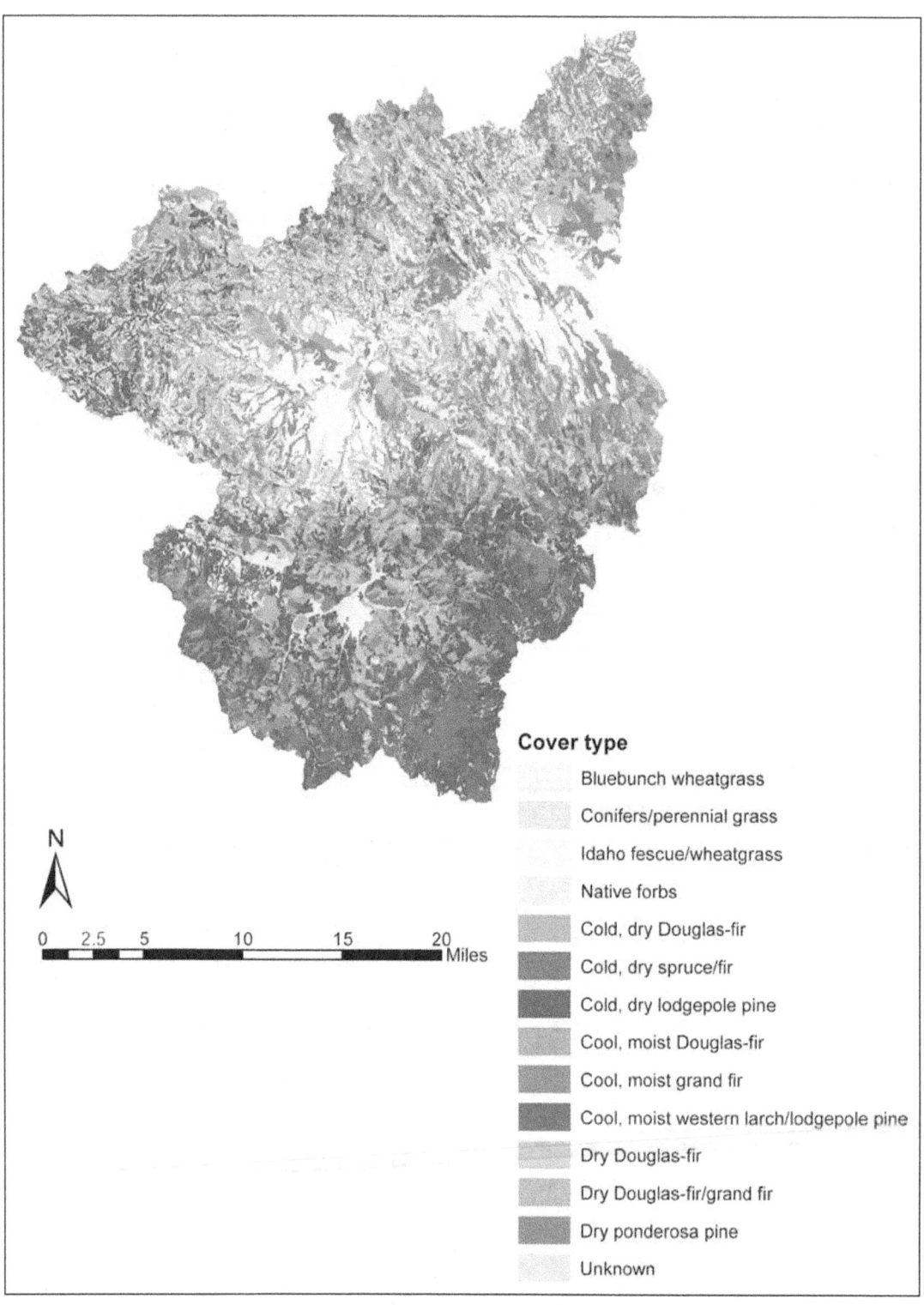

Cover type

Bluebunch wheatgrass

Conifers/perennial grass

Idaho fescue/wheatgrass

Native forbs

Cold, dry Douglas-fir

Cold, dry spruce/fir

Cold, dry lodgepole pine

Cool, moist Douglas-fir

Cool, moist grand fir

Cool, moist western larch/lodgepole pine

Dry Douglas-fir

Dry Douglas-fir/grand fir

Dry ponderosa pine

Unknown

Figure 7   Example of existing vegetation cover type classes in the Interior Northwest Landscape Analysis System study area Upper Grande Ronde subbasin Oregon Classes developed during the study may differ from those shown

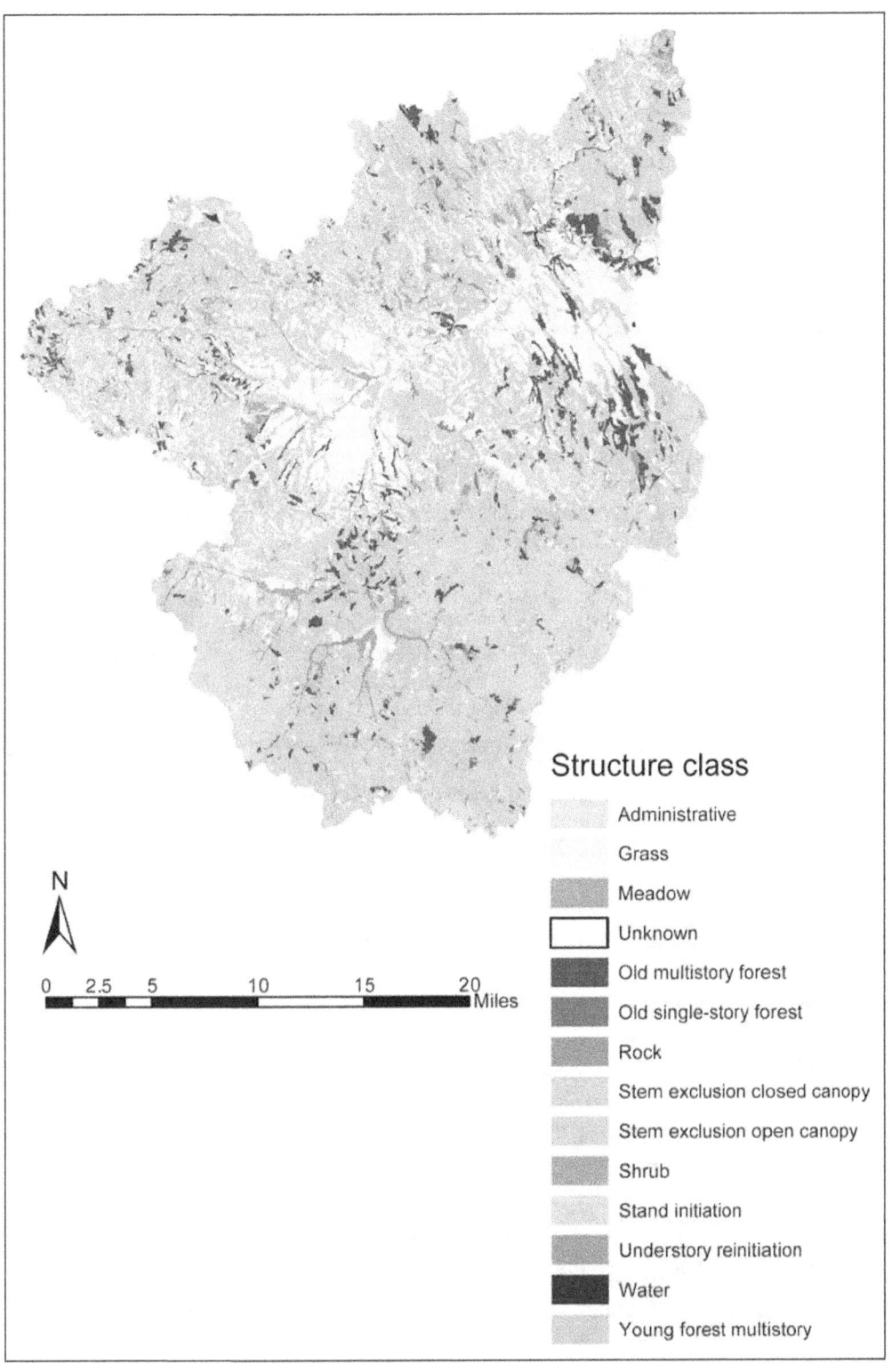

Structure class

Administrative

Grass

Meadow

Unknown

Old multistory forest

Old single-story forest

Rock

Stem exclusion closed canopy

Stem exclusion open canopy

Shrub

Stand initiation

Understory reinitiation

Water

Young forest multistory

Figure 8   Examp e of existing vegetation structure c asses in the Interior Northwest Landscape Ana ysis System study area Upper Grande Ronde subbasin Oregon C asses deve oped during the study may differ from those shown

at any point. Depending on disturbance probabilities and consequences, very little or no vegetation may actually accumulate in the long-term stable state at the end point of succession. In our example (fig. 6), insect and disease activity may reset interior ponderosa pine (*Pinus ponderosa* Dougl. ex Laws.)/stem-exclusion forest to the stand-initiation condition. In contrast to successional development, disturbances, including management, are probabilistic and possible at each time step, depending on vegetation state. A separate model (states and transitions) is developed for each modeling stratum (groups of potential vegetation types in the study area, see Hall 1998). We anticipate 15 or more modeling strata in the study area (figs. 7, 8, and 9). The example used for illustration (fig. 6) has been substantially simplified. Most models will be considerably more complex. Many of the models we use will contain "transition thresholds" influenced by site degradation or invasive plants, beyond which recovery to previous plant community conditions is difficult or impossible (e.g., Laycock 1991). Hann et al. 1997 and Hemstrom et al. (in press) used several such models to depict vegetation change across the interior Columbia basin.

State and Transition Modeling Systems and Recent Applications

A number of STM systems have been developed in the past 5 to 10 years and applied on Western landscapes either as research or planning tools, including SIMulating vegetative Patterns and Processes at Landscape ScaLEs (Barrett 2001, Chew 1995), LANDscape SUccession Model (Barrett 2001, Keane et al. 1996), and VDDT (Beukema and Kurz 1995). We will use VDDT (Beukema and Kurz 1995) and the associated TELSA (Kurz et al. 2000). The VDDT planning tool is a nonspatial model that allows building and testing STM for a set of environmental strata. The TELSA planning tool is a spatial application of VDDT that includes spatial analyses and spatial contagion of disturbances. Both models contain visual interfaces and other features that make them relatively easy to use. In addition, they have been used in landscape assessments and land management planning in the interior Northwest. The interior Columbia basin landscape assessment (Hann et al. 1997) built VDDT models for a broad cross section of range and forest lands in the interior Northwest. These and similar models are being used by some national forests for revisions to their land management plans (e.g., Merzenich et al., in press). Use of STM is a significant departure for national forest land management planning from past efforts where harvest scheduling models were predominantly used (e.g., Johnson et al. 1986). Harvest scheduling models made extensive use of timber inventories and linear programming to explore resource tradeoffs and marginal costs, as mandated under the planning regulations at the time.

Objectives and Research Approach

We used the following research approach:

1. Build STM by using the VDDT and TELSA modeling systems to simulate future forest, woodland, shrubland, and herbland vegetation conditions across the entire Upper Grande Ronde study area.

2. Link vegetation projections with SafeD (Bettinger et al. Chapter 4) and other resource effects models to examine the use of those models to calibrate STM for forested environments.

3. Explore ways to add states and transitions for large herbivores, invasive plants, and streamside/aquatic systems.

4. Examine stochastic effects and model sensitivity to disturbance probabilities.

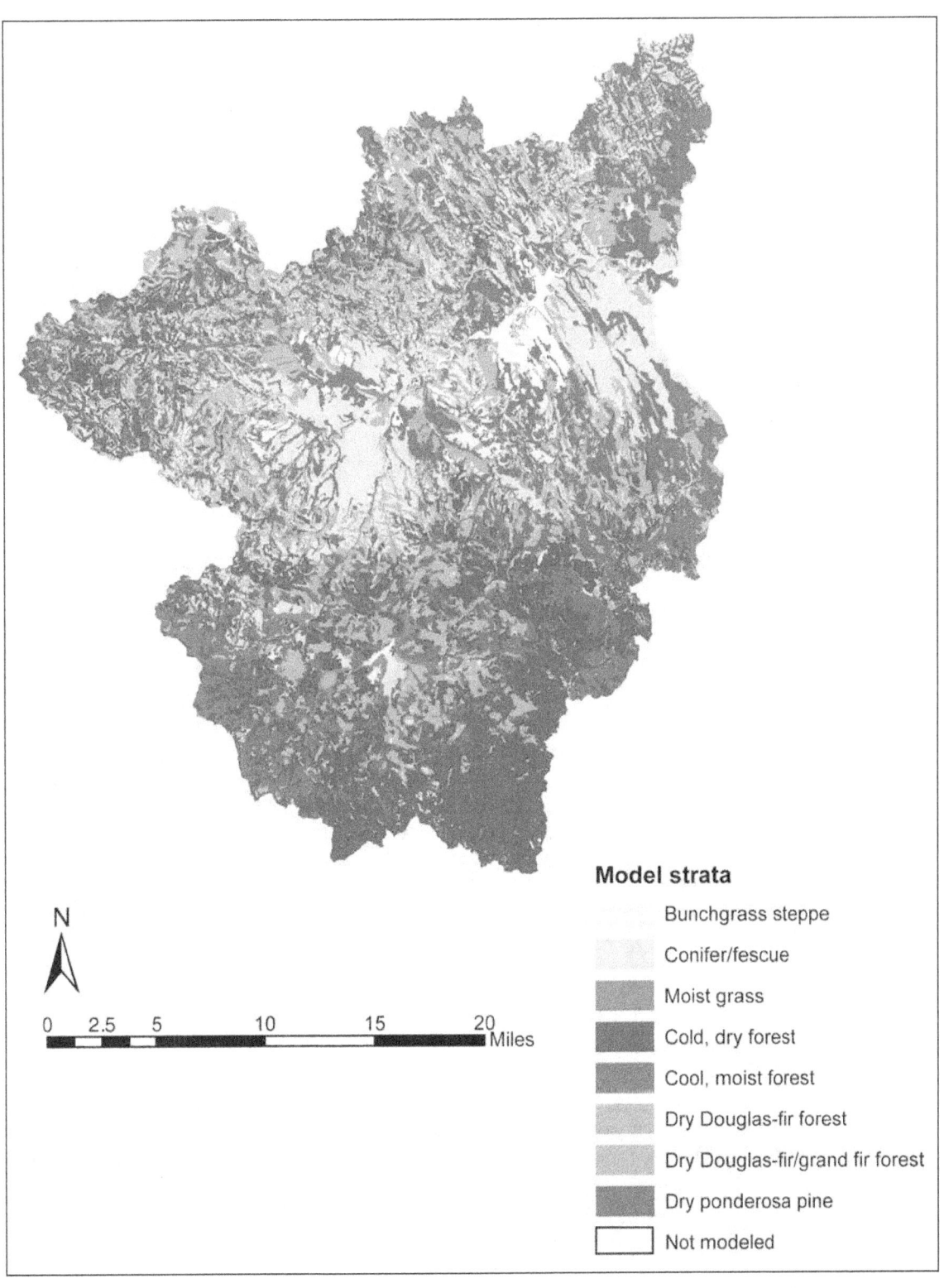

Model strata

Bunchgrass steppe

Conifer/fescue

Moist grass

Cold, dry forest

Cool, moist forest

Dry Douglas-fir forest

Dry Douglas-fir/grand fir forest

Dry ponderosa pine

Not modeled

N

0   2.5   5   10   15   20
                                          Miles

Figure 9   Example of potential vegetation modeling strata in the Interior Northwest Landscape Analysis System study area Upper Grande Ronde subbasin Oregon Classes developed during the study may differ from those shown

Build State and Transition Models

A number of tasks are required to build VDDT models for use in the INLAS project. Prototype models that might be useful starting points have been built for the interior Columbia basin assessment (Hann et al. 1997) and for the forested lands in the Blue Mountains province.[2] These models will be examined for applicability given the vegetation and environments in the Upper Grande Ronde. A first approximation set of STMs for the Upper Grande Ronde could come from adoption of suitable existing models. We expect that these first-generation models will require considerable refinement, especially those for woodlands, shrublands, and grasslands. A period of model review using the available literature and expert opinion will help refine these initial models to produce a second generation. We will include a variety of management activities by adding them as new pathways and, if necessary, vegetation states. The current version of both VDDT and TELSA can accept more than 400 vegetative states and a number of transitions limited only by computation time—likely more than sufficient for our purposes. We will design vegetation classes based on the need to add detail for wildlife habitat and other models, starting from those in the current Blue Mountains models. We recognize the importance of large dead wood in ecosystem processes and wildlife habitat. We will build structural classes that include abundant large dead wood for one or two decades following some kinds of stand-replacement disturbances.

Link State and Transition Model and Process-Based Models

Professional judgment often has been used to define vegetation states and to derive transition probabilities among vegetation states in existing STM. Although the dominant successional or disturbance transitions might be established in the literature for some vegetation types, many other transitions are not well described. Consequently, expert opinion often is used in model development and calibration. The cumulative effect of many small errors in estimated transition probabilities may undermine the reliability of simulations. Although annual wildfire probabilities often have been developed by using historical fire data, other transitions are more difficult to quantify, and few data are available.

We will examine and adjust states and transition probabilities, including those for various management activities, through the use of process-based models. The Forest Vegetation Simulator (FVS) (Crookston and Stage 1999) provides detailed estimates of tree establishment, growth, and mortality based on forest inventory and other data. Simulations from FVS are forest-based mensurational analyses of tree and stand growth as a function of density effects, disturbance effects, management treatments, and other factors that affect tree and stand growth. Stand-level simulations from FVS or SafeD will be used to refine transition probabilities or state conditions for forested lands to make forest-land projections more accurate. Unfortunately, similar process-based models might not be available for nonforest model strata. In this case, we will continue to rely on expert judgment and will document the sources and assumptions used.

In addition, vegetation classes in existing models are based on classical successional stages (e.g., Hann et al. 1997). We hope to examine this choice more closely given the kinds of stands that develop under human influences, some of which may not have good analogs in natural successional sequences. Detailed stand-level projections from FVS and SafeD models might provide a range of stand structures that should be included in STM for forested areas. We envision development of structural classes that represent stand architecture rather than successional stages that may or may not be representative of current and future east-side forest stands.

---

[2] **Merzenich, J. 2003** Persona communication P anning regiona ana yst USDA Forest Service Pacific Northwest Region P O Box 3623 Port and OR 97208

Objective 2 also will require linking model strata to timber inventories. It should be possible to link STM structure and composition classes to plot-level vegetation data from existing forest inventory data. We plan to examine the use of most similar-neighbor analyses (Moeur and Stage 1995, Ohmann and Gregory 2002) to link model strata and tree lists from plot data. We will use multivariate statistical processes to assign tree lists and other information from sampled sites to nonsampled sites based on similarities of environment, photointerpreted attributes, satellite imagery, and other features. This process may both (1) improve the accuracy of current forest composition and structure estimates by using existing plot samples and (2) allow more explicit description of future forest conditions for timber supply and harvest scheduling. True color aerial photographs at a scale of 1:15,840, black and white ortho photography at 1:24,000, and field stand examination data will be used to develop vegetation maps. A subsample of 10 to 20 percent of the photointerpreted polygons will be checked in the field to provide an assessment of photointerpretation accuracy.

Invasive Plants

Native vegetation and associated resources are experiencing significant degradation over wide areas of the interior West from nonnative invasive plants. The cumulative effects go beyond vegetative change because habitat for terrestrial vertebrates and other species is affected (Drake et al. 1989), fire regimes are altered (Billings 1994, Bunting et al. 1987, Pellant 1990), and other ecological processes may be disrupted (Billings 1994, Masters and Sheley 2001). Although the interior Columbia basin project included nonnative invasive plants in some STM, we will examine the potential interaction of invasive plants with other disturbances and management activities. State and transition models are a good choice for initial efforts to model invasive plant interactions across large landscapes because they can be assembled from sparse literature and data and expert opinion.

Ungulate Herbivory

Hobbs (1996) argued that native ungulates are critical agents of change in ecosystems via three processes: regulation of process rates, modification of spatial mosaics, and action as switches controlling transitions between alternative ecosystem states. Huntly (1991) identified the impact of herbivores on plant regeneration as a powerful yet little-studied mechanism of influence on vegetation composition, structure, and diversity. Wild and domestic ungulates should be considered potential agents of chronic disturbance (Riggs et al. 2000).

Cattle grazing often reduces cover of grasses and shrubs as well as total vegetation biomass (Jones 2000). Riggs et al. (2000) reported that in grand fir (*Abies grandis* (Dougl. ex D. Don) Lindl.) forests of northeast Oregon, understory biomass in ungulate exclosures was 2.1 times greater inside than outside, and forest-floor biomass was 1.5 times greater inside than outside. Shrub biomass was influenced more by ungulates than was grass or forb biomass. Augustine and McNaughton (1998) concluded that altered species composition of plant communities in response to selective foraging by ungulates is a general feature of plant-ungulate relations. The authors stated that by ungulates altering the competitive relations among plants, differential tolerance of co-occurring plant species becomes an important determinant of the responses of both woody and herbaceous plant communities to herbivory. Augustine and McNaughton (1998) also summarized ungulate effects on overstory species and listed several species of coniferous and deciduous trees that were herbivory intolerant. Ungulate herbivory is also a driving force shaping vegetation pattern in coastal coniferous forests (Schreiner et al. 1996, Woodward et al. 1994). Research by these authors indicated that ungulates maintained a reduced standing crop, increased forb species richness, and determined the distribution, morphology, and reproductive performance of several shrub species. Woodward et al. (1994) further stated that the extent to which herbivores can change ecosystem processes in forests likely depends on the scales of other disturbances.

Herbivory-induced changes in plant community composition have important habitat ramifications for a number of plant and animal species. Changes in understory structure and litter accumulations may be important to bird and small mammal populations. Individual species of plants and entire plant communities may be at risk under intensive herbivory. Examples of plant species at risk of elimination or severe decline under intensive herbivory include aspen (*Populus tremuloides* Michx.), bitterbrush (*Purshia tridentata* (Pursh) DC.), Pacific yew (*Taxus brevifolia* Nutt.), and mountain mahogany (*Cercocarpus* spp. Kunth) (Parks et al. 1998). Negative effects on vertebrate species that depend on these plants (e.g., cavity nesters in aspen stands, Wisdom et al. 2000) may occur. Inclusion of ungulate herbivory disturbances in STM for the Upper Grande Ronde will allow examination of two important questions:

1. What changes in composition and structure of plant communities occur as a result of herbivory at local and regional scales?

2. How does the grazing regime interact with frequency, intensity, and distribution of episodic disturbances to influence development of plant communities at local and regional scales?

The first question will initially be addressed through a synthesis of existing research data and findings from the Starkey project on diet selection and resource selection functions for ungulates in the Blue Mountains (e.g., from Johnson et al. 1995, Rowland et al. 2000, Wisdom 1998). Data will yield estimates of plant composition with and without herbivory, and the likelihood of herbivory effects occurring in various forest plant communities. The second question will be addressed through development of STM for the Upper Grande Ronde that explicitly includes ungulate herbivory, based on data synthesized for the first question. Plant succession in forests likely operates as a set of states and transitions, much like the models developed and validated for nonforest ecosystems (Laycock 1991, Westoby et al. 1989). Indeed, it now seems possible that the descriptions of many "climax" associations are questionable on this basis (Peek et al. 1978, Riggs et al. 2000, Schreiner et al. 1996). Although our first interest is in building herbivory models for application in the Upper Grande Ronde, we intend to ultimately apply these models at stand, watershed, and basin scales for the entire Blue Mountains province. The models should have some general application throughout the Rocky Mountain west.

Riparian Vegetation and Geomorphology

Riparian and aquatic issues have become critical in the inland Northwest (INFISH 1995, PACFISH 1995), and many upland land management activities have impacts on riparian and aquatic resources. Bettinger et al. (1998) attempted to account for impacts of management and disturbance on stream temperatures across large landscapes but did not project changes in riparian habitat. We will incorporate major physical and biological processes of riparian zones in an STM framework. Many analogies can be formed between existing STM for upland vegetation and the dynamics of valley-floor landforms and riparian plant communities. It may be possible to describe long-term riparian geomorphic and vegetation states, disturbance probabilities, and transitions among states for specific strata of riparian potentials. Drainage networks might be divided into discrete networks with different disturbance regimes similar to the stratification of potential vegetation types. Stream segments might be classified according to both their existing and potential characteristics and their succession described with transition probabilities based on hydrological disturbance regimes. Changes in riparian characteristics could consider both fluvial (e.g., floods) and nonfluvial (e.g., fire) disturbances. Treatment priorities might be based on channel instability and geomorphic and vegetation potentials. In addition, it might be possible to link upland episodic disturbance (e.g., wildfire) and riparian characteristics.

Linkages to Other Modules and Corporate Data

The STM module will generate several spatial and nonspatial data sets that should link well to other INLAS modules. The VDDT and TELSA models project the structural condition and cover type of grassland, shrubland, woodland, and forest vegetation. The VDDT model generates area estimates (hectares) for combinations of structure and cover in several environmental strata (as indicated by potential vegetation) by using an annual time step. It also tracks the area affected by individual disturbance transitions for each simulation year. Outputs are available in text files that can be readily transformed into databases. The TELSA model produces the same kinds of information and GIS coverages (e.g., maps) that can be used to examine spatial patterns of vegetation structure and composition as well as disturbances that drive vegetation change. We will adjust outputs of vegetation conditions and disturbances to fit the needs of wildlife habitat modeling and other modules to the degree that our models can produce appropriate information.

The VDDT and TELSA planning tools use vegetation structure classes that are derived from those suggested by Oliver and Larson (1996) as modified by O'Hara et al. (1996) and used in the interior Columbia basin scientific assessment (Quigley and Arbelbide 1997). Our modification of those structure classes will split some forest structures into classes for wildlife habitat modeling based on diameter of dominant trees. Discussions with USDA Forest Service Pacific Northwest Region planning personnel indicate that our structural classification should fit well with proposed corporate data standards.[3] The Natural Resource Information System (NRIS) proposes the use of the O'Hara et al. (1996) structure classes as one of the acceptable corporate data standards. In addition, a draft structural classification for the Pacific Northwest Region uses tree diameter breaks that are compatible with our structure classes. Our potential vegetation classes also should fit well with corporate data standards because we use aggregates of ecoclasses (Hall 1998).

Our vegetation cover type classes match those currently in use by Blue Mountains national forests (see footnote 2). However, they may not fit well with standard cover types that may be used in the future by the USDA Forest Service Pacific Northwest Region (see footnote 3). The Region's draft standards match NRIS standards and consist of Society of American Foresters (Eyre 1980) and Society for Range Management (Shiflet 1994) cover types. We found those cover types, which were designed for categorizing vegetation cover across the entire United States, to be insufficiently refined for mapping wildlife habitat and stratifying economic product potential at the scale of our study area.

Validation and Sensitivity Analysis

Model validation is important in evaluating the accuracy and reliability of model projections. Landscape simulation models can be difficult to validate empirically because projections of current conditions into the future may take decades to evaluate, and unforeseen disturbances or management approaches may generate different futures. If we could establish vegetation structure and composition conditions for the Upper Grande Ronde area at some point in the past, we might project those conditions to the present and evaluate differences from current conditions. However, the historical track of disturbances may be only one of many that could have occurred. Actual past disturbances may not have even been those that had a high probability of occurring. Given these difficulties and the relatively short timeframe for our work, we take two approaches to evaluating model projections. First, we will compare the projections from different vegetation

---

[3] **Connelly, W. 2003** Persona communication Economist and ana yst USDA Forest Service Pacific Northwest Region P O Box 3623 Port and OR 97208

modeling approaches to look for differences and similarities that may require further examination. Secondly, we will calibrate STM models with stand-scale forest models (e.g., FVS) that have been widely published and evaluated elsewhere.

Our modeling process will be based on stochastic or probabilistic disturbances. Vegetation transitions will be expressed in terms of probabilities. Both VDDT and TELSA have the capability of generating many Monte Carlo simulations by using random number seeds in calculating probabilities. We plan to repeatedly run individual management and disturbance scenarios to examine the effects of stochastic variation on model results. Our intent is to express model results as probabilistic rather than providing only one result for each scenario. In addition, we plan to vary key disturbance probabilities by one or two standard deviations from the calculated or assigned values to gauge model sensitivity.

Products and Audience

Land and wildlife managers in the Blue Mountains province are the targeted users of the research findings and management tools produced from the activities outlined in this paper. Clients include managers of public, private, and tribal lands in the Blue Mountains province, encompassing economic and social interests related to management of timber, livestock, wild ungulates, salmon, vertebrates, and plants of conservation concern. In particular, the Blue Mountains national forests are beginning revision of land management plans. The STM may offer some advantages for land management planning. The modeling framework can be applied to a variety of vegetation types and environments. The models are more easily understood than previous planning models and may provide for better public involvement in the analysis process. The coarse resolution of the internal modeling states in the STM makes them relatively easy to build, edit, and execute. Technical users also may include scientists, public groups, and resource specialists. Application of the concepts and relations developed as part of this research and associated management tools will also extend beyond the Blue Mountains to similar environments in other provinces of the Pacific Northwest and intermountain West.

Acknowledgments

Peter Bettinger, Lowell Suring, and Steve Wondzell provided helpful review comments. Funding for this project was provided by the U.S. Department of Agriculture, Forest Service, Pacific Northwest Research Station.

Metric Equivalents

When you know:	Multiply by:	To find:
Miles	1.609	Kilometers

Literature Cited

Alig, R.J.; Zheng, D.; Spies, T.A.; Butler, B.J. 2000. Forest cover dynamics in the Pacific Northwest west side: regional trends and projections. Res. Pap. PNW-RP-522. Portland, OR: U.S. Department of Agriculture, Forest Service, Pacific Northwest Research Station. 22 p.

Augustine, D.J.; McNaughton, S.J. 1998. Ungulate effects on the functional species composition of plant communities: herbivore selectivity and plant tolerance. Journal of Wildlife Management. 62: 1165-1183.

Barrett, T.M. 2001. Models of vegetative change for landscape planning: a comparison of FETM, LANDSUM, SIMPPLLE, and VDDT. Gen. Tech. Rep. RMRS-GTR-76-WWW. Ogden, UT: U.S. Department of Agriculture, Forest Service, Rocky Mountain Research Station. 14 p.

Bettinger, P.; Graetz, D.; Ager, A.A.; Sessions, J. 2004. The SafeD forest landscape planning model. In: Hayes, J.L.; Ager, A.A.; Barbour, R.J., tech. eds. Methods for integrating modeling of landscape change: Interior Northwest Landscape Analysis System. Gen. Tech. Rep. PNW-GTR-610. Portland, OR: U.S. Department of Agriculture, Forest Service, Pacific Northwest Research Station: 41-63. Chapter 4.

Bettinger, P.; Sessions, J.; Boston, K. 1997. Using tabu search to schedule timber harvests subject to spatial wildlife goals for big game. Ecological Modelling. 94: 111-123.

Bettinger, P.; Sessions, J.; Johnson, K.N. 1998. Ensuring the compatibility of aquatic habitat and commodity production goals in eastern Oregon with a tabu search procedure. Forest Science. 44: 96-112.

Beukema, S.J.; Kurz, W.A. 1995. Vegetation dynamics development tool user's guide, version 2.0 beta. 76 p. Unpublished report. On file with: ESSA Technologies Ltd., No. 300-1765 West 8th Avenue, Vancouver, BC, V6J 5C6, Canada.

Billings, W.D. 1994. Ecological impacts of cheatgrass and resultant fire on ecosystems in the western Great Basin. In: Monsen, S.B.; Kitchen, S.G., eds. Proceedings—ecology and management of annual rangelands. Gen. Tech. Rep. INT-GTR-313. Ogden, UT: U.S. Department of Agriculture, Forest Service, Intermountain Research Station: 22-30.

Bunting, S.C.; Kilgore, B.M.; Bushey, C.L. 1987. Guidelines for prescribed burning sagebrush steppe rangelands in the northern Great Basin. Gen. Tech. Rep. INT-231. Ogden, UT: U.S. Department of Agriculture, Forest Service, Intermountain Forest and Range Experiment Station. 33 p.

Cattelino, P.M.; Noble, I.R.; Slatyer, R.O.; Kessell, S.R. 1979. Predicting the multiple pathways of plant succession. Environmental Management. 3: 41-50.

Chew, J.D. 1995. Development of a system for simulating vegetative patterns and processes at landscape scales. Missoula, MT: The University of Montana. 182 p. Ph.D. dissertation.

Crookston, N.L.; Stage, A.R. 1999. Percent canopy cover and stand structure statistics from the Forest Vegetation Simulator. Gen. Tech. Rep. RMRS-GTR-24. Fort Collins, CO: U.S. Department of Agriculture, Forest Service, Rocky Mountain Research Station. 15 p.

Drake, J.; Mooney, H.; di Castri, E. [et al.], eds. 1989. Ecology of biological invasions: a global perspective. SCOPE 37. New York: John Wiley and Sons. 528 p.

Eyre, F.H. 1980. Forest cover types of the United States and Canada. Washington, DC: Society of American Foresters. 148 p.

Graetz, D.H. 2000. The SafeD model: Incorporating episodic disturbances and heuristic programming into forest management planning for the Applegate River watershed, southwestern Oregon. Corvallis, OR: Department of Forest Resources, Oregon State University. 127 p. M.S. thesis.

Hall, F.C. 1998. Pacific Northwest ecoclass codes for seral and potential natural communities. Gen. Tech. Rep. PNW-GTR-418. Portland, OR: U.S. Department of Agriculture, Forest Service, Pacific Northwest Research Station. 290 p. Vol. 2.

Hann, W.J.; Jones, J.L.; Karl, M.G. [et al.]. 1997. Landscape dynamics of the basin. In: Quigley, T.M.; Arbelbide, S.J., tech. eds. An assessment of ecosystem components in the interior Columbia basin and portions of the Klamath and Great Basins. Gen. Tech. Rep. PNW-GTR-405. Portland, OR: U.S. Department of Agriculture, Forest Service, Pacific Northwest Research Station: 337-1055. (Quigley, T.M., tech. ed.; Interior Columbia Basin Ecosystem Management Project: scientific assessment).

Hemstrom, M.A.; Wisdom, M.J.; Hann, W.J. [et al.]. [In press]. Sagebrush-steppe vegetation dynamics and restoration potential in the interior Columbia basin, USA. Conservation Biology.

Hobbs, N.T. 1996. Modification of ecosystems by ungulates. Journal of Wildland Management. 60: 695-713.

Horn, H.S. 1975. Markovian properties of forest succession. In: Cody, M.L.; Diamond, J.M., eds. Ecology and evolution of communities. Cambridge, MA: Harvard University Press: 196-211.

Huntly, N. 1991. Herbivores and the dynamics of communities and ecosystems. Annual Review of Ecology and Systematics. 22: 477-503.

Inland Native Fish Strategy (INFISH). 1995. Environmental assessment: decision notice and finding of no significant impact. Interim strategies for managing fish-producing watersheds in eastern Oregon and Washington, Idaho, western Montana and portions of Nevada. [Place of publication unknown]: U.S. Department of Agriculture, Forest Service, Intermountain, Northern, and Pacific Northwest Regions. [Irregular pagination].

Johnson, B.K.; Ager, A.; Crim, S.A. [et al.]. 1995. Allocating forage among wild and domestic ungulates—a new approach. In: Edge, W.D.; Olson-Edge, S.L., eds. Proceedings, sustaining rangeland ecosystems symposium. SR 953. Corvallis, OR: Oregon State University: 166-169.

Johnson, K.N.; Stuart, T.W.; Crim, S.A. 1986. FORPLAN version 2: an overview. Washington, DC: U.S. Department of Agriculture, Forest Service, Land Management Planning Systems Section. 98 p.

Jones, A. 2000. Effects of cattle grazing on North American arid ecosystems: a quantitative review. Western North American Naturalist. 60: 155-164.

Keane, R.E.; Long, D.G.; Menakis, J.P. [et al.]. 1996. Simulating coarse-scale dynamics using the Columbia River Basin Succession Model—CRBSUM. Gen. Tech. Rep. INT-GTR-340. Ogden, UT: U.S. Department of Agriculture, Forest Service, Intermountain Research Station. 50 p.

Kurz, W.A.; Beukema, S.J.; Klenner, W. [et al.]. 2000. TELSA: the tool for exploratory landscape scenario analysis. Computers and Electronics in Agriculture. 27: 227-242.

Laycock, W.A. 1991. Stable states and thresholds of range condition on North American rangelands: a viewpoint. Journal of Range Management. 44(5): 427-433.

Masters, R.A.; Sheley, R.L. 2001. Invited synthesis paper: principles and practices for managing rangeland invasive plants. Journal of Range Management. 54: 502-517.

Merzenich, J.; Kurz, W.; Beukema, S. [et al.]. [In press]. Determining forest fuel treatments for the Bitterroot front using VDDT. In: Arthaud, G.J.; Barrett, T.M., eds. Proceedings of the 8th symposium. Dordrecht, The Netherlands: Kluwer Academic Publishers.

Mladenoff, D.J.; He, H.S. 1999. Design and behavior of LANDIS, an object-oriented model of forest landscape disturbance and succession. In: Mladenoff, D.J.; Baker, W.L., eds. Advances in spatial modeling of forest landscape change: approaches and applications. Cambridge, United Kingdom: Cambridge University Press: 125-162.

Moeur, M.; Stage, A.R. 1995. Most similar neighbor: an improved sampling inference procedure for natural resource planning. Forest Science. 41(2): 337-359.

Noble, I.R.; Slatyer, R.O. 1980. The use of vital attributes to predict successional changes in plant communities subject to recurrent disturbances. Vegetatio. 43: 5-21.

O'Hara, K.L.; Latham, P.A.; Hessburg, P.I.; Smith, B.G. 1996. A structural classification of inland Northwest forest vegetation. Western Journal of Applied Forestry. 11(3): 97-102.

Ohmann, J.L.; Gregory, M.J. 2002. Predictive mapping of forest composition and structure with direct gradient analysis and nearest-neighbor imputation in coastal Oregon, USA. Canadian Journal of Forest Research. 32: 725-741.

Oliver, C.D.; Larson, B.C. 1996. Forest stand dynamics. Updated edition. New York: John Wiley and Sons, Inc. 520 p.

(PACFISH) USDA Forest Service and USDI Bureau of Land Management. 1995. Decision notice/Decision Record, FONSI, EA, Appendices for the Interim strategies for managing anadromous fish-producing watersheds in eastern Oregon and Washington, Idaho, and portions of California. Washington, DC: [Irregular pagination].

Parks, C.G.; Bednar, L.; Tiedemann, A.R. 1998. Browsing ungulates–an important consideration in dieback and mortality of Pacific yew (*Taxus brevifolia*) in a northeastern Oregon stand. Northwest Science. 72: 190-197.

Peek, J.M.; Johnson, F.D.; Pence, N.N. 1978. Successional trends in a ponderosa pine/bitterbrush community related to grazing by livestock, wildlife, and to fire. Journal of Range Management. 31: 49-53.

Pellant, M. 1990. The cheatgrass-wildfire cycle: Are there any solutions? In: McArthur, E.D.; Romney, R.M.; Smith, S.D.; Tueller, P.T., comps. Proceedings, symposium on cheatgrass invasion, shrub die-off, and other aspects of shrub biology and management. Gen. Tech. Rep. INT-276. Ogden, UT: U.S. Department of Agriculture, Forest Service, Intermountain Research Station: 11–18.

Quigley, T.M.; Arbelbide, S.J., tech. eds. 1997. An assessment of ecosystem components in the interior Columbia basin and portions of the Klamath and Great Basins. Gen. Tech. Rep. PNW-GTR-405. Portland, OR: U.S. Department of Agriculture, Forest Service, Pacific Northwest Research Station: 337-1055. Vol. 2. (Quigley, T.M., tech. ed.; Interior Columbia Basin Ecosystem Management Project: scientific assessment).

Riggs, R.A.; Tiedemann, A.R.; Cook, J.G. [et al.]. 2000. Modification of mixed-conifer forests by ruminant herbivores in the Blue Mountains ecological province. Res. Pap. PNW-RP-527. Portland, OR: U.S. Department of Agriculture, Forest Service, Pacific Northwest Research Station. 77 p.

Rowland, M.M.; Wisdom, M.J.; Johnson, B.K.; Kie, J.G. 2000. Elk distribution and modeling in relation to roads. Journal of Wildlife Management. 64: 672-684.

Schreiner, E.G.; Krueger, K.A.; Happe, P.J.; Houston, D.B. 1996. Understory patch dynamics and ungulate herbivory in old-growth forests of Olympic National Park, Washington. Canadian Journal of Forestry Research. 26: 255-265.

Sessions, J.; Johnson, K.N.; Franklin, J.F.; Gabriel, J.T. 1999. Achieving sustainable forest structures on fire prone landscapes while pursuing multiple goals. In: Mladenoff, D.J.; Baker, W.L., eds. Spatial modeling of forest landscape change. Cambridge, United Kingdom: Cambridge University Press: 210-255.

Shiflet, T.N. 1994. Rangeland cover types of the United States. Denver, CO: Society for Range Management. 152 p.

U.S. Department of Agriculture, Forest Service; U.S. Department of the Interior, Bureau of Land Management [USDA and USDI]. 2000. Interior Columbia basin final environmental impact statement, BLM/OR/WA/Pt-01/010+1792. Portland, OR. [Irregular pagination].

Wedin, H. 1999. Stand level prescription generation under multiple objectives. Corvallis, OR: Department of Forest Resources, Oregon State University. 178 p. M.S. thesis.

Westoby, M.; Walker, B.; Noy-Meir, I. 1989. Opportunistic management for rangelands not at equilibrium. Journal of Range Management. 42: 266-276.

Wisdom, M.J. 1998. Assessing life-stage importance and resource selection for conservation of selected vertebrates. Moscow, ID: University of Idaho. 118 p. Ph.D. dissertation.

Wisdom, M.J.; Holthausen, R.S.; Wales, B.C. [et al.]. 2000. Source habitats for terrestrial vertebrates of focus in the interior Columbia basin: broad-scale trends and management implications. Gen. Tech. Rep. PNW-GTR-485. Portland, OR: U.S. Department of Agriculture, Forest Service, Pacific Northwest Research Station. 434 p.

Woodward, A.; Schreiner, E.G.; Houston, D.B.; Moorhead, B.B. 1994. Ungulate-forest relationships in Olympic National Park: retrospective exclosure studies. Northwest Science. 68: 97-110.

Chapter 3: Application of the Forest Vegetation Simulator and Related Tools for Integrated Modeling of Forest Landscapes

Alan A. Ager[1]

Abstract

This chapter describes the use of stand-level growth simulators to address landscape planning issues, and outlines work by the Interior Northwest Landscape Analysis System (INLAS) project to enhance the functionality of the Forest Vegetation Simulator and related tools to meet the needs for landscape analysis tools. Stand-level growth models are widely used in the Forest Service and other agencies, and they are logical candidates to use as the core for an integrated framework of the kind envisioned for INLAS. However, a number of modifications are needed to facilitate wider application of these tools to address strategic planning and forest management issues. These proposed modifications include improved data linkages and streamlined methods for building scenarios and summarizing results and are described in this chapter.

Keywords: Landscape simulation, landscape ecology, Forest Vegetation Simulator, forest planning.

Introduction

There is growing interest in applying landscape ecology and simulation methods to forest management problems (Liu et al. 2000, Mladenoff and Baker 1999, Spies et al. 2002). Simulation methods provide the broad and flexible framework needed to model natural disturbances, forest succession, and management on large landscapes. Specific problems of interest include studying the effects of natural disturbance on aquatic and terrestrial habitat reserves (Johnson et al. 1998, Maffei and Tandy 2002) and developing spatially explicit schedules for fuel-reduction treatments (Finney Chapter 9). Analyzing these problems by using traditional methods used in forest operations research (Dykstra 1984) is difficult owing to the stochastic nature of disturbance processes and the need for spatial detail in strategic planning models. Many new simulation modeling lineages have evolved over the past 10 to 15 years, and the application of these models is continuing to grow in scale and complexity, resulting in many sophisticated systems for

[1] **Alan A. Ager** is an operations research ana yst U S Department of Agricu ture Forest Service Forestry and Range Sciences Laboratory 1401 Geke er Lane La Grande OR 97850

simulating forest succession, management, and disturbance on large landscapes in the Western United States (Bettinger et al. Chapter 4, Graetz 1999, Hof and Bevers 1998, Kurz et al. 2000, Liu et al. 2000, McCarter 1997, Sessions et al. 1999, Spies et al. 2002, Weise et al. 2000). The growing frequency of severe wildfires on interior forests has created a need for strategic planning models that examine the costs and benefits of fuel treatments on large landscapes (Johnson et al. 1998, Sessions et al. 1999) and development of spatially explicit fuel-treatment strategies that best meet multiple resource goals and constraints, including regulatory standards for terrestrial and aquatic species. These problems have complex spatiotemporal dimensions that must consider forest management, natural disturbances, and forest succession over time on large landscapes.

Focusing on recent work in the Western United States, there are two commonly used approaches to simulate changes in forest vegetation. The first, a **state and transition** approach, stratifies forest and other vegetation into states (e.g., forest structure, cover type) that change according to transitions representing disturbance, management, and succession. State and transition models were used for the Columbia River basin assessment (Hann et al. 1997), which led to improved software, and more recently, application for forest plan revisions. State and transition models and their application in the Interior Northwest Landscape Analysis System (INLAS) project are described by Hemstrom et al. (Chapter 2).

A second approach involves the application of tree-level growth simulators (Hann et al. 1995, Stage 1973, Wedin 1999) to model each and every stand on a landscape (Crookston and Havis 2002, Crookston and Stage 1991). Because these methods are relatively well established and readily available, they are logical choices to address specific kinds of resource analyses. However, our review of these tools and methods suggested that simulating management scenarios on forested landscapes remains a complex process. Many specialists on national forest ranger districts who do analyses of alternative management scenarios are largely baffled by the array of existing tools and required data formats, as well as how they can be adapted to project-level work.

This paper briefly summarizes the development and application of stand-level simulation models and their application to management problems in forests in the Western United States. Subsequent sections describe specific improvements to existing methods to help build a coherent modeling framework and facilitate wider application of stand-level models to address strategic planning issues on watersheds with multiple ownerships.

Stand-Level Landscape Simulation and Planning Models

The stand-level simulation approach has been used in a number of applied research projects over the past 10 to 15 years; however, much of this work is either not published or not described in detail in symposia and other documents. In the simplest approach, landscapes were modeled with stand simulators by simply batch processing all the stands in an area and linking the results to geographic information system (GIS) stand maps. Extending Forest Vegetation Simulator (FVS) to landscapes was advanced with the developments of the Landscape Management System (McCarter et al. 1997), the Parallel Processing Extension (PPE) to the FVS (Crookston and Stage 1991), the Prognosis Environmental Indicators model (Greenough et al. 2002), and SUPPOSE, a visual interface to FVS (Crookston 1997). The Parallel Processing Extension added important functionality (Crookston and Stage 1991) in that it provided the means to consider contagion, treatment priorities, and overall landscape condition during the simulation.

Graetz (1999) later demonstrated how stand-level models could be incorporated into landscape optimization systems (Bettinger et al. Chapter 4).

Much of the functionality in current landscape models is derived from the numerous FVS extensions and postprocessors that allow for scaling the simulation system to the problem at hand. An array of simulation capabilities, including the dynamics of fuels and fire effects, (Beukema et al. 1997a), insect and disease mortality (Roberts 2002), economics (Fight and Chmelik 1998, Renner and Martin 2002), etc., enhance the utility of this overall approach for landscape applications. Linkages to visualization systems (McGaughey 2002, 2004) and interfaces like SUPPOSE (Crookston 1997) or the Landscape Management System (McCarter 1997) make it possible to conduct simple landscape simulations with a broad array of capabilities.

One common feature among stand-level modeling projects is that tree lists are usually imputed for stands where data are missing by using a most-similar-neighbor (Crookston and Havis 2002, Moeur and Stage 1995) or K-nearest-neighbor (Ohmann and Gregory 2002) approach. Imputing means that the tree list is obtained from an existing sample of tree lists rather than estimating a new tree list. This process is necessary because tree list data rarely exist for every stand in a project. There have been several recent advances in methods to impute stand data (Crookston et al. 2002, Temesgen and LeMay 2002). More work is needed in this area to determine the effects of imputation errors on different outputs of landscape simulations.

The functionality of the stand-level approach began to more closely match that of traditional forest planning models with the work of Liu et al. (2000), Graetz (1999), Wedin (1999), and others to optimize the scheduling of treatments to meet landscape goals. In this approach, alternative management scenarios are simulated for each stand, and heuristic search algorithms are used to find a combination that best meets the landscape goals. Goal functions are formulated to allow for multiple-weighted goals. Several projects are now using heuristic methods (e.g., Hummel et al. 2002) to sort through simulations a posteriori to find prescriptions that maximize single- or multiple-weighted objectives. In the work of Graetz (1999) and Wedin (1999), the growth and mortality code was extracted from FVS and incorporated into a stand optimizer. This general lineage of landscape simulation/optimization models is reviewed by Bettinger et al. (Chapter 4).

Another significant enhancement to stand-level models was attained when spatially explicit stochastic disturbance was incorporated into landscape planning models (Graetz 2000, Johnson et al. 1998, Sessions et al. 1999). Periodic wildfire was simulated with the Fire Area Simulator (FARSITE, Finney 1999) and fire mortality functions were used to update tree lists after each wildfire. This work represented a significant convergence between landscape ecology models with those used in forest planning and harvest scheduling (Mladenoff and Baker 1999). Spatially explicit models for insect disturbance also have been integrated into landscape simulations (Beukema et al. 1997b, Smith et al. 2002).

Work continues on many aspects of incorporating nonforest products values into landscape simulation models (Greenough et al. 2002). Of particular interest are understory vegetation components, hydrology, wildlife models, and carbon pools. Greenough et al. (2002) provide an example of incorporating an array of environmental indicators into a stand-level simulation system.

Application of stand-level simulation methods to landscapes continues to grow in scale and number. For instance, the Coastal Landscape and Modeling Study (CLAMS) project (Spies et al. 2002) used stand-level modeling (pixels) to simulate 2.6 million ha of the coastal Oregon region.

Improvements to Stand-Level Growth Simulators for Landscape Applications

Somewhere in the various modeling lineages described in this volume lie the needs of ranger district specialists and forest planners who require the stand-level capabilities of FVS and some of the landscape capabilities in experimental models like those described by Bettinger et al. (Chapter 4). Many agency-sponsored development efforts toward this end have not had wide success owing to complex data structures, inflexibility, administrative overhead, accessibility, and other factors. At the same time, experimental systems used for research projects are neither designed for wide deployment nor to address more than a relatively narrow set of questions. Some of the issues that need resolution include appropriate data sources, tree list imputation, mechanics of building spatial scenarios, and linking various resource models. Methods are needed to quickly formulate, execute, and interpret realistic scenarios on large forested watersheds that contain multiple ownerships and complex arrays of management goals and intentions. For instance, a typical watershed in a Western national forest contains numerous management allocations, each having unique long-term management objectives ranging from fiber production, to scenic quality, to protection of habitat for federally listed species. The matrix of forest conditions and management goals is tedious to replicate in a landscape simulation. Further, an efficient simulation system for policy analysis requires a mechanism to rapidly alter the management matrix to test alternative scenarios.

Of prime importance is the ability to model fire and fuel dynamics over time and to visualize treatment response. Landscape planning models need the capability to measure wildfire hazard, as well as simulate prescribed fire and wildfire spread and effects on vegetation and fuels. These capabilities exist with the Fire and Fuels Extension (FFE) to the FVS (Beukema et al. 1997a), FLAMMAP (http://fire.org), and FARSITE (Finney 1999). However, for all these programs, there are significant implementation issues and little published case study in areas like the Blue Mountains. A major obstacle to extending stand-level simulators to landscapes is the problem of organizing spatial simulation units into landscapes and controlling their disposition over time. Simulation units are formed by overlaying GIS layers for stands, management intentions, riparian buffers, treatment alternatives, ownership boundaries, and other layers. The problem is complicated by fine-scale mosaics of federal land management goals and state, federal, tribal, industrial, and nonindustrial private land ownerships within a typical watershed. The resulting matrix of forest conditions and management goals can have several hundred elements for a given HUC4 watershed, making it tedious to formulate a given scenario. Furthermore, analysis of alternative scenarios requires repeatedly changing the array of management intensities to different land strata. Existing interfaces to the FVS like SUPPOSE (Crookston 1997) can simplify the process of organizing stands and management intentions into landscape scenarios by using policy labels (Vandenriesche 2002), although enhancements could significantly simplify the process.

Research Approach and Products

This work focuses on improving operational aspects of the FVS and related software in the context of landscape simulations, as well as adding functionality for resource problems that are of particular concern for the Blue Mountains region. The work will have relevance to efforts that are repackaging other stand-level simulators for landscape applications. Our approach will emphasize, but not be limited to, the improvement of existing software, data linkages, and documentation in terms of a case study. This work will complement the model development work described by Bettinger et al. (Chapter 4) and Hemstrom et al. (Chapter 2) concerned with larger scales and questions that demand features like optimization. The work will be targeted toward specific analyses, like fuels-reduction projects, where existing stand-level tools can be scaled up to address the issues at hand.

Key areas that will be addressed include the following:

1. Framework. A framework will be produced that describes the application of existing simulation tools for rapid development and simulation of management scenarios on land-scapes having multiple ownerships. The framework will be a manual of methodology, including a synthesis and compilation of case studies. It also will identify ways to improve linkages among existing data sets and software. The framework will review approaches to address issues such as measuring wildfire risk, simulating prescribed fire, treatment constraints, and landscape visualization.

2. Software development. Modifications to existing software will be explored to build a coherent, functional set of software tools that can be applied to a typical project to capture the differences between various treatment scenarios in terms of potential wildfire risk, fuel loadings, insect mortality, visual impacts, financial outcomes, and other attributes. A significant component of this work will be adding to the capabilities of the FVS PPE. Linkages among FVS-related and other software will be examined to find ways to improve integration of different resource models.

3. Application. The tools will be applied on the Upper Grande Ronde watershed in parallel with other INLAS modeling work to analyze a variety of land management scenarios and their long-term outcomes.

Audience

The primary audience for the products of this work are district specialists charged with National Environmental Policy Act analyses of land management scenarios and forest planners who require detailed projections of forest conditions through time under alternative management scenarios.

English Equivalent

When you know:	Multi by:	To get:
Hectares (ha)	2.47	Acres

Literature Cited

Bettinger, P.; Graetz, D.; Ager, A.A.; Sessions, J. 2004. The SafeD forest landscape planning model. In: Hayes, J.L.; Ager, A.A.; Barbour, R.J., tech. eds. Methods for integrating modeling of landscape change: Interior Northwest Landscape Analysis System. Gen. Tech. Rep. PNW-GTR-610. Portland, OR: U.S. Department of Agriculture, Forest Service, Pacific Northwest Research Station: 41-63. Chapter 4.

Beukema, S.J.; Greenough, J.A.; Robinson, D.C.E. [et al.]. 1997a. An introduction to the fire and fuels extension to FVS. In: Teck, R.; Moeur, M.; Adams, J., comps. Proceedings: Forest Vegetation Simulator conference. Gen. Tech. Rep. INT-GTR-373. Ogden, UT: U.S. Department of Agriculture, Forest Service, Intermountain Research Station: 191-195.

Beukema, S.J.; Greenough, J.A.; Robinson, D.C.E. [et al.]. 1997b. The westwide pine beetle model: a spatially-explicit contagion model. In: Teck, R.; Moeur, M.; Adams, J., comps. Proceedings: Forest Vegetation Simulator conference. Gen. Tech. Rep. INT-GTR-373. Ogden, UT: U.S. Department of Agriculture, Forest Service, Intermountain Research Station: 126-130.

Crookston, N.L. 1997. SUPPOSE: an interface to the Forest Vegetation Simulator. In: Teck, R.; Moeur, M.; Adams, J., comps. Proceedings: Forest Vegetation Simulator conference. Gen. Tech. Rep. INT-GTR-373. Ogden, UT: U.S. Department of Agriculture, Forest Service, Intermountain Research Station: 7-14.

Crookston, N.L.; Havis, R.N., comps. 2002. Second Forest Vegetation Simulator conference. Proc. RMRS-P-25. Fort Collins, CO: U.S. Department of Agriculture, Forest Service, Rocky Mountain Research Station. 208 p.

Crookston, N.L.; Moeur, M.; Renner, D. 2002. User's guide to the most similar neighbor imputation program version 2. Gen. Tech. Rep. RMRS-GTR-96. Moscow, ID: U.S. Department of Agriculture, Forest Service, Rocky Mountain Research Station. 35 p.

Crookston, N.L.; Stage, A.R. 1991. User's guide to the Parallel Processing Extension of the prognosis model. Gen. Tech. Rep. INT-281. Ogden, UT: U.S. Department of Agriculture, Forest Service, Intermountain Forest and Range Experiment Station. 87 p.

Dykstra, D.P. 1984. Mathematical programming for natural resource management. New York: McGraw-Hill, Inc. 318 p.

Fight, R.D.; Chmelik, J.T. 1998. Analysts guide to FEEMA for financial analysis of ecosystem management activities. Gen. Tech. Rep. FPL-GTR-111. Madison, WI: U.S. Department of Agriculture, Forest Service, Forest Products Laboratory. 5 p.

Finney, M.A. 1999. Mechanistic modeling of landscape fire patterns. In: Mladenoff, D.; Baker, W., eds. Spatial modeling of forest landscape change: approaches and applications. Cambridge, United Kingdom: Cambridge University Press: 186-209.

Finney, M.A. 2004. Landscape fire simulation and fuel treatment optimization. In: Hayes, J.L.; Ager, A.A.; Barbour, R.J., tech. eds. Methods for integrating modeling of landscape change: Interior Northwest Landscape Analysis System. Gen. Tech. Rep. PNW-GTR-610. Portland, OR: U.S. Department of Agriculture, Forest Service, Pacific Northwest Research Station: 117-131. Chapter 9.

Graetz, D. 1999. The SafeD model: incorporating episodic disturbances and heuristic programming into forest management planning for the Applegate River watershed, southwestern Oregon. Corvallis, OR: Oregon State University, College of Forestry. 127 p. M.S. thesis.

Greenough, J.; Kurz, W.; Robinson, D. [et al.]. 2002. Prognosis EI: a detailed watershed-level environmental indicators model. In: Crookston, N.L.; Havis, R.N., comps. Second Forest Vegetation Simulator conference. Proc. RMRS-P-25. Fort Collins, CO: U.S. Department of Agriculture, Forest Service, Rocky Mountain Research Station: 122-125.

Hann, D.W.; Hester, A.S.; Olsen, C.L. 1995. ORGANON user's manual. Ed. 5.0. Corvallis, OR: Department of Forest Resources, Oregon State University. 127 p.

Hann, W.J.; Jones, J.L.; Karl, M.G. [et al.]. 1997. Landscape dynamics of the basin. In: Quigley, T.M.; Arbelbide, S.J., tech. eds. An assessment of ecosystem components in the interior Columbia basin and portions of the Klamath and Great Basins. Gen. Tech. Rep. PNW-GTR-405. Portland, OR: U.S. Department of Agriculture, Forest Service, Pacific Northwest Research Station: 337-1055. Vol 2. (Quigley, T.M., tech. ed.; Interior Columbia Basin Ecosystem Management Project: scientific assessment).

Hemstrom, M.; Ager, A.A.; Vavra, M. [et al.]. 2004. A state and transition approach for integrating landscape models. In: Hayes, J.L.; Ager, A.A.; Barbour, R.J., tech. eds. Methods for integrating modeling of landscape change: Interior Northwest Landscape Analysis System. Gen. Tech. Rep. PNW-GTR-610. Portland, OR: U.S. Department of Agriculture, Forest Service, Pacific Northwest Research Station: 17-32. Chapter 2.

Hof, J.; Bevers, M. 1998. Spatial optimization for managed ecosystems. New York: Columbia University Press. 258 p.

Hummel, S.; Calkin, D.; Barbour, J. 2002. Landscape analysis with FVS and optimization techniques: efficient management planning for the Gotchen Late Successional Reserve. In: Crookston, N.L.; Havis, R.N., comps. Second Forest Vegetation Simulator conference. Proc. RMRS-P-25. Fort Collins, CO: U.S. Department of Agriculture, Forest Service, Rocky Mountain Research Station: 78-82.

Johnson, K.N.; Sessions, J.; Franklin, J.; Gabriel, J. 1998. Integrating wildfire into strategic planning for Sierra Nevada forests. Journal of Forestry. 96(1): 42-49.

Kurz, W.A.; Beukema, S.J.; Klenner, W. [et al.]. 2000. TELSA: the tool for exploratory landscape scenario analysis. Computers and Electronics in Agriculture. 27: 227-242.

Liu, G.; Nelson, J.D.; Wardman, C.W. 2000. A target-oriented approach to forest ecosystem design—changing the rules of forest planning. Ecological Modelling. 127: 269-281.

Maffei, H.; Tandy, B. 2002. Methodology for modeling the spatial and temporal effects of vegetation management alternatives on late successional habitat in the Pacific Northwest. In: Crookston, N.L.; Havis, R.N., comps. Second Forest Vegetation Simulator conference. Proc. RMRS-P-25. Fort Collins, CO: U.S. Department of Agriculture, Forest Service, Rocky Mountain Research Station: 69-77.

McCarter, J.B. 1997. Integrating forest inventory growth and yield, and computer visualization into a landscape management system. In: Teck, R.; Moeur, M.; Adams, J., comps. Proceedings: Forest Vegetation Simulator conference. Gen. Tech. Rep. INT-GTR-373. Ogden, UT: U.S. Department of Agriculture, Forest Service, Intermountain Research Station: 159-167.

McGaughey, R.J. 2002. Creating visual simulations of fuel conditions predicted by the fire and fuels extension to the Forest Vegetation Simulator. In: Crookston, N.L.; Havis, R.N., comps. Second Forest Vegetation Simulator conference. Proc. RMRS-P-25. Fort Collins, CO: U.S. Department of Agriculture, Forest Service, Rocky Mountain Research Station: 8-13.

McGaughey, R.J. 2004. Seeing the forest and the trees: visualizing stand and landscape conditions. In: Proceedings, views from the ridge: considerations for planning at the landscape level. Portland, OR: Western Forestry and Conservation Association; U.S. Department of Agriculture, Forest Service, Pacific Northwest Research Station. 133 p.

Mladenoff, D.; Baker, W. 1999. Development of forest and landscape modeling approaches. In: Mladenoff, D.; Baker, W., eds. Spatial modeling of forest landscape change: approaches and applications. Cambridge, United Kingdom: Cambridge University Press: 1-13.

Moeur, M.; Stage, A.R. 1995. Most similar neighbor: an improved sampling inference procedure for natural resource planning. Forest Science. 41(2): 337-359.

Ohmann, J.L.; Gregory, M.J. 2002. Predictive mapping of forest composition and structure with direct gradient analysis and nearest neighbor imputation in coastal Oregon, USA. Canadian Journal of Forest Research. 32: 725-741.

Renner, D.L.; Martin, F.C. 2002. Using the fuels and fire effects and economic (ECON) extensions to the Forest Vegetation Simulator (FVS) to evaluate the impacts of silvicultural regimes. In: Crookston, N.L.; Havis, R.N., comps. Second Forest Vegetation Simulator conference. Proc. RMRS-P-25. Fort Collins, CO: U.S. Department of Agriculture, Forest Service, Rocky Mountain Research Station: 97-103.

Roberts, J.C. 2002. Using a multichange agent approach with the Forest Vegetation Simulator on the Boise National Forest, Idaho. In: Crookston, N.L.; Havis, R.N., comps. Second Forest Vegetation Simulator conference. Proc. RMRS-P-25. Fort Collins, CO: U.S. Department of Agriculture, Forest Service, Rocky Mountain Research Station: 53-56.

Sessions, J.; Johnson, K.N.; Franklin, J.F.; Gabriel, J.T. 1999. Achieving sustainable forest structures on fire-prone landscapes while pursuing multiple goals. In: Mladenoff, D.; Baker, W.L., eds. Spatial modeling of forest landscape change: approaches and applications. Cambridge, United Kingdom: Cambridge University Press: 210-255.

Smith, E.L.; McMahan, A.J.; Eager, T. 2002. Landscape analysis application of the westwide pine beetle FVS extension. In: Crookston, N.L.; Havis, R.N., comps. Second Forest Vegetation Simulator conference. Proc. RMRS-P-25. Fort Collins, CO: U.S. Department of Agriculture, Forest Service, Rocky Mountain Research Station: 62-67.

Spies, T.A.; Reeves, G.H.; Burnett, K.M. [et al.]. 2002. Assessing the ecological consequences of forest policies in a multi-ownership province in Oregon. In: Liu, J.; Taylor, W.W., eds. Integrating landscape ecology into natural resource management. Cambridge, United Kingdom: Cambridge University Press: 179-207.

Stage, A.R. 1973. Prognosis model for stand development. Res. Pap. INT-137. Ogden, UT: U.S. Department of Agriculture, Forest Service, Intermountain Forest and Range Experiment Station. 32 p.

Temesgen, H.; LeMay, V. 2002. Linking prognosis BC to aerial attributes for timber supply analysis in British Columbia. In: Crookston, N.L.; Havis, R.N., comps. Second Forest Vegetation Simulator conference. Proc. RMRS-P-25. Fort Collins, CO: U.S. Department of Agriculture, Forest Service, Rocky Mountain Research Station: 126-127.

Vandenriesche, D. 2002. Using the labeling capabilities and Parallel Processing Extension of the Forest Vegetation Simulator for resource supply analyses. In: Crookston, N.L.; Havis, R.N., comps. Second Forest Vegetation Simulator conference. Proc. RMRS-P-25. Fort Collins, CO: U.S. Department of Agriculture, Forest Service, Rocky Mountain Research Station: 127-132.

Wedin, H. 1999. Stand level prescription generation under multiple objectives. Corvallis, OR: Oregon State University. 178 p. M.S. thesis.

Weise, D.R.; Kimberlin, R.; Arbaugh, M.J. [et al.]. 2000. A risk-based comparison of potential fuel treatment trade-off models. In: Neuenschwander, L.F.; Ryan, K.C., tech. eds. Proceedings of the joint fire science conference and workshop. Boise, ID: University of Idaho and the International Association of Wildland Fire: 1-7.

Chapter 4: The SafeD Forest Landscape Planning Model

Pete Bettinger, David Graetz, Alan Ager, and John Sessions[1]

Abstract

We describe quantitative methods in landscape planning and the application of simulation and optimization to analyze alternative policy and management on large landscapes. Landscape planning models can help people see and think in whole-landscape terms and give them a common reference point for discussing conflicting values. Forested landscape conditions are projected through space and time and provide a way to help evaluate the differences among alternative forest policies, and accomplish certain management planning objectives with respect to landscape-level processes and goals. Evaluating alternative forest management policies across the interior West landscape is complicated by the need to recognize the role of stochastic disturbances such as fire, insect, and disease outbreaks. We describe the development of the Simulation and analysis of forests with episodic Disturbances (SafeD) model for the Interior Northwest Landscape Analysis System project. The SafeD model is a multiscale, hybrid simulation/optimization model that addresses both optimization of silvicultural prescriptions at the stand level and the spatial scheduling of these prescriptions on large landscapes to meet multiobjective goals.

Keywords: Forest landscape planning, fire, natural disturbances, forest planning.

Introduction

Resolving the myriad of forest policy problems in the Western United States is hindered by the inability of land managers, policymakers, and planners to analyze tradeoffs of alternative management scenarios on large, heterogeneous landscapes over long time-frames. With the growing emphasis on managing large landscapes, it has become difficult to identify, visualize, and resolve conflicts on landscapes where there is interest in

[1] **Pete Bettinger** is an associate professor Danie B Warne Schoo of Forest Resources University of Georgia Athens GA 30602 **David Graetz** is a graduate research assistant Department of Forest Resources **John Sessions** is a professor Department of Forest Engineering Oregon State University Corva is OR 97331 **Alan A. Ager** is an operations research ana yst U S Department of Agricu ture Forestry and Range Sciences Laboratory 1401 Geke er Lane La Grande OR 97850

multiple, long-term goals. In addition, the current patchwork of regulatory policies, existing landscape conditions, and landownership patterns has created a new matrix of operational constraints that virtually prohibit active restoration of risk-prone habitat (Quigley et al. 2001). In many cases, the federal regulations that protect aquatic and terrestrial habitats are frequently in conflict with management intentions aimed at moderating the threat of severe wildfires or other disturbances. On typical national forest lands in eastern Oregon, resource protection prevents fuel treatments and stocking control on over 75 percent of the nonwilderness lands (Wilson et al., in press), thereby perpetuating the cycle of fuels buildup and catastrophic wildfire. Low-value products from typical restoration activities and finite Forest Service budgets further reduce the areas that can be treated to control density and maintain healthy forest stands.

The past decade has seen the rise of landscape planning models that use simulation and optimization methods to help dissect policy and management goals. Landscape planning models evolved from a fusion of landscape ecology models and forest planning efforts (Mladenoff and Baker 1999, Sessions et al. 1999) and allow for the deduction of results otherwise unattainable owing to the complexity of the planning problem on large landscapes (Mladenoff and He 1999). The goal of these models is to provide a mechanism to simulate landscape change in response to varying levels of management, disturbance, and succession (Mladenoff and Baker 1999, Mladenoff and He 1999, Quigley et al. 1996, Roberts and Betz 1999, Sessions et al. 1999). These models hold promise for solving policy issues, such as those related to the management of disturbance-prone landscapes, while simultaneously meeting the concerns for forest and range sustainability and the viability of terrestrial and aquatic species.

Although these hybrid simulation/planning models are clearly valuable tools to sort out the strategic visions for multiownership watersheds, there remain many gaps, as well as barriers, to more widespread application. One area that deserves attention is the process for allocating an array of stand management goals over space and time to meet landscape-level goals. Management decisions at the stand level, as well as succession and disturbance processes, ultimately drive landscape change, and the linkage between decisions at the stand level and their influence on the attainment of landscape goals is poorly understood. Clearly, decisions at both scales are important components of landscape-scale planning. The integration of stand-level optimization processes and landscape-level optimization processes has yet to be demonstrated.

In this paper, we summarize analytical methods used in landscape planning and describe how this work is being further developed for the Interior Northwest Landscape Analysis System (INLAS) project area. The goal of this work is to create a multiscale (i.e., stand and landscape) model that can be used to sort out management issues on large forest and rangeland areas in the interior West. We discuss the concept of stand-versus landscape-level optimization in meeting multiobjective goals and the integration of these two modeling scales within the INLAS project. Our goal is to apply this modeling method to address the following questions:

1. Can alternative management scenarios designed at the stand level have a significant effect on measures of forest ecosystem health, commodity production, and cumulative effects when portrayed spatially at a landscape level? That is, do stand-level objectives prevent the attainment of landscape-level goals?

2. Do landscape-level objectives prevent the attainment of stand-level goals?

3. When measured at the landscape level, can the threat of fire and cumulative water-shed effects be reduced through alternative management policies? Can the spatial distribution of management activities, within and across ownerships, significantly affect measures of forest ecosystem health, commodity production, and cumulative effects?

4. Do landownership patterns and behavior affect forest ecosystem health, commodity production, and cumulative effects, when portrayed spatially at a landscape level?

5. To what extent are commodity production, fire threat, cumulative effects, and fish and wildlife habitat goals compatible?

The answers to these questions will contribute to the ongoing discussion concerning sustainable management of Western landscapes. The flow of this paper proceeds first by discussing the literature associated with the optimization of stand-level goals, then the optimization of landscape-level goals. These two sets of goals are assumed to operate at different spatial scales and thus may not be complementary. We then describe an approach we are developing to integrate the two concepts by using a hybrid landscape simulation/optimization model. Landscape simulation or optimization models may offer some advantages for land management planning. In particular, the modeling framework can be designed to address a variety of management objectives and constraints, incorporate spatial representations of the landscape, and model processes at various scales. The fine resolution that landscape simulation and optimization models can support makes them more complex, yet can provide more detailed analyses of alternative policies. The model we propose developing will support an evaluation of policies in the interior West within the INLAS project.

Stand-Level Optimization

Stand-level optimization methods are used to develop optimal management prescriptions for individual stands, given a set of management goals. Stand-level optimization methods have evolved with the changing demands placed on forests. Initially the goals were to maximize economic or commodity production values but more recently have placed emphasis on noncommodity values. The approaches that can be used to develop optimal stand-level management prescriptions include the Hooke and Jeeves method (Haight et al. 1992, Hooke and Jeeves 1961), dynamic programming (Amidon and Akin 1968; Arthaud and Klemperer 1988; Brodie and Kao 1979; ; Brodie et al. 1978; Brukas and Brodie 1999; Chen et al. 1980a, 1980b; Gong 1992; Haight et al. 1985; Hool 1966; Kao and Brodie 1979; Yoshimoto et al. 1990), nonlinear programming (Kao and Brodie 1980), or specialized heuristics (Bare and Opalach 1987). Many of these approaches key off of whole stand growth-and-yield models or stand age/structure models, which do not tend to provide the tree-level data conditions necessary to facilitate the use of fire behavior models.

Most stand-level optimization methods reported in the literature focus on meeting forest economic or commodity production goals rather than the nontimber goals, such as a reduction in the threat of fire, which is becoming more important in the interior West. In fact, the optimization models that key off of individual tree growth-and-yield models (table 1) were developed with fixed-decision criteria, mainly economic, in mind. There are, however, some exceptions. Haight et al. (1985), for e.g., tracked biological indicators in the development of stand prescriptions although they were not influential in developing the management prescriptions. More recently, Haight et al. (1992) incorporated nontimber outputs into the development of optimal prescriptions by using penalty func-

Table 1—Stand-level optimization research and associated decisions when considering the use of individual tree growth-and-yield simulation models

Decision	Reference
Rotation age, or growing-stock level	Martin and Ek (1981)
	Haight et al. (1985)
	Arthaud and Klemperer (1988)
	Haight and Monserud (1990)
	Yoshimoto et al. (1990)
	Valsta (1992)
Thinning type	Haight et al. (1985)
	Arthaud and Klemperer (1988)
	Haight and Monserud (1990)
	Yoshimoto et al. (1990)
	Valsta (1992)
Planting density	Valsta (1993)
Multispecies management	Haight and Monserud (1990)
	Yoshimoto et al. (1990)
Uneven-age management	Buongiorno and Michie (1980)
	Bare and Opalach (1987)

tions to ensure the attainment of goals. And finally, Gong (1992) developed a multi-objective dynamic programming system to recognize nontimber values. However, Gong (1992) also noted a limitation on the number of dynamic programming state variables that could be used.

The types of forest stand-level goals we should consider for all landowners in the interior West could range from economic (maximize net present value) to biological (maximize mean annual increment) to ecological (minimize fire threat, maximize number of large trees produced). Providing flexibility in the established stand-level optimization techniques requires some level of developmental work, thus access to the computer code associated with the growth models. Also, linking these established techniques to a landscape-level simulation model is problematic. For example, an ideal landscape planning approach may require that the list of trees associated with each forest stand be tracked through time to enable an evaluation of fire hazard and other environmental effects. The number of stand tree lists to simultaneously track could easily exceed 100,000. An optimal prescription for each stand would need to be developed and perhaps adjusted as conflicts with landscape-level goals arise and as natural disturbances are modeled across the landscape. The ability to quickly access a stand's tree list and develop an optimal prescription, while attempting to achieve landscape-level goals, is therefore a priority.

A stand goal within (SafeD) is defined by some set of attributes that are desired of a stand at some future point (or points). An example may be to have a stand that has 60 percent of its basal area in western larch (*Larix occidentalis* Nutt.) with the remaining 40 percent in Douglas-fir (*Pseudotsuga menziesii* (Mirb.) Franco) and grand fir (*Abies grandis* (Dougl. ex D. Don) Lindl.). There is almost an unlimited number of stand goals that can be developed for any one stand—the only restriction is that goals must be based on attributes that are attainable from the data that describe the specific stand of interest (i.e., the "tree list").

Why are stand goals important for INLAS? One objective in INLAS is to create prescriptions for the current landscape that can be evaluated as if they were actually implemented on the ground. This will be done through computer simulation. Stand goals are crucial to the development of specific prescriptions because they give us a target and decision criteria for deciding if certain management actions are needed and in what quantities. In essence, stand goals quantify the desired conditions of a particular stand. When we optimize a stand prescription, we are essentially measuring attainment (or departure) from the stand goal. The closer we are to the goal, the better the prescription.

For any given stand in the INLAS study area, a stand goal may read, "Create a stand that minimizes its departure from a target Stand Density Index (SDI) value and concurrently maximizes the value of the stand–subject to a minimal harvest volume, when harvest is planned."

Mathematically this would be written as:

$$max \quad \sum_{p=1}^{n} \left((w1) * VALUE - (w2) * SDI\_DE \right)$$

$$\text{Subject to: } H_p \geq MinHarv_p \qquad \forall \, p \, ,$$

where

p = a single period,

n = the total number of periods,

$w1$ and $w2$ = weights to emphasize importance of each attribute,

$VALUE$ = an attribute that describes the value of the stand,

SDI_DE = an attribute calculated by squaring the SDI deviation (which is the difference between the obtained SDI and the target SDI),

H_p = the harvest level from the stand during period p, and

$MinHarv_p$ = a minimum harvest level threshold during period p.

Landscape-Level Optimization

In most landscape planning processes, much consideration is given to the decision variables and the rules for assigning management activities to decision variables, the quantitative rules for selecting new plan configurations, and the length of time the activity selection process (i.e., search process) is allowed to proceed (i.e., how long the computer program is run). Quantitative relationships, or rules, to constrain or guide the assignment of activities across a landscape can be categorized in many ways; one such categorization is whether the relationships require spatial information. The use of spatial information can make goal achievement a complex procedure in forest planning applications, but is important for simulating landscape-level processes.

The spatial arrangement of wildlife habitat and forest management activities is important for a number of reasons, including complying with regulatory restrictions and organizational policies and addressing aesthetic concerns. Forest regulations, for instance, are placing increasingly restrictive limits on the size and spatial relationships of harvest units on both private and public lands (Daust and Nelson 1993). The National Forest Management Act (1976) provides guidance regarding the appropriate harvest unit size on national forest lands, and the Oregon Forest Practices Act (State of Oregon 1999) provides similar guidance for privately owned lands. As a result of a need to manage forest land within regulatory frameworks, forest management planning now often attempts to achieve landscape management goals by placing spatial constraints on the scheduling of management activities (O'Hara et al. 1989).

Landscape-level planning models that allow the optimization of a spatial arrangement of activities to meet a set of management objectives vary from the more traditional optimizations techniques, such as linear or mixed-integer programming (e.g., Hof et al. 1994), to the nontraditional, but increasingly common heuristic programming techniques (e.g., Murray and Church 1995). Classical models such as the Timber Resource Allocation Method (RAM) (Navon 1971) and the Forest Planning Model (FORPLAN) (Johnson et al. 1980) were designed to address the problem of optimal scheduling of harvests with forestwide constraints. These models were used from the 1960s to 1990s and are classical in the sense that they use linear programming to allocate resources and activities to timber stands, and to a limited extent, recognize spatial relationships. However, recognition of spatial features in forest planning generally requires the use of integer-decision variables. Thus as the problem size increases, the potential solution space also increases, but at a disproportionately greater rate (Lockwood and Moore 1993). Mixed-integer programming and integer programming techniques have been used to help solve these problems and produce feasible management plans, but these techniques have substantive limitations (directly related to problem size) when applied to large landscapes (Lockwood and Moore 1993).

To explore the capabilities of traditional techniques, Hof and Joyce (1992) described nonlinear formulations aimed at accounting for the amount of edge, the juxtaposition of different habitat types, the dispersal distance among habitat types, and the minimum size of a patch of habitat. Hof et al. (1994) also described a mixed-integer programming approach that incorporates probabilistic objective functions for wildlife viability concerns. These approaches were theoretical in nature yet expanded the research boundaries and provide valuable insight into a much broader range of capabilities of linear, integer, and nonlinear programming methods. The limitations of these techniques persist, however, and both heuristics and simulation models have since been explored as possible alternatives.

Heuristics

The use of heuristics (solution methods that do not guarantee optimality of objectives has been achieved) in landscape planning is becoming more prevalent, particularly in planning processes where the potential solution space is large, or spatial constraints exist. Many types of complex, nonlinear goals (e.g., spatial and temporal distribution of elk (*Cervus elaphus*) habitat, as described in Bettinger et al. 1997), which have traditionally been considered too complex to solve with traditional optimization techniques, are now being incorporated into heuristics. In recent years, heuristics have been applied to scheduling problems related to forest management (Hoganson and Rose 1984), forest transportation (Murray and Church 1995; Nelson and Brodie 1990; Pulkki 1984; Weintraub et al. 1994, 1995), wildlife conservation and management (Arthaud and Rose 1996, Bettinger et al. 1997, Haight and Travis 1997), aquatic system management (Bettinger et al. 1998b), and the achievement of biological diversity goals (Kangas and Pukkala 1996). Monte Carlo simulation, tabu search (TS), and simulated annealing (SA) are three of the more popular heuristics. Three other more recently developed heuristics, the great deluge algorithm (GDA), threshold accepting, and genetic algorithms, also seem to operate as well as the others. Some effort also is being made to integrate the aspects of each into hybrid heuristic techniques, although this research is in its preliminary stages in natural resource management. Although the use of heuristics does not guarantee that a global optimum solution can be located for a particular landscape planning problem, heuristics can produce feasible (and often very good) solutions to complex problems, in a reasonable amount of time.

Simulated annealing is a search technique that began to be widely used during the early 1980s in operations research fields (Dowsland 1993). The foundation for SA was first published by Metropolis et al. (1953) in a scheduling algorithm that simulated the cooling of materials in a heat bath–a process known as annealing. The SA technique is a Monte Carlo method that uses a localized search process, where a subset of solutions is explored by moving from one solution to a neighboring solution with a simple change of a characteristic of a single-decision variable (1-opt moves), such as the timing of harvest of a management unit.

Threshold accepting (TA) is similar to SA, and was introduced by Dueck and Scheuer (1990). The TA technique also uses a localized search process but uses a slightly different, and somewhat simpler, set of acceptance rules for a new solution than does SA. Threshold accepting accepts every new (proposed) solution that is **not much worse** than the previous solution (within a preset limit of the value of the current solution), whereas in SA, the probability that a lower quality proposed solution would replace the current solution is a function of the quality of the solution and a stochastic element.

The great deluge algorithm is similar to SA in that it uses a localized search process. The GDA was introduced by Dueck (1993) and derives its name from the conceptual framework on which the algorithm works. Consider a problem where the objective is to find the highest elevation in a fictitious landscape by simply walking around and measuring elevations. Logically you would want to continuously measure higher and higher ground rather than lower ground. The GDA starts at some unknown location in the landscape, and subsequently weather conditions would be modeled as though it is "raining without end," flooding the landscape and making it easier to locate the higher elevations. As the water rises, the GDA moves around the landscape (the solution space) trying to "keep its feet dry" (by only walking on higher and higher ground), and eventually finding what it considers the highest spot on the landscape, or an estimate of the global optimum solution to a planning problem.

Tabu search has been successfully applied to a number of scheduling problems outside of forestry and wildlife management, such as those in telecommunications, transportation, shop sequencing, machine scheduling, and layout and circuit design problems (Glover 1990, Glover and Laguna 1993). Within forestry it has been applied to timber harvest scheduling problems with adjacency (green-up) requirements (Murray and Church 1995), as well as for developing forest plans that have landscape goals for elk (Bettinger et al. 1997) and aquatic habitat (Bettinger et al. 1998b). Tabu search with 1-opt moves such as the harvest timing of a management unit, short-term memory, and aspiration criteria is a good scheduling technique, but generally not as good as SA, TA, or GDA (Bettinger et al. 2002). Using 2-opt (the swapping of choices among two decision variables) (and greater) moves has allowed TS to produce results as good as SA, TA, or GDA (Bettinger et al. 2002), but at a fairly large computing cost (Bettinger et al. 1999). One advantage of TS is that it is well suited to parallel processing.

Genetic algorithms (GA) were developed initially by Holland (1975) in the 1970s. Diverse fields such as music generation, genetic synthesis, strategic planning, and machine learning have benefited from the application of GAs to the scheduling of resources (Srinivas and Patnaik 1994). The GAs have been applied to a limited extent in forestry (Falcão and Borges 2000, Lu and Eriksson 2000, Mullen and Butler 1999). Although GAs have proven to be fairly good in developing moderately complex forest plans (Bettinger et al. 2002), it is more difficult to implement GAs than SA, TA, or GDA. A hybrid GA/TS heuristic technique that utilizes 1-opt and 2-opt TS processes as well as a GA crossover process (Boston and Bettinger 2002) also has shown promise for developing moderately complex forest plans.

Simulation Models

Simulation models that schedule forest management activities similar to heuristics and traditional mathematical programming techniques can be developed to provide the spatial and temporal context to help guide policymakers who are given the task of evaluating strategic alternatives. These models might be considered favorable to use in situations where stochastic elements are modeled, making optimization difficult. Simulation models generally are developed to capture relevant features of the dynamic nature of some "target system" under study (Birta and Özmizrak 1996), and their reliability is highly dependent on the degree to which the models reflect reality (Li et al. 1993). Gaining reliability in a simulation model is not a trivial task. For example, ecological consequences can differ dramatically depending on the pattern of land use activities imposed on a landscape (Franklin and Forman 1987); thus one measure of reliability is in modeling realistic land use activities.

Many simulation models have been developed in the last two decades to model events or behaviors across landscapes. Franklin and Forman's (1987) was one of the first to simulate the ecological consequences of forest management activities on a landscape, and indicated that the pattern of management applied to landscapes can result in varying ecological consequences. Others (Flamm and Turner 1994; Gustafson and Crow 1994, 1996; Gustafson et al. 2000; Johnson et al. 1998; Li et al. 1993; Turner 1987; Wallin et al. 1994) have since developed models for forested landscapes that simulate a variety of activities or disturbances at various spatial and temporal scales. Simulation models have been widely used in other natural resource areas as well. For example, they have been developed to focus on other types of disturbances and landscapes, such as gypsy moth (*Lymantria dispar*) outbreaks (Zhou and Liebhold 1995) and grasslands (Gao et al. 1996). As with heuristics, the use of simulation models does not guarantee that a global optimum solution can be located for a particular landscape planning problem; in fact, most simulation models do not claim to be attempting to locate optimal solutions. Simulation models can, however, produce feasible (and often very good) solutions to complex problems, in a reasonable amount of time.

Some common drawbacks, however, of forest landscape simulation models include:

- Resolution of the landscape scale is low.

- Integration of activities within a hierarchical spatial structure is low. For example, small basic simulation units might be aggregated into larger management units, which might be aggregated into larger management units, which might be aggregated into even larger harvest blocks.

- Only a few variables are used to track and allocate activities, such as transition probabilities or stand age.

- Use of other socioeconomic or ecological information to track and allocate activities is low.

- Landownership is not explicitly recognized.

- Spatial allocation of harvests is stochastic.

- Key landscape variables, such as topography and stream networks, are not recognized.

- Regeneration harvest sizes are determined by using a normal distribution of harvest sizes.

- Broad management strategies are stochastically implemented.

- Initial conditions of the landscape are randomly assigned.

Two projects have been undertaken in the past 5 years to develop simulation models to overcome most of these limitations. The Coastal Landscape Analysis and Modeling Study (CLAMS) (http://www.fsl.orst.edu/clams/), centered in the Coast Range of Oregon, is developing the LAndscape Management Policy Simulator (LAMPS) model to evaluate alternative forest management policies across all landownerships, long timeframes (100 years), and large areas (2 million ha). The LAMPS model does not, however, incorporate stochastic fire events in the simulation of management policies. The Applegate Project (http://www.cof.orst.edu/research/safcfor/) developed a hybrid landscape optimization/ simulation modeling system called "Simulation and analysis of forests with episodic Disturbances," or SafeD (Graetz 2000), that incorporated stochastic fire events. Table 2 presents a comparison of a few of the more important aspects of four forest landscape simulation models: "Safe Forests" (Johnson et al. 1998), LANDIS (Gustafson et al. 2000), LAMPS (Bettinger and Lennette 2002), and SafeD.

Approach and Design of a Landscape Planning Model

The approach we are suggesting would be useful in evaluating the aggregate effects of policies across a forested landscape and centers on the ability to use spatial simulation or optimization techniques. This type of approach can provide managers, policymakers, and planners with the ability to think about forests and their management in ways unimagined only a few decades ago. Often called "landscape assessment and planning," these approaches help people see and think in whole-landscape terms (not simply single ownerships) and give them a common reference.

In support of the INLAS project, we are proposing the development of a spatial landscape simulation model that will use spatial analysis techniques to model forest change across all ownerships and over long timeframes. Although the model will use both strategic (long-range, coarse-scale) and tactical (short-range, fine-scale) planning methods, it is more appropriate to call it a midscale, or regional, simulation model than a fine-scale tactical planning model. Successful implementation requires effective interdisciplinary collaboration that addresses the economic, ecological, and social dimensions of proposed management policies. Bettinger (1999) proposed that four elements were required at appropriate levels for a system to be implemented effectively: people, databases,

Table 2—A comparison of recently developed landscape simulation models

	Simulation model			
Comparison criteria	Safe forest	LANDIS	LAMPS[a]	SafeD[b]
Spatial data components:				
Analysis area (ha)	400 000	600 000	600 000	200 000
Data structure	Vector	Raster	Vector	Raster
Minimum mapping unit	Varies	200 x 200 m	25 x 25 m[c]	25 x 25 m
Model characteristics:				
Recognize ecological and economic goals	Both	Ecological	Both	Both
Optimize multiple goals	Yes	No	No	Yes
Represent forest management activities	Yes	Yes	Yes	Yes
Represent landowner behavior	No	No	Yes	No
Represent stochastic events	Yes	Yes	Yes	Yes
Represent fire disturbances (spatially)	Partially	Yes	No	Yes
Represent insect disturbances (spatially)	No	No	No	Yes

[a] LAMPS = LAndscape Management Po icy Simu ator
[b] SafeD = Simu ation and ana ysis of forests with episodic Disturbances
[c] Raster databases are converted to vector databases for use in the LAMPS mode

technology, and an organizational commitment to the project. This paper mainly addresses the development of appropriate technology for modeling management and stochastic disturbances at the midscale in the interior West. Although the four elements are interdependent, our assumption is that data development, hiring and management of highly trained personnel, and a commitment by the main supporters of the INLAS project (USDA Forest Service, Oregon Department of Forestry, and College of Forestry at Oregon State University) will be supplied at the appropriate levels and appropriate times. No system is perfect, as Bettinger and Boston (2001) point out, but how setbacks are addressed is important in maintaining a level of progress consistent with project time lines.

On completion of the model, managers, policymakers, and planners will have the capability to (1) evaluate the effects of fuel treatments on wildfire behavior; (2) identify economic, ecological, and social constraints associated with the application of various policies; and (3) locate areas (perhaps watersheds) that are particularly difficult to manage under various constraints. With this in mind, we now concentrate on the technical development of a spatial landscape simulation model, its components, and the types of activities we envision modeling. Obviously a recognition of economic, ecological, and social goals is important. However, given that a project of this scope involves multiple collaborators, a linkage from one model to the other is more likely; facilitating the linkage between models is important. In addition, landowner objectives may range from relatively simple (maximize net present value) to more complex (maximize timber volume produced with acceptable fire threat, or minimize fire threat with high volumes produced), and the ability to develop an analysis that recognizes the need to optimize multiple goals. The representation of a range of forest management activities is also important because a wider set of potential management activities may facilitate the achievement of certain goals. And finally, the ability to recognize or model stochastic events is becoming more important as these events shape the condition of forests much more than activities by humans. Spatially representing fire spread and insect outbreaks as a function of forest conditions and landscape characteristics is important. Obviously the previous forest management practices can affect the risk of a stochastic event occurring; thus when projecting future conditions, the planned activities will also likely affect these risk levels.

The Simulation and Analysis of Forests with Episodic Disturbances Model

As noted earlier, the main objective of this paper is to develop a spatial forest landscape simulation model that allows the portrayal of processes (management activities, stochastic events, etc.) and subsequent analysis of silvicultural treatments at both the stand and landscape levels. The approach and design of this modeling effort build on the efforts of Graetz (2000), who developed a preliminary model (SafeD) to incorporate fire and insect disturbances in a landscape planning system. The SafeD model evolved from the efforts of the Sierra Nevada Ecosystem Project (Sessions et al. 1999) and the Applegate Project (Graetz 2000). The SafeD model is a spatially explicit, hybrid simulation/optimization model that allows the achievement of multiple resource goals at both the stand and landscape levels, while recognizing stochastic disturbances, and management behavior. It uses a distance-independent individual tree growth model (similar to the Forest Vegetation Simulator) to facilitate the development of optimal stand prescriptions, a heuristic scheduling model to allocate prescriptions across the landscape, and a raster-based fire-spread model called Fire Area Simulator (FARSITE, Finney 1998) to model fire on the landscape. This modeling framework is attractive because it can schedule management activities that attempt to meet long-term landscape goals under an uncertain future of stochastic disturbances.

To recognize the achievement of optimal stand-level prescriptions, optimal landscape-level objectives, and to recognize stochastic events, the operation of the SafeD model is segmented into four processing stages (fig. 10). To recognize the importance of both stand- and landscape-level goals, SafeD first develops a set of optimal prescriptions for each stand. It then allocates the prescriptions to the landscape to achieve landscape-level goals. Stochastic events are then applied to the landscape in a spatial manner. Finally, the stand- and landscape-level goals are reevaluated and adjusted, if necessary, to reflect the changes that have occurred on the landscape and in affected stands.

Optimizing Stand-Level Goals

Within SafeD, prescriptions for timber stands are dynamically generated by a stand optimization model that uses a combination of the region-limited strategy and path (RLS-PATH) algorithm (Yoshimoto 1990). A number of potential stand-level objectives can be recognized, and an optimal prescription for each can be developed. One challenge for the INLAS science team and collaborators will be in defining the types of stand-level objectives that should be modeled. The types of objectives modeled in the Applegate Project (Graetz 2000) included limiting fire hazard, limiting insect and wind-throw hazard, enhancing wildlife habitat, improving fish habitat, and maximizing net present value. To achieve these objectives, tree harvesting and snag creation rates were varied, and the resulting residual tree growth monitored. Goal achievement was then measured by using both live- and dead-tree characteristics.

Because an optimal stand-level management prescription is developed for all stand-level objectives, a second challenge becomes deciding which prescription to actually apply to each stand. For example, if we had three potential objectives (maximize net present value [a single goal for a stand], minimize fire hazard [a single goal for a stand], or maximize net present value with an acceptable fire hazard [multiple goals for a stand]), three

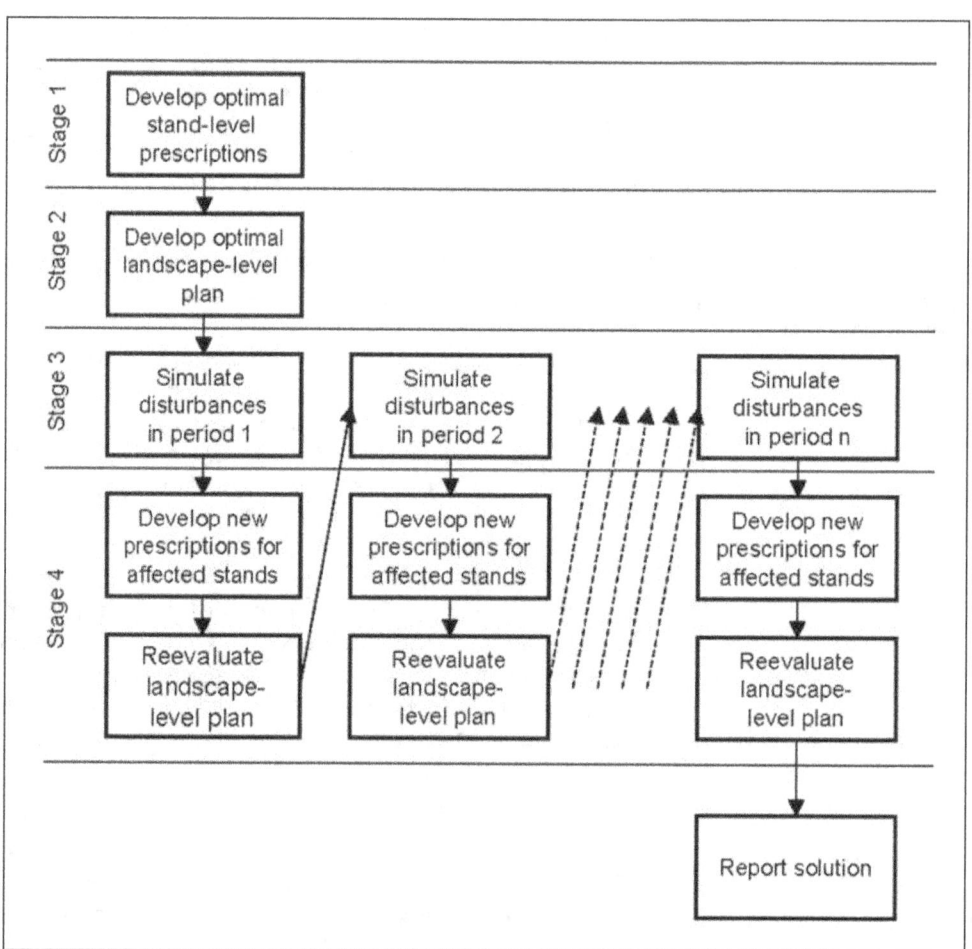

Figure 10   Four-stage process of the Simu ation and ana ysis of forest with episodic Disturbance mode

optimal prescriptions would be developed for each stand on the landscape. Only one of these prescriptions can be applied to each stand, however. The prescription choice will be based on its contribution to overall landscape goals when applied to a stand, which may be a function of the spatial location of each stand.

Optimizing Landscape-Levels Goals

The second stage of SafeD consists of a landscape simulation model that distributes the optimal stand-level prescriptions through time and space given landscape-level goals and constraints. It is often confusing to those not closely familiar with forest planning efforts that stand- and landscape-level objectives are not necessarily compatible. A brief example may help clarify this notion. Let's say we have four hypothetical stands, each containing a different set of stand conditions. Applying stand-level optimization techniques to each to maximize net present value, e.g., may lead to a schedule that indicates each should be clearcut immediately. Although this may seem extreme, these prescriptions are optimal for each stand and represent decisions that are independent of the other stands. If the overall landscape objective of the landowner is to spread the harvests out evenly over time to avoid surges and dips in timber production, one or more of the optimal stand-level prescriptions could not be used, and some other prescription needs to be developed to represent the management of these stands. Therefore although optimal stand prescriptions can be generated, it is highly unlikely that they will lead directly to an optimal landscape-level scheduling solution (unless both stand- and landscape-level objectives are exactly the same).

The SafeD model designs planning problems as Model I nonlinear integer problems, where individual stands are tracked through time as they are regenerated or disturbed. The spatial location of each stand, as well as certain stand structural conditions, is important in adequately modeling management behavior and natural disturbance events.

It is clear from the previously provided summary of the literature that traditional techniques, such as linear or integer programming, are not appropriate for management planning at the landscape scale when integer variables are required to represent spatial landscape features. Therefore, a heuristic scheduling technique, the GDA, was chosen for use as the landscape-level optimization technique in the SafeD model. In the Applegate Project implementation of SafeD (Graetz 2000), the following objective function was used:

maximize:

$$\sum_{k=1}^{m}\sum_{j=1}^{q}\sum_{t=1}^{n} r_{k,j,t}\, x_{k,j,t} \;, \tag{3}$$

where

k = a stand;

m = total number of stands in a landscape;

j = a prescription;

q = total number of possible prescriptions;

t = a time period;

n = total number of time periods in a planning horizon;

r_{kjt} = the value of some stand attribute residing in stand k, when managed under prescription j, during time period t; and

x_{kjt} = a binary (0-1) variable indicating whether prescription j was assigned to stand k during time period t.

A variety of constraints can be included in the SafeD model; however, the current version of the SafeD model uses only two. The first is a constraint limiting the number of prescriptions applied to a stand in each time period,

$$\sum_{j=1}^{q} x_{k,j,t} = 1 \qquad \forall\, k,t \;, \tag{4}$$

and the second is a constraint on the level of equivalent roaded acres (ERA) that resulted from management activities. The ERA (McGurk and Fong 1995) is a measure used by the national forests to estimate cumulative impacts to a landscape, and to some extent, explains the hydrologic recovery of watersheds. There has been some debate, however, about the ability of ERA to be correlated with changes in measures of aquatic habitat (sediment and temperature) (Bettinger et al. 1998a). Within SafeD, an ERA constraint was applied in each time period and to each subwatershed:

$$\left[\frac{\sum\limits_{k=1}^{p} ERA_{k,t} \, A_k}{\sum\limits_{k=1}^{p} A_k} \right] \leq ERA\_Threshold_{t,w} \, , \qquad \forall \, t, w \qquad (5)$$

where

k = a stand,

p = the total number of stands in a subwatershed,

t = a time period,

w = a watershed,

$ERA_{k\,t}$ = the contribution to equivalent roaded acres by stand k during time period t,

A_k = the area of stand k, and

$ERA\_Threshold_{t\,w}$ = the upper limit on equivalent roaded acres allowed in subwatershed w during time period t.

Other constraints could be added to the SafeD model to guide the scheduling of management activities during the landscape-level optimization process. These may include timber harvest volume flow constraints, harvest adjacency (green-up) constraints, or the maintenance of a distribution of habitat patch sizes. Constraints also can be applied to individual landowner groups, or land allocations within landowner groups. Collaborators of the INLAS project will be called on to provide guidance in the development of appropriate landscape-level processes that must be recognized in future versions of SafeD; the landscape-level objectives and constraints will arise from these discussions.

Recognizing Stochastic Events

The third stage of SafeD distributes stochastic events across time and space. The brief description of stochastic events that follows is not meant to minimize their importance in a landscape planning effort. Within the SafeD model, fire events are applied in a spatial manner across the landscape in response to climatic variables and the management activities prescribed for each stand. Insect disturbance models were based on expert advice and are designed to simulate the expected growth-and-yield losses from forests over the long run. Episodic mortality of trees is embedded in the SafeD model to occur during drought periods (which are determined in a stochastic manner). Mild and severe drought periods will trigger the application of insect disturbances to the landscape. During these insect events, the structural condition of each stand in the landscape is examined, and a decision is made regarding the application of accelerated mortality rules.

Wildfires are applied to the landscape in the SafeD model by using the FARSITE model developed by Finney (1998). The FARSITE model is a fire growth-and-spread model that requires a spatial database describing the landscape. It includes methodology that allows the modeling of surface fire spread, crown fire spread, fire spotting, and fuel moisture content. Enabling the use of FARSITE requires knowing how many fires will occur during a specific period, how long they will burn, and where the initiation points are on the landscape. Probability distributions were used in the Applegate Project (Graetz 2000) to determine these parameters.

A number of sources of information are brought to bear on the modeling of stochastic events, including expert knowledge and functional relationship models. The literature on the effects of fire and insect events on landscapes is broad, yet little exists when one considers including these events in a forest landscape planning model. Some examples include Armstrong et al. (1999) who modeled the effects of natural disturbances (fires) on boreal landscapes nonspatially by assuming a distribution of forest types would be regenerated each year, and Reed and Errico (1986) who modeled the effects of fire in a linear programming model (again, nonspatial), but found that although fire losses may be stochastic, a close approximation to an optimal solution for a forest plan can be developed by using deterministic fire distributions that closely resemble the stochastic disturbance levels.

Reoptimize Stand-Level Prescriptions

The fourth stage of SafeD provides for a reoptimization of stand-level objectives in those stands affected by the distribution of stochastic events across the landscape. Landscape-level objectives are then reexamined, and prescriptions reassigned to reflect attainment of these goals.

Products and Audience

The approach we describe represents a refined forest landscape simulation model that is able to prescribe, schedule, and locate treatments dynamically in response to stochastic disturbances (fire, insects, etc.). This type of planning or policy analysis model will be useful in efforts aimed at evaluating the aggregate effects of policies across a forested landscape, and can provide managers, policymakers, and planners with the ability to think about forests and their management in ways unimagined only a few decades ago. Often called "landscape assessment and planning," this type of approach helps people see and think in whole-landscape terms (not simply single ownerships) and promotes a common understanding of the basic processes that underlie landscape change.

We will apply SafeD to evaluate several alternative forest management policies and practices of each landowner in the pilot test area. The economic, ecological, and social effects will be measured for management scenarios that achieve specific goals related to fuels reduction, riparian management, threatened and endangered species habitat, and other values. At the initiation of the INLAS project, the intent (from the Oregon State University modeling perspective) was to support the Oregon Department of Forestry's effort at evaluating landscape management alternatives for eastern Oregon, thus supporting the Forestry Program for Oregon and providing spatial projections of how the landscape might look under different management scenarios. It is hoped that simulations from SafeD also could provide national forest managers direction for choosing forest landscape management systems that address the tradeoffs associated with timber production, fire risk, and ecosystem health.

Analysis of alternative policies is the primary product of this modeling effort and will likely be a learning process for all involved. Outputs from the modeling effort will include a set of GIS databases that provide an indication of the effects of alternative management policies on the forest resources of eastern Oregon. Associated with these GIS databases are forest structural conditions (as represented by tree lists) that can facilitate further analyses of the effects of policies on wildlife and aquatic habitat resources on forested lands. Evaluating the impact of policies in a spatial context will require thinking about forests and forest resources in a manner heretofore difficult to perform. Although sets of data describing economics and commodity production levels will allow a relative comparison of alternative policy scenarios, examining alternative policies at a landscape scale (with maps) will likely require both quantitative and qualitative approaches.

A secondary product of the modeling effort involves a separate analysis of silvicultural treatments at the stand level. Here our goal is to understand which management practices are most beneficial (from a variety of perspectives: reducing fire hazard, maximizing net present value, etc.) to implement across broad classes of forests. Examining the resulting stand-level decisions, in light of forest-level goals and landscape disturbances, may provide management direction for both federal and private landowners, where multiple-resource goals influence the management of interior West forests.

The tertiary products developed by the modeling effort will be knowledge, algorithms, and software for modeling the effects of stand management and development on fine litterfall tree mortality, and snag longevity. The decay of large dead wood certainly is important for modeling wildlife, insects, and disease response to management and disturbance processes. Snags are tracked through time in the stand-level prescription model. Down wood, however, is not tracked through time, nor is the decay of either resource. The decay of wood is important for various biological effects models. The type of "bottom-up" analysis that would be provided (from trees to landscapes) and the growth projections that will ensue after natural disturbances may be useful in calibrating the INLAS state and transition modeling effort (Hemstrom et al. Chapter 2). Estimates of decay rates for fine litter, coarse woody debris, and snags would also then logically follow and provide a mechanism for summarizing these conditions over space and time, then facilitate an evaluation of the effects of management on wildlife species that utilize these resources. In addition, there has been only a limited amount of work aimed at incorporating fuel dynamics into the prediction of fire occurrence and behavior. In fact, usually only the mean rates of litter inputs and decomposition are used in modeling efforts, with no provision for variation based on stand structure and density levels (e.g., Keane et al. 1996). Yet, stand density strongly influences fuel accumulation (Maguire 1994) and litter decomposition (Piene 1978). Thus the development of models that estimate the effects of stand management on the production and decay of these resources is important.

The development of landscape simulation or optimization models requires a major collaboration between scientists, planners, managers, and policymakers to ensure that the kind of model developed will have widespread application and acceptance at the spatiotemporal scales at which it is used. As with most large-scale landscape modeling efforts, collaborators of the INLAS project will be called on to provide guidance in their areas of expertise. In large projects, with 10 to 20 internal collaborators and numerous outside interest groups shaping the look and feel of an analysis system, the expected goals of the project will likely change. For example, a fire specialist will be asked to assist in fine-tuning parameters related to the fire spread model. As refinements are made to these and other important components of an overall landscape modeling system, previously developed model components may need to be adjusted.

Although the modeling system we describe is well suited to address a wide spectrum of issues relating to the dynamics of change in coniferous forests, there remain a number of gaps in our knowledge about important disturbance factors that affect other significant resources. Of most interest are invasive plants, large herbivores, and hydrologic processes that regulate stream geomorphology and associated riparian conditions. Data and models are lacking to incorporate the effects of these factors into detailed simulation models like SafeD that model processes like stand growth in a continuous scale. In the absence of refined data and models, an alternative approach to building a landscape model that considers these factors is described by Hemstrom et al. (Chapter 2). Finally, for demonstration purposes, stochastic processes are incorporated into the results only once. For extensive analysis purposes, multiple runs will be required to assess the capacity of the landscape to not only produce the goals suggested by the policymakers but also to evaluate the projected dynamics of change that affect natural resources.

Two rather difficult issues to address are those related to sensitivity analysis and validation of the SafeD process. Sensitivity analyses give the customer of the simulation system products a sense of the importance of variables in the model. At present, no sensitivity analysis has been planned. Given the number of variables included in the fire model, the stand-level prescription generator, and the SafeD landscape model, the number of potential scenarios that can be modeled is infinite. The difficulty for a sensitivity analysis effort will be in determining which parameters to keep constant, and which to vary. It may be more difficult to determine which to keep constant in a sensitivity analysis, because it assumes that these variables are reflective of the human or natural system. Validation of large forest landscape models has generally been limited to an assessment of how well the model simulates what is typically known (e.g., recent harvest levels, recent areas treated with various management prescriptions). It has been suggested that one should use simulation models to evaluate paths from past conditions to the present. This would allow one to evaluate how well the models can explain past behavior of landscapes and may provide a good clue as to how they can help explain future behavior. However, projecting a historical landscape to the present is problematic. One would need databases that describe the landscape 20, 30, or more years ago to do this, an effort not planned within the INLAS project. Thus validation of large-scale forest landscape planning models is elusive. A number of verification processes are used to determine whether submodels within the larger SafeD modeling framework are working as intended, by comparing various output products to the models (e.g., the Forest Vegetation Simulator) from which the processes were derived. In addition, the cumulative results from a landscape simulation (harvest volumes, areas treated, fire risk, etc.) will be evaluated for reasonableness, which while not a validation, may suggest how well the simulation model is performing.

Acknowledgments

The authors thank Jamie Barbour and Jane Hayes for their guidance in developing this paper, and Kevin Boston, J. Douglas Brodie, and Miles Hemstrom for their thoughtful reviews.

English Equivalents

When you know:	Multiply by:	To get:
Hectares (ha)	2.47	Acres
Meters (m)	3.28	Feet

Literature Cited

Amidon, E.L.; Akin, G.S. 1968. Dynamic programming to determine optimum levels of growing stock. Forest Science. 14: 287-291.

Armstrong, G.W.; Cumming, S.G.; Adamowicz, W.L. 1999. Timber supply implications of natural disturbance management. The Forestry Chronicle. 75: 497-504.

Arthaud, G.J.; Klemperer, W.D. 1988. Optimizing high and low thinnings in loblolly pine with dynamic programming. Canadian Journal of Forest Research. 18: 1118-1122.

Arthaud, G.J.; Rose, D. 1996. A methodology for estimating production possibility frontiers for wildlife habitat and timber value at the landscape level. Canadian Journal of Forest Research. 26: 2191-2200.

Bare, B.B.; Opalach, D. 1987. Optimizing species composition in uneven-aged forest stands. Forest Science. 33: 958-970.

Bettinger, P. 1999. Distributing geographic information systems capabilities to field offices: benefits and challenges. Journal of Forestry. 97(6): 22-26.

Bettinger, P.; Boston, K. 2001. A conceptual model for describing decisionmaking situations in integrated natural resource planning and modeling projects. Environmental Management. 28: 1-7.

Bettinger, P.; Boston, K.; Sessions, J. 1999. Intensifying a heuristic forest harvest scheduling search procedure with 2-opt decision choices. Canadian Journal of Forest Research. 29: 1784-1792.

Bettinger, P.; Graetz, D.; Boston, K. [et al.]. 2002. Eight heuristic planning techniques applied to three increasingly difficult wildlife planning problems. Silva Fennica. 36: 561-584.

Bettinger, P.; Johnson, K.N.; Sessions, J. 1998a. Evaluating the association among alternative measures of cumulative watershed effects on a forested watershed in eastern Oregon. Western Journal of Applied Forestry. 13: 15-22.

Bettinger, P.; Lennette, M. 2002. LAndscape Management Policy Simulator (LAMPS), version 1.1 user's manual. Corvallis, OR: Department of Forest Resources, Oregon State University. 97 p.

Bettinger, P.; Sessions, J.; Boston, K. 1997. Using tabu search to schedule timber harvests subject to spatial wildlife goals for big game. Ecological Modeling. 94: 111–123.

Bettinger, P.; Sessions, J.; Johnson, K.N. 1998b. Ensuring the compatibility of aquatic habitat and commodity production goals in eastern Oregon with a tabu search procedure. Forest Science. 44: 96–112.

Birta, L.G.; Özmizrak, F.N. 1996. A knowledge-based approach for the validation of simulation models: the foundation. ACM Transactions of Modeling and Computer Simulation. 6(1): 76–98.

Boston, K.; Bettinger, P. 2002. Combining tabu search and genetic algorithm heuristic techniques to solve spatial harvest scheduling problems. Forest Science. 48: 35-46.

Brodie, J.D.; Adams, D.; Kao, C. 1978. Analysis of economic impacts on thinning and rotation for Douglas-fir, using dynamic programming. Forest Science. 24: 513-522.

Brodie, J.D.; Kao, C. 1979. Optimizing thinning in Douglas-fir with three-descriptor dynamic programming to account for accelerated diameter growth. Forest Science. 25: 665-672.

Brukas, V.; Brodie, J.D. 1999. Economic optimisation of silvicultural regimes for Scots pine using dynamic programming. Baltic Forestry. 5(1): 28-34.

Buongiorno, J.; Michie, B.R. 1980. A matrix model of uneven-aged forest management. Forest Science. 26: 609-625.

Chen, C.M.; Rose, D.W.; Leary, R.A. 1980a. Derivation of optimal stand density over time—a discrete stage, continuous state dynamic programming solution. Forest Science. 26: 217-227.

Chen, C.M.; Rose, D.W.; Leary, R.A. 1980b. How to formulate and solve optimal stand density over time problems for even-aged stands using dynamic programming. Gen. Tech. Rep. NC-56. St. Paul, MN: U.S. Department of Agriculture, Forest Service, North Central Research Station. 17 p.

Daust, D.K.; Nelson, J.D. 1993. Spatial reduction factors for strata-based harvest schedules. Forest Science. 39(1): 152-165.

Dowsland, K.A. 1993. Simulated annealing. In: Reeves, C.R., ed. Modern heuristic techniques for combinatorial problems. New York: John Wiley and Sons, Inc.: 20-69.

Dueck, G. 1993. New optimization heuristics: the great deluge algorithm and the record-to-record travel. Journal of Computational Physics. 104: 86-92.

Dueck, G.; Scheuer, T. 1990. Threshold accepting: a general purpose optimization algorithm appearing superior to simulated annealing. Journal of Computational Physics. 90: 161-175.

Falcão, A.O.; Borges, J.G. 2000. Designing an evolution program for solving integer forest management scheduling models: an application in Portugal. Forest Science. 47: 158-168.

Finney, M.A. 1998. FARSITE: Fire Area Simulator–model development and evaluation. Res. Pap. RMRS-RP-4. Ogden, UT: U.S. Department of Agriculture, Forest Service, Rocky Mountain Research Station. 47 p.

Flamm, R.O.; Turner, M.G. 1994. Alternative model formulations for a stochastic simulation of landscape change. Landscape Ecology. 9: 37-46.

Franklin, J.F.; Forman, R.T.T. 1987. Creating landscape patterns by forest cutting: ecological consequences and principles. Landscape Ecology. 1: 5-18.

Gao, Q.; Li, J.; Zheng, H. 1996. A dynamic landscape simulation model for the alkaline grasslands on Songnen Plain in northeast China. Landscape Ecology. 11: 339-349.

Glover, F. 1990. Tabu search–Part II. ORSA Journal of Computing. 2(1): 4-32.

Glover, F.; Laguna, M. 1993. Tabu search. In: Reeves, C.R., ed. Modern heuristic techniques for combinatorial problems. New York: John Wiley and Sons, Inc.: 70-150.

Gong, P. 1992. Multiobjective dynamic programming for forest resource management. Forest Ecology and Management. 48: 43-54.

Graetz, D.H. 2000. The SafeD model: incorporating episodic disturbances and heuristic programming into forest management planning for the Applegate River watershed, southwestern Oregon. Corvallis, OR: Department of Forest Resources, Oregon State University. 127 p. M.S. thesis.

Gustafson, E.J.; Crow, T.R. 1994. Modeling the effects of forest harvesting on landscape structure and the spatial distribution of cowbird brood parasitism. Landscape Ecology. 9: 237-248.

Gustafson, E.J.; Crow, T.R. 1996. Simulating the effects of alternative forest management strategies on landscape structure. Journal of Environmental Management. 46: 77-94.

Gustafson, E.J.; Shifley, S.R.; Mladenoff, D.J. [et al.]. 2000. Spatial simulation of forest succession and timber harvesting using LANDIS. Canadian Journal of Forest Research. 30: 32-43.

Haight, R.; Brodie, J.D.; Dahms, W. 1985. A dynamic programming algorithm for optimization of lodgepole pine management. Forest Science. 31: 321-330.

Haight, R.; Monserud, R. 1990. Optimizing any-aged management of mixed-species stands: II. Effects of decision criteria. Forest Science. 36: 125-144.

Haight, R.G.; Monserud, R.A.; Chew, J.D. 1992. Optimal harvesting with stand density targets: managing Rocky Mountain conifer stands for multiple forest outputs. Forest Science. 38: 554-574.

Haight, R.G.; Travis, L.E. 1997. Wildlife conservation planning using stochastic optimization and importance sampling. Forest Science. 43(1): 129-139.

Hemstrom, M.; Ager, A.; Vavra, M. [et al.]. 2004. The application of state and transition models for integrated landscape simulation. In: Hayes, J.L.; Ager, A.A.; Barbour, R.J., tech. eds. Methods for integrating modeling of landscape change: Interior Northwest Landscape Analysis System. Gen. Tech. Rep. PNW-GTR-610. Portland, OR: U.S. Department of Agriculture, Forest Service, Pacific Northwest Research Station: 17-32. Chapter 2.

Hof, J.G.; Bevers, M.; Joyce, L.; Kent, B. 1994. An integer programming approach for spatially and temporally optimizing wildlife populations. Forest Science. 40: 177-191.

Hof, J.G.; Joyce, L.A. 1992. Spatial optimization for wildlife and timber in managed forest ecosystems. Forest Science. 38: 489–508.

Hoganson, H.M.; Rose, D. 1984. A simulation approach for optimal timber management scheduling. Forest Science. 30(1): 220-238.

Holland, J.H. 1975. Adaptation in natural and artificial systems. Ann Arbor, MI: University of Michigan Press. [Pages unknown].

Hooke, R.; Jeeves, T.A. 1961. "Direct search" solution of numerical and statistical problems. Journal of the Association for Computing Machinery. 8: 212-229.

Hool, J.N. 1966. A dynamic programming—Markov chain approach to forest production control. Forest Science Monograph 12. 26 p.

Johnson, K.N.; Jones, D.B.; Kent, B. 1980. A user's guide to the forest planning model (FORPLAN). Fort Collins, CO: U.S. Department of Agriculture, Forest Service, Land Management Planning. [Pages unknown].

Johnson, K.N.; Sessions, J.; Franklin, J.; Gabriel, J. 1998. Integrating wildfire into strategic planning for Sierra Nevada forests. Journal of Forestry. 96(1): 42-49.

Kangas, J.; Pukkala, T. 1996. Operationalization of biological diversity as a decision objective in tactical forest planning. Canadian Journal of Forest Research. 26: 103-111.

Kao, C.; Brodie, J.D. 1979. Determination of optimal thinning entry interval using dynamic programming. Forest Science. 25: 672-674.

Kao, C.; Brodie, J.D. 1980. Simultaneous optimization of thinnings and rotation with continuous stocking and entry intervals. Forest Science. 26: 338-346.

Keane, R.E.; Morgan, P.; Running, S.W. 1996. FIRE-BGC—a mechanistic ecological process model for simulating fire succession on coniferous forest landscapes of the northern Rocky Mountains. Res. Pap. INT-484. Ogden, UT: U.S. Department of Agriculture, Forest Service, Intermountain Research Station. 122 p.

Li, H.; Franklin, J.F.; Swanson, F.J.; Spies, T.A. 1993. Developing alternative forest cutting patterns: a simulation approach. Landscape Ecology. 8: 63-75.

Lockwood, C.; Moore, T. 1993. Harvest scheduling with spatial constraints: a simulated annealing approach. Canadian Journal of Forest Research. 23: 468–478.

Lu, F.; Eriksson, L.O. 2000. Formulation of harvest units with genetic algorithms. Forest Ecology and Management. 130: 57-67.

Maguire, D.A. 1994. Branch mortality and potential litterfall from Douglas-fir trees in stands of varying density. Forest Ecology and Management. 70: 41-53.

Martin, G.L.; Ek, A.R. 1981. A dynamic programming analysis of silvicultural alternatives for red pine plantations in Wisconsin. Canadian Journal of Forest Research. 11: 370-379.

McGurk, B.J.; Fong, D.R. 1995. Equivalent roaded area as a measure of cumulative effect of logging. Environmental Management. 19: 609-621.

Metropolis, N.; Rosenbluth, A.; Rosenbluth, M. [et al.]. 1953. Equation of state calculations by fast computing machines. Journal of Chemical Physics. 21: 1087-1092.

Mladenoff, D.; Baker, W. 1999. Development of forest and landscape modeling approaches. In: Mladenoff, D.; Baker, W., eds. Spatial modeling of forest landscape change: approaches and applications. Cambridge, United Kingdom: Cambridge University Press: 1-13.

Mladenoff, D.; He, H.S. 1999. Design, behavior and application of LANDIS, an object-oriented model of forest landscape disturbance and succession. In: Mladenoff, D.; Baker, W., eds. Spatial modeling of forest landscape change: approaches and applications. Cambridge, United Kingdom: Cambridge University Press: 125-162.

Mullen, D.S.; Butler, R.M. 1999. The design of a genetic algorithm based spatially constrained timber harvest scheduling model. In: Seventh symposium on systems analysis in forest resources. Gen. Tech. Rep. NC-205. St. Paul, MN: U.S. Department of Agriculture, Forest Service, North Central Research Station: 57-65.

Murray, A.T.; Church, R.L. 1995. Heuristic solution approaches to operational forest planning problems. OR Spektrum. 17: 193–203.

National Forest Management Act of 1976 [NFMA]. Act of October 22, 1976: 16 U.S.C. 1600.

Navon, D.I. 1971. Timber RAM... a long-range planning method for commercial timber lands under multiple-use management. Res. Pap. PSW-70. Berkeley, CA: U.S. Department of Agriculture, Forest Service, Pacific Southwest Research Station. 22 p.

Nelson, J.; Brodie, J.D. 1990. Comparison of a random search algorithm and mixed integer programming for solving area-based forest plans. Canadian Journal of Forest Research. 20: 934-942.

O'Hara, A.J.; Faaland, B.A.; Bare, B.B. 1989. Spatially constrained timber harvest scheduling. Canadian Journal of Forest Research. 19: 715-724.

Piene, H. 1978. Effects of increased spacing on carbon mineralization rates and temperature in a stand of young balsam fir. Canadian Journal of Forest Research. 8: 398-406.

Pulkki, R. 1984. A spatial database—heuristic programming system for aiding decision-making in long-distance transport of wood. Acta Forestalia Fennica 188. 89 p.

Quigley, T.M.; Haynes, R.W.; Graham, R.T., tech. eds. 1996. Integrated scientific assessment for ecosystem management in the interior Columbia basin and portions of the Klamath and Great Basins. Gen. Tech. Rep. PNW-GTR-382. Portland, OR: U.S. Department of Agriculture, Forest Service, Pacific Northwest Research Station. 303 p.

Quigley, T.M.; Haynes, R.W.; Hann, W.J. 2001. Estimating ecological integrity in the interior Columbia River basin. Forest Ecology and Management. 153: 161-178.

Reed, W.J.; Errico, D. 1986. Optimal harvest scheduling at the forest level in the presence of fire. Canadian Journal of Forest Research. 16: 266-278.

Roberts, D.; Betz, D. 1999. Simulating landscape vegetation dynamics of Bryce Canyon National Park with the vital attributes/fuzzy systems model VAFS/LANDSIM. In: Mladenoff, D.; Baker, W., eds. Advances in spatial modeling of forest landscape change: approaches and applications. Cambridge, United Kingdom: Cambridge University Press. 99-124.

Sessions, J.; Johnson, K.N.; Franklin, J.F.; Gabriel, J.T. 1999. Achieving sustainable forest structures on fir-prone landscapes while pursuing multiple goals. In: Mladenoff, D.; Baker, W., eds. Spatial modeling of forest landscape change: approaches and applications. Cambridge, United Kingdom: Cambridge University Press: 210-255.

Srinivas, M.; Patnaik, L.M. 1994. Genetic algorithms: a survey. Computer. (June): 17-26.

State of Oregon. 1999. Revised statutes, Chapter 527: insect and disease control; forest practices. http://www.leg.state.or.us/ors/527.html. (January 10, 2002).

Turner, M.G. 1987. Spatial simulation of landscape changes in Georgia: a comparison of 3 transition models. Landscape Ecology. 1: 29-36.

Valsta, L.T. 1992. A scenario approach to stochastic anticipatory optimization in stand management. Forest Science. 38: 430-447.

Valsta, L.T. 1993. Stand management optimization based on growth simulators. Res. Pap. 453. Helsinki, Finland: The Finnish Forest Research Institute, Information Systems Group. 51 p.

Wallin, D.O.; Swanson, F.J.; Marks, B. 1994. Landscape pattern response to changes in pattern generation rules: land-use legacies in forestry. Ecological Applications. 4: 569-580.

Weintraub, A.; Jones, G.; Magendzo, A. [et al.]. 1994. A heuristic system to solve mixed integer forest planning models. Operations Research. 42: 1010-1024.

Weintraub, A.; Jones, G.; Meacham, M. [et al.]. 1995. Heuristic procedures for solving mixed-integer harvest scheduling–transportation planning models. Canadian Journal of Forest Research. 25: 1618-1626.

Wilson, D.; Maguire, D.; Barbour, J. [In press]. Assessment of the small-diameter timber harvest from restoration treatments in densely-stocked stands on national forests in eastern Oregon. Western Journal of Applied Forestry.

Yoshimoto, A.; Haight, R.G.; Brodie, J.D. 1990. A comparison of the pattern search algorithm and the modified path algorithm for optimizing an individual tree model. Forest Science. 36: 394-412.

Zhou, G.; Liebhold, A.M. 1995. Forecasting the spatial dynamics of gypsy moth outbreaks using cellular transition models. Landscape Ecology. 10: 177-189.

Chapter 5: Assessment Techniques for Terrestrial Vertebrates of Conservation Concern

Barbara C. Wales and Lowell H. Suring[1]

Abstract

The quantity and quality of habitat for many wildlife species have changed throughout the interior Western United States over the last 150 years owing to a variety of natural and human-caused disturbances. Results from regional landscape models indicate that many species in this region are currently at risk of extirpation. Little is known, however, about how landscape mosaics and patterns of vegetation contribute to the viability of wildlife populations at finer scales. The increased ability to model vegetation and disturbances, including insects and fire, allows the opportunity to explore how potential changes in vegetation structure and composition may affect wildlife populations at finer scales. We identify methods to describe and evaluate habitat abundance, quality, and distribution across area and time, considering alternative management goals and assumptions at a landscape scale. Landscape simulation modeling results associated with a prototype subbasin in northeastern Oregon will be used to develop a decision-support tool to help managers and scientists design and schedule management activities that provide for conservation and recovery of terrestrial vertebrates.

Keywords: Decision support, habitat modeling, species of concern, wildlife.

Introduction

In recent work associated with the Interior Columbia Basin Ecosystem Management Project (ICBEMP), an approach was developed to evaluate how wildlife habitat for species of conservation concern is distributed across the interior Columbia basin (Raphael et al. 2001, Wisdom et al. 2000) (tables 3 and 4). These analyses provided insight into the abundance, quality, and distribution of habitats and to the status of associated terrestrial species across the basin. Findings demonstrated large declines in old forests,

[1] **Barbara C. Wales** is a wildlife biologist, U S Department of Agriculture, Forest Service, Pacific Northwest Research Station, Forestry and Range Sciences Laboratory, 1401 Gekeler Lane, La Grande OR 97850 **Lowell H. Suring** is a wildlife ecologist, U S Department of Agriculture, Forest Service, Terrestrial Wildlife Unit, Forestry Sciences Laboratory, 316 East Myrtle Street, Boise ID 83702

Table 3—Species of conservation concern occurring in the Upper Grande Ronde assessment area and considered for use in the development of INLAS

Common name	Habitat association	Federal status	Oregon Department of Fish and Wildlife status	Oregon Natural Heritage rank
Amphibians;				
Columbia spotted frog	Riparian	SoC	SU	S2?
Birds;				
Bald eagle	Riparian	T	T	S3B,S4N
Black-backed woodpecker	Broad-elevation, old forest		SC	S3
Brown creeper	Broad-elevation, old forest			S4
Brown-headed cowbird	All habitats			S5
Flammulated owl	Broad-elevation, old forest		SC	S4B
Great gray owl	Broad-elevation, old forest		SV	S3
Northern goshawk	Broad-elevation, old forest	SoC	SC	S3
Olive-sided flycatcher	Broad-elevation, old forest	SoC	SV	S4
Pileated woodpecker	Broad-elevation, old forest		SV	S4?
Pine grosbeak	Broad-elevation, old forest			S2?
Pygmy nuthatch	Low-elevation, old forest		SC	S4?
Three-toed woodpecker	Broad-elevation, old forest		SC	S3
White-headed woodpecker	Low-elevation, old forest	SoC	SC	S3
Williamson's sapsucker	Broad-elevation, old forest		SU	S4B,S3N
Willow flycatcher	Riparian	SoC	SV	S4
Mammals:				
American marten	Broad-elevation, old forest		SV	S3
Canada lynx	High-elevation forest	T	T	S1
Fringed myotis	Forest, woodland, and sagebrush	SoC	SV	S2?
Long-eared myotis	Forest, woodland, and sagebrush	SoC	SU	S3
Long-legged myotis	Forest, woodland, and sagebrush	SoC	SU	S3
Silver-haired bat	Broad-elevation, old forest	SoC	SU	S4?
Western small-footed myotis	Forest, woodland, and sagebrush	SoC	SU	S3
Yuma myotis	Riparian	SoC		S3

State Natura Heritage ranks
S1= critica y imperi ed
S2 = imperi ed
S3 = vu nerab e
S4 = apparent y secure
S5 = secure
? = inexact rank
B = breeding range
N = nonbreeding range

Federa status
SoC = isted as species of concern by the U S Fish and Wi d ife Service
T = isted as threatened by the U S Fish and Wi d ife Service

Oregon status
SC = sensitive species critica category
SV = sensitive species vu nerab e category
SU = sensitive species undetermined status
T = isted as threatened by Oregon Department of Fish and Wi d ife

Table 4—Scientific names of species of conservation concern

Common name	Scientific name
Amphibians:	
Columbia spotted frog	*Rana luteiventris*
Birds:	
Bald eagle	*Haliaeetus leucocephalus*
Black-backed woodpecker	*Picoides arcticus*
Brown creeper	*Certhia americana*
Brown-headed cowbird	*Molothrus ater*
Flammulated owl	*Otus flammeolus*
Great gray owl	*Strix nebulosa*
Northern goshawk	*Accipiter gentilis*
Olive-sided flycatcher	*Contopus borealis*
Pileated woodpecker	*Dryocopus pileatus*
Pine grosbeak	*Pinicola enucleator*
Pygmy nuthatch	*Sitta pygmaea*
Three-toed woodpecker	*P. tridactylus*
White-headed woodpecker	*P. albolarvatus*
Williamson's sapsucker	*Sphyrapicus thyroideus*
Willow flycatcher	*Empidonax traillii*
Mammals:	
American marten	*Martes americana*
Canada lynx	*Lynx canadensis*
Fringed myotis	*Myotis thysanodes*
Long-eared myotis	*M. evotis*
Long-legged myotis	*M. volans*
Silver-haired bat	*Lasionycteris noctivagans*
Western small-footed myotis	*M. subulatus*
Yuma myotis	*M. yumanensis*

native grasslands, and native shrub lands at 1-km resolution. This information has provided a basis for potential additional analysis and development of management direction at smaller scales and greater resolution.

The Interior Northwest Landscape Analysis System (INLAS) provides an opportunity to develop and implement a prototype approach for applying and focusing the results of the ICBEMP to regional and local natural resource planning efforts, in particular for updating land and resource management plans on national forests throughout the Northwest. Land managers working at these finer scales (e.g., province or national forest) need tools to help them evaluate habitat for terrestrial vertebrates at midscales. To provide for the conservation of all species across their ranges, as per the National Forest Management Act (NFMA 1976) regulations, national forest land managers require analyses that will incorporate areas large enough to encompass several home ranges of all species of concern. Such analyses also will provide insight into the potential contribution other public and private lands may make to the conservation of species and their habitats.

Prototype Study Area

The Upper Grande Ronde subbasin has been selected as the study area for initial development and application of INLAS. There are approximately 40 terrestrial vertebrate species of concern within the Upper Grande Ronde subbasin (see Wisdom et al. 2000). This initial list received additional screening against the State of Oregon Heritage Status Rank (Association for Biodiversity Information 2001) for species ranked S1–S3 (e.g., vulnerable or below) and against the state of Oregon sensitive species list (Oregon Department of Fish and Wildlife 1997) for species ranked vulnerable or critical. Occurrence of each of the resulting species within the study area was verified with local species checklists (e.g., Bull and Wisdom 1992) and the results of the Oregon Gap Analysis program (Kagan et al. 1999). Probability of occurrence also was evaluated based on habitats available in the study area. These screens resulted in a list of 24 potential species for analysis (table 3). Most of the species of conservation concern within the Upper Grande Ronde also occur throughout large areas within the interior West, and many of these species have home ranges that span multiple subwatersheds or larger scales. The tools developed through this project will be used to facilitate planning and evaluation of various management activities and should be useful at multiple scales. Such planning tools will be useful to help restore and conserve natural landscape patterns and functions over the long term.

Research Objectives

We propose to develop methods to describe and evaluate habitat abundance, quality, and distribution through time considering different management objectives and activities. To accomplish this, we will address the following:

- How will the current quantity, quality, and distribution of habitats that contribute to the long-term persistence of species of concern change in the future under different management regimes in the Upper Grande Ronde subbasin?

- How do the effects of roads, recreation, fire, insects, disease, timber harvest, grazing, and other disturbances (and their interactions) influence the viability and vulnerability of terrestrial vertebrates of concern in the Upper Grande Ronde subbasin?

- Develop analytical tools that are user-friendly and flexible to accommodate available data in other locations, thereby facilitating widespread application.

- Describe how effective broad-scale habitat models are in providing a useful context for mid- and fine-scale analyses and land management planning.

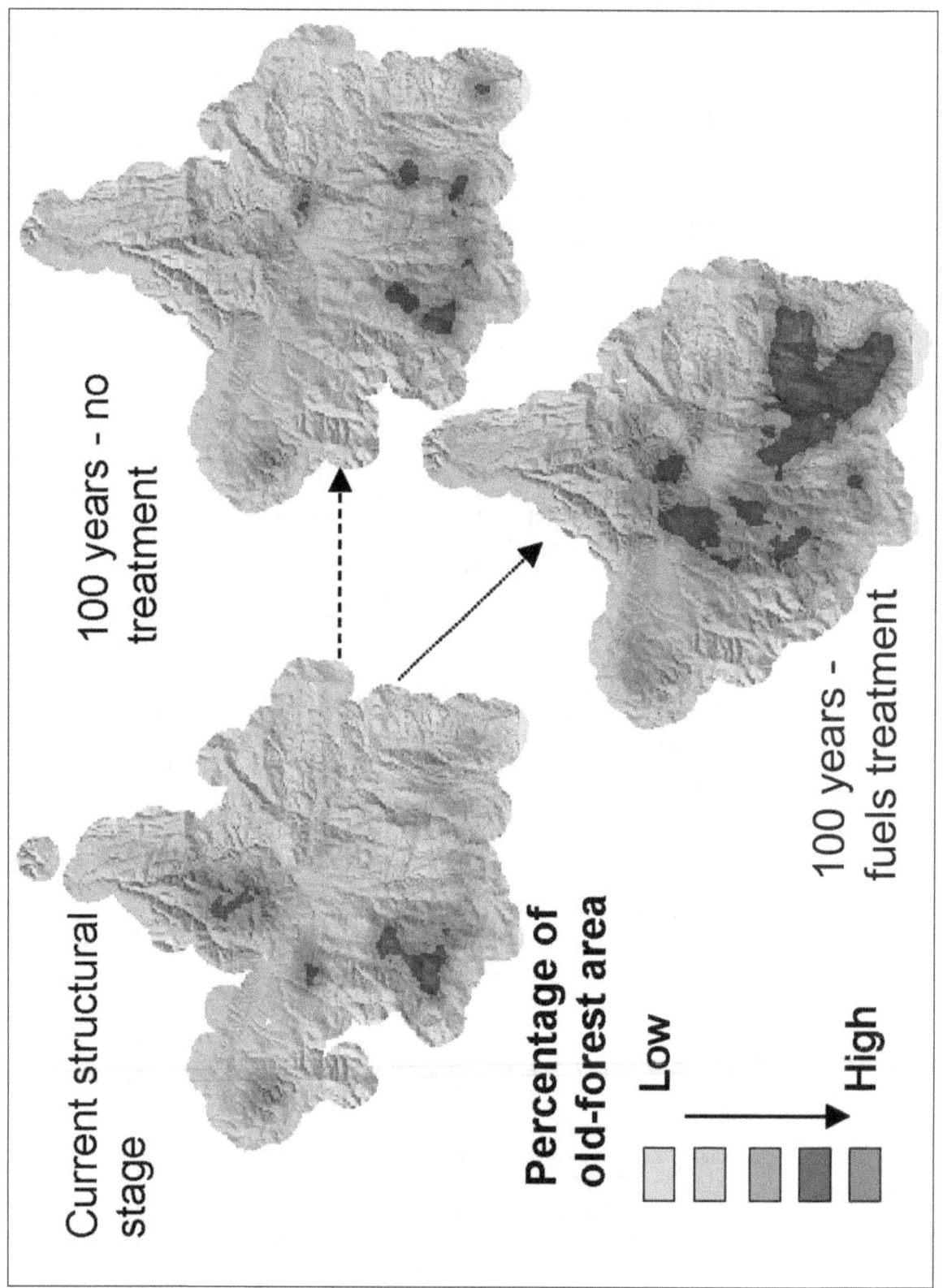

Current structural stage

100 years - no treatment

100 years - fuels treatment

Percentage of old-forest area

Low

High

Figure 11—One potential modeling output comparing suitable habitat for an old-forest-dependent species for the current period and as estimated under two different management scenarios in 100 years.

Methods

Evaluating landscape change may be more important than current landscape structure in developing an understanding of long-term population dynamics of terrestrial vertebrates (Dunn et al. 1991, Knick and Rotenberry 2000). By using a combination of geographic information system spatial modeling and decision-support models (DSMs), we will evaluate changes in wildlife habitat under different management regimes through time as well as develop assessment processes for wildlife species at a subbasin scale. Figure 11 displays how one potential output might look comparing two different management scenarios through time. We will explore the use of Bayesian belief networks (BBNs), a type of DSM, as well as other more traditional modeling techniques such as habitat suitability index models. See Wondzell and Howell (Chapter 6) for more discussion regarding the use of DSMs.

Bayesian modeling is just one of numerous types of wildlife habitat modeling that can calculate an index of population response.[2] It can provide a modeling approach that (1) displays major influences on the persistence of wildlife populations and their values and interactions, (2) combines categorical and continuous variables, (3) combines empirical data with expert judgment, often from multiple experts; and (4) expresses predicted outcomes as likelihoods as a basis for risk analysis and risk management (Marcot et al. 2001). The models can rely on outputs from other models, such as projected vegetation, to estimate the amount of habitat available, and other environmental factors, to estimate the quality of habitat (Raphael et al. 2001). It is likely models will be developed at two scales, site-specific and subbasin, which will be hierarchically nested. The site-specific model will estimate habitat quantity and quality at the scale of a pixel (or stand), whereas the subbasin model will summarize those results to assess the overall conditions within a subbasin. Figure 12 shows an example of a site-specific belief network modified from the work of Raphael et al. (2001). Within the subbasin model, it is possible to assess the connectivity of high-quality habitats, another important aspect for some wildlife species.

The wildlife models will rely heavily on the outcomes of the vegetation modeling described by Hemstrom et al. (Chapter 2) and Bettinger et al. (Chapter 4). Many of the species of concern in our study area are dependent on snags and coarse woody debris (CWD). Because insects, disease, and fire are imbedded in the vegetation modeling efforts, snags will be addressed. We will develop methods to quantify snag and CWD development within the vegetation models. In addition, a companion project in the same study area will be developing landscape models to predict snag and CWD densities in relation to vegetation type and landscape characteristics, such as distance to nearest roads and towns, elevation, and slope, which we will build into our habitat models (Bate and Wisdom 2001). We also will be working to develop close links with other resource modules such as recreation, social, and riparian. Although little empirical data exist on species distribution across the subbasin, we will use any available data to help build the models and use existing models such as those developed by McGrath et al. (2003), Sallabanks et al. (2002), and Roloff and Haufler (1997) (also footnote 2). Our knowledge on species environmental requirements and population dynamics differs widely per species, so some models will be better developed than others.

---

[2] Ro off G J 2001 Breeding habitat potentia mode for northern goshawks in the Idaho Southern Batho ith [Pages unknown] Unpub ished document On fi e with: Timber and Resources Boise Cascade Corporation 1564 Tom inson Road Mason MI 48854

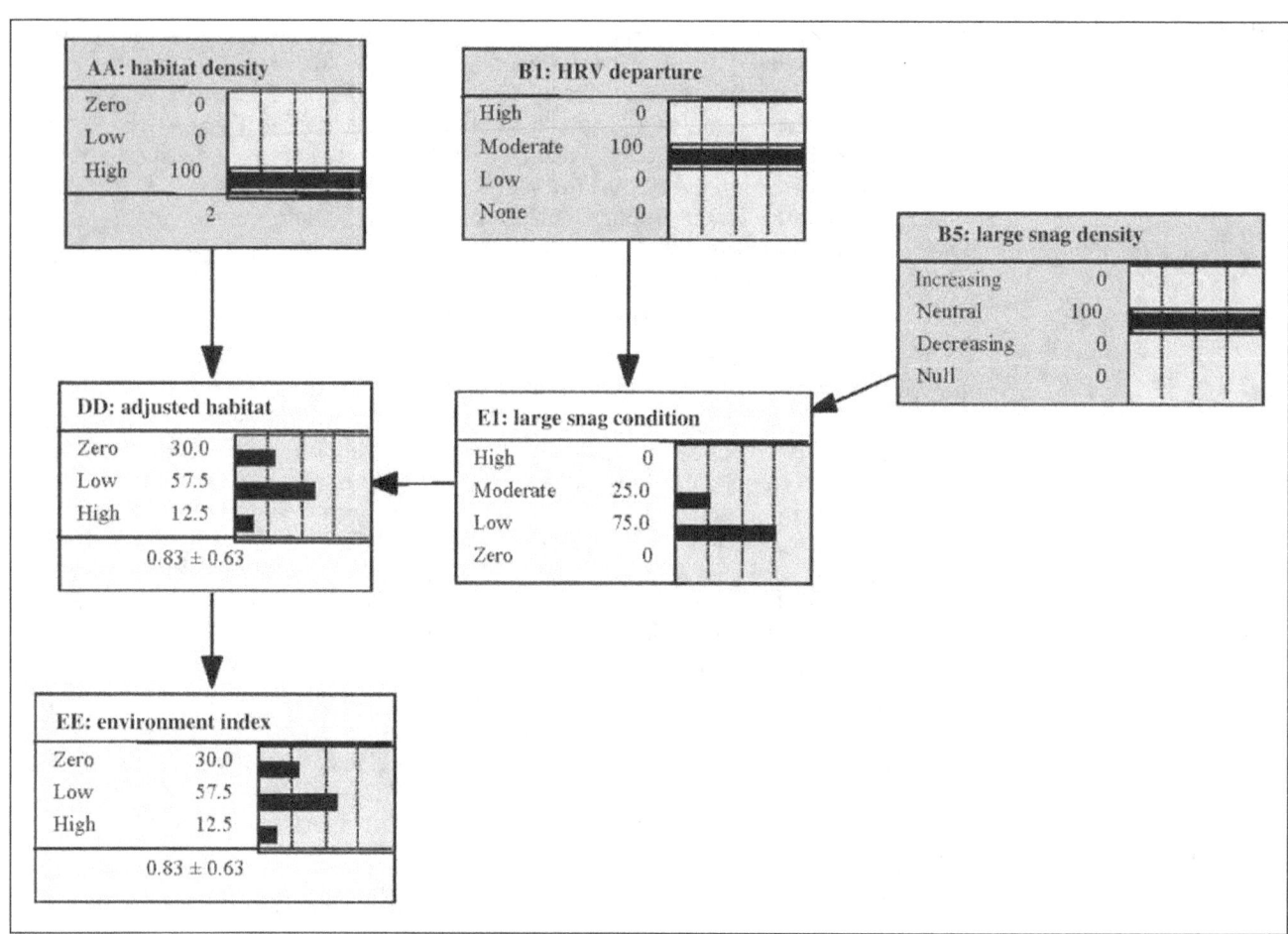

Figure 12   Example of a Bayesian belief network model adapted from Raphael et al. (2001) This example was used to quantify habitat quality and quantity within a subwatershed for pygmy nuthatch

The performance of BBN models, as well as alternative approaches to BBN models, also may be evaluated where alternative models exist that are compatible with vegetation data generated by the INLAS base models (e.g., Hemstrom et al. Chapter 2 and Bettinger et al. Chapter 4). Performance of BBN and other models may be evaluated in various ways, including the use of Bayesian statistics (Lee 2000), or through other analyses of model predictions versus empirical observations (Rowland et al. 2003, Wisdom et al. 2002). Tests of model performance will provide an opportunity to explore how different procedures for modeling wildlife habitat compare in terms of their results, veracity, and compatibility with INLAS models for other resources. In addition, the models developed during this analysis will be evaluated through a companion project to be conducted in the study area by scientists from the University of Idaho, which will provide information in developing a final set of user-friendly models.

Products and Audience

As a result of this work, we will provide prototype decision-support models that can be used to describe the amount, distribution, and quality of habitat for terrestrial vertebrates throughout the interior West. These analytical tools will help managers and scientists design and schedule management activities that will provide for the conservation of terrestrial species at a landscape scale through time. We will apply this prototype to the Upper Grande Ronde subbasin. The models we build will give a relative index to habitat quality or species persistence, depending on the scale.

Acknowledgments

M. Wisdom, R. Riggs, and G. Roloff provided comments on the manuscript.

English Equivalent

When you know:	Multiply by:	To get:
Kilometers (km)	0.06125	Miles

Literature Cited

Association for Biodiversity Information. 2001. NatureServe: an online encyclopedia of life (Web application), version 1.4. Arlington, VA. http://www.natureserve.org/. (July 6).

Bate, L.J.; Wisdom, M.J. 2001. Pre-proposal to investigate snag-log-road relations at stand and landscape scales in the interior Columbia basin. Portland, OR: U.S. Department of Agriculture, Forest Service, Pacific Northwest Research Station. On file with: Michael Wisdom, USDA Forest Service, Forestry and Range Sciences Laboratory, 1401 Gekeler Lane, La Grande, OR 97850.

Bettinger, P.; Graetz, D.; Ager, A.A.; Sessions, J. 2004. The SafeD forest landscape planning model. In: Hayes, J.L.; Ager, A.A.; Barbour, R.J., tech. eds. Methods for integrating modeling of landscape change: Interior Northwest Landscape Analysis System. Gen. Tech. Rep. PNW-GTR-610. Portland, OR: U.S. Department of Agriculture, Forest Service, Pacific Northwest Research Station: 41-63. Chapter 4.

Bull, E.L.; Wisdom, M.J. 1992. Fauna of the Starkey Experimental Forest and Range. Gen. Tech. Rep. PNW-GTR-291. Portland, OR: U.S. Department of Agriculture, Forest Service, Pacific Northwest Research Station. [Not paged].

Dunn, C.P.; Sharpe, D.M.; Guntenspergen, G.R. [et al.]. 1991. Methods for analyzing temporal changes in landscape pattern. In: Turner, M.G.; Gardner, R.H., eds. Quantitative methods in landscape ecology: the analysis and interpretation of landscape heterogeneity. New York: Springer-Verlag: 173-198.

Hemstrom, M.; Ager, A.A.; Vavra, M. [et al.]. 2004. State and transition approach for integrating landscape models. In: Hayes, J.L.; Ager, A.A.; Barbour, R.J., tech. eds. Methods for integrating modeling of landscape change: Interior Northwest Landscape Analysis System. Gen. Tech. Rep. PNW-GTR-610. Portland, OR: U.S. Department of Agriculture, Forest Service, Pacific Northwest Research Station: 17-32. Chapter 2.

Kagan, J.S.; Hak, J.C.; Csuti, B. [et al.]. 1999. Oregon Gap Analysis Project final report: a geographic approach to planning for biological diversity. Portland, OR: Oregon Natural Heritage Program. 72 p.

Knick, S.T.; Rotenberry, J.T. 2000. Ghosts of habitat past: contribution of landscape change to current habitats used by shrubland birds. Ecology. 81: 220-227.

Lee, D. 2000. Assessing land-use impacts on bull trout using Bayesian belief networks. In: Ferson, S.; Burgman, M., eds. Quantitative methods for conservation biology. New York: Springer: 127-147.

Marcot, B.G.; Holthausen, R.S.; Raphael, M.G. [et al.]. 2001. Using Bayesian belief networks to evaluate fish and wildlife population viability under land management alternatives from an environmental impact statement. Forest Ecology and Management. 153: 29-42.

McGrath, M.T.; DeStefano, S.; Riggs, R.A. [et al.]. 2003. Spatially explicit influences on northern goshawk nesting habitat in the interior Pacific Northwest. Wildlife Monographs. 154. 63 p.

National Forest Management Act of 1976 [NFMA]. Act of October 22, 1976; 16 U.S.C. 1600.

Oregon Department of Fish and Wildlife. 1997. Sensitive species. Portland, OR. 9 p.

Raphael, M.G.; Wisdom, M.J.; Rowland, M.M. [et al.]. 2001. Status and trends of habitats of terrestrial vertebrates in relation to land management in the Interior Columbia River basin. Forest Ecology and Management. 153: 63-87.

Roloff, G.J.; Haufler, J.B. 1997. Establishing population viability planning objectives based on habitat potentials. Wildlife Society Bulletin. 25: 895-904.

Roloff, G.J.; Wilhere, G.F.; Quinn, T.; Kohlmann, S. 2001. An overview of models and their role in wildlife management. In: Johnson, D.H.; O'Neil, T.A., eds. Wildlife-habitat relationships in Oregon and Washington. Corvallis, OR: Oregon State University Press: 512-536.

Rowland, M.M.; Wisdom, M.J.; Johnson, D.H. [et al.]. 2003. Evaluation of landscape models for wolverine in the interior Northwest U.S.A. Journal of Mammalogy. 84(1): 92-105.

Sallabanks, R.; Riggs, R.A.; Cobb, L.E. 2002. Bird use of forest structural classes in grand fir forests of the Blue Mountains, Oregon. Forest Science. 48(2): 311-322.

Wisdom, M.J.; Holthausen, R.S.; Wales, B.C. [et al.]. 2000. Source habitats for terrestrial vertebrates of focus in the interior Columbia basin: broad-scale trends and management implications. Gen. Tech. Rep. PNW-GTR-485. Portland, OR: U.S. Department of Agriculture, Forest Service, Pacific Northwest Research Station. 3 vol. 1119 p. (Quigley, T.M., tech. ed. Interior Columbia Basin Ecosystem Management Project: scientific assessment).

Wisdom, M.J.; Wales, B.C.; Rowland, M.M. [et al.]. 2002. Performance of greater sage-grouse models for conservation assessment in the Interior Columbia basin, USA. Conservation Biology. 16: 1232-1242.

Wondzell, S.; Howell, P. 2004. Developing a decision-support model for assessing condition and prioritizing the restoration of aquatic habitat in the interior Columbia basin. In: Hayes, J.L.; Ager, A.A.; Barbour, R.J., tech. eds. Methods for integrating modeling of landscape change: Interior Northwest Landscape Analysis System. Gen. Tech. Rep. PNW-GTR-610. Portland, OR: U.S. Department of Agriculture, Forest Service, Pacific Northwest Research Station: 73-81. Chapter 6.

Chapter 6: Developing a Decision-Support Model for Assessing Condition and Prioritizing the Restoration of Aquatic Habitat in the Interior Columbia Basin

Steven M. Wondzell and Philip J. Howell[1]

Abstract

The INLAS Aquatic Module is part of the larger Interior Northwest Landscape Analysis System (INLAS)—a multidisciplinary effort to develop midscale analytical tools to project succession and disturbance dynamics across landscapes in the interior Northwest. These tools are intended to be used to examine change in ecological and socioeconomic systems under various policy or management options (Barbour et al. Chapter 1). For the Aquatics Module, we are developing tools to assess midscale aquatic habitat in the context of the biophysical characteristics of streams and watersheds and landscape-scale processes, including natural disturbances such as fire, and alternative management scenarios. We will apply these analytical tools to a demonstration area (the Upper Grande Ronde River subbasin), where we will assess factors influencing conditions of aquatic habitat and water quality and evaluate the potential cumulative effects of alternative management scenarios on aquatic habitat, hydrology, and erosion. The tools we are developing are intended to help natural resource specialists and managers define the types of management most likely to be compatible with guidelines for aquatic species and their habitat and management objectives for other resources.

Keywords: Decision-support models, aquatic habitat, water quality, salmon, steelhead, bull trout, alternative management scenarios.

Introduction

Chinook salmon (*Oncorhynchus tshawytscha*) (Walbaum), steelhead (*O. mykiss* [formerly *Salmo gairdneri* Richardson), and bull trout (*Salvelinus confluentus* (Suckley)) have been eliminated from much of their historical range and are now listed as threat-

[1] **Steven M. Wondzell** is a research aquatic ecologist U S Department of Agriculture Forest Service Pacific Northwest Research Station Forest Sciences Laboratory 3625 93rd Ave O ympia WA 98512 **Philip J. Howell** is a fisheries bio ogist U S Department of Agricu ture Forest Service Pacific Northwest Region 1401 Geke er Lane La Grande OR 97850

ened or endangered within most of the interior Columbia River basin (USDA and USDI 2000). Other native fishes also have declined (Lee et al. 1997). Many factors have contributed to declines, including (1) overharvest; (2) blocked access and increased mortality of migrating fish from dams; (3) interactions between wild fish and hatchery stocks, which appear to impair fitness of wild stocks; and (4) degradation of spawning and rearing habitat (Federal Caucus 2000). Degraded water quality is closely linked to issues surrounding degraded spawning and rearing habitat. Thousands of miles of streams throughout the Columbia River basin, including the Upper Grande Ronde subbasin (Grande Ronde Water Quality Committee 2000), have been listed as impaired by the states under section 303d of the Clean Water Act for failing to meet water quality standards (Lee et al. 1997). Streams in USDA Forest Service (USDA FS) ownership are most commonly listed for failure to meet standards for sediment/siltation/turbidity, water temperature, and flow (Lee et al. 1997).

The USDA FS and other federal agencies, including National Marine and Fisheries Service (NMFS), U.S. Fish and Wildlife Service (USF&WS), and USDI Bureau of Land Management (BLM) have been developing broad-scale approaches to address aquatic and other land management issues within the region (FCRPS Biological Opinion 2000, Federal Caucus 2000, USDA and USDI 2000). These broad-scale plans recognize the importance of maintaining existing high-quality habitat in tributaries of the Columbia basin and restoring habitat that is currently degraded.

The success of broad-scale management depends on the ability of natural resource specialists to convert broad-scale management direction into mid- and fine-scale management practices. To do this, natural resource specialists, managers, and planners must be informed as to the nature and extent of potential impacts resulting from current management practices and proposed changes in those practices (Rieman et al. 2001). Specifically, natural resource specialists need to be able to assess (1) the ability of a stream (or watershed) to support species of interest and other desired resource values, (2) the current condition, and (3) the potential impacts of management decisions on future conditions. Managers and planners must be able to use this information to determine the type and location of management activities most likely to meet desired objectives and to prioritize these activities on the basis of multiple and sometimes conflicting objectives.

Management actions occur in systems with high natural variability and that have been altered by a number of historical and current land and water management practices. Thus, predictions of the potential effects of management actions are fraught with uncertainty associated with the ecological responses and the complexity of multiple management objectives and strategies under consideration (Rieman et al. 2001). To aid evaluations, land managers in the inland Northwest need tools that formalize these complex relationships into a common framework that describes aquatic habitat in the context of landscape processes and conditions, potential effects of management actions, and sources of uncertainty. There are currently no analytical tools available that provide managers the ability to assess conditions of aquatic habitats at mid to fine scales (i.e., 4th to 6th hydrologic unit codes or HUCs) in a landscape context and to analyze potential cumulative effects of management decisions, including forest harvest, fuels reduction, herbivory, and riparian management, on aquatic species and their habitats.

The goal of the proposed research is to develop a decision-support tool to help inform management decisions at midscales. The proposed research is guided by four primary questions:

- How have changes in landscape processes, such as fire, over the last 100 to 150 years affected aquatic habitat and populations of aquatic species?

- What and where are the principal opportunities to maintain and restore aquatic species and water quality?

- What are the cumulative effects of alternative management approaches on aquatic habitat and water quality?

- How can stream restoration opportunities be better integrated with management for other resources?

Review of Alternative Modeling Approaches

A variety of modeling approaches are available to address the questions we pose above. Below, we briefly review these modeling approaches and evaluate their suitability for this project.

Mechanistic Models

Existing tools are unable to adequately address the questions listed above for various reasons. First, many models are narrowly focused and thus do not include other factors that are likely to influence aquatic and riparian habitat. For example, the Stream Segment Temperature Model (SSTemp) (USGS 1999) is typical of reach-scale temperature models that calculate shading/sun exposure to the stream surface and use temperature and volume of water flowing into a reach to estimate a new temperature at the bottom of a reach. These models reliably predict the effect of site-scale modifications on stream temperatures within relatively short stream reaches. However, they are not designed to analyze temperature changes within entire stream networks. Secondly, most existing models have been designed to answer questions at different scales. For example, the aquatic-effects analysis model developed for the interior Columbia basin (Rieman et al. 2001) operates at too coarse a scale, whereas models such as SSTemp work at too fine a scale for subbasin planning. Thirdly, most mechanistic models are too complex, requiring extensive data and a high degree of expertise to run and analyze, both of which are frequently not available. Examples of these models include network-scale stream-temperature models such as SNTemp (USGS 2000) or distributed hydrology models, such as the Distributed Hydrology Soil Vegetation Model (DHSVM) (Wigmosta et al. 1994). The DHSVM, e.g., is designed to predict event-based stream discharges and annual water yield at watershed scales but requires detailed inputs of soil and topographic characteristics and is driven by spatially distributed energy and precipitation budgets. The DHSVM would need to be calibrated to match observed hydrographs and then validated by predicting hydrographs for a different series of storms or a different watershed. However, it would usually be difficult to obtain local calibration data, and the calibrated model will not be readily transferable to other watersheds. Fourthly, most existing models lack followup support for technology transfer to agency management units to help natural resource specialists parameterize the models to local conditions and then run the models. Finally, only a few empirical models have been developed for the interior West that relate landscape variables and processes to aquatic habitat or species because the empirical basis for these relationships is limited. All these factors limit the use of complex, mechanistic models as planning tools that can be applied to subbasins across the entire Columbia River basin.

Each of the models described above offers some utility toward analyzing a specific problem related to land management practices and their effect on aquatic habitat. None of these models, however, attempts to link landscape processes and the range of land management practices to cumulative effects on either habitat capacity or water quality. We do not know of a linked series of models that would enable a user to simultaneously examine multiple, midscale land management issues and their effect on aquatic habitat capacity and water quality.

Expert System, Expert Evaluation, and Statistical Models

Recently, several models (for example, the Ecosystem Diagnosis and Treatment [EDT] Method, the Plan for Analyzing and Testing Hypotheses [PATH], and the Cumulative Risk Initiative [CRI]) have been developed to help inform decisions related to salmon management in the Columbia River basin. The EDT model (Mobrand Biometrics 1999) was designed to compare effects of alternative strategies for managing hatcheries, hydropower, and harvest. The EDT model was designed to be a comprehensive model, accounting for spatial and temporal interactions between habitat conditions, competition, and predation, and projecting cumulative effects (ISAB 2001). Consequently, the model is relatively complex, requiring qualitative and quantitative habitat information about species, which are represented as a set of rules relating survival to habitat conditions. The model is fine scale, utilizing habitat information at the 6th HUC (HUC6 level) and some 40 habitat parameters (ISAB 2001). The EDT model will be required in future subbasin assessments in the Columbia River basin, and work is currently underway to integrate EDT into a broader assessment framework to evaluate fish and wildlife species across aquatic, riparian, and terrestrial environments (Marcot et al. 2002). Although EDT is a habitat-based model, it was not designed to link instream features to processes occurring in upland areas—processes such as fire and other natural disturbances or land management activities such as harvest or grazing. Also, EDT does not directly assess uncertainty in predicted outcomes, and because the model is complex, it is difficult to ground-truth all input data and to review or edit rules linking habitat to the survival of fish species (ISAB 2001). These factors would make EDT difficult to use in INLAS.

The PATH and CRI models are statistical modeling approaches focused on population dynamics of anadromous salmonids. The PATH model (Marmorek et al. 1998) was designed to examine Snake River listed salmon and steelhead and to evaluate management options for these species as affected by survival in specific life stages. The model's main focus is the survival of fish migrating through the mainstem river corridor and the influence of variations in the management and operation of the hydropower system on fish survival. The CRI model statistically examines the survival of fish in freshwater habitats as one generalized component of the overall extinction risk for all listed anadromous salmonids in the Columbia River basin (CRI 2000). However, CRI does not link survival to specific habitat attributes nor does it consider how habitat might change under different management scenarios. These factors make PATH and CRI unsuitable for use in INLAS.

Decision-Support Models

Decision-support models (DSMs) are based on decision analysis and provide possible alternatives to the more traditional modeling approaches described above. Decision analysis can be broadly divided into two components: (1) risk analysis and (2) risk management. Risk analysis is the process of identifying the results of alternative decisions. Thus, risk analysis can help natural resource specialists examine the expected effects of different management strategies (Varis and Kuikka 1999). Further, because risk analysis uses explicit, quantitative methods to examine uncertainty (Clemen 1996), risk analysis can be used to assess the influence of various sources of uncertainty (e.g., variability) on the probability of achieving specific outcomes given a particular decision. Additionally, risk analysis can be used to estimate the value of additional information (e.g., monitoring, watershed analysis). Risk analysis, however, cannot choose the "best" management strategy. Risk management is the process of assessing the value of possible outcomes. A formal risk management plan requires that decisionmakers (i.e., managers) define their attitudes about risks and assign quantifiable values (e.g., an economic cost or a societal benefit) to each possible outcome identified in the risk analysis.

The use of DSMs to conduct risk analysis for the INLAS aquatic module offers several specific advantages that meet our modeling needs. The DSMs can:

- Provide a quantitative framework to describe the current understanding of the complex interrelationships between landscape properties and aquatic habitat, to explicitly define these relationships within the model structure, and then to test the influence of each variable on expected outcomes.

- Use outputs from other models (e.g., the projected changes in vegetation, fire severity and extent, management activities, and other variables from other INLAS modules) to project changes in aquatic habitat units at selected points in time.

- Use expert opinion to parameterize input variables when empirical data are lacking. Additionally, the influence of those opinions and the underlying assumptions are explicit and consistent within the model. The model is transparent in that key assumptions and the values of all variables, including those based on expert opinion, are displayed.

- Incorporate empirical data, mechanistic models, meta-analyses, and subjective probabilities from experts into a single model, integrate information from several disciplines, and use that information to analyze alternative management scenarios.

- Be used to test effects of alternative assumptions on outcomes.

- Determine the relative contribution of each variable to model outcomes through sensitivity analysis of model variables.

At least two DSMs have been developed and are currently in use in the Pacific Northwest and interior Columbia basin. The Ecosystem Management Decision Support System (EMDS) (Reynolds 1999, Reynolds et al. 2000), developed by the Pacific Northwest Research Station, is a fuzzy logic rule-based model providing decision-support tools for landscape analysis and restoration priority setting. However, the aquatic applications to date have primarily focused on disturbance from landslides and debris flows, rather than fire, in basins west of the Cascade Range. Further, current applications of EMDS are driven primarily by inchannel variables, such as large wood and pools, rather than upland characteristics and management activities. Aquatic applications also have not been integrated with other resource areas (e.g., vegetation management, terrestrial species).

A Bayesian belief network (BBN) model was developed for the aquatic effects analysis of management alternatives proposed in the environmental impact statement for the interior Columbia basin (Rieman et al. 2001). This model has been used to evaluate broad-scale effects of federal land management alternatives on aquatic habitat and species for the interior Columbia basin. However, the model is designed for broad-scale analyses of Interior Columbia Basin Ecosystem Management Project (ICBEMP) management alternatives. Also, the model does not directly examine the effects of specific management practices. Rather it uses measures of management activity, such as road density, to project habitat condition over large spatial scales. Although neither the existing versions of EMDS nor the ICBEMP BBN model are sufficient to meet our objectives, they are examples of the types of DSMs most likely to meet the modeling needs identified above.

Modeling Approach

We will develop a DSM to evaluate the effects of alternative land-management scenarios on salmonid habitat at the subbasin scale within the interior Columbia basin. The work described here is focused on risk analysis. Objectives include:

Objectives

- Develop midscale analytic tools to:

    - Assess aquatic habitat condition in the context of the biophysical characteristics of streams and watersheds and landscape-scale processes.

    - Compare potential cumulative effects of alternative management scenarios on aquatic habitat.

    - Help define where and what types of land and water management treatments may be most compatible with aquatic habitat considerations (e.g., key habitats and limitations of species, sensitive soils, existing roads).

- Develop analytic tools that can incorporate new information to resolve key uncertainties in an adaptive management framework.

- Develop analytic tools that are spatially explicit (i.e., can analyze and report information at various fine and mid scales),

- Develop analytic tools that are sufficiently flexible to accommodate a variety of available data and that facilitate widespread application,

- Complement other existing midscale aquatic analytic tools (EDT and EMDS).

Methods

The initial phase of decision-model development will be to identify the decision context(s), responses to be modeled and management alternatives. Decision models will then be structured specifically to address each decision situation and to link with other INLAS modules. Conditional dependencies will be parameterized by using the existing data from the region and data gathered from published studies via meta-analysis (Gelman et al. 1995). Where empirical data or other model output are lacking, expert opinion will be solicited from a panel of species and habitat experts and used to parameterize variables included in the models (Morgan and Henrion 1990). To explicitly incorporate uncertainty, relationships between environmental variables and habitat capacity will be modeled as conditional dependencies (probabilities), combined in a BBN (influence diagram) (Haas 2001), dynamic optimization model (Williams 1996), or similar decision-model form. Sensitivity analysis will then be performed on these models.

Links to Other INLAS Modules

Although the streams make up only a tiny percentage of the total land base of the Upper Grande Ronde watershed, they can be impacted by land use activities occurring anywhere within the watershed. Thus, the decision-support tool developed for the INLAS Aquatic Module needs to be linked directly to many other INLAS modules. Potential direct linkages between the vegetation, disturbance, riparian, wood utilization, herbivory, recreation, and economic modules are illustrated (fig. 13). We will use inputs from these INLAS modules to characterize watershed attributes that directly or indirectly influence the aquatic system and then analyze those projected landscapes to evaluate likely habitat capacity and water quality effects for short-term (e.g., 5- to 10-year) and long-term (e.g., 100-year) timeframes that would result from specific management scenarios. Aquatic habitat capacity potential also is affected by physical attributes of the subbasin, attributes such as slope steepness, soil types, and valley floor widths, which are fixed

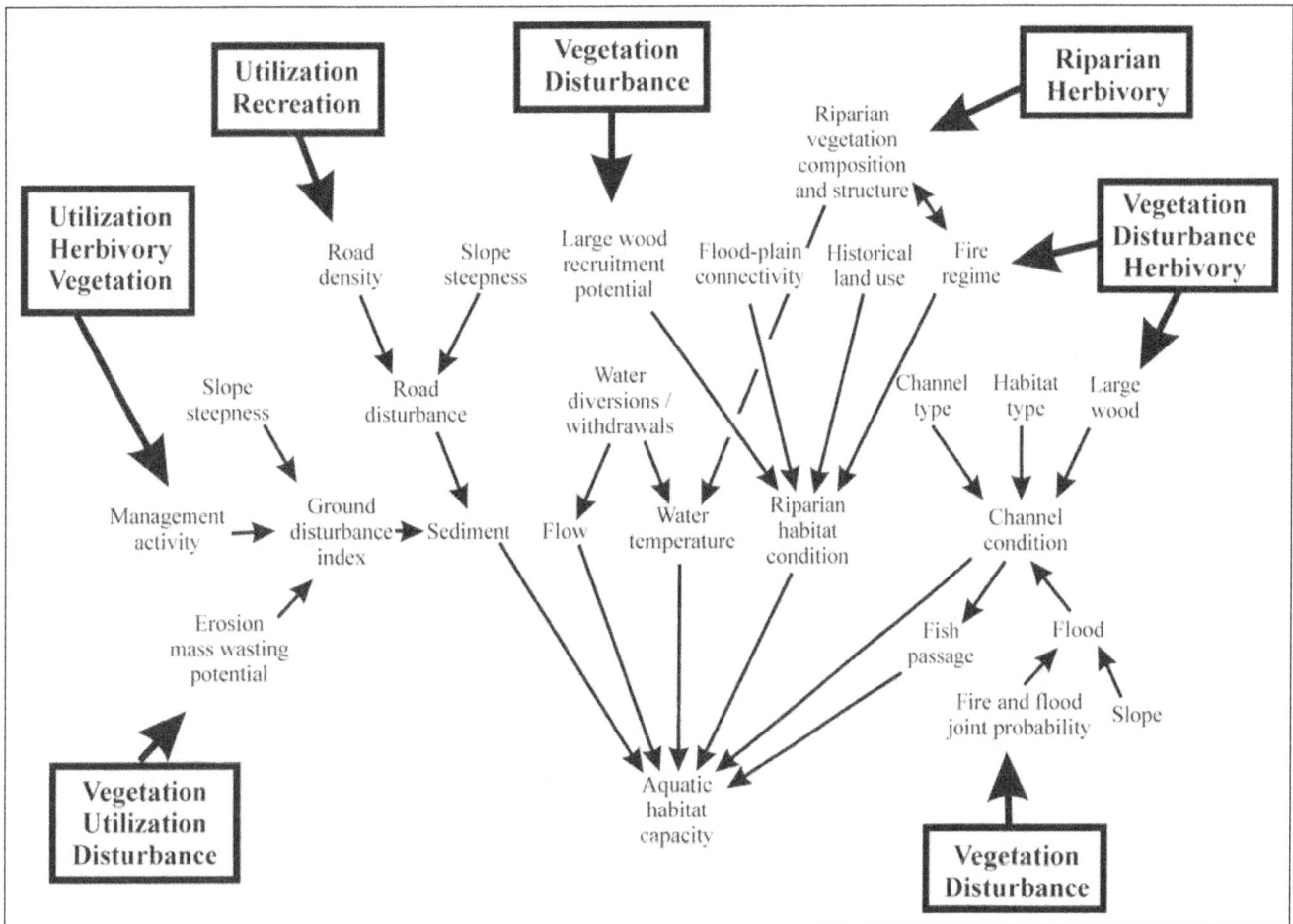

Figure 13 Example of possible linkages between physical conditions and management practices and aquatic habitat capacity to be used for decision analysis (The actual decision analysis framework will be developed with the use of expert panels during the project) Potential links to other Interior Northwest Landscape Analysis System modules are illustrated (bold text in boxes)

physical attributes and insensitive to management-caused changes. Many of the other INLAS modules require similar descriptive information. Spatially explicit databases will be compiled for the INLAS project and available to all INLAS modules so that effects of specific management scenarios will be based on identical watersheds.

Expected Outputs

We will develop DSMs and provide detailed documentation of those models including methods used to incorporate data into the decision models, the sensitivity analysis, and evaluation of the relative value (cost benefit) of collecting additional data to better parameterize model variables. The latter also will be used to make recommendations regarding future studies or monitoring efforts.

We also will develop a user-friendly electronic version of the DSMs for use by Forest Service biologists.

The DSMs will be applied to the Upper Grande Ronde subbasin to evaluate the influence of alternative management scenarios developed to address aquatic and other resource issues.

Acknowledgments

We acknowledge review comments from Miles Hemstrom, Jim Peterson, and Bruce Rieman, and especially comments and discussions with Bruce Marcot, all of which greatly improved this manuscript.

Literature Cited

Barbour, R.J.; Maguire, D.; Singleton, R. 2004. A framework for the development and application of INLAS. In: Hayes, J.L.; Ager, A.A.; Barbour, R.J., tech. eds. Methods for integrating modeling of landscape change: Interior Northwest Landscape Analysis System. Gen. Tech. Rep. PNW-GTR-610. Portland, OR: U.S. Department of Agriculture, Forest Service, Pacific Northwest Research Station: 1-16. Chapter 1.

Clemen, R.T. 1996. Making hard decisions: an introduction to decision analysis. 2nd ed. Belmont, CA: Duxbury. 688 p.

Cumulative Risk Initiative [CRI]. 2000. Cumulative risk initiative: a standardized quantitative analysis of risks faced by salmonids in the Columbia River basin. Seattle, WA: Northwest Fisheries Science Center, NMFS-NOAA. http://www.nwfsc.noaa.gov/cri/pdf_files/CRI2000.pdf. (June 9, 2003).

Federal Caucus. 2000. Vols. 1-2. Conservation of Columbia basin fish, final basinwide salmon recovery strategy. Portland, OR: Federal Caucus/Bonneville Power Administration. http://www.salmonrecovery.gov/Final_Strategy_Vol_1.pdf, http://www.salmonrecovery.gov/Final_Strategy_Vol_2.pdf. (June 9, 2003).

Federal Columbia River Power System [FCRPS] Biological Opinion. 2000. Reinitiation of consultation on operation of the federal Columbia River power system, including the juvenile fish transportation program, and 19 Bureau of Reclamation projects in the Columbia Basin. National Marine Fisheries Service. http://www.nwr.noaa.gov/1hydrop/hydroweb/docs/Final/2000Biop.html. (June 9, 2003).

Gelman, A.B.; Carlin, J.S.; Stern, H.S.; Rubin, D.B. 1995. Bayesian data analysis. Boca Raton, FL: Chapman and Hall. 552 p.

Grande Ronde Water Quality Committee. 2000. Upper Grande Ronde River subbasin water quality management plan. Portland, OR: Oregon Department of Environmental Quality. http://www.deq.state.or.us/wq/tmdls/UprGR/UprGRWQMP.pdf. (June 9, 2003).

Haas, T.C. 2001. A Web-based system for public-private sector collaborative ecosystem management. Stochastic Environmental Research and Risk Assessment. 15: 101-131.

Independent Scientific Advisory Board [ISAB]. 2001. Model synthesis report: an analysis of decision-support tools used in Columbia River basin salmon management. Report 2001-1. Portland, OR: Northwest Power Planning Council; National Marine Fisheries Service. 124 p. http://www.nwcouncil.org/library/isab/isab2001-1.pdf. (June 9, 2003).

Lee, D.C.; Sedell, J.R.; Rieman, B.E. [et al.]. 1997. Broadscale assessment of aquatic species and habitats. In: Quigley, T.M.; Arbelbide, S.J., tech. eds. 1997. An assessment of ecosystem components in the interior Columbia basin and portions of the Klamath and Great Basins. Gen. Tech. Rep. PNW-GTR-405. Portland, OR: U.S. Department of Agriculture, Forest Service, Pacific Northwest Research Station: 1057-1496. Vol. 3. (Quigley, T.M., tech. ed; Interior Columbia Basin Ecosystem Management Project: scientific assessment).

Marcot, B.G.; McConnaha, W.E.; Whitney, P.H. [et al.]. 2002. A multi-species framework approach for the Columbia River basin: integrating fish, wildlife, and ecological functions [CD-ROM]. Portland, OR: Northwest Power Planning Council. http://www.edthome.org/framework. (June 9, 2003).

Marmorek, D.R.; Peters, C.N.; Parnell, I., eds. 1998. PATH final report for fiscal year 1998. Vancouver, BC: ESSA Technologies Ltd. 263 p.

Mobrand Biometrics, Inc. 1999. The EDT method. http://www.edthome.org/framework/Appendicies/Appendix pdfs/Appendix_A.pdf. (June 9, 2003).

Morgan, M.G.; Henrion, M. 1990. Uncertainty: a guide to dealing with uncertainty in quantitative risk and policy analysis. Cambridge, United Kingdom: Cambridge University Press. 344 p.

Reynolds, K.M. 1999. EMDS users guide (version 2.0): knowledge-based decision support for ecological assessment. Gen. Tech. Rep. PNW-GTR-470. Portland, OR: U.S. Department of Agriculture, Forest Service, Pacific Northwest Research Station. 63 p.

Reynolds, K.M.; Jensen, M.; Andreasen, J.; Goodman, I. 2000. Knowledge-based assessment of watershed condition. Computers and Electronics in Agriculture. 27: 315-333.

Rieman, B.; Peterson, J.T.; Clayton, J. [et al.]. 2001. Evaluation of potential effects of federal land management alternatives on trends of salmonids and their habitats in the interior Columbia River basin. Forest Ecology and Management. 153: 43-62.

U.S. Department of Agriculture, Forest Service; U.S. Department of the Interior, Bureau of Land Management. 2000. Interior Columbia basin supplemental draft environmental impact statement. The Interior Columbia Basin Ecosystem Management Project. Washington, DC: U.S. Government Printing Office. [Irregular pagination].

U.S. Geological Survey [USGS]. 1999. Stream segment temperature model. Fort Collins, CO: U.S. Department of the Interior, Biological Resources Division, Fort Collins Science Center. Model documentation. http://www.fort.usgs.gov/products/pubs/4041/4041.pdf and code. http://www.fort.usgs.gov/products/software/SNTEMP/sntemp.asp. (June 9, 2003).

U.S. Geological Survey [USGS]. 2000. Stream segment temperature model. Fort Collins, CO: U.S. Department of the Interior, Biological Resources Division, Fort Collins Science Center. Model documentation. http://www.fort.usgs.gov/products/pubs/4090/4090.asp and code. http://www.fort.usgs.gov/products/software/SNTEMP/sntemp.asp. (June 9, 2003).

Varis, O.; Kuikka, S. 1999. Learning Bayesian decision analysis by doing: lessons from environmental and natural resources management. Ecological Modelling. 199: 177-195.

Wigmosta, M.; Vail, L.; Lettenmaier, D.P. 1994. A distributed hydrology-vegetation model for complex terrain. Water Resources Research. 30: 1665-1679.

Williams, B.K. 1996. Adaptive optimization of renewable natural resources: solution algorithms and a computer program. Ecological Modelling. 93: 101-111.

Chapter 7: Modeling the Effects of Large Herbivores

Martin Vavra, Alan A. Ager, Bruce Johnson, Michael J. Wisdom, Miles A. Hemstrom, and Robert Riggs[1]

Abstract

Knowledge about the effects of ungulate herbivores on forest and range vegetation in the Blue Mountains in northeastern Oregon is reviewed, and future research needs to improve our understanding of herbivory on ecosystem processes are identified. Herbivores have had a major influence on the development of current vegetation conditions, yet their effects are largely ignored in most planning analyses, especially the wild ungulates. We discuss alternative modeling approaches to help understand herbivory as a disturbance process and identify gaps in knowledge and data that need attention before models can be fully integrated with landscape planning systems. For the Interior Northwest Landscape Analysis System we plan to develop the framework for a conceptual model of herbivory effects on succession. This model should run at multiple scales but ultimately function to deliver landscape-level products. The model ultimately will consider herbivore density and distribution as inputs.

Keywords: Herbivory, succession, disturbance, modeling, ungulates.

Introduction

Herbivory by wild and domestic ungulates has profound effects on ecosystem patterns and processes and direct economic implications for production of nearly every commodity and amenity associated with forests and rangelands in the Pacific Northwest. Many

[1] **Martin Vavra** is a research range scientist **Michael J. Wisdom** is a research wi d ife bio ogist and **Alan A. Ager** is an operations research ana yst U S Department of Agricu ture Forest Service Pacific Northwest Research Station Forestry and Range Sciences Laboratory **Bruce Johnson** is a fish and wi d ife bio ogist Oregon Department of Fish and Wi d ife 1401 Geke er Lane La Grande OR 97850 **Miles A. Hemstrom** is a research eco ogist U S Department of Agricu ture Forest Service Pacific Northwest Research Station Forest Science Laboratory 620 SW Main Suite 400 Port and OR 97205 **Robert Riggs** is a research wi d ife bio ogist Boise Bui ding So utions Northeast Oregon/Idaho Region 1917 Jackson Street La Grande OR 97850

factors determine the level of herbivory, and in turn, the magnitude of herbivory effects on ecosystems. Impacts associated with the management of ungulate herbivory in relation to ecosystem properties potentially involve millions of dollars. Moreover, the effects of ungulate herbivory on the dynamics of plant succession have strong legal and policy implications related to federal requirements to maintain viable populations of native species. Mandates by the Endangered Species Act (1973) and National Forest Management Act (1976) make the issue of ungulate herbivory of interest to nearly every user and manager of forests and rangelands.

Enough data are available to develop a conceptual framework for linking proposed herbivory research with potential management products and address three major parts of ungulate-ecosystem relationships: (1) direct effects of ungulate herbivory on ecosystems, (2) factors affecting ungulate herbivory, and (3) integration of relevant, unpublished data and existing publications to augment parts 1 and 2. Our paper focuses on herbivory by three ungulates that dominate landscapes of the Blue Mountains and Pacific Northwest: elk (*Cervus elaphus*), mule deer (*Odocoileus hemionus*), and cattle.

Positive results of appropriate management of these three ungulate species need to be fully recognized and articulated. A wealth of existing but unpublished data needs to be integrated with existing publications and findings from future research. Specifically, models need to be built and validated that project effects of ungulate herbivory at multiple scales, particularly stand, watershed, and basin scales. Such products can be used as endpoints for management application in wildfire rehabilitation and prescribed fire and fuels-reduction programs. They also can be developed as large-scale hypotheses for further testing and validation through adaptive management. In this manner, our proposed research and potential management products have a strong foundation in research but are of direct utility to managers of ungulates, ungulate herbivory, and the forest ecosystems in which ungulates occur.

Model development will occur in a progressive manner. First, broad-scale models of ungulate resource selection that predict spatially explicit distributions of ungulates on landscapes will be constructed from information available from the Starkey Project (Johnson et al. 2000). Ongoing research and published information (Riggs et al. 2000) will be used to develop a model of herbivore forage preference and resulting forage depletion. These models form the underpinning of models that predict the effects of herbivory on flora and fauna at landscape scales such as found in range allotments. An ungulate keystone effects model will then be targeted as a primary end product. Such a model could be used to understand the effects of herbivory on other resources of interest (e.g., timber production, avian species richness, or nutrient recycling) and to assess the degree to which successional trajectories and vegetation states can be maintained or altered in desired ways.

Herbivory Effects on Forest and Range

Succession in forests has been traditionally assumed to progress predictably to climax plant associations (Clements 1936). Evidence is growing that succession can be controlled or altered dramatically by chronic herbivory (Augustine and McNaughton 1998, Hobbs 1996, Jenkins and Starkey 1996, Peek et al. 1978, Riggs et al. 2000, Schreiner et al. 1996). Variation in the herbivory regime (i.e., variation in the herbivore species, and timing, duration, or intensity of grazing) can vary the pattern and rate of successional change, and even vary the apparent endpoint (i.e., trajectory) of succession. Thus, to predict landscape vegetation dynamics with confidence, one must understand the herbivory regime and its influence on succession in the form of vegetation states, transitions, and potential thresholds. Knowledge of the role of chronic herbivory in altering succession is critical to managers dealing with the results of wildfires, prescribed fires, and fuels-reduction projects as well as understanding current steady states.

Current conditions in forests of the Western United States are associated with a high risk of catastrophic events that could dramatically change ecosystem patterns and processes (Hann et al. 1997, Hemstrom et al. 2001). Years of fire suppression and resulting forest ingrowth, combined with tree mortality caused by insect and disease outbreaks, have contributed to widespread development of forest conditions that deviate dramatically from background or historical range of variability (Quigley and Arbelbide 1997). These current conditions are associated with a high risk of lethal fire events (Hann et al. 1997). The role of herbivory in developing current conditions is not well understood but is implicated (Belsky and Blumenthal 1997).

Management actions may be taken to reduce tree density and fuels and to increase prescribed burning as means of reducing fire risk during the next several years and decades. Concomitant with such management activities, however, will be the continuing risk of conflagrations in areas yet to be treated, given the substantial portion of forest landscapes that may not receive management attention because of limitations of time, money, and practicality of application. Consequently, vast acreages have been and may continue to be altered by wildfire (Hemstrom et al. 2001). For example, 17 percent of the Wallowa-Whitman National Forest has burned in the last 10 years. These disturbances will set in motion secondary plant succession that can result in trajectories influenced by herbivory.

Hobbs (1996) made the case that native ungulates are critical agents of change in ecosystems via three processes: regulation of process rates, modification of spatial mosaics, and action as switches controlling transitions between alternative ecosystem states. Huntly (1991) identified the impact of herbivores on plant regeneration as a powerful yet little-studied mechanism of influence on vegetation composition, structure, and diversity. Wild and domestic ungulates should be considered agents of chronic disturbance, capable of influencing succession, nutrient cycles, and habitat characteristics to extents equal to episodic fire or timber harvest (Riggs et al. 2000).

An extensive review by Jones (2000) revealed that grass and shrub cover as well as total vegetation biomass are often reduced by cattle grazing. Riggs et al. (2000) reported that understory biomass at seven grand fir (*Abies grandis* (Dougl. ex D. Don) Lindl.) and Douglas-fir (*Pseudotsuga menziesii* (Mirb.) Franco.) exclosure sites averaged 2.1 times greater inside than outside, and forest-floor biomass was 1.5 times greater inside than outside the exclosure sites. Shrub biomass was influenced more by ungulates than was grass or forb biomass. Photos from exclosures illustrate the effect of large herbivores on forest understory vegetation (fig. 14). Augustine and McNaughton (1998) concluded that altered species composition of plant communities in response to selective foraging by ungulates is a general feature of plant-ungulate relations. They stated that by ungulates altering the competitive relations among plants, differential tolerance of co-occurring plant species becomes an important determinant of the responses of both woody and herbaceous plant communities to herbivory. They also summarized ungulate effects on overstory species and listed several species of coniferous and deciduous trees that were herbivory-intolerant. Ungulate herbivory is also a driving force shaping vegetation pattern in coastal coniferous forests (Schreiner et al. 1996, Woodward et al. 1994). Research by

Figure 14 Visua comparison of vegetative structure inside (top) and outside
(bottom) ungu ate-proof exc osures fo owing 30 years of protection from ungu ate
herbivory at the Hoodoo site Wa a Wa a Ranger District Umati a Nationa Forest
Oregon Photographed by Robert A Riggs

these authors indicated that ungulates maintain a reduced standing crop, increase forb species richness, and determine the distribution, morphology, and reproductive performance of several shrub species. Woodward et al. (1994) further stated that the extent to which herbivores can change ecosystem processes in forests likely depends on the scales of other disturbances. However, we hope to demonstrate that it is the balance between the scale of episodic disturbance and the density of ungulates that is the primary driver of change.

Of particular interest in areas like the Blue Mountains are the interactions between grazing and conifer stand density (Belsky and Blumenthal 1997, Karl and Doescher 1993, Krusi et al. 1996, Madany and West 1983, Rummell 1951, Savage and Swetnam 1990, Zimmerman and Neueschwander 1984). There is increasing evidence that under certain conditions, the net effect of long-term cattle grazing is higher conifer density (Belsky and Blumenthal 1997) and concomitant increase in the risk of large-scale crown fires and insect epidemics. The role of other ungulates (deer, elk) has not been demonstrated but can be implicated (Augustine and McNaughton 1998, Hobbs 1996, Riggs et al. 2000). Higher rates of conifer seedling survival associated with some large herbivore grazing regimes probably result from the combined impacts of selective avoidance of conifer foliage by herbivores and decreased ground-fire frequency as a consequence of reduction in understory fine fuels (i.e., grass, see Zimmerman and Neuenschwander 1984) and less seedling competition from preferred forage species. It is interesting to note that if grazing does indeed promote short-term overstocking of conifer stands that, without intervention management such as precommercial or commercial thinning, such stands are likely to be ultimately predisposed to disease and insect epidemics and crown fires. As a result, ecosystems subjected to intensely chronic herbivory may be predisposed to more marked oscillations in the amount and distribution of transitory range, although this is arguably influenced by the fuels mosaic and ignition rate as well as the herbivory regime. Along with potential for periodic instability of the plant-animal equilibrium are instabilities in forest structure.

With the potential for herbivory-induced changes in plant composition of forest understories and overstories, important habitat ramifications for a number of plant and animal species occur. Changes in understory structure and litter accumulations may be important to bird and small mammal populations (DeCalesta 1994, Fagerstone and Ramey 1996). Individual species of plants and entire plant communities may be at risk under intensive herbivory. Native steppe species in the interior Northwest are not adapted to frequent and close grazing (Mack and Thompson 1982). Examples of plant species in the Blue Mountains that are at risk of elimination or severe decline under intensive herbivory include aspen (*Populus tremuloides* Michx.), Pacific yew (*Taxus brevifolia* Nutt.), bitterbrush (*Purshia tridentata* (Pursh) DC.), and mountain mahogany (*Cercocarpus* spp. Kunth) (Parks et al. 1998). Negative effects on vertebrate species that depend on these plants (e.g., cavity nesters in aspen stands) are implied (Wisdom et al. 2000).

Herbivory Models   We identified two modeling approaches that could be useful to address research and management questions related to herbivory in the Blue Mountains province. The first uses a state and transition approach (Laycock 1991, Westoby et al. 1989) and builds on an existing model of succession and disturbance in the Blue Mountains (Hemstrom et al. Chapter 2). The second is a fine-scale individual animal foraging model that brings together previous work on foraging behavior of ungulates with data from Starkey on forage production and animal distributions (Johnson et al. 1996, 2000). These two approaches are described in more detail below.

State and Transition Models

Plant succession in forests likely operates as a set of states and transitions, much like the models developed and validated for rangeland ecosystems (Laycock 1991, Westoby et al. 1989). Indeed, it now seems possible that the veracity of many "climax" associations is questionable on this basis (Peek et al. 1978, Riggs et al. 2000, Schreiner et al. 1996).

State and transition models (Laycock 1991, Westoby et al. 1989) for specific forest plant communities can be built from the succession-disturbance regime models that were developed and applied to forest landscapes of the interior Columbia basin (Hann et al. 1997; Hemstrom et al. 2001, in press). These models were designed as state and transition models. The models projected successional change for each potential vegetation type and management prescription that was associated with each unique combination of disturbance regimes of herbivory, fire, disease, insects, and human activities. The models were built and parameterized with the use of the Vegetation Dynamics Development Tool (VDDT) (Beukema and Kurz 1995, as cited and used by Hann et al. 1997; Hemstrom et al. 2001, in press) and projected through time in a spatially explicit manner by using the Columbia River Basin Succession Model (CRBSUM) (Keane et al. 1996) and corollary rule sets (Hann et al. 1997).

An example state and transition model of ponderosa pine (*Pinus ponderosa* Dougl. ex Laws.) forests in the Blue Mountains is shown in figure 15. This model was built by using the VDDT program (Beukema and Kurz 1995). This is the type of model that we will modify to construct herbivory-disturbance-regime models that integrate the effects of herbivory on succession after episodic disturbances of fire, insects, disease, and human activities. This type of model provides the greatest utility for multiscale management inferences. This modeling approach has several advantages: (1) effects of all disturbance regimes and management prescriptions for all vegetation types can be accounted for at any spatial and temporal scale desired, provided sufficient empirical data exist for their substantiation; (2) the role of herbivory can be explicitly modeled in relation to all potential interactions with other disturbance regimes and management; (3) sensitivity and validation of herbivory effects relative to the interactive effects with other disturbance regimes can be tested; and (4) spatial and temporal scales of herbivory/disturbance effects can be modeled. Ultimately, these models could be applied at the stand, watershed, and basin scales for the entire Blue Mountains province provided that their predictions can be substantiated empirically. The models should have some general application throughout the Rocky Mountain West.

Starkey Foraging Model

A second approach to modeling the effects of herbivory involves building on earlier work at Starkey to simulate forage consumption and performance of ungulates on summer range conditions (Johnson et al. 1996). In contrast to the state and transition approach, this work is built on basic processes of herbivores moving across landscapes and foraging for preferred plants in preferred habitats. This modeling approach uses empirical models of animal distributions, forage production, and animal energetics, coupled with process-based models of foraging behavior to simulate foraging by cattle, elk (*C.elepnas*), and deer (*Odocoileus* spp.) at the landscape scale (5000 to 50 000 ha). The original formulation of the Starkey Foraging Model (SFM) was completed within a linear programming framework (Johnson et al. 1996) and later refined within a simulation framework that modeled individual animals, their movements, and foraging behavior at the bite level (fig. 16). Much of this work is based on previous models of movement and foraging behavior (Cooperrider and Bailey 1984; Kueffer 2000; Seagle and McNaughton 1992; Spalinger and Hobbs 1992; Van Dyne et al. 1984a, 1984b). The model considers foraging site selection, forage consumption, energy balance, and forage regrowth on a daily time

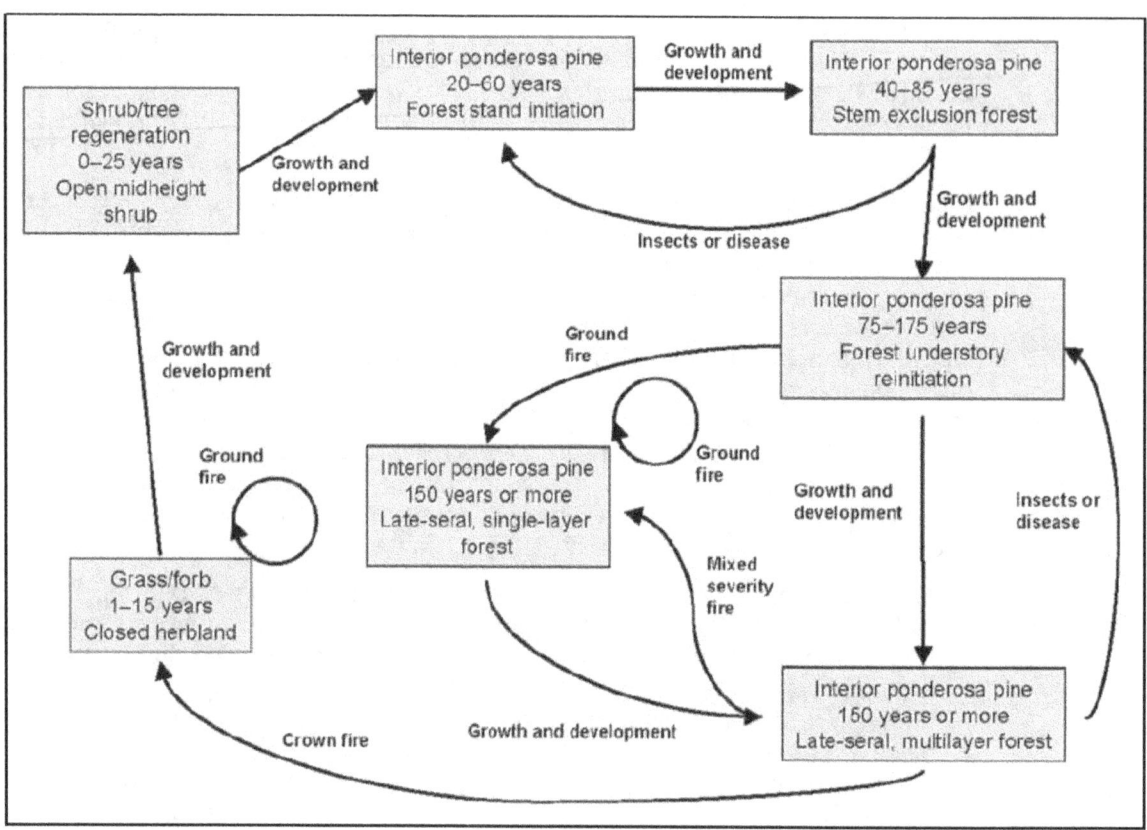

Figure 15 A hypothetica state and transition mode for the interior ponderosa pine forest (from Hemstrom et a Chapter 2)

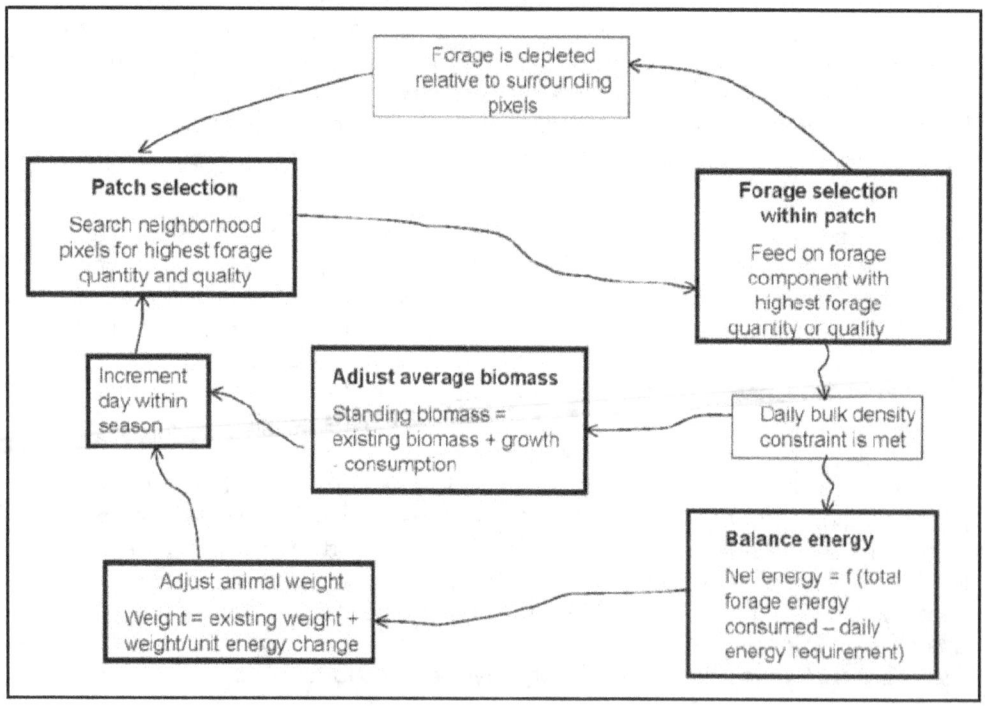

Figure 16 Simu ation sequence for se ecting forage in the Starkey Foraging Mode and the resu ting energy ba ance and resu ting gain or oss of body mass for grazing ungu ate on a dai y time step

step by using an array of empirical and conceptual information. Habitat preferences for elk, deer, and cattle were modeled by using resource selection functions developed at the Starkey Project (Coe et al. 2001, Johnson et al. 2000). Resource selection functions were developed on a monthly time step for elk, deer, and cattle (fig. 17) and represent the probability of an animal visiting a particular pixel.

Forage production was estimated by using several empirical models built from Starkey data (1993-2000) and the literature. Data from Starkey were used to build functions that predicted herbage production as a function of Julian day (figs. 18 to 20). These data came from clipped plots at Starkey and were constructed for grasslands, ponderosa pine, and riparian ecotypes as represented in the area sampled. The equations for grasslands, ponderosa pine, and riparian ecotypes were extrapolated to the seven plant association groups in the model: moist meadows (MM), dry meadows (MD), bunchgrass and shrub lands (GB), warm dry forests with grass (WDG), warm dry forests with shrub understory (WDS), cool moist forest with grass understory (CMG), cool moist forest with shrub understory (CMS), and subsequently partitioned into forbs, grass, and shrubs by using scaling factors developed from Hall (1973) and Johnson and Hall (1990). The growth functions also were adjusted for canopy closure on a pixel basis by using relationships developed at four grazing exclosures at Starkey and the data of Pyke and Zamora (1982) (fig. 21). Forage quality, as measured by in vitro digestible energy (IVDE) of forage, was obtained from the literature (Holechek et al. 1981, Sheehy 1987, Svejcar and Vavra 1985, Westenskow 1991) and data at Starkey (fig. 22). Digestible energy was calculated from IVDE by using the methods of McInnis et al. (1990).

The dynamics of animal foraging are modeled as a two-step process that involves the selection of feeding patches and subsequent selection of forage within the feeding patch. The form of this two-stage model was motivated by literature and concepts in optimal foraging theory and ecology of ungulates (Gross et al. 1993, 1995; Shipley and Spalinger 1995; Spalinger and Hobbs 1992). Feeding patches were defined as 30- by 30-m pixels, a size chosen to be compatible with geographical information system (GIS) data on vegetation strata. Movement to foraging patches was modeled by using a neighborhood search algorithm that searched a 300-m radius for pixels that maximized the expression:

$$\frac{(RSF_{spm})^{a_s} \ \text{x} \ (DE_{pm})^{\ b_s} \ \text{x} \ (F_{pm})^{c_s}}{(Distance_{i,j})^{1/d_s}} \ ,$$

where

$(RSF_{spm})^a$ = resource selection function score $(0 \geq RSF^a \leq 1)$ for pixel p, species s, month m;

DE_{pm} = digestible energy in mcal/kg forage for pixel p and month m;

$(F_{pm})^c$ = forage (kg/ha) present on pixel p and month m; and

$(Distance_{i,j})^{1/d}$ = distance (m) required to move from the current pixel (i) to the pixel (j) being evaluated.

The a, b, and c are species-specific, real valued weighting coefficients that are used to control the relative importance of habitat, forage quality, and forage energy content and movement distances in the foraging process. All these factors influence the selection of feeding sites by elk, deer, and cattle (Johnson et al. 1996). Initial simulations with the

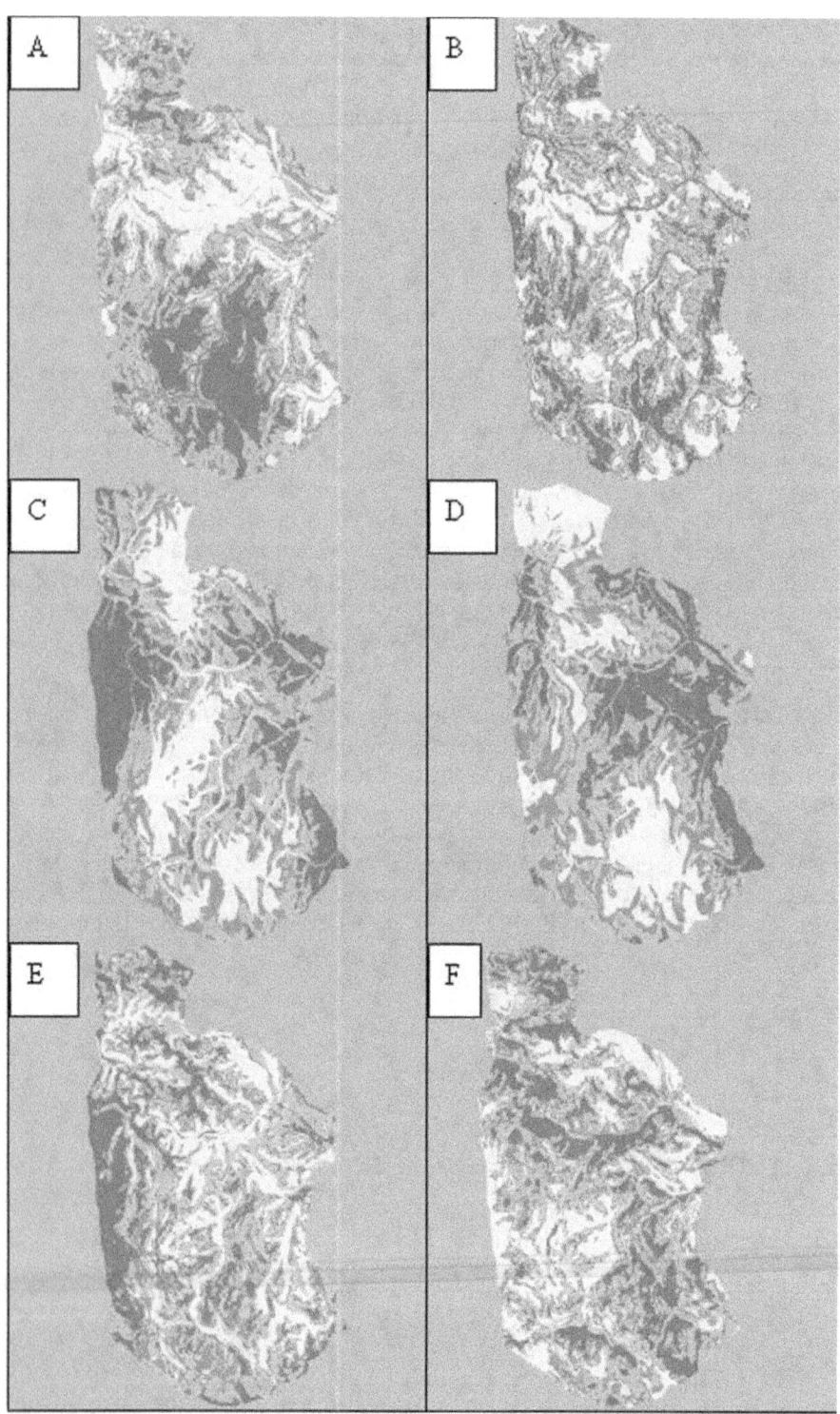

Figure 17 Predicted distributions of catt e in June (A) and August (B) mu e deer in May (C) and August (D) and e k in May (E) and August (F) from resource se ection functions Co ors depict probabi ity of use from high (brown) moderate y high (green) moderate y ow (red) and ow (ye ow)

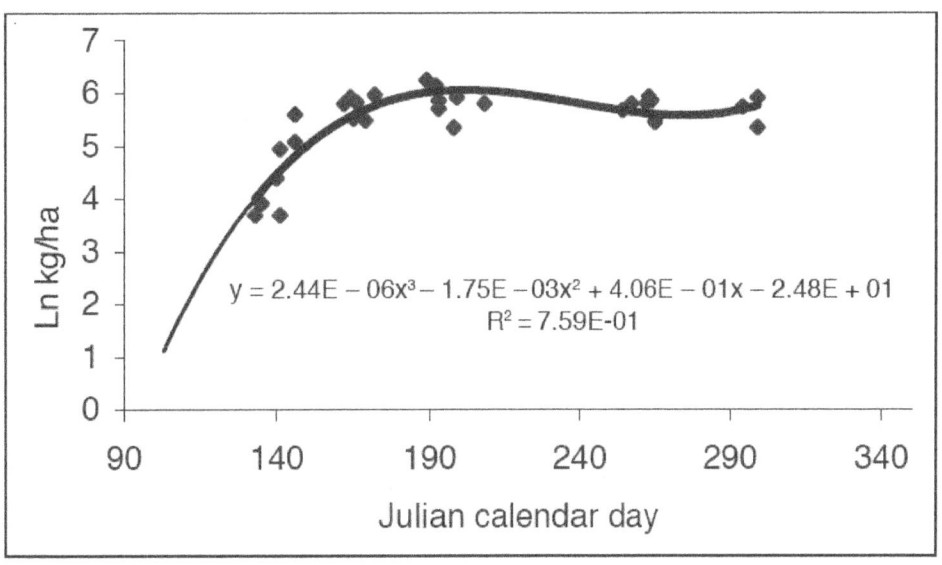

Figure 18   Herbage production in ponderosa pine habitat co ected from c ipped p ots at the Starkey Experimenta Forest and Range during 1993 99

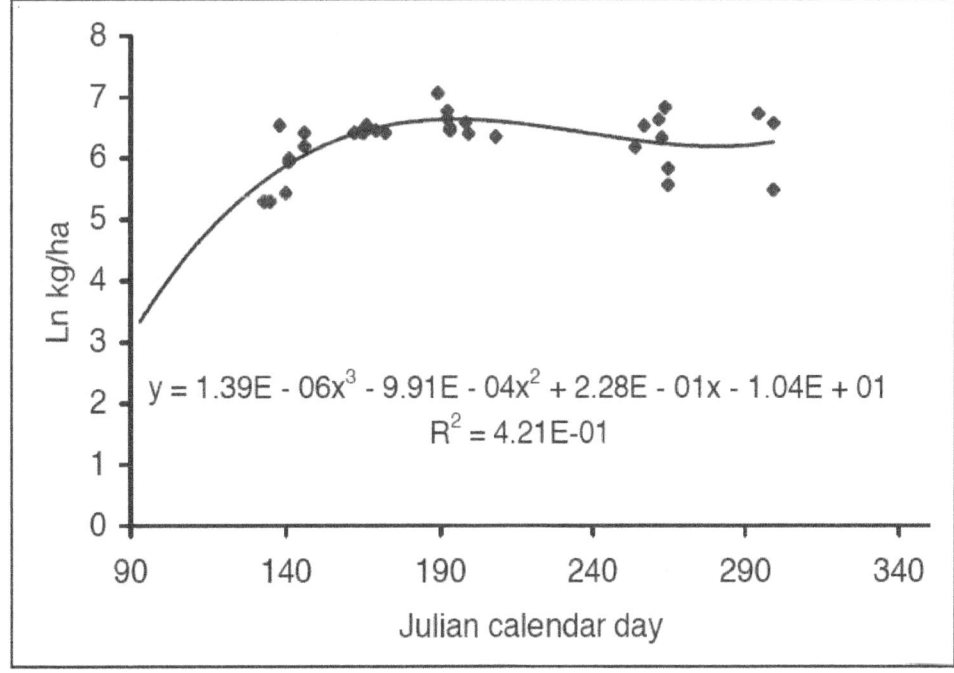

Figure 19   Herbage production in grass ands at the Starkey Experimenta Forest and Range estimated from data co ected from c ipped p ots during 1993 99

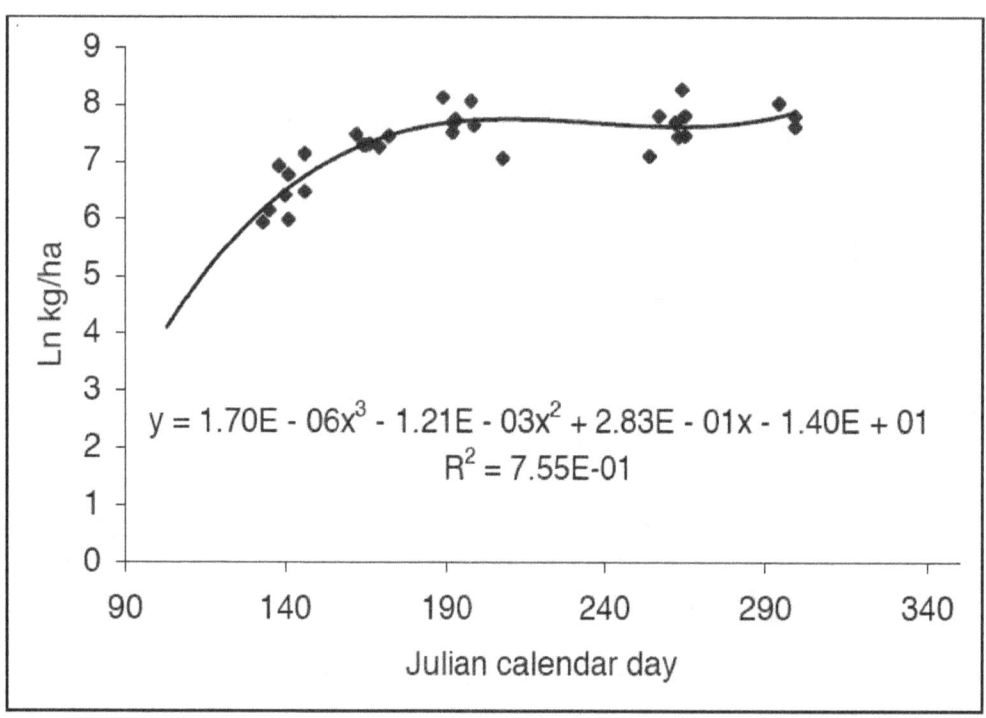

Figure 20 Estimated forage production in riparian areas co ected from c ipped p ots determined for Starkey Experimenta Forest and Range during 1993 99

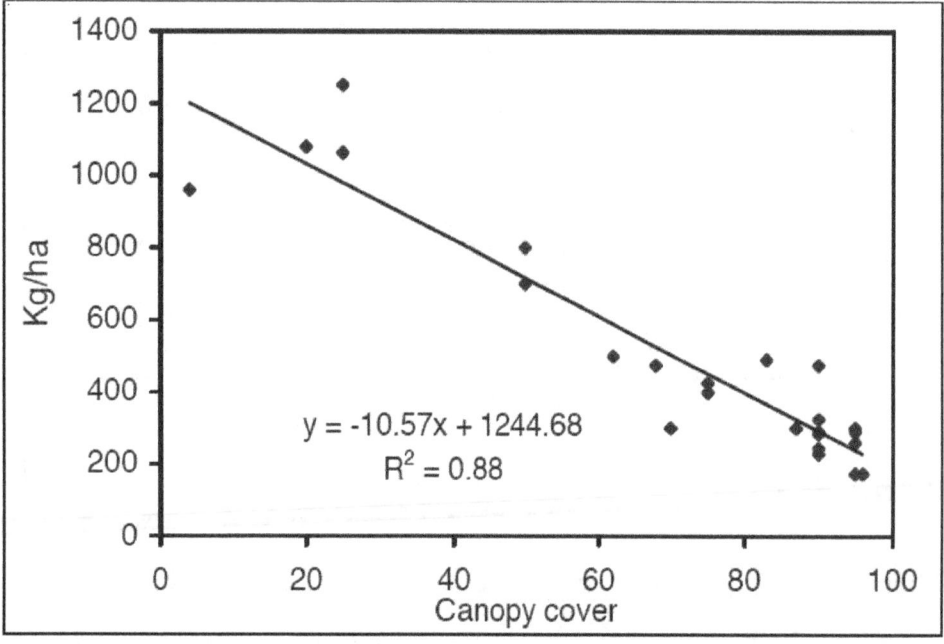

Figure 21 Predicted herbage production in grand fir habitat as a function of canopy cover Data for canopy cover >50 percent were adapted from Pyke and Zamora (1982) and the four data points in the upper eft of the graph are unpub ished da a from Starkey Experimenta Forest and Range

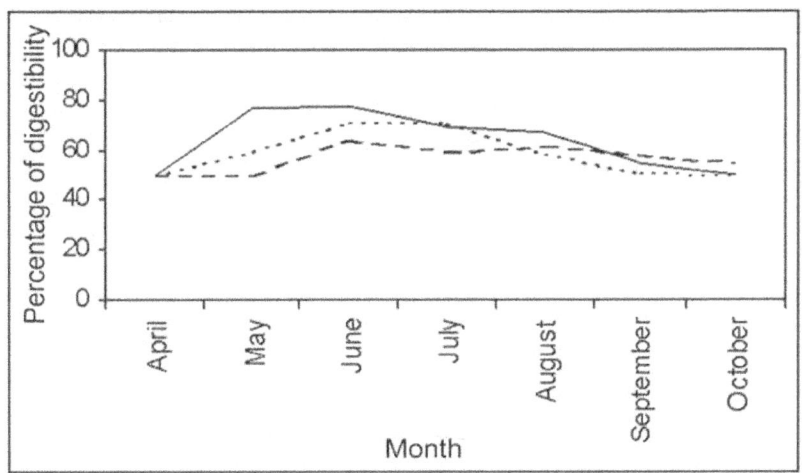

Figure 22 Hypothetica examp e of in vitro digestibi ity of grasses (dashed ine) forbs (so id ine) and shrubs (dotted ine) in coo moist forests at Starkey Experimenta Forest and Range Forage digestibi ity estimates were from unpub ished data co ected at Starkey Experimenta Forest and Range (Ho echek et a 1981 Krueger and Bedunah 1988 Skov in 1967 Svejcar and Vavra 1985 Urness 1984 and Wa ton (1962)

SFM used coefficients of 1.0 for all species. Once a foraging pixel was selected, consumption of forage (grass, forbs, and shrubs) was modeled as a Monte Carlo process that simulated successive bites that removed forage types in proportion to the product of total forage available times forage digestible energy. Specifically,

$$P_{ts} = \frac{(F_{pm})^{w_s} (DE_{ptm})}{\sum_{1}^{t}[(F_{pm})^{w_s} (DE_{ptm})]}, \tag{2}$$

where

P_{ts} = probability of removing forage type t for species s $(0 \geq P_{ts} \leq 1)$;

F = forage on pixel p at month m;

DE_{ptm} = digestible energy in mcal/kg for forage type t, pixel p, and month m; and

W_s = species-specific weighting factor.

The initial simulations used W_s = (body weight)$^{0.75}$. This resulted in deer emphasizing forage quality versus cattle emphasizing forage bulk. Elk, with their intermediate body weight, were simulated as having a foraging behavior in between that of deer and cattle. Bite size was held constant for each species (elk – 0.22 g, deer = 0.06 g, cattle = 0.53 g), although in future work, the type II functional response between bite size and plant size could be coupled with a maximum number of bites constraint to reduce foraging efficiency for smaller plant size (Gross et al. 1993). Foraging on a particular pixel ceased when either 90 percent of the forage was consumed or the total energy was 20-percent below average for all pixels in the 300-m-radius neighborhood. Using the foraging rules described above, animals foraged until they reached 3 percent of body weight per day. When average forage quality for a particular animal and day was below 55 percent, the bulk forage constraint was reduced to 2.5 percent. Animal energy balances were calculated daily and used monthly energy requirements prorated to a daily basis (table 5). Daily energy balance was calculated by using the energy conversion equation as:

$$Me = 1000^x \text{ kg forage} \times (0.038 \times \%DE + 0.18)/1.22, \tag{3}$$

where

DE = digestible energy (mcal/kg forage).

Negative energy balances were translated into a weight loss by using a conversion of 6000 mcal/kg. Positive daily energy balances were translated into a weight gain by using the conversion 12 000 mcal/kg.

Test simulations with this model (figs. 23 and 24) for a summer grazing system (April 15 to November 15, 210 days) were performed by using a herd of 500 cows, 450 elk, and 250 deer. Initial weights were set at 450, 230, and 60 kg per animal for cows, elk, and deer. The initial simulations showed good correspondence with known levels of forage consumption and animal weight gains (losses) on the Starkey area (7800 ha). The simulations also show the effect of lower forage production on foraging patterns by elk and deer (figs. 23 and 24). Although much work remains on this modeling approach, the initial simulations indicated that it is feasible to build a fine-scale foraging model for cattle, elk, and deer that can simulate consumption of individual plants on large landscapes through time.

Research Needs

Managers need information on herbivory to understand its impacts on succession, forest productivity, and biodiversity. Research should focus on, among other things, providing tools to better understand the role of herbivory in shaping plant communities in interior Northwest forests. Primary questions of interest are:

1. What are the patterns of resource selection by deer, elk, and cattle that influence composition and structure of plant communities at multiple scales?

2. What changes in composition and structure of plant communities occur as a result of herbivory at local and regional scales?

3. How does the herbivory regime interact with frequency, intensity, and distribution of episodic disturbances to influence development of plant communities at local and regional scales?

Questions 1 and 2 can be addressed through a synthesis of existing research data and findings from the Starkey Project on resource selection functions for ungulates in the Blue Mountains (Johnson et al. 2000, Rowland et al. 2000, Wisdom 1998). These data can provide estimates of plant composition with and without herbivory and the likelihood of herbivory effects occurring in various forest plant communities. We will develop products for questions 1 and 2. Question 3 requires the development of a multiscale model of ungulate herbivory, based on data synthesized for questions 1 and 2 and by using the modeling frameworks discussed above. This question will be addressed through the development of a conceptual herbivory model.

Table 5—Daily energy demands of adult female deer, cow, and elk by month

Species	April	May	June	July	August	September	October
				mcal per day			
Cattle	23	23	23	22	21	19	18
Elk	6.7	7.3	10.2	10.3	9.3	7.5	7.0
Deer	3.2	3.3	4.8	4.9	4.3	3.6	3.1

Sources: Hudson and White 1985a 1985b; Ne son and Leege 1982; Sheehy 1987; Wa mo et a 1977

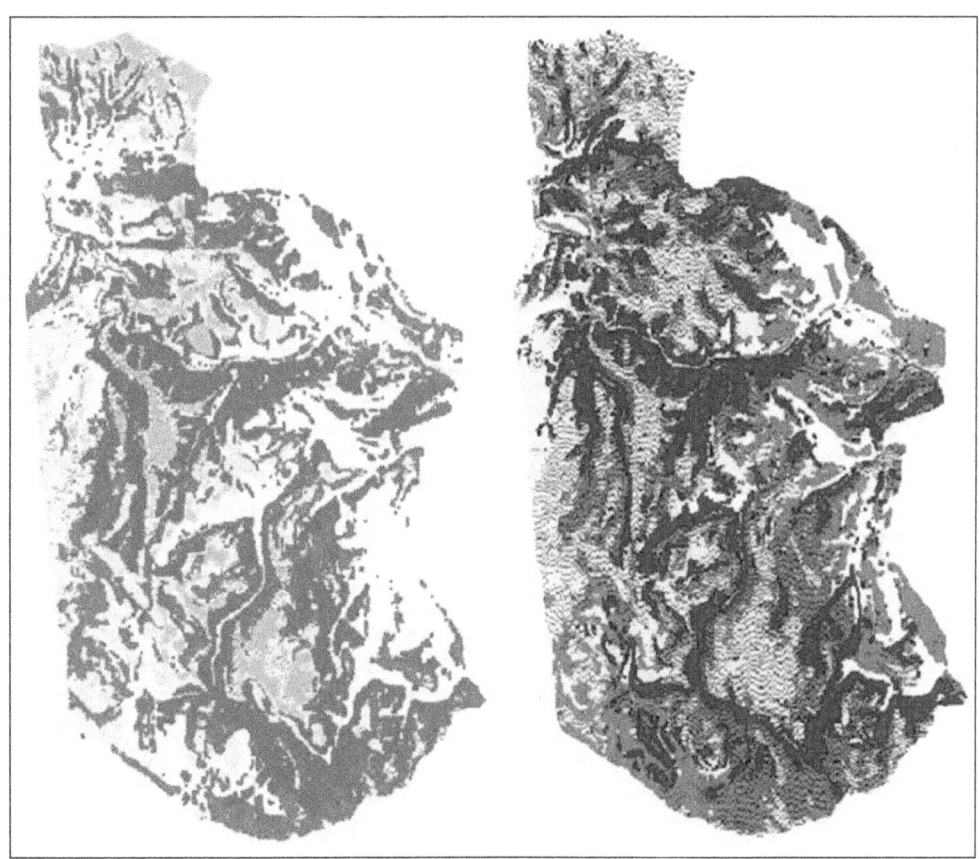

Figure 23 Resu ts of simu ating foraging by 450 e k at Starkey for Apri 15 Ju y 15 by using the Starkey Foraging Mode Images show the areas foraged over time Co ors depict the sequence in which forage was removed (green 0 to 20 days ye ow 21 to 40 days brown 41 to 60 days and b ue >60 days) for norma forage production (eft) and drought conditions (10 percent of norma forage production right pane)

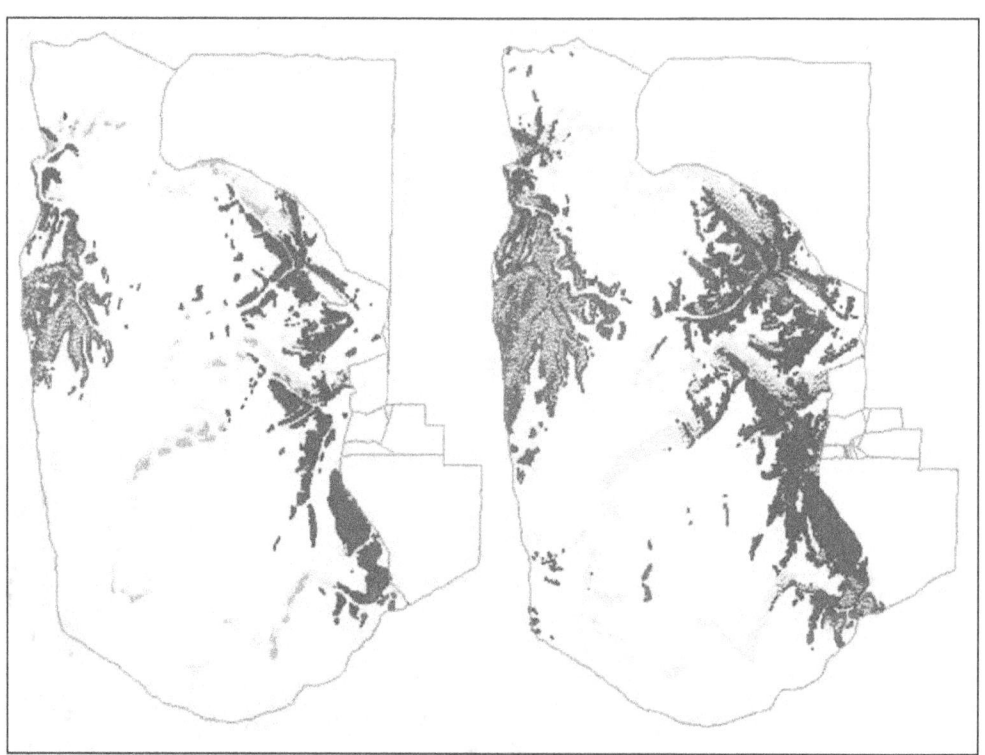

Figure 24—Resu ts of simu ating foraging by 250 mu e deer at Starkey for Apri 15–Ju y 15 using the Starkey Foraging Mode Images show the areas foraged over time Co ors depict the sequence in which forage was removed (green 0 to 20 days ye ow 21 to 40 days brown 41 to 60 days and b ue >60 days) for norma forage production (eft) and drought conditions (10 percent of norma forage production right pane)

For the state and transition approach, appending new states and transitions specific to herbivory would provide a prototype framework and identify the major gaps in terms of unknown transitions and states. The transitions will be modeled within the context of a disturbance, where assumptions about the frequency and magnitude can be changed to simulate specific management scenarios analogous to prescribed fire or wildfire. In contrast to other types of disturbances, the herbivory transitions will not be periodic or involve epidemics and will be associated with relatively low transition probabilities. There will exist states that can only be achieved after long periods of chronic herbivory.

Further work on the SFM needs to focus on refining the coarse stratification of vegetation types (forbs, grass, and shrubs) for both production and consumption by herbivores. Information to fill this gap can come from literature and ongoing studies at Starkey and industrial forest land. For instance, diet selection data are available from the study of Riggs et al. 2000, although these data are for a limited set of plant associations in the Blue Mountains. These data are in the form of species depletion curves for individual taxa (fig. 25). Incorporation into the SFM would require extending the array of forage types for individual species. However, although this might accomplish species-specific consideration of plant biomass for a given season, the long-term multiseasonal effects on particular species would require additional modeling of the plant response to grazing. If virtually all of a species is consumed over successive years, we need to know how long it will take before the species is extirpated from a particular foraging patch, and how the extirpation progress relates to the abundance of a species in neighboring patches. The life

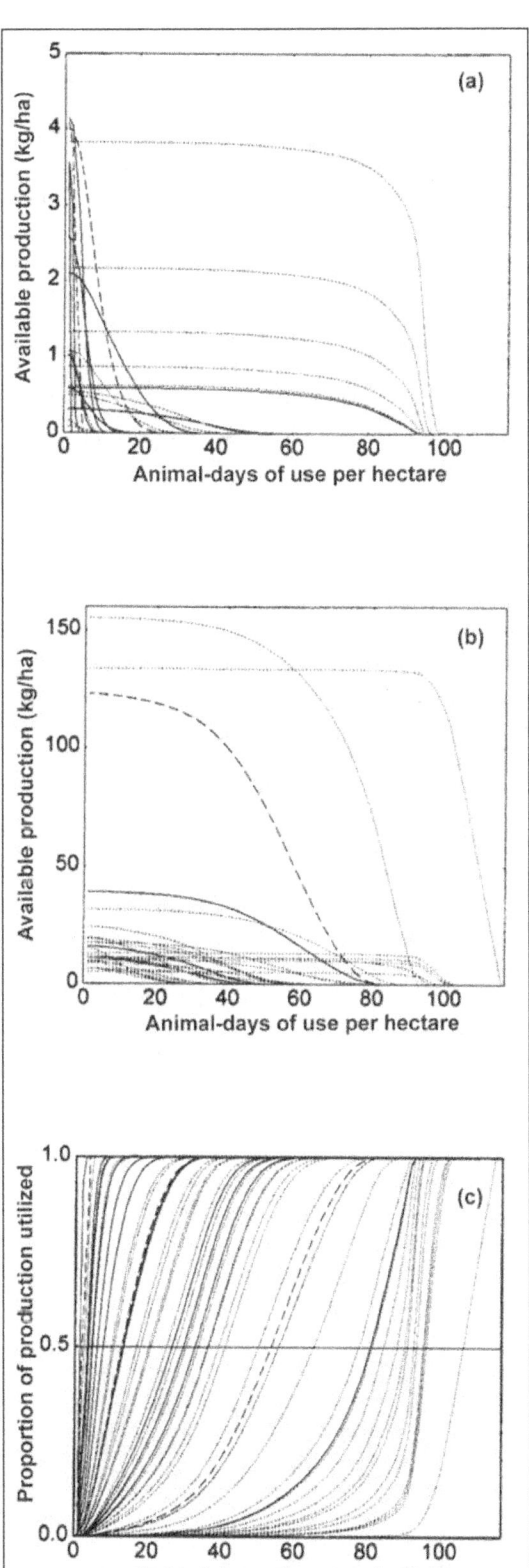

Figure 25   Mode profi es for taxon-specific dep etion of (a) rare and (b) common p ant taxa and (c) corresponding who e-community uti ization within 2 years of c earcut timber harvest of an *Abies grandis* forest Mottet study site Umati a Na-tiona Forest Dep etion and uti ization of shrubs (so id ines) graminoids (dashed ines) and forbs (stipp ed ines) were mode ed on empirica estimates of e k forage preferences anima -days of e k grazing and tota production partitioned among p ant taxa in the postdisturbance community Rare high y preferred p ant taxa are dep eted at re ative y high rates Preference-abundance re ationships among spe-cies particu ar y during the first few years fo owing episodic disturbance may determine to a arge extent the potentia for a ternate successiona pathways in disturbance-adapted mixed-conifer forests (Riggs et a 2000) Such definitive mode ing at the community eve requires re iab e estimation of grazing preferences and re iab e know edge of anima density and distribution Current databases are inadequate and further fie d work is required Graphs excerpted from Riggs et a (2000)

history of each shrub needs to be considered to model response to grazing. Qualitative information on species response to grazing is included in plant association guides for the Blue Mountains in terms of whether species increase or decrease when subjected to grazing pressure. Forage production data also need refinements in terms of modeling the growth of the major plant species. These data also are limited but available in plant association guides (e.g., Hall 1973). In addition, studies are underway at Boise Cascade to build empirical models of nonconifer plant production and composition for a subset of the plant communities in the Blue Mountains.

Linking a spatial foraging model like that developed at Starkey with tree growth simulators (e.g., the Forest Vegetation Simulator [FVS]) is a complex problem. The simulation of herbivory as a spatial disturbance within a stand-level simulation model will require the kind of formulation described by Bettinger et al. (Chapter 4) to simulate wildfire within a vegetation growth model like FVS. Integration of herbivory models into vegetation growth models presents a significant challenge for future work.

Products and Audience

Forest, rangeland, and wildlife managers in the Blue Mountains province are the targeted users of the research findings and management tools produced from the activities outlined in this paper. Clients include managers of public, private, and tribal lands in the Blue Mountains province, encompassing economic and social interests related to management of timber, livestock, wild ungulates, salmon, and vertebrates and plants of conservation concern. Technical users of the research findings and products outlined here include spatial analysts, planners, and resource specialists of public, private, and tribal lands in the Blue Mountains. Application of the concepts and relations developed as part of this research and associated management tools also will extend beyond the Blue Mountains to similar environments in other provinces of the Pacific Northwest and intermountain West. These extensions will target the above-named clients in these similar environments.

English Equivalents

When you know:	Multiply by:	To get:
Hectares (ha)	2.47	Acres
Meters (m)	3.28	Feet
Grams (g)	.0352	Ounces
Grams (g)	.0022	Pounds
Kilogram (kg)	2.205	Pounds

Literature Cited

Augustine, D.J.; McNaughton, S.J. 1998. Ungulate effects on the functional species composition of plant communities: herbivore selectivity and plant tolerance. Journal of Wildlife Management. 62: 1165-1183.

Belsky, A.J.; Blumenthal, D.M. 1997. Effects of livestock grazing on stand dynamics and soils in upland forests of the interior. Western Conservation Biology. 11: 315-327.

Bettinger, P.; Graetz, D.; Ager, A.A.; Sessions, J. 2004. The SafeD forest landscape planning model. In: Hayes, J.L.; Ager, A.A.; Barbour, R.J., tech. eds. Methods for integrating modeling of landscape change: Interior Northwest Landscape Analysis System. Gen. Tech. Rep. PNW-GTR-610. Portland, OR: U.S. Department of Agriculture, Forest Service, Pacific Northwest Research Station: 41-63. Chapter 4.

Beukema, S.J.; Kurz, W.A. 1995. Vegetation dynamics development tool user's guide, version 2.0 beta. 76 p. Unpublished report. On file with: ESSA Technologies Ltd., No. 300-1765 West 8th Avenue, Vancouver, BC, Canada V6J 5C6.

Clements, F.E. 1936. Nature and structure of the climax. Journal of Ecology. 24: 252-284.

Coe, P.K.; Johnson, B.K.; Kern, J.W. [et al.]. 2001. Responses of elk and mule deer to cattle in summer. Journal of Range Management. 54: A51-A76.

Cooperrider, A.Y.; Bailey, J.A. 1984. A simulation approach to forage allocation. In: National Research Council/National Academy of Sciences, eds. Developing strategies for rangeland management. Boulder, CO: Westview Press: 525-560.

DeCalesta, D.S. 1994. Effect of white-tailed deer on songbirds within managed forests in Pennsylvania. Journal of Wildlife Management. 58: 711-718.

Endangered Species Act of 1973 [ESA]; 16 U.S.C. 1531-1536, 1538-1540.

Fagerstone, K.A.; Ramey, C.A. 1996. Rodents and lagomorphs. In: Krausman, P.R., ed. Rangeland wildlife. Denver, CO: Society of Range Management: 83-132.

Gross, J.E.; Shipley, L.A.; Hobbs, T.N. [et al.]. 1993. Functional response of herbivores in food-concentration patches: tests of a mechanistic model. Ecology. 74(3): 778-791.

Gross, J.E.; Zank, C.; Hobbs, N.T.; Spalinger, D.E. 1995. Movement rules for herbivores in spatially heterogeneous environments: responses to small scale patterns. Landscape Ecology. 10(4): 209-217.

Hall, F.C. 1973. Plant communities of the Blue Mountains in eastern Oregon and southeastern Washington. R-6 Area Guide 3-1. Portland, OR: U.S. Department of Agriculture, Forest Service, Pacific Northwest Region. 62 p.

Hann, W.J.; Jones, J.L.; Karl, M.G. [et al.]. 1997. Landscape dynamics of the basin. In: Quigley, T.M.; Arbelbide, S.J., tech. eds. An assessment of ecosystem components in the interior Columbia basin and portions of the Klamath and Great Basins. Gen. Tech. Rep. PNW-GTR-405. Portland, OR: U.S. Department of Agriculture, Forest Service, Pacific Northwest Research Station: 337-1055. Vol 2. (Quigley, T.M., tech ed.; Interior Columbia Basin Ecosystem Management Project: scientific assessment).

Hemstrom, M.; Ager, A.A.; Vavra, M. [et al.]. 2003. State and transition approach for integrating landscape models. In: Hayes, J.L.; Ager, A.A.; Barbour, R.J., tech. eds. Methods for integrating modeling of landscape change: Interior Northwest Landscape Analysis System. Gen. Tech. Rep. PNW-GTR-610. Portland, OR: U.S. Department of Agriculture, Forest Service, Pacific Northwest Research Station: 17-32. Chapter 2.

Hemstrom, M.A.; Korol, J.J.; Hann, W.J. 2001. Trends in terrestrial plant communities and landscape health indicate the effects of alternative management strategies in the interior Columbia River basin. Forest Ecology and Management. 153: 105-126.

Hemstrom, M.A.; Wisdom, M.J.; Rowland, M.M. [et al.]. [In press]. Sagebrush-steppe vegetation dynamics and potential for restoration in the interior Columbia basin, USA. Conservation Biology.

Hobbs, N.T. 1996. Modification of ecosystems by ungulates. Journal of Wildlife Management. 60: 695-713.

Holechek, J.L.; Vavra, M.; Skovlin, J. 1981. Diet quality and performance of cattle on forest and grassland range. Journal of Animal Science. 53: 291-298.

Hudson, R.J.; White, R.G. 1985a. Computer simulation of energy budgets. In: Hudson, R.J.; White, R.G., eds. Bioenergetics of wild herbivores. Boca Raton, FL: CRC Press: 261-290.

Hudson, R.J.; White, R.G. 1985b. Bioenergetics of wild herbivores. Boca Raton, FL: CRC Press. 314 p.

Huntly, N. 1991. Herbivores and the dynamics of communities and ecosystems. Annual Review of Ecology and Systematics. 22: 477-503.

Jenkins, K.; Starkey, E. 1996. Simulating secondary succession of elk forage values in a managed forest landscape, western Washington. Environmental Management. 20: 715-724.

Johnson, B.K.; Ager, A.A.; Crim, S. [et al.]. 1996. Allocating forage among wild and domestic ungulates—a new approach. In: Edge, W.D.; Olson-Edge, S.L., eds. Proceedings of the sustaining rangeland ecosystems symposium. SR953. Corvallis, OR: Oregon State University: 166-168.

Johnson, B.K.; Kern, J.W.; Wisdom, M.J. [et al.]. 2000. Resource selection and spatial separation of mule deer and elk in spring. Journal of Wildlife Management. 64: 685-697.

Johnson, C.G., Jr.; Hall, F.C. 1990. Plant associations of the Blue Mountains. R6 Ecol. Area 3. Portland, OR: U.S. Department of Agriculture, Forest Service, Pacific Northwest Region. 116 p.

Jones, A. 2000. Effects of cattle grazing on North American arid ecosystems: a quantitative review. Western North American Naturalist. 60: 155-164.

Karl, M.G.; Doescher, P.S. 1993. Regulating competition on conifer plantations with prescribed cattle grazing. Forest Science. 39: 405-418.

Keane, R.E.; Long, D.G.; Menakis, J.P. [et al.]. 1996. Simulating course-scale vegetation dynamics using the Columbia River Basin Succession Model–CRBSUM. Gen. Tech. Rep. INT-GTR-340. Ogden, UT: U.S. Department of Agriculture, Forest Service, Intermountain Research Station. 50 p.

Krueger, J.K.; Bedunah, D.J. 1988. Influence of forest site on total nonstructural carbohydrate levels of pinegrass, elk sedge, and snowberry. Journal of Range Management. 41: 144-149.

Krusi, B.O.; Schutz, M.; Gramiger, H.; Achermann, G. 1996. Was bedeuten Huftiere fur den Lebensraum National Park. Cratschla. 4: 51-64.

Kueffer, C. 2000. Modellierung der Habitatsnutzung des Rothirsches *Cervus elaphus* L. im Gebiet des Schweizerischen Nationalparkes—Ein individuenbasierter Ansatz. ETH Zurich: Institute of Terrestrial Ecology. 230 p. M.S. thesis.

Laycock, W.A. 1991. Stable states and thresholds of range condition on North American rangelands: a viewpoint. Journal of Range Management. 44: 427-434.

Mack, R.; Thompson, J. 1982. Evolution in steppe with few large, hooved mammals. American Naturalist. 119: 757-773.

Madany, M.H.; West, N.E. 1983. Livestock grazing-fire regime interactions within montane forests of Zion National Park, UT. Ecology. 64(4): 661-667.

McInnis, M.L.; Quigley, T.M.; Vavra, M.; Sanderson, H.R. 1990. Predicting beef cattle stocking rates and live weight gains on eastern Oregon rangelands: description of a model. Simulation: 137-145.

National Forest Management Act of 1976 [NFMA]; Act of October 22, 1976; 16 U.S.C. 1600.

Nelson, J.R.; Leege, T.A. 1982. Nutritional requirements and food habitats. In: Thomas, J.W.; Toweill, D.E., eds. Elk of North America: ecology and management. Harrisburg, PA: Stockdale Press: 323-368.

Parks, C.G.; Bednar, L.; Tiedemann, A.R. 1998. Browsing ungulates–an important consideration in dieback and mortality of Pacific yew (*Taxus brevifolia*) in a northeastern Oregon stand. Northwest Science. 72: 190-197.

Peek, J.M.; Johnson, F.D.; Pence, N.N. 1978. Successional trends in a ponderosa pine/bitterbrush community related to grazing by livestock, wildlife, and to fire. Journal of Range Management. 31: 49-53.

Pyke, D.A.; Zamora, B.A. 1982. Relationships between overstory structure and understory production in the grand fir/myrtle boxwood habitat type of northcentral Idaho. Journal of Range Management. 35: 769-773.

Quigley, T.M.; Arbelbide, S.J., tech. eds. 1997. An assessment of ecosystem components in the interior Columbia basin and portions of the Klamath and Great Basins. Gen. Tech. Rep. PNW-GTR-405. Portland, OR: U.S. Department of Agriculture, Forest Service, Pacific Northwest Research Station. 335 p. Vol 1. (Quigley, T.M., tech. ed.; Interior Columbia Basin Ecosystem Management Project: scientific assessment).

Riggs, R.; Tiedemann, A.R.; Cook, J.G. [et al.]. 2000. Modification of mixed-conifer forests by ruminant herbivores in the Blue Mountains ecological province. Res. Pap. PNW-RP-527. Portland, OR: U.S. Department of Agriculture, Forest Service, Pacific Northwest Research Station. 77 p.

Rowland, M.M.; Wisdom, M.J.; Johnson, B.K.; Kie, J.G. 2000. Elk distribution and modeling in relation to roads. Journal of Wildlife Management. 64: 672-684.

Rummell, R.S. 1951. Some effects of livestock grazing on ponderosa pine forest and range in central Washington. Ecology. 32(4): 594-607.

Savage, M.; Swetnam, T.W. 1990. Early 19th century fire decline following sheep pasturing in Navajo ponderosa pine forest. Ecology. 71(6): 2374-2378.

Schreiner, E.G.; Krueger, K.A.; Happe, P.J.; Houston, D.B. 1996. Understory patch dynamics and ungulate herbivory in old-growth forests of Olympic National Park, Washington. Canadian Journal of Forest Research. 26: 255-265.

Seagle, S.W.; McNaughton, S.J. 1992. Spatial variation in forage nutrient concentrations and the distribution of Serengeti grazing ungulates. Landscape Ecology. 7: 229-241.

Sheehy, D.P. 1987. Grazing relationships of elk, deer, and cattle on seasonal rangelands in northeastern Oregon. Corvallis, OR: Oregon State University. 269 p. Ph.D. dissertation.

Shipley, L.A.; Spalinger, D.E. 1995. Influence of size and density of browse patches on intake rates and foraging decisions of young moose and white-tailed deer. Oecologia. 104: 112-121.

Skovlin, J.M. 1967. Fluctuations in forage quality on summer range in the Blue Mountains. Res. Pap. PNW-44. Portland, OR: U.S. Department of Agriculture, Forest Service, Pacific Northwest Forest and Range Experiment Station. 20 p.

Spalinger, D.E.; Hobbs, N.T. 1992. Mechanisms of foraging in mammalian herbivores: new models of functional response. American Naturalist. 140: 325-348.

Svejcar, T.; Vavra, M. 1985. Seasonal forage production and quality on four native and improved plant communities. Tech. Bull. 149. Corvallis, OR: Oregon State University, Agricultural Experiment Station. 24 p.

Urness, P.J. 1984. Managing lodgepole pine ecosystems for game and range values. In: Baumgartner, D.M.; Krebill, R.G.; Arnott, J.T.; Westman, G.F., eds. Lodgepole pine: the species and its management. Pullman, WA: Washington State University: 297-304.

Van Dyne, G.M.; Burch, W.; Fairfax, S.K.; Huey, W. 1984a. Forage allocation on arid and semiarid public grazing lands: summary and recommendations. In: National Research Council/National Academy of Sciences, eds. Developing strategies for rangeland management. Boulder, CO: Westview Press: 1-26.

Van Dyne, G.M.; Kortopates, P.T.; Smith, F.M. 1984b. Quantitative frameworks for forage allocation. In: National Research Council/National Academy of Sciences, eds. Developing strategies for rangeland management. Boulder, CO: Westview Press: 289-416.

Wallmo, O.C.; Carpenter, L.H.; Regelin, W.L. [et al.]. 1977. Evaluation of deer habitat on a nutritional basis. Journal of Range Management. 30: 122-127.

Walton, R.L. 1962. The seasonal yield and nutrient content of native forage species in relation to their synecology. Corvallis, OR: Oregon State University. 92 p. M.S. thesis.

Westenskow, K.J. 1991. Conditioning bunchgrass on elk winter range. Corvallis, OR: Oregon State University. 109 p. M.S. thesis.

Westoby, M.; Walker, B.; Noy-Meir, I. 1989. Opportunistic management for rangelands not at equilibrium. Journal of Range Management. 42: 266-276.

Wisdom, M.J. 1998. Assessing life-stage importance and resource selection for conservation of selected vertebrates. Moscow, ID: University of Idaho. 118 p. Ph.D. dissertation.

Wisdom, M.J.; Holthausen, R.S.; Wales, B.C. [et al.]. 2000. Source habitats for terrestrial vertebrates of focus in the interior Columbia basin: broad-scale trends and management implications. Gen. Tech. Rep. PNW-GTR-485. Portland, OR: U.S. Department of Agriculture, Forest Service, Pacific Northwest Research Station. 156 p. Vol. 1. (Quigley, T.M., tech ed.; Interior Columbia Basin Ecosystem Management Project: scientific assessment).

Woodward, A.; Schreiner, E.G.; Houston, D.B.; Moorhead, B.B. 1994. Ungulate-forest relationships in Olympic National Park: retrospective exclosure studies. Northwest Science. 68: 97-110.

Zimmerman, G.T.; Neueschwander, L.F. 1984. Livestock grazing influences on community structure, fire intensity, and fire frequency within the Douglas-fir/ninebark habitat type. Journal of Range Management. 37: 104-110.

Click to continue

Chapter 8: Simulating Mortality From Forest Insects and Diseases

Alan A. Ager, Jane L. Hayes, and Craig L. Schmitt[1]

Abstract

We describe methods for incorporating the effects of insects and diseases on coniferous forests into forest simulation models and discuss options for including this capability in the modeling work of the Interior Northwest Landscape Analysis System (INLAS) project. Insects and diseases are major disturbance agents in forested ecosystems in the Western United States, and over time, are responsible for major changes in forest composition and structure. Incorporating their effects into forest simulation models is difficult, especially the representation of large, episodic insect epidemics. Much empirical data on insect mortality is available for modelers, and an array of mortality models have been incorporated into indivdual tree growth simulators. Scaling these models to simulate epidemics on landscapes requires, among other things, parameters that describe the amplitudes and periodicities of pathogen/pest population cycles. Incorporating insect and disease effects into forest simulation models makes it possible to explore ways to minimize epidemic conifer mortality and secondary interactions with other disturbances. In addition, the inclusion of other resource goals and financial considerations makes it possible to analyze the costs and benefits of forest management activities that target stands with high risk of mortality. We discuss options for modeling insect and disease mortality within the INLAS project.

Keywords: Forest insects and diseases, forest stand simulation, tree mortality, landscape simulation.

[1] **Alan A. Ager** is an operations research ana yst and **Jane L. Hayes** is a research bio ogica scientist U S Department of Agricu ture Forest Service Pacific Northwest Research Station Forestry and Range Sciences Laboratory **Craig L. Schmitt** is a p ant patho ogist U S Department of Agricu ture Forest Service B ue Mountains Pest Management Service Center 1401 Geke er Lane La Grande OR 97850

Introduction

Simulating the potential impacts of insects and diseases on forests like those in the Blue Mountains of northeast Oregon is challenging. Defoliators (Torgersen 2001), bark beetles (*Dendroctonus* spp.) (Hayes and Daterman 2001), mistletoe (*Arceuthobium* spp.) (Parks and Flanagan 2001), and root diseases (Thies 2001) all have unique population dynamics, epidemiology, and effects on forest vegetation. Interactions among these disturbance agents as well as with management activities and physical disturbances such as wildfire and windthrow are also significant. Collectively, insects and diseases are major determinants of forest composition and structure over time, and thus warrant serious attention in forest planning and landscape simulation efforts (Quigley et al. 2001). Previous federal and state planning efforts may have underestimated the potential effects of insects and diseases in projections of future forest conditions, which may have reduced the effectiveness of these plans (Gast et al. 1991).

In this paper, we review methods to model conifer mortality caused by major forest insects and diseases within the framework of landscape planning models such as those described in Ager (Chapter 3), Bettinger et al. (Chapter 4), and Hemstrom (Chapter 2). Much of this work involves integrating and parameterizing existing mortality and risk models implemented elsewhere, such as in the Forest Service Forest Vegetation Simulator (FVS) (Wykoff et al. 1982). However, major gaps exist in the area of modeling spatial spread rates data for some insect species, and the process of simulating the complex cycles of insect populations and disease centers on a large landscape is a challenge for any landscape planning effort. The following discussion treats forest insects separately from forest diseases. We focused on major pests in the Blue Mountains based on historical survey data (Gast et al. 1991) with the broad goal of summarizing existing tools, identifying major gaps, and proposing research and development to create a robust set of methods for modeling mortality caused by forest insects and diseases.

Extensive descriptions and reviews of insects and diseases and their effects on forest trees in the Blue Mountains can be found in Filip et al. (1996), Gast et al. (1991), Hayes and Daterman (2001), Parks and Flanagan (2001), Thies (2001), and Torgersen (2001). Aerial survey maps of insect infestations provide a detailed chronology of infestations over a 50-year period for the Blue Mountains (USDA FS 2003a).

Insect Mortality Models

Pertinent aspects of insect biology in the context of landscape planning models center on the dynamics of infestations and include the periodicity and amplitude of the infestation cycles, the spatial pattern of the initial infestation centers, and the resulting damage they cause in terms of mortality and reduced vigor. The divergent life histories of the major mortality-causing insects complicate an integrated modeling approach in landscape planning models.

Tree-level mortality models for the major mortality-causing insects are all implemented in FVS extensions that are described in detail elsewhere (USDA FS 2003b) There are many case histories of modeling insect- and disease-caused mortality at the stand (e.g., Cameron et al. 1990, Gast et al. 1991; also see Hayes and Daterman 2001, Torgersen 2001), and to a lesser extent, landscape scale (Beukema et al. 1997, Eager and Angwin 1997, Graetz 2000, Smith et al. 2002). Landscape simulations are usually accomplished by imputing tree lists for stands where data are incomplete. Insect mortality models can be built ad hoc in FVS when no formal model exists by using the COMPUTE statements and the event monitor to trigger mortality on specific host trees when stand conditions meet an established susceptibility criterium. The existing FVS model extensions differ in their state of validation and complexity and require many parameters to trigger outbreaks and regulate the mortality. Recent efforts have focused on simulating multiple pests (e.g., Roberts 2002, Roberts and Weatherby 1997), examining interactions among pests (e.g., Eager and Angwin 1997), and modeling the spatial spread of insects (e.g., Smith et al. 2002). The use of the FVS Parallel Processor (Crookston and Stage 1991) vastly simplifies the modeling of insect spread among stands within the FVS system.

Modeling endemic insect mortality requires parameters that define stand and tree susceptibility and mortality rates among the tree type within the stand. Modeling epidemics implies a spatial extent beyond an individual stand, and additional parameters are required to control (1) triggering of an outbreak; and (2) duration, intensity, and frequency of occurrence (Roberts and Weatherby 1997). In the case of the westwide pine beetle model (Beukema et al. 1997), a spatially explicit model that considers stand contagion, parameters also are needed to control the rate of spread. Parameters needed to simulate insect epidemics are described individually below.

Determining Susceptibility Levels to Epidemic Events

Stand susceptibility models use stand attributes such as average size and density of host species and physical site factors including ecoclass, slope, aspect, and elevation in determining susceptibility to insect outbreaks. In a few cases, spatial information such as the distance to the nearest infestation also is considered (e.g., Shore et al. 2000). In FVS, stand susceptibility models can be built and implemented by using FVS COMPUTE statements that calculate relevant stand metrics (Roberts and Weatherby 1997).

Triggering an Outbreak

Outbreaks can be triggered as a function of susceptibility levels or by using assumptions about intrinsic insect population cycles (Monserud and Crookston 1982). The resultant mortality is dependent on other factors such as susceptibility levels and outbreak duration and intensity. Epidemic triggers can be regulated independently of endemic mortality by changing the probability of the two levels of mortality and associated intensity of the outbreaks. Some FVS model extensions have keywords that specify whether stands are part of widespread or local outbreaks. Assumptions that are tailored to specific insect pests are usually made about the interval between outbreaks and their duration. The outbreak is manifested in mortality if susceptibility conditions are appropriate. Roberts and Weatherby (1997) provide examples of simulating insect outbreaks by using the FVS extensions.

Duration of Outbreaks

Population dynamics, spread, and host availability affect duration of infestations. The FVS insect extensions have defaults for duration. For instance, the default for Douglas-fir beetle (*Dendroctonus pseudotsugae* Hopkins) pest extension (Marsden et al. 1994) is 4 years in the Blue Mountain variant. In the western spruce budworm (*Choristoneura occidentalis* Freeman) extension (Crookston et al. 1990, Sheehan et al. 1989), the duration is related to a hazard rating system where low hazard generates a 5-year, moderate a 10-year, and high a 15-year duration. Management activities that alter susceptibility after an outbreak begins can alter the duration. Mortality of the host also affects duration of outbreak.

Intensity of Outbreaks

Intensity is usually expressed as a function of the number of host trees killed by tree species and diameter class per FVS cycle. Some models such as the Western Spruce Budworm Extension can incorporate other types of damage like top kill and decreased growth from defoliation. Intensity is modeled in concert with spread rate among stands as part of simulating an epidemic. Damage is affected by using mortality functions in the FVS extensions, either within an FVS extension or within outside software.

Spread

At least two methods have been applied to simulate the spread of an insect epidemic. One approach uses Monte Carlo methods that simulate gradual growth of the infestation among the population of stands in the simulation (Roberts and Weatherby 1997). This approach does not consider stand contagion but rather uses random selection of stands that meet susceptibility criteria. The probability of an infestation can be changed in this process to alter the rate at which stands become infested. Multiple probabilities can be used in a similar Monte Carlo process to trigger low-level endemic mortality as well as large epidemics. A more sophisticated approach to insect spread that considers stand contagion was developed in the westwide Pine Beetle Model (Beukema et al. 1997, Smith et al. 2002). Stands are simultaneously simulated by using the FVS parallel processor, and stand-to-stand spread of beetles is simulated.

Disease Mortality Models

The major tree diseases in the Blue Mountains are root disease and dwarf mistletoe. Although dwarf mistletoe is primarily modeled as causing growth reduction, root disease is simulated as causing mortality. Principal root diseases include Armillaria root disease caused by *Armillaria ostoyae*, laminated root rot caused by *Phellinus weirii* (Murr.) Gilb., Annosus root disease caused by *Heterobasidion annosum* (Fr.) Bref., and black stain root disease caused by *Leptographium wageneri* Kendrick M.J. Wingfield. Extensive reviews of these diseases and their occurrences in the Blue Mountains can be found in Hagle and Goheen (1986), Hessburg et al. (1994), Campbell and Liegel (1996), Filip et al. (1996), and Thies (2001). Fundamental differences in the biology between insects and diseases call for different modeling methods. Although contagion is a factor with diseases, the spread is too slow to consider as part of a landscape process (e.g., 2 feet per year). Diseases can be modeled as endemic mortality, meaning that the mortality is chronic, not episodic, and mortality is an intrastand or intrapolygon, rather than an interstand or interpolygon process. In contrast to disease, the most important component in simulation models for insects is the relationship between mortality and management activities. High levels of management activities can bring about more infections and mortality (Thies 2001), whereas in insect pests, management is largely viewed as a way to reduce spread.

As with insects, extensive modeling capability for diseases exists in FVS (Frankel 1998, Hawksworth et al. 1995). The western root disease model in FVS simulates the effects of Armillaria root disease, laminated root rot, and Annosus root disease (Frankel 1998). Considerable effort is required to build keyword files and calibrate these models for application on large landscapes. Management to control diseases (e.g., boron treatments) can be simulated with FVS extensions. Given the slow rate of disease spread, many of the concerns with insect pests in terms of interstand spread and cyclical epidemics are not an issue with diseases.

Insect and Disease Risk Models

The previous discussion focused on the modeling of tree mortality from insects and diseases. Depending on the overall objectives, the insect and disease considerations in landscape planning can often be addressed by using only measures of infestation or infection risk rather than predicting actual tree mortality. Risk models measure the long-term outlook for the effects from pests and offer a relatively simple approach to characterize forest conditions in terms of a latent potential to experience mortality, and are often used when tree-level mortality modeling is not practical. Numerous risk rating models for insects and diseases have been developed and widely applied in coniferous forests in the intermountain West and elsewhere (see Hayes and Daterman 2001, Hessburg et al. 1994, Lehmkuhl et al. 1994, Steele et al. 1996). These models are typically used in watershed or National Environmental Policy Act (NEPA)-related analysis to help identify susceptible stands and assign treatment priorities. Most models output categorical values that measure relative risk, and a few quantify risk in probabilistic terms. Risk assessments are used to identify treatment priorities to reduce hazards from infestations or epidemics. Many, but not all of the models, have been tested through field validation and are published with accompanying software. Risk models have been added to FVS as event monitor applications for the mountain pine (*Dendroctonus ponderosae* Hopkins) and spruce (*D. rufipennis* (Kirby)) beetle. There is also integrated pest risk software that calculates multiple insect and disease risk ratings (Ager 1996, Hessburg et al. 1994, Scott et al. 1998).

Data requirements for the risk models differ ranging from coarse photointerpreted stand characteristics such as canopy closure to detailed stand metrics such as the basal area of host species within a specific diameter range. In addition, many models require physiographic inputs like slope, aspect, elevation, and other physical attributes. A number of risk models have subcomponents that independently measure risk from susceptibility to better assess probability of mortality.

Although risk models offer a rapid way to address insect and disease considerations in landscape planning projects, their shortcoming is that they generally do not consider population levels and cycles, and therefore only measure the longer term risk of an infestation and mortality.

Landscape Modeling Systems

State transition models of landscape vegetation (Hemstrom et al. Chapter 2) use discrete vegetation classes and transition probabilities to model change from succession, management, and disturbance (Kurz et al. 2000). In contrast to tree-level growth models like FVS, the growth and mortality of individual trees is encapsulated in the transition probabilities. The use of states and transitions reduces the complexity of landscape simulations, although there remains a significant challenge to estimate and validate transition probabilities. There are several case studies using a state and transition approach to modeling forest landscape change by using the Vegetation Dynamics Development Tool (VDDT) and the Tool for Exploratory Landscape Analysis (TELSA) (Kurz et al. 2000). A prototype TELSA model built for the Upper Grande Ronde considered insect mortality from spruce budworm and Douglas-fir beetle; and spruce beetle and mountain pine beetle in ponderosa (*Pinus ponderosa* Dougl. ex Laws.) and lodgepole pine (*P. contorta* Dougl. ex Loud.). Insect epidemics were simulated, and mortality was represented by changing the vegetative state of infested stands based on host mortality. Parameters for simulating epidemics were obtained from data on historical infestations including USDA Forest Service, Pacific Northwest Region aerial survey maps (USDA FS 2003a) and other historical information (e.g., Gast et al. 1991). Pertinent information for each insect vector included periodicity of outbreaks and the percentage of host type infested during an outbreak. Initial results from this model show how different management scenarios change future extent and severity of insect epidemics and the effects of alternative forest management schedules.

Alternatives to the state and transition approach are stand-level models that use individual-based tree growth models to simulate multiple stands on a landscape. Incorporating insect- and disease-caused mortality into these models is relatively straightforward. For instance, a simple landscape simulation with insect and disease mortality can be built by simulating all the stands in a landscape with FVS and FVS pest extensions (Roberts and Weatherby 1997). This approach can be enhanced to consider spreading of infestations by using the FVS parallel processing extension, as in the westwide pine beetle model (Smith et al. 2002). When combined with the array of other FVS extensions and postprocessors (USDA FS 2003c), the multistand approach of using FVS and the parallel processing extension provides a flexible system that can address a variety of scenarios.

More complex are the stand-alone optimization models such as the Simulation and analysis of forests with episodic Disturbances (SafeD) model (Bettinger et al. Chapter 4, Graetz 2000, Wedin 1999), which derive their growth equations from FVS code but do not have direct linkages to FVS and the pest extensions. In SafeD, insect and disease mortality was modeled as an endemic process as part of stand growth (Wedin 1999), and epidemic or periodic mortality from insects or diseases was not considered.

Research Approach

Options for Different Modeling Frameworks

Each of the methods (FVS-related software, state transitions models, landscape simulation/optimization models) for simulating vegetation change for the INLAS project requires different amounts and kinds of development to enable modeling of insect and disease mortality. The major tasks required to incorporate insect- and disease-caused mortality by using FVS-related software approach (Ager Chapter 3) involve issues of local calibration and experience to run the FVS extensions for Douglas-fir beetle, western spruce budworm, Douglas-fir tussock moth (*Orgyia pseudotsugata* McDunnough), and mountain pine beetle on lodgepole pine. Additionally, ad hoc models for mountain pine beetle on ponderosa pine, western pine beetle (*D. brevicomis* LeConte) on ponderosa pine, and spruce beetle on Engelmann spruce (*Picea engelmannii* Parry ex Engelm.), such as those illustrated by Roberts and Weatherby (1997) for ponderosa pine, need to be evaluated on local stand conditions. A major part of this work will be estimation of parameters for epidemic lengths, periodicities, and spread rates for Blue Mountain conditions. For INLAS, we will experiment with FVS insect extensions in concert with the development of FVS-related landscape simulation tools.

Stand-alone landscape optimization models such as those described by Bettinger et al. (Chapter 4) pose a larger problem within the context of INLAS. Although modeling **endemic** mortality can be accomplished by using mortality functions derived from the literature, modeling epidemics in stand-alone optimization models will require substantial work and is probably beyond the scope of this project. A first step would be converting FVS insect extensions to run within other stand-alone programs. Parameters are then needed for epidemic lengths, periodicities, and spread rates for Blue Mountain conditions. With this accomplished, epidemics could be simulated much like wildfire as described by Bettinger et al. (Chapter 4), where simulations are stopped each decade to run the FARSITE fire model (Finney Chapter 9). Insect mortality could be simulated every cycle, with epidemic parameters carrying over from cycle to cycle. Supporting epidemic parameters described above, including spread rate, intensity, and duration, are needed. An alternative that would take advantage of many of the FVS insect and disease models could be achieved by using the pest extensions in FVS to process tree lists from a stand-alone optimization model at each cycle. Specifically the Douglas-fir beetle, western spruce budworm, and western pine beetle can be applied to tree lists generated by SafeD and used to trigger single-cycle tree damage and mortality. Components of the FVS insect and disease models that consider more than one cycle would need to be incorporated into the optimization model. For instance, the scheduling of periodic outbreaks could be implemented by writing the appropriate keyword files for FVS. The integration of insect and disease mortality into forest simulation/optimization models would provide a way to explore how different landscape goals are affected by these disturbance agents. Both stand and landscape goals can incorporate financial or other considerations to allow the estimation of the marginal cost of reducing insect and disease effects. Landscape goals also can be combined into multiobjective goals. For instance, stand goals would minimize susceptibility, whereas landscape goals could alter the spatial arrangement of susceptible stands to minimize spread (see Bettinger et al. Chapter 4). Landscape planning models can explore alternative scenarios by applying management activities targeting specific insect pests. Results from simulations could be applied by forest managers, pest management practitioners, and researchers concerned with landscape planning and simulation.

State and transition models require specific transitions to represent mortality of the different insect and disease agents (Hemstrom et al. Chapter 2). Like the other modeling approaches, the major part of this work is estimating characteristics of epidemics for Blue Mountain conditions. We discuss approaches to estimating these parameters below.

Estimating Parameters for Insect Epidemic Cycles

As mentioned earlier, a key component of any effort to model insect and disease mortality is parameters that describe the lengths, periodicities, and spread rate of epidemics for each insect of concern for local conditions. This section presents the result of a preliminary work to quantify these parameters by using data on past infestations. Although ultimately the size of epidemics is dependent on host type availability and secondary factors that influence epidemic growth (e.g., weather, spatial patterns of host, natural disturbance), realistic values must be used for epidemic cycles.

The importance of host availability and other factors is illustrated with historical conditions in the Blue Mountains. For example, it is assumed that the large historical outbreaks of western pine beetle have not been repeated in recent times owing to a decrease in large-diameter ponderosa pine. In contrast, infestations by defoliators have increased with the extent of defoliator host type (e.g., true firs) (e.g., Powell 1994). Spruce beetle epidemics are often triggered by wind events that result in a large number of downed spruce (e.g., Gast et al. 1991). Another example is Douglas-fir beetle, where trees weakened during defoliator outbreaks seem especially susceptible to Douglas-fir beetles (e.g., Wright et al. 1984). Hence, bark beetle activity is often observed after several years of budworm or tussock moth defoliation in the Blue Mountains.

Despite the dependence of outbreak size on host and other factors, we tried to gain some preliminary insight into the spatiotemporal patterns of insect epidemics by surveying historical outbreaks. For instance, it would be of interest to know how epidemics are manifested in terms of the numbers of individual infestation sites and the average size. Using data from the annual Aerial Insect Detection Survey conducted by the USDA Forest Service Pacific Northwest Region and Oregon Department of Forestry, we summarized and examined patterns of past insect infestations in the Blue Mountains. Additional information was obtained from Gast et al. (1991). These data clearly show the difference between epidemic and endemic infestations, and that endemic levels for one insect may exceed endemic levels for others (table 6, fig. 26). Bark beetles have relatively active endemic populations in the Blue Mountains compared to defoliators, and the acres affected during an epidemic range from a twentyfold to thirtyfold increase for some species, whereas others can cause a onefold to several hundredfold increase. Endemic levels of defoliators are so low that damage is not visible. Clearly, the defoliator cycles are high amplitude, and in the case of spruce budworm, have a long cycle. Although epidemics were characterized by increases in both infestation size and number of sites, the latter appears more important than the former. For instance, the individually mapped beetle infestations are all about 1.5 to three times larger for the epidemic versus endemic periods, whereas the number of polygons increased by an average of six times. We note that this difference could be an artifact of the mapping procedure. Also, the spatial arrangement of host stands could account for a major component of the size versus number contrast.

Table 6—Summary of aerial survey insect damage surveys showing population parameters[a]

Species	Population status	Average duration	Average periodicity	Number of polygons	Proportion of years	Average mapped unit	Total area
		– – – – – Years – – – – –			Percent	– – – – Acres – – – –	
Douglas-fir beetle	Endemic			108	43.75	70	7,560
	Epidemic	8	15	661	65.25	265	175,165
Fir engraver beetle	Endemic			137	79.20	190	26,030
	Epidemic	5	20	951	21.80	257	244,407
Western pine beetle	Endemic			108	75.00	143	15,444
	Epidemic	4	16	299	25.00	364	108,836
Mountain pine beetle in lodgepole pine	Endemic			68	70.80	200	13,600
	Epidemic	9	63	749	29.20	561	420,189
Mountain pine beetle in ponderosa pine	Endemic			216	78.70	154	33,264
	Epidemic	5	14	986	21.30	315	310,590
Spruce beetle	Endemic			23	85.40	225	5,175
	Epidemic	6+	Variable: disturbance-related	129	14.60	348	44,892
Douglas-fir tussock moth	Endemic			0	81.10	0	0
	Epidemic	3	9	353	18.90	557	196,621
Western spruce budworm	Endemic			0	56.60	0	0
	Epidemic	12	36	583	43.40	4,858	2,832,214

[a] Data were obtained between 1954 and 2001 and pertain to a forested ands in the B ue Mountains province Low damage (BS-L and BS-1) for western spruce budworm were not inc uded because they do not genera y indicate host morta ity

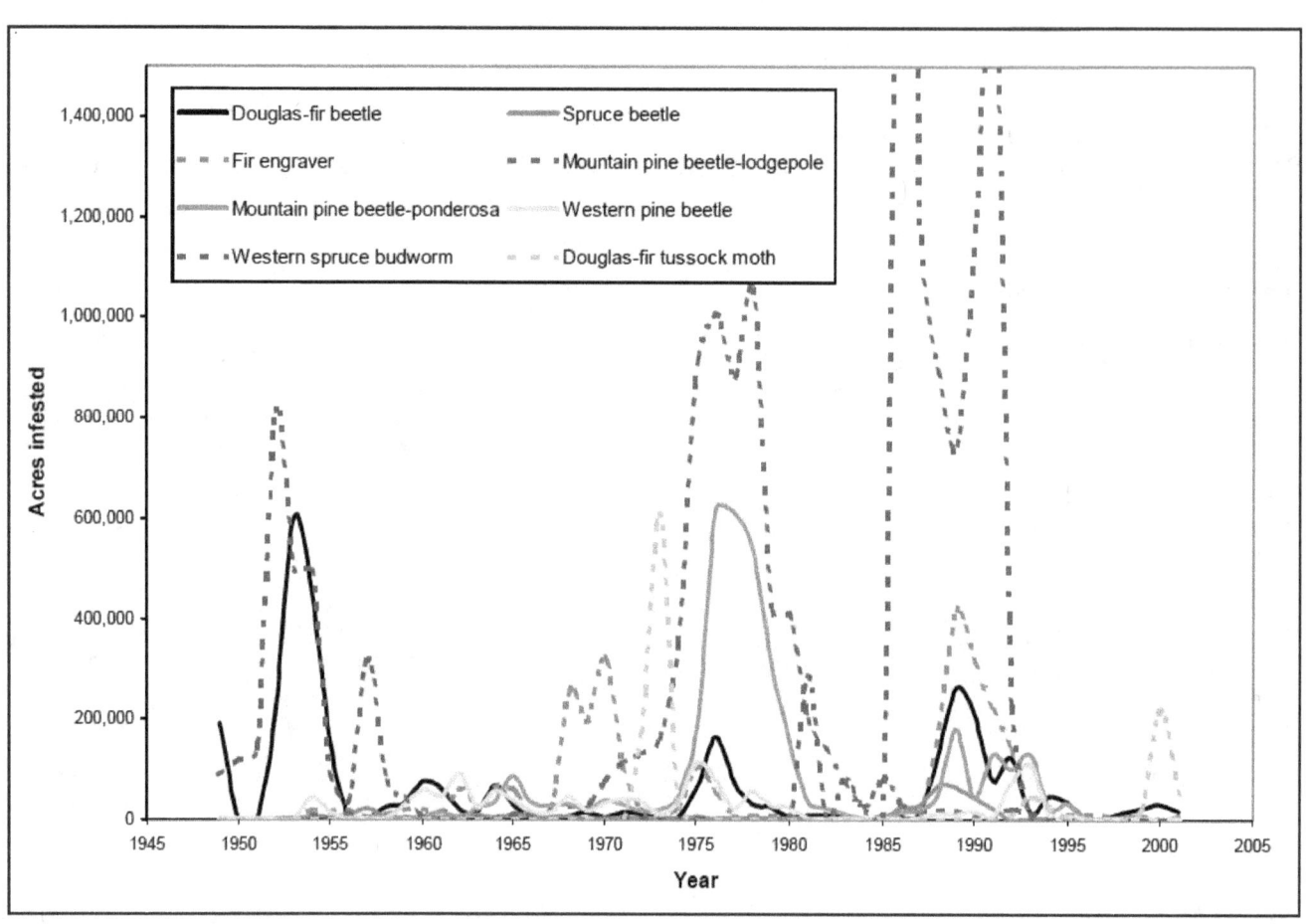

Figure 26—Acres infested with major insect pests as derived from aerial survey information and Gast et al. (1991). Peak values of about 3 million acres for western spruce budworm were truncated to improve visibility of other data. Budworm damage codes for low damage (BS-L, BS-1) were omitted.

At a minimum, table 6 and figure 26 illustrate qualitative features of insect infestations and illustrate the stochastic nature of this particular natural disturbance. In addition, the data show the relative importance of modeling spatial spread and contagion among the various insect pests. Defoliators like western spruce budworm that are capable of rapid spread over very large areas probably do not warrant detailed modeling of spread because most or all host are infested over a short period. In contrast, insects that have longer infestations per area affected (i.e., broad peaks, such as mountain pine beetle in lodgepole pine and fir engraver beetle [*Scolytus ventralis* LeConte in true fir]) show longer infestation periods per total acres infested, suggesting constraints to spreading are regulating these infestations more than in the western spruce budworm. Here, more detailed spread models might be warranted.

It should be noted that the data show population status data for the Blue Mountains as a whole, and it is possible to have localized epidemics that result in significant damage. Douglas-fir tussock moth epidemics have characteristically developed in several discrete and different areas within the Blue Mountains over the last century. However, in most cases, epidemic populations of various insects and associated damage develop concurrently or occur over large areas within the Blue Mountains.

One additional factor that must be considered with these data is that aerial survey sketch mapping has evolved over the years as new technology has been developed. For example, this new technology has allowed more accurate portrayal of discrete pockets of infestation, whereas in the early days of surveying, these were grouped in large polygons; thus, polygons have decreased in size and increased in number.

Proposed Work

The goal of incorporating insect and disease mortality in landscape simulation models in the context of INLAS is to better understand the long-term interactions of insects, disease, management, and other disturbances, and forest succession. Through the INLAS project, we will continue to investigate the historical epidemic data and try to produce parameters for each of the major insect pests. Work on diseases will probably be minimal given their relatively minor effect on mortality. We will explore methods to assess uncertainty in the insect epidemic data. Given a set of reasonable parameters, epidemics will be simulated by using the simulation framework described in Ager (Chapter 3) for the INLAS project area. These simulations will use the FVS pest extensions and will be completed for a set of management scenarios (Barbour et al. Chapter 1). The outputs will provide the data to examine how long-term levels of insect mortality might be affected by different intensities and kinds of forest management at the subbasin scale.

Acknowledgments

Helpful reviews of an earlier version of this paper were provided by Don Scott and Nick Crookston.

Metric Equivalents

When you know:	Multiply by:	To find:
Acres	0.405	Hectares
Feet	.3048	Meters

Literature Cited

Ager, A.A. 1996. Operations manual for UPEST. Pendleton, OR: U.S. Department of Agriculture, Forest Service, Umatilla National Forest. 16 p.

Ager, A.A. 2004. Stand-level approaches to simulating forest landscapes in the Western U.S. In: Hayes, J.L.; Ager, A.A.; Barbour, R.J., tech. eds. Methods for integrating modeling of landscape change: Interior Northwest Landscape Analysis System. Gen. Tech. Rep. PNW-GTR-610. Portland, OR: U.S. Department of Agriculture, Forest Service, Pacific Northwest Research Station: 33-40. Chapter 3.

Barbour, R.J.; Ager, A.A.; Hayes, J.L. 2004. A framework for the development and application of INLAS: the Interior Northwest Landscape Analysis System. In: Hayes, J.L.; Ager, A.A.; Barbour, R.J., tech. eds. Methods for integrating modeling of landscape change: Interior Northwest Landscape Analysis System. Gen. Tech. Rep. PNW-GTR-610. Portland, OR: U.S. Department of Agriculture, Forest Service, Pacific Northwest Research Station: 1-16. Chapter 1.

Bettinger, P.; Graetz, D.; Ager, A.A.; Sessions, J. 2004. The SafeD forest landscape planning model. In: Hayes, J.L.; Ager, A.A.; Barbour, R.J., tech. eds. Methods for integrating modeling of landscape change: Interior Northwest Landscape Analysis System. Gen. Tech. Rep. PNW-GTR-610. Portland, OR: U.S. Department of Agriculture, Forest Service, Pacific Northwest Research Station: 41-63. Chapter 4.

Beukema, S.J.; Greenough, J.A.; Robinson, D.C.E. [et al.]. 1997. The westwide pine beetle model: a spatially-explicit contagion model. In: Teck, R.; Moeur, M.; Adams, J., comps. Proceedings: Forest Vegetation Simulator conference. Gen. Tech. Rep. INT-GTR-373. Ogden, UT: U.S. Department of Agriculture, Forest Service, Intermountain Research Station: 126-130.

Cameron, D.E.; Stage, A.R.; Crookston, N.L. 1990. Performance of three mountain pine beetle damage models compared to actual outbreak histories. Res. Pap. INT-435. Ogden, UT: U.S. Department of Agriculture, Forest Service, Intermountain Research Station. 13 p.

Campbell, S.; Liegel, L., tech. coords. 1996. Disturbance and forest health in Oregon and Washington. Gen. Tech. Rep. PNW-GTR-381. Portland, OR: U.S. Department of Agriculture, Forest Service, Pacific Northwest Research Station and Pacific Northwest Region; Oregon Department of Forestry; Washington Department of Natural Resources. 105 p.

Crookston, N.L.; Colbert, J.J.; Thomas, P.W. [et al.]. 1990. User's guide to the western spruce budworm modeling system. Gen. Tech. Rep. INT-274. Ogden, UT: U.S. Department of Agriculture, Forest Service, Intermountain Research Station. 40 p.

Crookston, N.L.; Stage, A.R. 1991. User's guide to the parallel processing extension of the prognosis model. Gen. Tech. Rep. INT-281. Ogden, UT: U.S. Department of Agriculture, Forest Service, Intermountain Research Station. 87 p.

Eager, T.J.; Angwin, P.A. 1997. Forest health assessment–Piney analysis area, Holy Cross Ranger District, White River National Forest. In: Teck, R.; Moeur, M.; Adams, J., comps. Proceedings: Forest Vegetation Simulator conference. Gen. Tech. Rep. INT-GTR-373. Ogden, UT: U.S. Department of Agriculture, Forest Service, Intermountain Research Station: 116-120.

Filip, G.M.; Torgersen, T.R.; Parks, C.A. [et al.]. 1996. Insect and disease factors in the Blue Mountains. In: Jaindl, R.G.; Quigley, T.M., eds. Search for a solution: sustaining the land, people, and economy of the Blue Mountains. Washington, DC: American Forests: 169-202.

Finney, M.A. 2004. Landscape fire simulation and fuel treatment optimization. In: Hayes, J.L.; Ager, A.A.; Barbour, R.J., tech. eds. Methods for integrating modeling of landscape change: Interior Northwest Landscape Analysis System. Gen. Tech. Rep. PNW-GTR-610. Portland, OR: U.S. Department of Agriculture, Forest Service, Pacific Northwest Research Station: 117-131. Chapter 9.

Frankel, S.J., tech. coord. 1998. Users guide to the western root disease model, version 3.0. Gen. Tech. Rep. PSW-165. Albany, CA: U.S. Department of Agriculture, Forest Service, Pacific Southwest Research Station. 164 p.

Gast, W.R., Jr.; Scott, D.W.; Schmitt, C. 1991. Blue Mountains forest health report: new perspectives in forest health. Portland, OR: U.S. Department of Agriculture, Forest Service, Malheur, Umatilla, and Wallowa-Whitman National Forests. [Irregular pagination].

Graetz, D.H. 2000. The SafeD model: incorporating episodic disturbances and heuristic programming into forest management planning for the Applegate River watershed, southwestern Oregon. Corvallis, OR: Department of Forest Resources, Oregon State University. 127 p. M.S. thesis.

Hagle, S.K.; Goheen, D.J. 1986. Root disease response to stand culture. In: Schmidt, W.C., comp. Proceedings: future forests of the mountain West: a stand culture symposium. Gen. Tech. Rep. INT-GTR-243. Ogden, UT: U.S. Department of Agriculture, Forest Service, Intermountain Research Station: 303-308.

Hawksworth, F.G.; Williams-Cipriani, J.C.; Eav, B.B. [et al.]. 1995. Dwarf mistletoe impact modeling system user's guide and reference manual. Internal Rep. MAG-95-2. Fort Collins, CO: U.S. Department of Agriculture, Forest Service, Forest Pest Management Methods Application Group. 120 p.

Hayes, J.L.; Daterman, G.E. 2001. Bark beetles (*Scolytidae* spp.) in eastern Oregon and Washington. Northwest Science. 75: 21-30.

Hemstrom, M.; Ager, A.A.; Vavra, M. [et al.]. 2004. State and transition approach for integrating landscape models. In: Hayes, J.L.; Ager, A.A.; Barbour, R.J., tech. eds. Methods for integrating modeling of landscape change:
Interior Northwest Landscape Analysis System. Gen. Tech. Rep. PNW-GTR-610. Portland, OR: U.S. Department of Agriculture, Forest Service, Pacific Northwest Research Station: 17-32. Chapter 2.

Hessburg, P.F.; Mitchell, G.R.; Filip, G.M. 1994. Historical and current roles of insects and pathogens in eastern Oregon and Washington forested landscapes. Gen. Tech. Rep. PNW-GTR-327. Portland, OR: U.S. Department of Agriculture, Forest Service, Pacific Northwest Research Station. 72 p.

Kurz, W.A.; Beukema, S.J.; Klenner, W. [et al.]. 2000. TELSA: the tool for exploratory landscape analysis scenario analysis. Computers in Electronics in Agriculture. 27: 227-242.

Lehmkuhl, J.F.; Hessburg, P.F.; Everett, R.L. [et al.]. 1994. Historical and current forested landscapes of eastern Oregon and Washington: Part I. Vegetation pattern and insect and disease hazard. Gen. Tech. Rep. PNW-GTR-328. Portland, OR: U.S. Department of Agriculture, Forest Service, Pacific Northwest Research Station. 88 p.

Marsden, M.A.; Eav, B.B.; Thompson, M.K. 1994. User's guide to the Douglas-fir beetle impact model. Gen. Tech. Rep. RM-250. Fort Collins, CO: U.S. Department of Agriculture, Forest Service, Rocky Mountain Research Station. 9 p.

Monserud, R.A.; Crookston, N.L. 1982. A user's guide to the combined stand prognosis and Douglas-fir tussock moth outbreak model. Gen. Tech. Rep. INT-127. Ogden, UT: U.S. Department of Agriculture, Forest Service, Intermountain Forest and Range Experiment Station. 49 p.

Parks, C.G.; Flanagan, P.T. 2001. Dwarf mistletoes, rust diseases, and stem decays in eastern Oregon and Washington. Northwest Science. 75: 31-37.

Powell, D.C. 1994. Effects of the 1980s western spruce budworm outbreak on the Malheur National Forest in northeastern Oregon. R6-FI&D-TP-12-94. Portland, OR: U.S. Department of Agriculture, Forest Service, Pacific Northwest Region, Forest Insects and Diseases Group. 176 p.

Quigley, T.M.; Hayes, J.L.; Starr, G.L. [et al.]. 2001. Improving forest health and productivity in eastern Oregon and Washington. Northwest Science. 75: 234-251.

Roberts, J.C. 2002. Using a multichange agent approach with the forest vegetation simulator on the Boise National Forest, Idaho. In: Crookston, N.L.; Havis, R.N., comps. Second Forest Vegetation Simulator conference. Proc. RMRS-P-25. Ogden, UT: U.S. Department of Agriculture, Forest Service, Rocky Mountain Research Station: 53-56.

Roberts, J.C.; Weatherby, J.C. 1997. Successional simulation using the Forest Vegetation Simulator and multi-pest scenarios for various levels of planning. In: Teck, R.; Moeur, M.; Adams, J., comps. Proceedings: Forest Vegetation Simulator conference. Gen. Tech. Rep. INT-GTR-373. Ogden, UT: U.S. Department of Agriculture, Forest Service, Intermountain Research Station: 111-115.

Scott, D.W.; Schmitt, C.L.; Ager, A. 1998. Analyzing insect and disease risks for watershed analysis with the UPEST risk calculator program. Rep. BMZ-98-1. La Grande, OR: U.S. Department of Agriculture, Forest Service, Wallowa-Whitman National Forest, Blue Mountains Pest Management Service Center. 18 p.

Sheehan, K.A.; Kemp, W.P.; Colbert, J.J.; Crookston, N.L. 1989. The western spruce budworm model: structure and content. Gen. Tech. Rep. PNW-GTR-241. Portland, OR: U.S. Department of Agriculture, Forest Service, Pacific Northwest Research Station. 70 p.

Shore, T.L.; Safranyik, L.; Lemieux, J.P. 2000. Susceptibility of lodgepole pine stands to the mountain pine beetle: testing of a rating system. Canadian Journal of Forest Research. 30: 44-49.

Smith, E.; McMahan, A.J.; Eager, T. 2002. Landscape analysis of the westwide pine beetle FVS extension. In: Crookston, N.L.; Havis, R.N., comps. Second Forest Vegetation Simulator conference. Proc. RMRS-P-25. Ogden, UT: U.S. Department of Agriculture, Forest Service, Rocky Mountain Research Station: 62-68.

Steele, R.; Williams, R.E.; Weatherby, J.C. [et al.]. 1996. Stand hazard rating for central Idaho forests. Gen. Tech. Rep. INT-GTR-332. Ogden, UT: U.S. Department of Agriculture, Forest Service, Intermountain Research Station. 29 p.

Thies, W.G. 2001. Root diseases in eastern Oregon and Washington. Northwest Science. 75: 38-45.

Torgersen, T.R. 2001. Defoliators in eastern Oregon and Washington. Northwest Science. 75: 11-20.

U.S. Department of Agriculture, Forest Service [USDA FS]. 2003a. Forest health protection. http://www.fs.fed.us/r6/nr/fid. (November).

U.S. Department of Agriculture, Forest Service [USDA FS]. 2003b. http://www.fs.fed.us/foresthealth/technology/products.htm. (November).

U.S. Department of Agriculture, Forest Service [USDA FS]. 2003c. http://www.fs.fed.us/fmsc/fvs/index.php. (November).

Wedin, H. 1999. Stand level prescription generation under multiple objectives. Corvallis, OR: Department of Forest Resources, Oregon State University. 178 p. M.S. thesis.

Wright, L.C.; Berryman, A.A.; Wickman, B.E. 1984. Abundance of the fir engraver, *Scolytus ventralis*, and the Douglas-fir beetle, *Dendroctonus pseudotsugae*, following tree defoliation by the Douglas-fir tussuck moth. Canadian Entomologist. 116: 293-305.

Wykoff, W.R.; Crookston, N.L.; Stage, A.R. 1982. User's guide to the stand prognosis model. Gen. Tech. Rep. INT-133. Ogden, UT: U.S. Department of Agriculture, Forest Service, Intermountain Forest and Range Experiment Station. 112 p.

Chapter 9: Landscape Fire Simulation and Fuel Treatment Optimization

Mark A. Finney[1]

Abstract

Fuel treatment effects on the growth and behavior of large wildland fires depend on the spatial arrangements of individual treatment units. Evidence of this is found in burn patterns of wildland fires. During planning stages, fire simulation is most often used to anticipate effects of fuel treatment units. Theoretical modeling shows that random patterns are inefficient in changing large-fire growth rates compared to strategic designs. For complex landscapes, computational methods are being developed to identify optimal placement of fuel treatment units that collectively disrupt fire growth similarly to the strategic patterns. By combining these algorithms with forest simulations over long periods (say 50 years), the long-term effects of various treatment strategies can be compared.

Keywords: Fire simulation, fire modeling, fuel treatments.

Introduction

Large wildland fires are archetypal landscape phenomena. Landscapes are large land areas that encompass properties that vary at scales finer than the landscape as a whole (e.g., vegetation and topography). Wildland fires often encompass spatial and temporal domains that are large compared to the landscape properties critical to their behavior (fuels, weather, and topography). As fires advance across the landscape, they encounter fine-scale variability in fuels, topography, and weather that produces complex patterns of behavior and effects (see review by Finney 1999). Simulation models can accommodate such high-frequency variation in the fire environment and thereby help us understand movement and behavior of individual fires in complex conditions (Finney 1998). Simulation models are the main tools used to anticipate the effects management of vegetation and forests has on large fire growth and behavior. Fire simulations, however, must be coupled with vegetation or forest growth simulations if long-term consequences of wildland fires and management are to be addressed (Johnson et al. 1998, Keane et al. 1996, Sessions et al. 1999). This paper will first summarize fire modeling and fuel management techniques and then discuss methods for incorporating fire growth simulations and fuel management optimization into landscape forest simulations.

---

[1] **Mark A. Finney** is a research forester U S Department of Agricu ture Forest Service Rocky Mountain Research Station Fire Sciences Laboratory P O Box 8089 Missou a MT 59807

Fire Simulations and Their Requirements

Wildland fire behavior has long been known to be a function of fuels, weather, and topography (Brown and Davis 1973). Fire behavior programs in use today, e.g., the fire behavior (BEHAVE) prediction and fuel modeling system (Andrews 1986), accept inputs for these factors and predict fire behavior characteristics. Fire behavior refers to the gross characteristics of fire, e.g., fireline intensity (kW/m, or power per unit length of the flaming front), spread rate (m/min^{-1}), spotting distance, fuel consumption (kg/m), and whether the fire is a surface or crown fire. These quantities are important to managing wildland fire fighting operations, to estimating ecological effects of fires, and to designing fuel treatments that change fire behavior. The BEHAVE program applies fire behavior models to a given point on the ground or in one dimension.

The Fire Area Simulator (FARSITE) program extends these models to calculate fire behavior in two dimensions or across an area of land. As a result, data on fuels, weather, and topography must be provided spatially, with weather and fuel moisture allowed to change with time. Fire behavior across two spatial dimensions varies by the relative direction of fire spread, e.g., heading with the wind or slope, or flanking normal or backing counter to the heading direction. Relative fire spread direction is important in determining the variability of behaviors and effects that occur as large wildland fires move across landscapes (Catchpole et al. 1982). Many techniques have been applied to the problem of two-dimensional fire growth (see reviews by Finney 1998, 1999). Techniques that represent the growth and behavior of the fire edge as a vector or wave front (Finney 2002a, Richards 1990, Sanderlin and Van Gelder 1977) produce less distortion of fire shape and response to temporally varying conditions than techniques that model fire growth from cell-to-cell on a gridded landscape. They are thus preferable for performing fire simulations for supporting fire management operations because they can realistically reflect changes in fire behavior resulting from suppression, fuel, and weather changes.

Fuel Management Activities and Changes to Fire Effects and Behavior at the Stand Level

Fuel management activities are designed to change the structure of wildland vegetation and biomass distribution for the purpose of altering potential fire behavior. The prescriptions and objectives for fuel management depend on the characteristics of the vegetation and fire regime. For forest ecosystems with low- and mixed-severity fire regimes (Agee 1998), fuel management prescriptions can be designed to improve survivability of trees following wildland fires, restore forest structure, and improve the success of fire suppression efforts. For high-severity fire regimes in brushland and forest ecosystems, fuel management objectives can change fire behavior, slowing overall fire growth and improving fire suppression. Fuel management techniques that have proven effective in changing wildland fire behavior and effects consist of prescribed burning (Davis and Cooper 1963, Deeming 1990, Helms 1979, Koehler 1993, Martin et al. 1989, Pollet and Omi 2002), thinning (Hirsch and Pengelly 1999, Keyes and O'Hara 2002), and other mechanical manipulation of living or dead vegetation (Brown and Davis 1973, Pyne et al. 1996). Forest fuel treatments that reduce canopy fuels must often be accompanied by surface fuel treatment; otherwise the surface fuel hazard can be increased (Alexander and Yancik 1977, van Wagtendonk 1996). There are three main targets of fuel management prescriptions that contribute to changes in discrete kinds of fire behavior (table 7).

The changes in potential fire behavior are produced at the stand level, or within the treated area. Fire behaviors before and after treatment can be modeled by using fire behavior prediction systems such as BEHAVE (Andrews 1986) and Nexus (Scott and Reinhardt 2001) to compare fire spread rates, intensities, and propensity for crown fire.

Although fuel management tends to produce immediate changes in fire behavior, fuel treatment effects are only temporary. Fuel conditions change over time as a result of fuel accretion, regrowth of understory vegetation, and ingrowth of young trees. More research

Table 7—General relationships among fuels, prescriptions, and intended changes to fire behavior from fuel treatments

Fuel target	Prescription	Change in fire behavior
Surface fuels (live grass and brush, and dead and downed woody material)	Prescribed burning, mechanical treatments remove, compact, or reduce continuity of surface fuels	Reduced spread rate and intensity, and limit ignition of tree crowns and other aerial fuels
Ladder fuels (small trees, brush, low limbs)	Thinning (small-diameter trees) and prescribed burning (scorching and killing small trees and brush) to decrease vertical continuity between surface and crown fuels	Limit ability for fire to transition from surface to crown fire by separating surface fuels from crown fuels
Canopy fuels (fine fuels like needles, and small twigs in tree crowns)	Thinning to reduce horizontal continuity of crowns (e.g., overstory thin)	Limit spread of crown fire

is required to understand the long-term efficacy of fuel treatments on fuel conditions and fire behavior so that scheduling of future management activities and maintenance can be determined.

Landscape Effects of Fuel Management

Landscape strategies for fuel treatments can be distinguished in terms of their intention to (1) contain fires or (2) to modify fire behavior. Fire containment has been attempted by arranging fuel treatments as fuel breaks (Agee et al. 2000, Green 1977, Omi 1996, Weatherspoon and Skinner 1996). Fuel breaks are designed to facilitate active fire suppression at predetermined locations by indirect tactics (e.g., burnout). An alternative is to modify fire behavior and fire progress across landscapes through strategic placement of treatments and patterns of treatments (Brackebusch 1973; Finney 2001a, 2001b; Hirsch et al. 2001). The latter strategy affords flexibility for integration into land management planning and does not rely on uncertainties of success in fire suppression to mitigate fire effects. The remainder of this paper will focus on strategic treatments.

Although behavior and effects of wildland fires can be changed within a particular treatment unit or stand, the behavior and progress of a much larger fire may not be affected by small treatment units. Fire progression maps often reveal that small units are circumvented by large wildland fires (Dunn 1989, Salazar and Gonzalez-Caban 1987) with little net effect on the overall growth of the fire (fig. 27). Instead, the progress of large wildland fires is only affected by treatments that are (1) comparable to the size of the fire or (2) by treatments that collectively disrupt the growth of fires (Brackebusch 1973, Finney 2001a, Gill and Bradstock 1998). Examples of landscape-scale effects of fuel management are evidenced in large national parks (e.g., Yosemite, Sequoia, and Kings Canyon) where fire management policies have allowed free-burning fires for nearly three decades (Parsons and van Wagtendonk 1996, van Wagtendonk 1995) and in Baja, California, chaparral where little fire suppression exists (Minnich and Chou 1997). Because large fires are of primary concern to fire and forest managers, the most important effects of fuel treatments can only be achieved if landscape-scale considerations are incorporated into

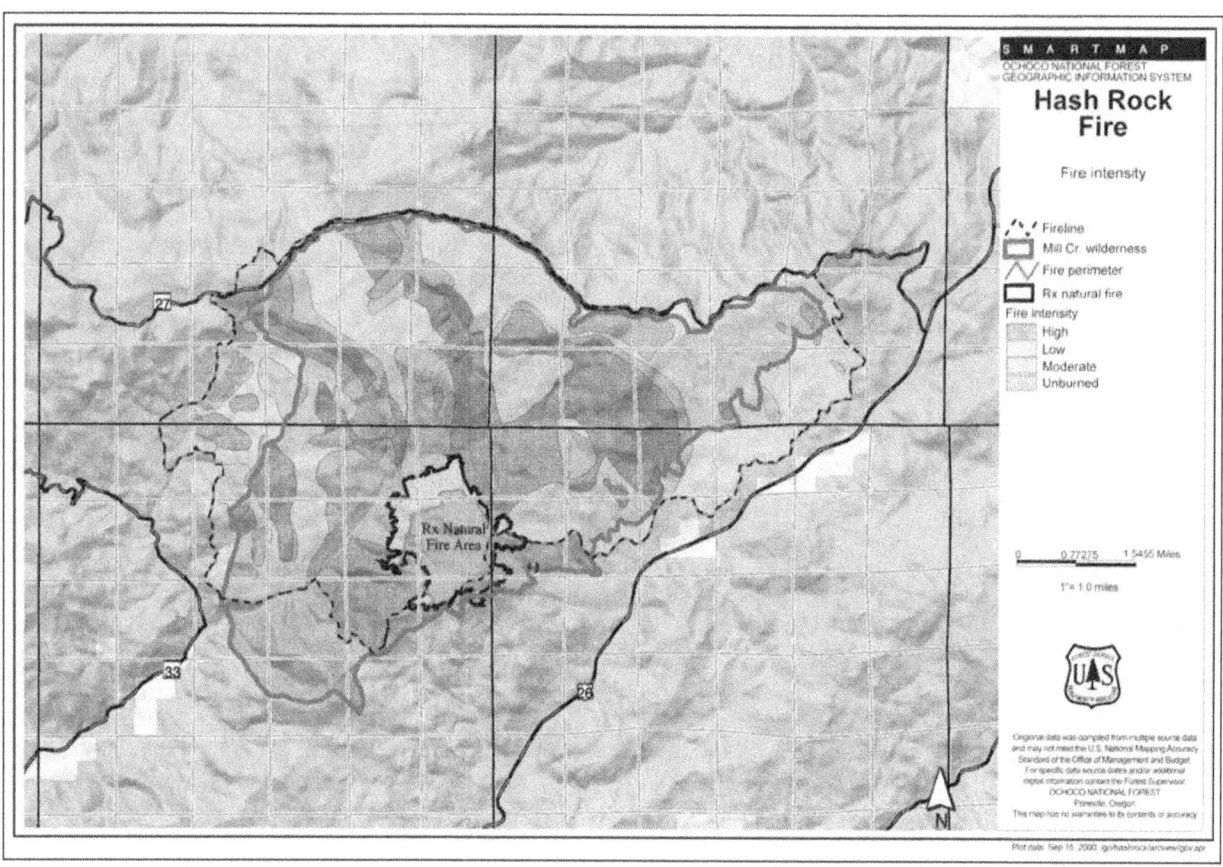

Figure 27   Fire severity at the Hash Rock fire (August 2000) near Prinevi e Oregon A prescribed natura fire (i e fire use for resource benefit) that occurred in 1995 produced important oca ized changes in fire behavior but had itt e effect on the progress of the Hash Rock Fire as a who e

the design and positioning of fuel treatments (Brackebusch 1973, Deeming 1990, Omi 1996, Omi and Kalabokidis 1998).

The effects of individual fuel treatment units on large fires must be modeled through simulation. Aside from the minimally managed fire regimes in a few national parks and wilderness areas, no full-scale landscape fuel management activities have been attempted. Thus, our only indications as to the effectiveness of treatments and patterns come from theoretical and modeling activities, and occasional experience of using forest harvest patterns for fire suppression (Bunnell 1998). Brackebusch (1973) advocated a mosaic pattern of managed fuel patches to disrupt fire growth. Gill and Bradstock (1998) discussed the amount of randomly arranged prescribed burns needed to disrupt fire growth. Hirsch et al. (2001) proposed strategically locating fuel treatment units in a "smart forest" approach to harvest scheduling and location. Theoretical work on fuel patterns (Finney 2001a, 2001b) indicates that spatial patterns of fuel treatments are critical to fire growth rates (i.e., the rate of spread of large fires) (fig. 28). Here, random fuel treatments are very inefficient in changing overall fire growth rates. Compared to the partially overlapped pattern, randomly arranged treatments permit fire to easily move laterally around treatments unless large portions of the landscape are treated. This is further illustrated by a comparison of large fire growth rates across the entire range of treatments (fig. 29). If fire spread rate is reduced to one-fifth within the treatment unit compared to the untreated surrounding landscape (as a direct effect of the treatment

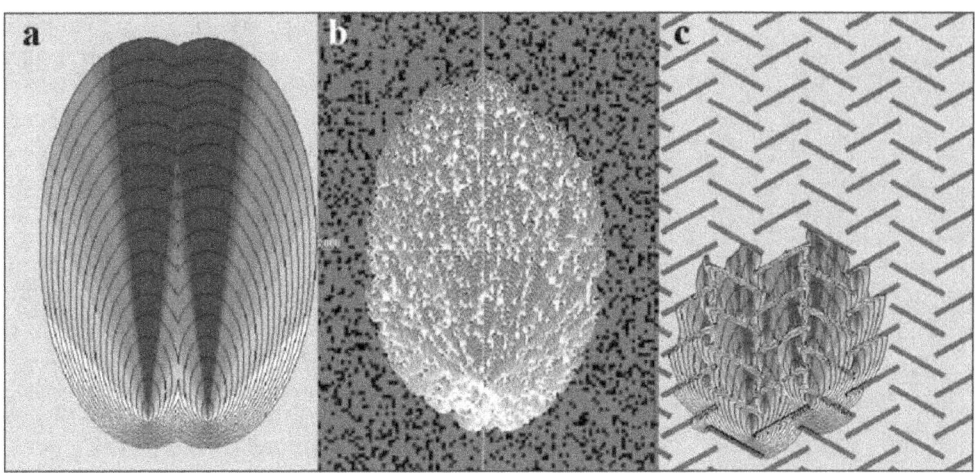

Figure 28 Simu ations of fire growth on different theoretica fue patterns Compared to (a) no treatment (b) random 20-percent treatment produces itt e effect on overa fire growth compared to (c) a theoretica partia -over ap treatment Random arrangements are ineffective because the fire can circumvent treatment areas

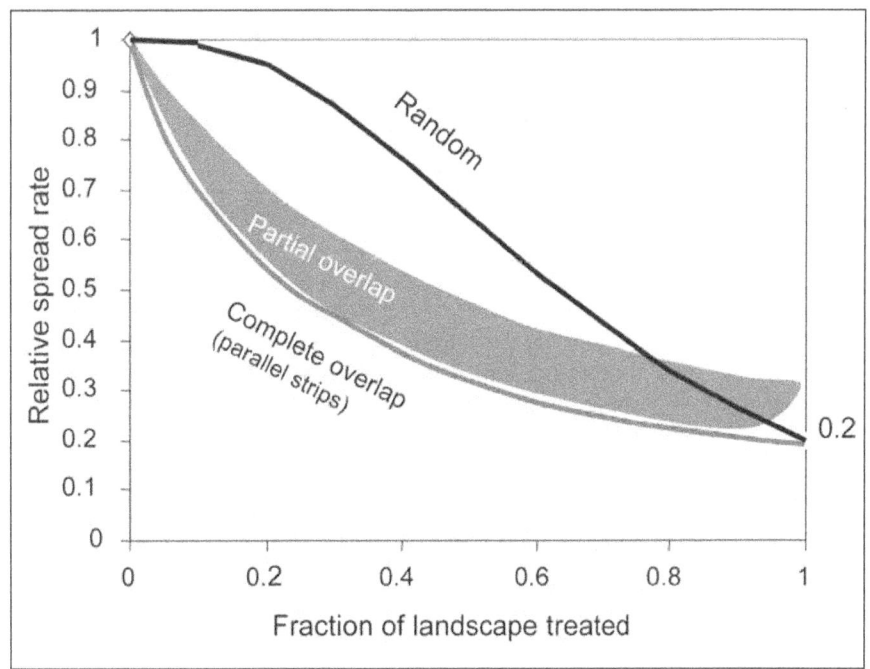

Figure 29 Overa fire spread rate as a function of treatment fraction for different spatia patterns of treatment units (from Finney 2001a 2003) reduces re ative spread rate to 0 2 Compared to patterns that require over ap among treatments the random treatment pattern produces itt e reduction in overa fire spread rate unti re ative y arge proportions of the andscape are treated (because fire goes around the treated patches)

prescription) 35-percent reduction in large fire growth rates is achieved by treating about 10 percent of the landscape in the strategic pattern compared to 50 percent in a random pattern (fig. 29). The strategic pattern is clearly more efficient (per area treated) than a random spatial arrangement of treatments. In nature, fire patterns created by free-burning fires in the large national parks and Baja (Minnich and Chou 1997, Parsons and van Wagtendonk 1996, van Wagtendonk 1995) obstruct fire growth because large percentages of the landscape are maintained by previous fires, despite the random locations of those fires and previously burned areas.

The effects of fuel and forest management activities on fire behavior are not restricted to the stand that is treated. Behavior characteristics of large wildland fires can be altered outside the treated area because of the way fire behavior changes depending on the relative fire spread direction. These constitute an "off-site" effect of treatments that are seen as changes in overall fire growth rate (fig. 28), flanking and backing fire burning with lower fireline intensity on the lee-side of treatment units (fig. 30), and in moderated fire effects on the lee-side of fuel changes (fig. 31). Such landscape-scale effects on large fires become important to the patch sizes and proportions of areas burned with different severities.

Effects of Spatial Locations and Patterns of Landscape Fuel Treatments

Despite the potential benefits of fuel management at the stand and landscape levels, limitations on the amounts and locations of treatment suggest that these activities must be carefully chosen to achieve the greatest effect and benefit. The problem might be approached as an optimization of effects given constraints on locations, amounts, and prescriptions that can be applied. Application of spatial optimization and strategies in forest management (Baskent 1999, Baskent and Jordan 1996, Snyder and ReVelle 1996) and fire management (Finney 2001a, Hirsch et al. 2001, Hof et al. 2000, Wilson and Baker 1998) is becoming more common. For a simple theoretical landscape consisting of two fuel types on flat terrain, a pattern of rectangular fuel treatment units can be optimized for size and placement (Finney 2001a). Such patterns are optimal in terms of efficiency and effectiveness in reducing large-fire growth rates compared to random fuel patterns (Finney 2001b, 2003). However, there are no analytical solutions to the optimization of fuel treatment locations on real landscapes that are complex in terms of fuels, topography, and weather. For real landscapes, where fuels, topography, and weather all differ, an optimization of this kind is complicated by the spatial and temporal nature of fire and its movement through a pattern of fuel treatments.

An optimization algorithm is under development for helping choose the placement of fuel treatments on real landscapes (Finney 2002b). One process now being considered consists of two steps: (1) use fire growth algorithms to identify the fastest travel routes across a landscape, and (2) use heuristic algorithms to optimize the locations and sizes of fuel treatments to block these routes. The fastest travel routes produced by fire growth algorithms suggest initial places for optimal placement of fuel treatments for delaying fire growth. The procedure requires the construction of a gridded landscape containing information on fuels and topography (fig. 32a). Specific weather conditions associated with the conditions targeted for fuel treatment performance, including wind direction, windspeed, humidity, and temperature are used to compute the fire behavior at each cell. Each cell contains fire spread rates in all directions assuming an elliptical fire shape (Finney 2002a) so that fire growth across the landscape can be computed from a generic ignition source. The fire growth algorithm is based on minimum fire travel time methods from graph theory (Finney 2002a, Moser 1991) that efficiently calculate fire growth and behavior for each cell (node) on the landscape. The paths producing the minimum fire travel time can then be processed to identify the "influence paths" or routes of fire travel

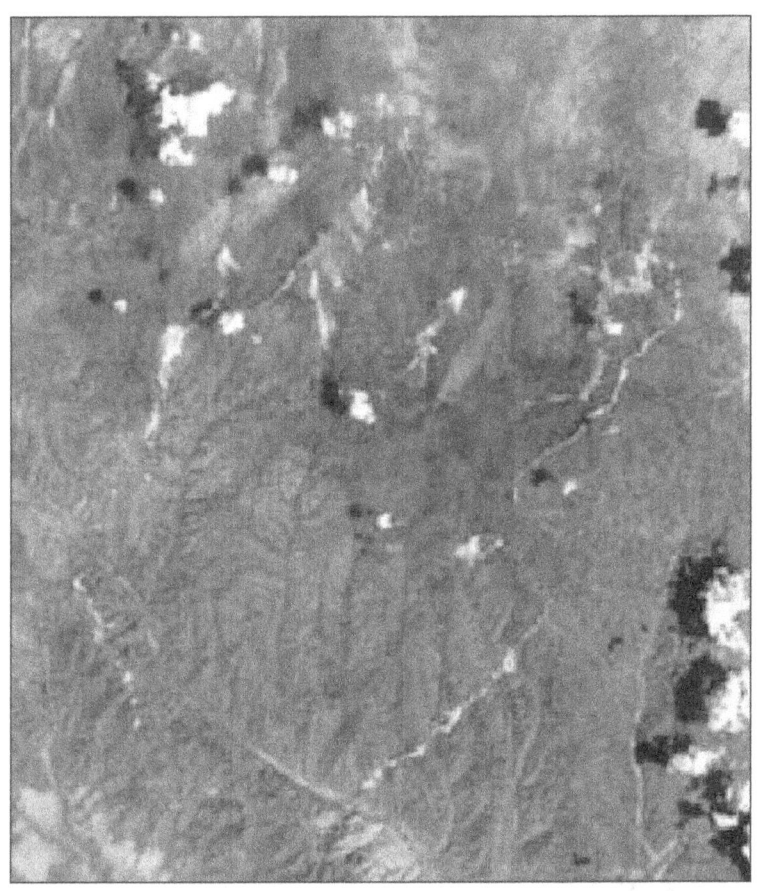

Figure 30 Landsat 7 image of the Rodeo fire in Arizona (June 21 2002) showing interior fire fronts around arrow-shaped is ands within the main fire These occur where fire fronts join after circumventing the is ands and are a andscape-sca e effect of varying fue s and fire behavior

Figure 31 A ridge within the A der Creek fire (Montana 2000) showing offsite effect of rocky areas (arrows) on fire effects and behavior Crown fire moved from ower eft to upper right and cou d not burn areas on ee side of rocky patches (photo by Co in Hardy USDA FS Missou a Fire Sciences Lab)

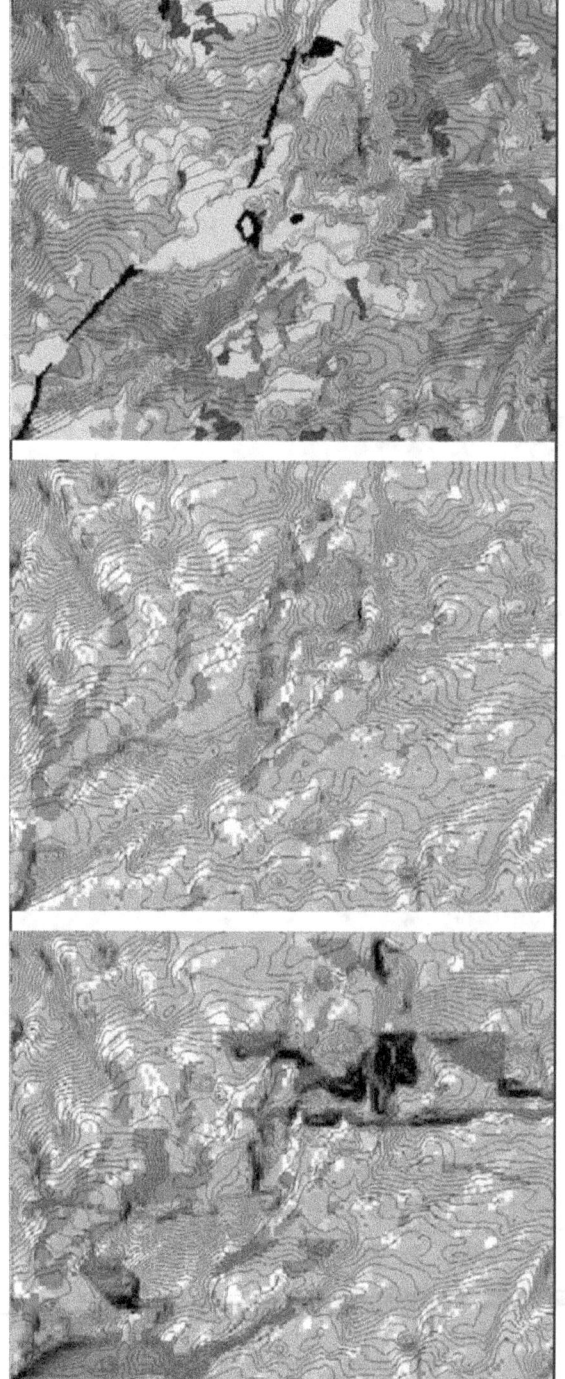

Figure 32a   Fue s and terrain data showing fire growth contours (progression in 1-hour time step from north to south)

Figure 32b   Fire inf uence paths ca cu ated from fire growth a gorithm Given the ignition configuration (bottom of andscape) fire burning through paths of high inf uence (red) u timate y burns more and area than areas around them These suggest p aces to p ace fue treatment units because a arge effect wou d be achieved by s owing fire spread through those areas compared to surrounding areas

Figure 32c   Fue treatments (fuchsia co or) optimized by using a genetic a gorithm for this andscape Treatments cause fire growth to take twice as ong as it wou d without treatments to cross this andscape whi e occupying about 15 percent of the tota   and area

that account for the most area burned later in time (fig. 32b). These paths are the starting locations for treatment units because of the large influence that blocking those paths has on area burned. The exact number, sizes, and patterns of those treatments, however, must be obtained through the use of a heuristic algorithm (fig. 32c).

Heuristic algorithms are used to find spatially optimal fuel treatment unit sizes and locations. At present, a genetic algorithm (Goldberg 1989) is being developed for evaluating collections of fuel treatment units to determine their effectiveness and efficiency at changing overall fire growth rates. The challenging part of this problem is the sequential nature of fire movement. Fuel treatment units located upwind divert fire growth and change the priorities for fuel treatments downwind (sizes and locations). Furthermore, the optimal spatial pattern is not necessarily composed of locally optimal treatment units. In other words, the importance of each unit is only realized in context of the entire pattern. An approach to this problem involves the use of recursion, starting the algorithm at downwind locations and allowing it to recurse toward the ignition location. At each location, a population of "best" treatment units is selected based on the best populations from previous locations (i.e., upwind or closer to the ignition). The performance of individual treatment patterns is assessed by using the fire growth algorithm to compare fire travel times among treatment alternatives. The genetic algorithm (GA) is used to refine the population of individual treatment units within a horizontal strip, where each treatment unit has characteristics of vertical location and size. Ultimately, the optimal solution is selected from the treatments that produce the overall best effect. The algorithm consists of the following steps:

- Evaluate the fire growth by using the minimum travel time algorithm for the landscape without treatment.

- Divide the landscape into a series of strips of random width running perpendicular to the main fire spread direction.

- Starting with the downwind strip (i.e., farthest from the ignition), use GA to optimize the fuel treatment locations and unit sizes for each of the fuel treatment configurations obtained from the GA on previous strips. Applying the GA to each strip requires recursion into preceding strips to find the optimal treatment locations and sizes. Each treatment configuration in each strip is evaluated by using the minimum travel time algorithm.

- Within each strip, create populations of treatment locations and sizes to evaluate and improve by using the GA. Treatment unit sizes are obtained by infilling the fire growth contours from a starting point (e.g., an influence path) by using the differential spread rate owing to treatment.

- Pick the best overall treatment pattern from all strips that maximize the fire travel time across the landscape as a whole.

The above algorithm is being developed for handling spatial constraints on treatment area and local treatment effectiveness (i.e., within a given stand and stand type). So far, the algorithm appears to identify fuel treatment units that efficiently retard overall fire growth (fig. 32c).

Integration of Fire and Landscape Simulations

Long-term consequences of forest and fuel management activities on wildland fire behavior can only be understood by either large-scale experimentation or through simulation modeling. Until experimental or operational treatment areas have been established on the ground and monitored, simulation modeling will be the only method available.

Many landscape simulation approaches are currently used for spatially modeling fire and long-term future forest development (Johnson et al. 1998, Jones and Chew 1999, Keane et al. 1997, Mladenoff and He 1999, Sessions et al. 1996, Thompson et al. 2000). Some of these have been proposed for modeling effects of treatments and for optimizing the scheduling of fuel treatments. At present, these simulations do not permit control for fuel treatment spatial patterns. As the above analysis of simple landscape patterns suggests, however, fuel treatments at the landscape scale have topological effects that are critical to changing fire growth. Improvements to landscape simulations include the prescription, scheduling, and location of treatments dynamically in response to unpredicted disturbances (fire, insects, etc.). Furthermore, the simulation must have fine-scale resolution of landscape units, as either grids (raster) or small polygons, to retain the fine resolution of spatially variable fire effects (Finney 1999).

The intent of a new modeling effort is to modify the simulation approach (Simulation and Analysis of Forests with Episodic Disturbances [SafeD]) described by Sessions et al. (1999) and Johnson et al. (1998) to incorporate a spatial optimization for fuel treatments (Finney 2002b). The SafeD model has been used previously to examine how fuelbreaks performed in the presence of wildfire and forest change (Johnson et al. 1998, Sessions et al. 1999). Currently, SafeD (Graetz 2000) is a spatially explicit simulation/optimization tool that features a stand prescription generator (Wedin 1999), forest growth-and-yield modeling by using the Forest Vegetation Simulator (FVS), a heuristic method of allocating activities across a landscape with multiple constraints, and a spatially explicit fire growth model FARSITE (Finney 1998). Together, these models allow for scheduling of fuel and harvesting treatments, simulation of wildfire events and effects, growth and mortality of vegetation, surface and crown fuel development, and specification of stand- and landscape-level objectives. The landscape goal-seeking component of SafeD couples heuristic techniques with goal programming to find near-optimal sets of stand and landscape prescriptions. Multiple stand management objectives can be specified for the simulations. Mechanical and prescribed fire treatment effects are modeled in SafeD by manipulation of tree lists (lists of density by size and species of trees) and surface fuel components. Wildfire effects are created by fireline intensity maps created by FARSITE simulations that are activated by the SafeD model.

Several additions to the SafeD model will be required to permit spatial optimization of fuel treatments. Optimal fuel treatment locations will be determined by inclusion of a spatial treatment algorithm (e.g., Finney 2002b).

Research Applications

A project funded by the Joint Fire Science Program (http://www.nifc.gov/joint_fire_sci/jointfiresci.html) will make use of the SafeD simulation system to address landscape fuel treatment scheduling and potential effects for several study areas. These study areas are located in the Blue Mountains in eastern Oregon (one of the INLAS study sites), Sanders County in western Montana, the Sierra National Forest in California, and southern Utah. The landscapes were chosen as samples of different ecosystems, fire regimes, mixtures of landownership, and fuel and forest management issues and constraints to examine, in a practical sense, how the outcomes of landscape fuel treatment programs can be expected to differ. A series of simulations for these landscapes will be performed to address the following questions:

- How important is fuel treatment topology to the potential effects of treatments on real landscapes?

- For different fuel treatment amounts and patterns, what fuel treatment effects (e.g., fire sizes, burned area, severity) can be expected with no constraint on treatment location or prescription?

- What fuel treatment effects are possible given current restrictions on fuel and forest management activities?

- What are the tradeoffs in fuel treatment effectiveness possible by relaxing some of the constraints?

The results of this project are intended to lead to practical methods for guiding fuel treatment planning across landscapes and for helping identify constraints on needed management activities through cooperation among the many competing interests in wildland management.

Conclusions

The fire behavior models presently available can be used to simulate fire growth, behavior, and effects at the landscape scale. Effects of fuel treatments on changes in fire behavior can be modeled for a variety of prescriptions and environmental conditions. The fire simulations also have been used to examine spatial effects of fuel treatment patterns, suggesting that fuel treatment topology can be important to effects on fire growth and behavior. Fire growth simulation and heuristic algorithms are being combined as a means to find optimal patterns of treatments in highly variable conditions found on real landscapes. These optimizations are to be combined with landscape simulation and scheduling programs to examine likely effects of spatial fuel treatment programs on wildland fire behaviors and effects at the landscape scale.

Acknowledgments

This work was partly funded by the Joint Fire Science Program and the USDA Forest Service, Rocky Mountain Research Station, Fire Sciences Laboratory, Fire Behavior Research Work Unit in Missoula, Montana.

English Equivalents

When you know:	Multiply by:	To find:
Meters (m)	3.28	Feet
Kilograms (kg)	2.205	Pounds
Kilowatts per meter (kW/m)	0.2889	British thermal unit per foot per second

Literature Cited

Agee, J.K. 1998. Fire strategies and priorities for forest health in the Western United States. In: Proceedings of the 13th fire and forest meteorology conference. Fairfax, VA: International Association of Wildland Fire, USA: 297-303.

Agee, J.K.; Bahro, B.; Finney, M.A. [et al.]. 2000. The use of fuelbreaks in landscape fire management. Forest and Ecology Management. 127: 55-66.

Alexander, M.E.; Yancik, R.F. 1977. The effect of precommercial thinning on fire potential in a lodgepole pine stand. Fire Management Notes. 38(3): 7-9, 20.

Andrews, P.L. 1986. BEHAVE: fire behavior prediction and fuel modeling system–BURN subsystem. Part 1. Gen. Tech. Rep. INT-194. Ogden, UT: U.S. Department of Agriculture, Forest Service, Intermountain Forest and Range Experiment Station. 130 p.

Baskent, E.Z. 1999. Controlling spatial structure of forested landscapes: a case study towards landscape management. Landscape Ecology. 14: 83-97.

Baskent, E.Z.; Jordan, G.A. 1996. Designing forest management to control spatial structure of landscapes. Landscape and Urban Planning. 34: 55-74.

Brackebusch, A.P. 1973. Fuel management: a prerequisite not an alternative to fire control. Journal of Forestry. 71(10): 637-639.

Brown, A.A.; Davis, K.P. 1973. Fire control and use. 2nd ed. New York: McGraw-Hill Book Company. 686 p.

Bunnell, D. 1998. Old-growth lodgepole pine and the Little Wolf Fire. In: Close, K.; Bartlette, R., eds. Proceedings of the 1994 interior West fire council meeting and program. Fairfax, VA: International Association of Wildland Fire, USA: 155-160.

Catchpole, E.A.; de Mestre, N.J.; Gill, A.M. 1982. Intensity of fire at its perimeter. Australian Forest Research. 12: 47-54.

Davis, L.S.; Cooper, R.W. 1963. How prescribed fire affects wildfire occurrence. Journal of Forestry. 61: 915-917.

Deeming, J.E. 1990. Effects of prescribed fire on wildfire occurrence and severity. In: Walstad, J.D.; Radosevich, S.R.; Sandberg, D.V., eds. Natural and prescribed fire in Pacific Northwest forests. Corvallis, OR: Oregon State University Press: 95-104. Chapter 8.

Dunn, A.T. 1989. The effects of prescribed burning on fire hazard in the chaparral: toward a new conceptual synthesis. In: Berg, N.H., tech. coord. Proceedings of the symposium on fire and watershed management. Gen. Tech. Rep. PSW-109. Albany, CA: U.S. Department of Agriculture, Forest Service, Pacific Southwest Research Station: 23-29.

Finney, M.A. 1998. FARSITE: Fire Area Simulator—model development and evaluation. Res. Pap. RMRS-RP-4. Fort Collins, CO: U.S. Department of Agriculture, Forest Service, Rocky Mountain Research Station. 47 p.

Finney, M.A. 1999. Mechanistic modeling of landscape fire patterns. In: Mladenoff, D.J.; Baker, W.L., eds. Spatial modeling of forest landscape change: approaches and applications. Cambridge, United Kingdom: Cambridge University Press: 186-209.

Finney, M.A. 2001a. Design of regular landscape fuel treatment patterns for modifying fire growth and behavior. Forest Science. 47(2): 219-228.

Finney, M.A. 2001b. Spatial strategies for landscape fuel treatments. In: Bento, J.; Botelho, H., eds. Workshop on tools and methodologies for fire danger mapping: proceedings of a workshop. Vila Real, Portugal: Universidad de Traj-os-montes el Alto-Douro, Departamento Forestal: 157-163.

Finney, M.A. 2002a. Fire growth using minimum travel time methods. Canadian Journal of Forest Research. 32: 1420-1424.

Finney, M.A. 2002b. Use of graph theory and genetic algorithms for finding optimal fuel treatment locations. In: Viegas, D.X., ed. Proceedings of the 4th international conference on fire research [CD ROM]. Rotterdam, The Netherlands: Millpress Science Publishers.

Finney, M.A. 2003. Calculation of fire spread rates across random landscapes. International Journal of Wildland Fire. 12(2): 167-174.

Gill, A.M.; Bradstock, R.A. 1998. Prescribed burning: patterns and strategies. In: 13th conference on fire and forest meteorology. Fairfax, VA: International Association of Wildland Fire, USA: 3-6.

Goldberg, D.E. 1989. Genetic algorithms in search, optimization and machine learning. Boston, MA: Addison-Wesley Publishing Co. 432 p.

Graetz, D.H. 2000. The SafeD model: incorporating episodic disturbances and heuristic programming into forest management planning for the Applegate River watershed, southwestern Oregon. Corvallis, OR: Oregon State University. 127 p. M.S. thesis.

Green, L.R. 1977. Fuelbreaks and other fuel modification for wildland fire control. Agric. Handb. 499. Washington, DC: U.S. Department of Agriculture, Forest Service. 79 p.

Helms, J.A. 1979. Positive effects of prescribed burning on wildfire intensities. Fire Management Notes. 40(3): 10-13.

Hirsch, K.; Kafka, V.; Tymstra, C. [et al.]. 2001. Fire-smart forest management: a pragmatic approach to sustainable forest management in fire-dominated ecosystems. The Forestry Chronicle. 77(2): 357-363.

Hirsch, K.; Pengelly, I. 1999. Fuel reduction in lodgepole pine stands in Banff National Park. In: Neuenschwander, L.F.; Ryan, K.C., tech eds. Proceedings of the joint fire sciences conference and workshop. Boise, ID: University of Idaho: 250-256.

Hof, J.; Omi, P.N.; Bevers, M.; Laven, R.D. 2000. A timing oriented approach to spatial allocation of fire management effort. Forest Science. 46(3): 442-451.

Johnson, K.N.; Sessions, J.; Franklin, J.; Gabriel, J. 1998. Integrating wildfire into strategic planning for Sierra Nevada forests. Journal of Forestry. 96(1): 42-49.

Jones, J.G.; Chew, J.D. 1999. Applying simulation and optimization to evaluate the effectiveness of fuel treatments for different fuel conditions at landscape scales. In: Neuenschwander, L.F.; Ryan, K.C., tech. eds. Proceedings of the joint fire science conference and workshop. Boise, ID: University of Idaho: 89-95.

Keane, R.E.; Morgan, P.; Running, S.W. 1996. FIRE-BGC—a mechanistic ecological process model for simulating fire succession on coniferous forest landscapes of the northern Rocky Mountains. Res. Pap. RP-INT-484. Ogden, UT: U.S. Department of Agriculture, Forest Service, Intermountain Research Station. 122 p.

Keyes, C.R.; O'Hara, K.L. 2002. Quantifying stand targets for silvicultural prevention of crown fires. Western Journal of Applied Forestry. 17(2): 101-109.

Koehler, J.T. 1993. Prescribed burning: a wildfire prevention tool? Fire Management Notes. 53-54(4): 9-13.

Martin, R.E.; Kauffman, J.B.; Landsberg, J.D. 1989. Use of prescribed fire to reduce wildfire potential. In: Berg, N.H., tech. coord. Proceedings of the symposium on fire and watershed management. Gen. Tech. Rep. PSW-109. Albany, CA: U.S. Department of Agriculture, Forest Service, Pacific Southwest Research Station: 17-22.

Minnich, R.A.; Chou, Y.H. 1997. Wildland fire patch dynamics in the chaparral of southern California and northern Baja California. International Journal of Wildland Fire. 7: 221-248.

Mladenoff, D.; He, H.S. 1999. Design, behavior and application of LANDIS, an object-oriented model of forest landscape disturbance and succession. In: Mladenoff, D.J.; Baker, W.L., eds. Spatial modeling of forest landscape change: approaches and applications. Cambridge, United Kingdom: Cambridge University Press: 125-162.

Moser, T.J. 1991. Shortest path calculation of seismic rays. Geophysics. 56(1): 59-67.

Omi, P.N. 1996. Landscape-level fuel manipulations in Greater Yellowstone: opportunities and challenges. In: Greenlee, J., ed. The ecological implications of fire in Greater Yellowstone. Proceedings of the 2nd biennial conference on the Greater Yellowstone ecosystem. Fairfax, VA: International Association of Wildland Fire, USA: 7-14.

Omi, P.N.; Kalabokidis, K.D. 1998. Fuels modification to reduce large fire probability. In: Viegas, D.X., ed. 3rd international conference on forest and fire research and 14th conference on fire and forest meteorology. Industrial, Portugal: ADAI–Associacao para o Desenvolvimento da Aerodinamica: 2073-2088. Vol 2.

Parsons, D.J.; van Wagtendonk, J.W. 1996. Fire research and management in the Sierra Nevada. In: Halvorson, W.L.; Davis, G.E., eds. Science and ecosystem management in the national parks. Tucson, AZ: University of Arizona Press: 25-48 Chapter 3.

Pollet, J.; Omi, P.N. 2002. Effect of thinning and prescribed burning on crown fire severity in ponderosa pine forests. International Journal of Wildland Fire. 11(1): 1-10.

Pyne, S.J.; Andrews, P.L.; Laven, R.D. 1996. Introduction to wildand fire. 2nd ed. New York: John Wiley and Sons, Inc. 769 p.

Richards, G.D. 1990. An elliptical growth model of forest fire fronts and its numerical solution. International Journal of Numerical Methods in Engineering. 30: 1163-1179.

Salazar, L.A.; Gonzalez-Caban, A. 1987. Spatial relationship of a wildfire, fuelbreaks, and recently burned areas. Western Journal of Applied Forestry. 2(2): 55-58.

Sanderlin, J.C.; Van Gelder, R.J. 1977. A simulation of fire behavior and suppression effectiveness for operation support in wildland fire management. In: Proceedings of the 1st international conference on mathematical modeling. St. Louis, MO: [Publisher unknown]: 619-630.

Scott, J.H.; Reinhardt, E.D. 2001. Assessing crown fire potential by linking models of surface and crown fire behavior. Res. Pap. RMRS-RP-29. Fort Collins, CO: U.S. Department of Agriculture, Forest Service, Rocky Mountain Research Station. 59 p.

Sessions, J.; Johnson, K.N.; Franklin, J.F.; Gabriel, J.T. 1999. Achieving sustainable forest structures on fire-prone landscapes while pursuing multiple goals. In: Mladenoff, D.J.; Baker, W.L., eds. Spatial modeling of forest landscape change: approaches and applications. Cambridge, United Kingdom: Cambridge University Press: 210-255.

Sessons, J.; Johnson, K.N.; Sapsis, D. [et al.]. 1996. Methodology for simulating forest growth, fire effects, timber harvest, and watershed disturbance under different management regimes. In: Sierra Nevada Ecosystem Project; final report to Congress. Addendum. Davis, CA: University of California, Centers for Water and Wildland Resources: [Pages unknown].

Snyder, S.; ReVelle, C. 1996. The grid packing problem: selecting a harvesting pattern in an area with forbidden regions. Forest Science. 42(1): 27-34.

Thompson, W.A.; Vertinsky, I.; Schreier, H.; Blackwell, B.A. 2000. Using forest fire hazard modeling in multiple use forest management planning. Forest Ecology and Management. 134: 163-176.

van Wagtendonk, J.W. 1995. Large fires in wilderness areas. Gen. Tech. Rep. INT-GTR-320. In: Brown, J.K.; Mutch, R.W.; Spoon, C.W.; Wakimoto, R.H., tech. coords. Proceedings: symposium on fire in wilderness and park management. Odgen, UT: U.S. Department of Agriculture, Forest Service, Intermountain Research Station: 113-116.

van Wagtendonk, J.W. 1996. Use of a deterministic fire growth model to test fuel treatments. In: Sierra Nevada Ecosystem Project; final report to Congress. Assessments and scientific basis for management options. Davis, CA: University of California, Centers for Water and Wildland Resources: 1155-1165. Vol. 2.

Weatherspoon, C.P.; Skinner, C.N. 1996. Landscape-level strategies for forest fuel management. In: Sierra Nevada Ecosystem Project; final report to Congress. Assessments and scientific basis for management options. Davis, CA: University of California, Centers for Water and Wildland Resources: 1471-1492. Vol 2.

Wilson, J.S.; Baker, P.J. 1998. Mitigating fire risk to late-successional forest reserves on the east slope of the Washington Cascade Range, USA. Forest Ecology and Management. 110: 59-75.

Chapter 10: Connection to Local Communities

Gary J. Lettman and Jeffrey D. Kline[1]

Abstract

The socioeconomic health of La Grande and other northeastern Oregon communities traditionally has been linked to the region's forests, which have provided economic activity related to timber outputs as well as recreation and other nontimber values. Forest management changes within the Interior Northwest Landscape Analysis System (INLAS) project area can affect socioeconomic changes in the region. This research will evaluate the regional economic impacts of current and alternative forest management alternatives implemented within the INLAS project area and describe prevailing attitudes and values toward forestry and forest management among the region's residents. The research will contribute to understanding the socioeconomic consequences of current and alternative forest management scenarios and can assist forest managers and policymakers in identifying potential compatibilities regarding joint production of multiple timber and nontimber forest outputs.

Keywords: Forest economics, input/output models, local economies, eastern Oregon.

Overview

The socioeconomic health of La Grande and other northeastern Oregon communities traditionally has been linked to the region's forests. Historically, lumber and wood products industries contributed significantly to the region's economic base. More recently, other forest resource-based industries, such as recreation and tourism, also have been recognized as important contributors to local economies. However, a two-thirds reduction in timber harvests in eastern Oregon (Oregon Department of Forestry 2001), coupled with poor economic conditions for the region's agriculture (Barney and Worth 2001), has led to increased concerns regarding the socioeconomic health of northeastern Oregon's communities. Current county-level unemployment rates in the region are between 8 and 16 percent (Bureau of Labor Statistics 2002). Alternative forest management scenarios could alter forest conditions and resource outputs in ways that result in both economic impacts to communities economically dependent on forestry activities, as well as

[1] **Gary J. Lettman** is a principa forest economist Oregon Department of Forestry 2600 State Street Sa em OR 97301; and **Jeffrey D. Kline** is a research forester U S Department of Agricu ture Forest Service Pacific Northwest Research Station Forestry Sciences Laboratory 3200 SW Jefferson Way Corva is OR 97331

in quality-of-life impacts that affect residents and visitors who recreate in the region's forests.

Although assessments of alternative forest management practices often have focused on evaluating regional economic impacts resulting from timber outputs, Oregonians also increasingly recognize forests as important cultural resources. Recent population growth coupled with growth of nonforestry economic sectors has reduced the proportion of Oregonians who are directly involved with the economic aspects of forests and forestry (Kline and Armstrong 2001). These and other socioeconomic changes have led to greater environmental orientations toward forests (Schindler et al. 1993, Steel et al. 1994). Recent statewide surveys, for example, suggest that Oregonians place high values on clean air and water, wilderness, and wildlife (Davis et al. 1999). Growing urban populations also can increase demands for outdoor recreation. In another survey, Oregonians cited natural beauty and recreation opportunities as the attributes they most value about living in the state (Oregon Business Council 1993). Similar changes in public values and attitudes toward forests have been observed nationally (Bengston 1994, Davis et al. 1991, Egan and Luloff 2000, Schindler et al. 1993).

How attitudes and values regarding forests might change over time relative to concerns for other issues of regional or statewide interest can reveal the degree to which local communities will trade off forest values of different types with other public objectives. Recent survey data gathered during the ongoing economic turndown, e.g., suggest that Oregonians currently rate economic issues, such as education funding and the recession, as more important than forest management and environmental issues (Davis et al. 2001). Understanding the socioeconomic consequences of current and alternative forest management scenarios in the Interior Northwest Landscape Analysis System (INLAS) project area is important to evaluating resulting regional and statewide impacts. However, understanding Oregonians' attitudes and values regarding forests, and how they change over time, is important to evaluating what range of forest practices and policies will be politically feasible in the future. Together, the two types of information provide a socioeconomic context for evaluating what forest management alternatives are appropriate and can assist managers and policymakers in identifying potential compatibilities regarding joint production of multiple forest outputs.

Objectives

The objectives of this research are to (1) build and calibrate economic impact models for state, county, and local economies to analyze the economic effects of current and alternative forest management scenarios; and (2) describe attitudes and values among the region's residents toward forests and forest management and consider what changes in these might mean for public forest management and policy in the future.

Research Approach

The planned research involves two principal tasks: (1) evaluate the economic impacts of alternative forest management scenarios and (2) describe and examine public attitudes and values toward forests.

Evaluate Economic Impacts

The economic impacts of alternative forest management scenarios will be examined by using output data describing the volume of timber and other forest commodities produced under different scenarios as input data into economic models describing local and regional economic activity. Harvested timber volume and other forest commodity measures will be estimated from tree lists data produced by INLAS vegetation models at each modeling interval. The analysis will describe community and regional economic impacts resulting from different levels of timber volume and other forest commodities produced under the alternative INLAS forest management scenarios tested.

Two types of economic models could be used to examine the economic impacts of current and alternative forest management scenarios. The first is a commercially available economic modeling system such as the Impact Analysis for Planning (IMPLAN) social accounting and economic impact system (Lindall and Olson 1993). This approach would enable relatively quick and easy development of input/output models, after updating and validating county-level data supplied with the modeling system. Such models provide "snapshots in time" of local economies, and their resulting multipliers can be used to evaluate economic impacts of changes in forest management practices. A disadvantage to using these models is that analyses can be satisfactorily done only at the county level, not for individual communities. Such models also may not fully account for informal economic activity, such as undocumented trade and unreported income, which may be characteristics of some forest-based activities involving recreation and nontimber forest products for example.

A second approach is to develop economic impact models by using community or regional economic surveys. Unlike commercially available modeling systems, survey-based models could be constructed for individual communities of interest. However, their disadvantage is their greater complexity and higher cost. Constructing survey data models involves obtaining data on the impacts of local purchases and sales of each economic sector to demands in all other economic sectors, including imports purchased and exports sold.

The choice between using a commercially available modeling system, such as IMPLAN, versus using a survey-based approach will depend on assessing available funding and staffing resources at the outset relative to information needs of the greater INLAS research effort. The IMPLAN system currently is being used in socioeconomic assessments in Wallowa, Union, and Grant Counties, and opportunities may exist to build on this ongoing work.

Examining Public Attitudes and Values

Analyzing only the short-term impacts of alternative forest management scenarios on local and regional economies, and only in terms of dollar flows, provides an incomplete picture of the socioeconomic effects of different forest management activities on nearby communities. For example, user values for fish and wildlife resources, recreation values for activities like fishing and hiking, and preservation values for the forest are examples of nonfinancial economic values that should be considered in evaluating future management activities. Measuring residents' willingness to pay for biodiversity and other nonmarket values through surveys is beyond the scope of work foreseen for INLAS. However, there are many examples of such analyses in published economics literature (Lettman 2001). These will be reviewed and summarized to illustrate some of the values people may hold for biodiversity and nonmarket forest outputs not generally included in financial-based economic analyses.

Additionally, telephone survey and focus group data already collected for the Oregon Department of Forestry (Davis et al. 2001) will be examined to help improve understanding of the attitudes and values of people in local communities toward forests and natural resource issues, and how these values might change over time. Because the data were collected for seven different regions in Oregon, including northeast Oregon, it will be possible to examine attitudes and values toward forest and natural resource management issues at the regional level and to compare regional and statewide focus group and survey results. In particular, survey results will be summarized for the northeast Oregon counties of Baker, Grant, Umatilla, Union, and Wallowa, and compared to results statewide.

The review and summary of public attitudes and values will not be linked directly to other INLAS models. Rather, they will provide background information describing the social context in which forest management and policy decisions are made.

Products and Users

The research will produce analyses of the regional economic impacts of alternative forest management scenarios and describe public attitudes and values toward forests. In particular, the economic impact analyses will produce economic impact multipliers and other quantitative results, whereas the examination of public attitudes and values will produce qualitative literature reviews, survey results, and other descriptive information. Specific products will include two reports: one report describing the regional economic impacts of current and alternative forest management and fire planning scenarios, as well as the technical aspects of the economic impact approaches taken; and one report describing public values and attitudes toward forests and forest management, which form the socioeconomic context in which management and policymaking will take place. Users of the information produced by this research will include the Governor of Oregon, the Oregon Departments of Forestry and Economic and Community Development, local community officials, national forest planners, and others concerned with the impacts of forest management on economic development and community stability.

Literature Cited

Barney and Worth, Inc. 2001. Inland Northwest economic adjustment strategy, 2001. Olympia, WA: Washington Department of Community, Trade, and Economic Development. 74 p.

Bengston, D.N. 1994. Changing forest values and ecosystem management. Society and Natural Resources. 7(6): 515-533.

Bureau of Labor Statistics. 2002. Local area unemployment statistics. Washington, DC. http://www.bls.gov/. (27 June 2003).

Davis, A.; Hibbits, T.; McCaig, P. 1999. Oregonians discuss forest values, management goals and related issues. Portland, OR: Forest Resources Institute. 19 p.

Davis, A.; Hibbits, T.; McCaig, P. 2001. A forestry program for Oregon: Oregonians discuss their options on forest management and sustainability. Portland, OR: Davis, Hibbitts and McCaig, Inc. 72 p.

Davis, L.S.; Ruth, L.W.; Teeguarden, D.; Henly, R.K. 1991. Ballot box forestry. Journal of Forestry. 89(12): 10-18.

Egan, A.F.; Luloff, A.E. 2000. The exurbanization of America's forests: research in rural social science. Journal of Forestry. 98(3): 26-30.

Kline, J.D.; Armstrong, C. 2001. Autopsy of a forestry ballot initiative: characterizing voter support for Oregon's Measure 64. Journal of Forestry. 99(5): 20-27.

Lettman, G.J., coord. 2001. Elliott State Forest management plan revision: connection to state and local economies. Salem, OR: Oregon Department of Forestry. 158 p.

Lindall, S.A.; Olson, D.C. 1993. Micro IMPLAN user's guide: version 91-F. Stillwater, MN: Minnesota IMPLAN Group, Inc. 417 p.

Oregon Business Council. 1993. Oregon values and beliefs: summary. Portland, OR: 39 p.

Oregon Department of Forestry. 2001. Oregon timber harvest reports, 1990-2000. Salem, OR. 3 p.

Schindler, B.; List, P.; Steel, B.S. 1993. Managing federal forests: public attitudes in Oregon and nationwide. Journal of Forestry. 91(7): 36-42.

Steel, B.S.; List, P.; Shindler, B. 1994. Conflicting values about federal forests: a comparison of national and Oregon publics. Society and Natural Resources. 7(2): 137-153.

Chapter 11: Conflicts and Opportunities in Natural Resource Management: Concepts, Tools, and Information for Assessing Values and Places Important to People

Roger N. Clark[1]

Abstract

The world today, in general, and natural resource management, in particular, seem to be about ever-increasing conflicts. As human populations grow, diversify, and move about the landscape, concerns mount about the impacts of people on water, forests, fish, wild-life, and other people. Strategies for resolving these impacts often result in polarized, either-or remedies, which lead to land use restrictions or closures. Controversy grows as people feel inappropriately excluded from areas and places they have used for years if not generations. In this paper, a number of concepts and approaches are briefly described for identifying and evaluating the values and places important to people. The work proposed as part of the Interior Northwest Landscape Analysis System project focuses on human population dynamics and the relationship between human uses and values and natural resources, with recreation used as a case example. This information, if used in the context of integrated planning, management, and research should help to develop and implement strategies for sustaining a more diverse array of biophysical and social options at multiple spatial and temporal scales.

Keywords: Recreation, integration, resource conflicts, population dynamics.

Introduction

The past 50 years have seen continuing and emerging conflicts in what people value and how they wish to use natural resources (Allen and Gould 1986). As our population grows and diversifies, demands on forests and other natural resources increase. Alarms are sounded from many quarters about the negative effects of people on a variety of values that accrue from public and private lands. Also as scientific information expands, new questions arise about the interactions (both positive and negative) between people and

[1] **Roger N. Clark** is a research socia scientist U S Department of Agricu ture Forest Service Pacific Northwest Research Station Pacific Wi d and Fire Sciences Laboratory 400 N 34th St Suite 201 Seatt e WA 98103

the natural resources upon which we depend for our survival and lifestyles. Just how real these problems are is subject to debate. Opposing interest groups' perspectives, concerns about the ideological positions of managers and scientists, and conflicting data make the public even more skeptical about who can be trusted to deal with the complex problems we face.

Many people are dissatisfied with how decisions are made about management of lands they care about (Wondolleck 1988, Wondolleck and Yaffee 2000). Management of roads and trails, riparian areas, and threatened and endangered species increasingly leads to difficult problems where the perception often prevails that **people must go**. This perception can lead to restrictions and closures that limit public access to resources such as valued places for recreation. Taking care of one system (i.e., social, biophysical, or economic) often leads to disenfranchising another. Polarization leads to either-or solutions to complex problems. This often leads to less than optimal solutions with clear winners and losers. Better ways are needed to identify not only the conflicts but also the compatibilities between biophysical and social values and uses. Many have argued that until we embrace people as being a part of ecosystems, rather than apart from, we will continue to breed conflict rather than accommodation (Clark et al. 1999).

Conflicts regarding forest values typically involve the interaction among three key elements: **people** (their distribution, values, organization, and behavior), **places** (both the geographic and symbolic sense), and **processes** (both ecological processes as well as human activities and institutions that affect people, places, and their interactions) (Stankey and Clark 1992). As we seek to better understand these conflicts and to more effectively fashion solutions that prevent or at least mitigate them, it is important that we understand how different management programs will affect each element. Conversely, we need to understand how changes in these elements can affect management programs. For example, how do changes in forest conditions affect employment opportunities in rural communities or the availability of recreation sites? How do changes in local populations or land use rules affect adjacent forests and forest management activities?

The work described in this paper focuses on ways to better understand the relationship between people and natural resources. What people value, their perspectives and perceptions, and what they actually do and where they do it must be considered. Approaches, tools, and information are needed to help managers, scientists, and citizens work through problem framing and problemsolving to identify and implement options that are less polarizing than at present (Wondolleck 1988; Yankelovich 1991, 1999).

The Interior Northwest Landscape Analysis System (INLAS) project is intended to assemble and apply concepts, frameworks, models, and other tools to enable resource managers to address complex biophysical and social values and uses at multiple scales. Some concepts and tools already exist, whereas others are needed to enable scientists and managers to better understand what concerns people have and how they can be better included in planning and management processes.

The work described in this paper will address three components: (1) What frameworks and concepts exist that can be applied to understand the relations between human concerns, values, and uses and biophysical conditions and processes? (2) What changes are occurring in the human population and what significance might that have for use and management of the area? and (3) How can places that are important to people for things such as recreation be identified, described, and evaluated with respect to other biophysical resources and uses?

Component 1: Frameworks and Concepts

There are various frameworks and concepts that provide ways to identify, understand, and evaluate the values and places important to people and how these interact with other resources. Several such concepts that seem to have value for the INLAS project are briefly described here.

Interactions and Integration

Periodically, particular words and phrases take on a special if uncertain significance to people. Integration is one such example. It is used in many circles and implies certain conditions or actions to those who use it. In research, we frequently cite the need for "better integration," or the desire for "integrated approaches" or "integrated teams." Nevertheless, exactly what makes something integrated remains elusive. In the absence of some clarity about and shared expectations for what we expect from integration, we run the risk of perpetuating another round of confusing rhetoric and meaningless slogans best suited to bumper stickers (Clark et al. 1999).

A more holistic understanding about human-natural resource interactions is needed. Such understanding will provide the foundation for developing and implementing integrated resource management programs and practices. There are many reasons why integrated approaches are increasingly desired.

- **The world is complex**. Either-or approaches are no longer tenable and can be unnecessarily divisive (owls vs. jobs, timber vs. recreation, fish vs. dams, riparian restoration vs. public access or recreation use). We need to embrace a wide range of values and uses to find ways to reject either-or solutions to complex problems. To understand multifaceted systems, we need models and approaches that allow us to isolate and explain the interactions within and among its parts. As we attend to biological and physical factors, we also must deal with the social, cultural, economic and institutional aspects of environmental values and uses. However, these things cannot only be considered after the fact as add-ons or things to mitigate for or against.

- **Substantive areas (basic processes, problems, issues, policies) require it**. Integrated approaches are about complex processes, connections, and inter-relationships. Stewardship and sustainability involve relationships between people, their environments, and processes that link them. Disciplinary, fragmented research (even if in sum all the parts are included) does not add up to understanding the complexity of the whole.

- **Traditional institutions often fragment rather than unite**. Such institutional behavior exists in education, management, and research organizations. Diverse perspectives are valid, and if we can tie them together, we will reveal new knowledge and provide answers to complex questions facing society.

This project focuses on improving understanding of how systems (biophysical, ecological, human) interact and the effects one has on the other. Lack of such knowledge leads to loss of options as a **tyranny of small decisions** are made to resolve perceived problems as conflicts occur between the biophysical and social systems. Ideology rather than science often guides such decisions. Past research and development have generally been disciplinary where experts start from world views, beliefs, etc. within like disciplines. We have an opportunity to better understand how these complex systems function together. This will lead to better understanding of when, where, and how multiple uses can be allowed without unacceptable adverse effects of one on the other.

For example, the recreation resource is unusual because it represents the combination of most, if not all, physical and biological resources and their management. Past management has tended to focus primarily on recreation and other public uses apart from all other resources. Expanding recreational and other opportunities for the public and addressing potential conflicts require an improved understanding of the complex system of which recreation is a part (Clark 1987).

There are various questions to be addressed regarding the interactions between people and natural resource values and uses. The basic question is under what conditions can public access and use of high-quality recreation settings and sites be provided without adverse effects on biophysical conditions and functions such as in riparian areas? To understand this, we need to better appreciate how these systems interact. How do these interactions vary at different spatial and temporal scales? What is acceptable both from a biophysical and social perspective? Moreover, we need improved frameworks and knowledge about the cumulative effects on and from recreation use and management, as well as on and from riparian use and management (Clark and Gibbons 1991).

Problem Framing Is a Critical First Step and Must Be Ongoing

Inadequately framed problems are a major obstacle to designing successful projects to better understand human-natural resource interactions (Bardwell 1991; Clark et al. 1999, in press; Senge 1990). Several things that might be considered to improve effective problem framing are briefly described below.

It is important not to commit to a particular direction until one gets the questions right. This means that we need to step back from individual or disciplinary definitions and join with other interests to ensure that we are not solving the "wrong" problem. We must learn from one another about how we define landscapes so that we can jointly determine opportunities and redefine problems and then develop explicit questions to drive joint actions.

To be effective, problem framing and resolution must include diverse perspectives and value systems. Because landscape values and meanings are highly variable, there is no "correct" definition. Although this suggests that diversity may be an obstacle, it may be an opportunity as well. What can unite us is recognition of the power of both individual and collective perspectives. Processes that are inclusive increase the possibility of improved understanding, greater representativeness in public participation, an opportunity to learn, and eventually identifying better ways to get desired outcomes (Wondolleck 1988).

A number of things make designing and implementing integrated approaches hard to do (Clark et al. 1999, in press). Ideologies and beliefs (world views) condition how we think and act (Socolow 1976). Such ways of thinking can become problematic if not dealt with constructively, but can enrich dialogue and problemsolving if embraced upfront. Striving to get answers and solutions before clarifying the questions and problems often derails the best intended efforts (Bardwell 1991). Scientific language and expertise make it difficult for interested citizens to easily engage in processes and activities that affect them. Technology can be a means to desired ends but can be a hindrance if the wrong questions are under study.

Problem framing is difficult and often inadequate to identify new questions and understanding. A major challenge is to understand the needs and questions to be addressed before lines are drawn on maps and data collection started. Such problem framing is the most important, yet least well-done step, particularly if all interested parties are not included up front. Problem framing must account for the world views and ideologies people have, or these will limit or preclude effectiveness in the longer run. Problem framing must be iterative and adaptive; it takes time and patience. If done well, clear and shared expectations will result.

To be effective, problem framing must account for diverse ways of knowing and diverse forms of knowledge. In this sense, scientific knowledge is only one component. It is necessary but not sufficient for understanding relationships between biophysical and social systems.

Landscapes Are in the Eye of the Beholder[2]

A central problem facing INLAS is to determine the scale of an area to understand the people-resource interactions (Clark et al. 1999, Jensen and Bourgeron 2001). Landscapes such as that represented by INLAS, and places within them, have meanings to people at every conceivable scale. Which is the "right" scale depends (Clark et al., in press). It takes on a different meaning for people who live in the region or beyond vs. those who live nearby. It differs for people who may care about but never visit the area. And for people who actually set foot on the land and visit the area, there may be strong attachments to particular places. The appropriate scale from a human perspective may not match nicely with biophysical considerations, at least within present planning and scientific approaches.

There is no one right definition for what a landscape is or the scale(s) appropriate for understanding relationships between humans and natural resources. Various needs and questions will define the appropriateness of landscape meanings and scales of analysis. Sometimes these needs are defined by scientists, and at other times by resource managers, and at still others by citizens. Technical definitions are important for technical analyses but not necessarily important to everyone; they often are a means to unclear ends.

In a sense, the meanings that landscapes hold are determined by those viewing the landscape or by interacting with it in other ways. Each meaning is different, not better or worse. To fully understand the values and meanings landscapes produce requires that analyses be inclusive of the people that interact with the landscape in diverse ways.

People think and act at multiple scales for many reasons (Stankey and Clark 1992). There is no one way to divide time and space that will account for the multiple values, concerns, and uses that people bring to the understanding of natural resources. Some ways to think about how landscapes can be considered from a social science perspective are briefly described below.

- **A suite of values is of importance to people**. There are a number of values that are important to people as they think about and use forests and other landscapes. These include commodity, public use, amenity, environmental quality, spiritual, and health values. Such values are attached to landscapes by different types of people and at different scales. For example, recreation can be thought of as people using microsites such as campsites or as driving for pleasure across larger landscapes. Moreover, the array of values often blends biophysical, economic, and social domains in different combinations across space, people, and time. This means that to understand the meaning and importance of these values requires expertise beyond the biophysical sciences.

---

[2] This section is adapted from Clark et al. (in press) and Stankey and Clark (1992)

- **People organize in many ways**. There are a variety of ways to think about how people (individuals) are combined at different scales and how a social organizational hierarchy can be described. These include individuals, family and household groups, neighborhoods, communities, counties/boroughs, states/provinces, nations, and ultimately, the globe. The interests people hold in the landscape at different scales and the decisions they make about how they interact with the landscape may cut across these different levels. Each level or scale is characterized by different emergent properties, such that the next higher scale is not simply an aggregation of the units at the next lower scale. There are often mismatches between these organizational units and biophysical scales that will need to be reconciled before any analysis begins if an integrated solution is desired.

- **People act at multiple spatial scales**. These include microsites, areas (e.g., a grove of trees, meadows), drainages, watersheds, landscapes (e.g., the Upper Grande Ronde), regions (e.g., the Blue Mountains), continents, and the globe. It is important to consider such ways of defining scales because different social, cultural, and institutional properties may emerge at each scale. Appropriate scales may be defined by the processes at work, interactions within and between components of complex biophysical and social systems, and policy and scientific needs.

- **Human lives and activities consider multiple temporal scales**. Ways of defining time include the past, today, tomorrow, weeks, seasons, years, decades, and generations. These may or may not coincide with how time is considered by specialists concerned with biophysical phenomena. Differences between biological and social scales of significance are frequently at the root of conflict—such as when forest plans are considered over a 50-year timeframe but budgets are appropriated annually. Considerations of time often influence how acceptable people believe forest management practices to be. Who can wait, e.g., for newly harvested forests to become old growth when people only live for a few decades?

- **Beware the ecological fallacy when drawing conclusions about people**. Meanings cannot simply be aggregated upward; people may define an entire watershed as a suitable place for timber harvesting, yet hold claims to spiritual, aesthetic, and recreational meanings at the site level. What may be true at a higher scale, such as the county level, may not be so at lower scales, such as the communities in the county; the attributes of a transportation system may not apply to the individual roads within; qualities of a dispersed recreation area may differ when one looks at specific sites; and the distribution of meanings across a landscape cannot necessarily be summed to arrive at an overall assignment of landscape meanings. It is likely in many cases that different processes work at different scales. The perspectives people have when they think at different scales influence judgments about the appropriateness and acceptability of change. In addition, what may be acceptable at one scale may not be so at another.

Habitats for People

In the INLAS project, recreation will be used as a case example for understanding the relationship between human uses and values and other resource uses and values. Recreation was chosen because of manager interest and the existence of methods for identifying recreation places people use.

Many of the concepts from the wildlife habitat literature (Thomas 1979) apply to recreation (Clark 1987, 1988). Several of these might be considered when managing for recreation habitats. Understanding these concepts could help managers evaluate the potential effects of alternative strategies and prescriptions on recreational opportunities (Clark and Stankey 1979).

142

- People have "home ranges." Resident populations tend to center recreation in the community; other users are migratory (tourists) and frequent sites well beyond their home ranges. The size of the home range is influenced by the relative availability of recreational opportunities desired by the population, competition among users for these opportunities, and mode and duration of travel.

- People use definable "travel corridors." Natural topographic features and human-created corridors channel air, water, critters, and people. The intersection of corridors (water crossings, power corridors, dams) or flows within them often reveals conflicts and compatibilities between public values and uses and other resource values. Access in general is constrained by travel routes (roads and trails) and by physical-biological conditions, such as steep slopes, dense vegetation, and bodies of water. Knowledge of present and potential travel corridors should help predict the effects of management practices on recreational use patterns.

- People are "territorial." They form strong attachments to favorite and often-visited places and usually do not wish to see them changed. It is important to identify the location and characteristics of such sites before any on-the-ground management occurs.

- "Hiding cover" is particularly important at campsites. People generally want privacy and quiet, and they try to separate themselves from other parties and from evidence of other resource uses. This seems to be as true for people in moderately developed areas as it is for people who prefer dispersed settings and wilderness.

- "Critical habitat" might be defined as a combination of attributes considered absolutely necessary for some types of recreation values and uses.

- "Edges" seem to influence recreational use. For example, sites near natural or artificial openings and riparian and coastal areas all appear to be used more frequently than other locations.

- People like "diversity" in the sites they visit and the activities they engage in.

- Site "preferences" may differ from actual "requirements." Requirements are elements essential to recreation; preferences add quality to a recreational experience. However, preferences for some people may be requirements for others.

- Habitats are "dynamic," and both natural changes and human-caused disturbances influence the nature of recreational settings. Indeed, the type and location of recreation activities can change with physical alterations. Such change can be managed both spatially and temporally to achieve desired goals.

- "Adaptation" occurs as recreation habitats are changed. Users can choose to stay in such areas and alter their expectations or move on (thus becoming "displaced") if the changes exceed their accepted limits. Although either outcome may be appropriate, the potential consequences of both should be evaluated to avoid destruction of irreplaceable opportunities.

These concepts can help us think about how people relate to landscapes at multiple scales and improve our ability to understand the effects of policy options and management practices on existing and potential public values and uses.

Settings and Places Important to People

People form strong opinions about places and the characteristics of places at multiple scales. They also are concerned about the appropriateness of resource management uses (in time and space) (Clark and Stankey 1979). Legacies on the land from past management (road management, area closures, timber harvesting) affect judgments in different ways. It is hard for some people to relate to large landscapes when they are concerned about favorite places. Place attributes and meanings (at multiple scales) influence choices people make (Clark and Downing 1985). However, the meanings people attach to specific places, and which define critical habitat needs, are often not correlated with certain types of biogeographical features mapped by biologists.

A variety of factors influence recreation use patterns (Clark 1988). Some of these are described below.

- The places where people choose to recreate are important. Most people tend to have special places they visit repeatedly (Clark et al. 1984). Often these are places people used as children and those where they now take their children. These places may be large landscapes or small sites. Favorite and often-visited sites are definable, and people form strong attachments to them (Clark et al. 1984, Clark and Stankey 1986). In many areas, recreationists have established their own campsites, and they are concerned about the relation between other resource uses and these sites; many want their favorite campsites protected from the effects of logging (or other resource uses) (Clark and Downing 1985, Clark and Stankey 1986, Clark et al. 1984).

- The type of access is the key to most recreation and strongly influences use patterns. For example, as a group, people who recreate in roaded forest lands want roads of various designs and standards, but they do not need to be paved in all cases.

- Site attributes affect, in many often predictable ways, how recreationists make choices (McCool et al. 1985, Stanley and McCool 1985). Some attract (scenery) or detract (bugs and poisonous snakes); some facilitate (road pullouts) or constrain (steep terrain) (Clark and Stankey 1986). Attributes that have been determined to be particularly important in dispersed areas include water (marine, riparian, lakes, streams), trees (of various species, densities, and age), flat areas, naturalness (or natural appearing), and privacy from others not in one's own party (much like wilderness users). Knowledge of these attributes aids in determining what is possible, desirable, or necessary at a particular location to protect, enhance, or create opportunities for recreation.

Recreation (both in terms of our choice of activity and places) often plays a major role in where people choose to live and take vacations. Relatively easy access to diverse natural environments explains why many people have chosen to reside where they do. The forests, lakes, streams, mountains, and all the associated wildlife provide a rich backdrop for the diverse recreation people seek. Special places and favorite activities provide the temporary retreat from pressures at work and at home.

So when managers of public (and in some cases private) lands consider changing what users have known and valued about those special places, users become alarmed. People remember other places that have been lost for one reason or another (Clark and Stankey 1979). Many questions come to mind: What will the changes mean to one's family? How long will it take before one can go there again? Do managers know about the places people like and why they like them? Can favorite places be protected? These and other questions are important because the places people value are more than rock, dirt, and trees that can easily be replaced. They have special meaning that even the best manager cannot easily discern (Downing and Clark 1979).

Acceptability—of What, for Whom, Why

Natural resource management programs are considered to be sustainable when they are ecologically sound, economically feasible, and socially acceptable. Social acceptability is an essential aspect of any successful implementation effort. The social acceptability judgment process is critical to the efforts to manage natural resource systems on an integrated, multiple-value basis. For instance, any given practice is likely evaluated on the basis of potential alternatives as well as the consequences of any given alternative on other resources, values, and benefits. If a proposal to limit public access to riparian corridors, e.g., is presented solely as a means of restoring aquatic habitat, some particular patterns of acceptability will emerge. However, if the proposal also includes the impacts such closures will have on historical recreation, then it is likely that some other pattern of acceptability will emerge. At present, such multiresource issues typically lack full consideration of social acceptability assessments, with the result that public opposition increases.

Understanding is limited about the factors affecting the formation of acceptability judgments, their resistance to change, and the conditions that lead to change. A conventional premise is that public judgments are primarily influenced by the level and accuracy of the technical and scientific information held by different citizen interests, or that they are predominantly the reflection of adverse aesthetic judgments. Existing research on social acceptability indicates that judgments are the product of a complex, multifaceted, and dynamic process, of which information—in the technical-scientific sense—or aesthetic appearances are only a part. The judgment formation process is greatly affected by the belief systems of individuals. In addition, the trust associated with individuals or organizations making decisions can have a major effect on what is and is not acceptable.

The nature and extent of change acceptable to recreationists and other forest users differs (Clark and Stankey 1979; Stankey et al. 1985, 2003). People seem to have different expectations for "macro" versus "micro" sites, and the microsite seems more susceptible to adverse change; i.e., management activities acceptable in the general area (such as evidence of logging or roads or restoration activities) may be considered intolerable at a campsite.

Acceptance of change varies both in time and space and depends on many factors (Kakoyannis et al. 2001, Shindler et al. 2002). Judgments about the acceptability of change depend on its nature, extent, cause, and location with respect to specific areas, the meanings people attach to landscapes at different scales, and places people value.

The research community has a significant role in helping create a more socially acceptable brand of forest management. Not that there is an insufficient amount of either theoretical research or applied research already to draw from. What is in short supply, however, is (1) well-defined, manager-friendly frameworks for conducting more socially acceptable processes and (2) the institutional will (i.e., commitment, time, and resources) for experimentation and implementation (Shindler et al. 2002).

Component 2: Population Dynamics[3]

The Pacific Northwest is experiencing rapid and far-reaching population changes (McCool et al. 1997). Population growth and redistribution affect both urban and rural areas. Accompanying this growth and change is a climate of increasing conflict over the region's once-abundant natural resources. Much of this conflict centers on changing societal values and expectations regarding the things public lands should produce (McGranahan 1999). Moreover, there is increased competition for the commodities, amenities, and recreational opportunities provided by those public lands.

Given this dynamic and challenging context, it is important to understand both how the population is changing and the potential implications these changes have for the management of forest lands in the Pacific Northwest (Troy 1998). As certain communities shift from rural to suburban or urban, what changes are likely to occur in attitudes and public uses regarding natural resource issues? What are the factors that are driving migration from urban to rural areas? Are the motivations for in-migration to rural communities driven by economic concerns or by the amenities of small towns and natural resources?

The fundamental concept driving the analysis of population dynamics is that changes in the makeup of human populations will be accompanied by changes in the attitudes and uses of residents toward the management of forest lands whether public or private. In addition, these changing attitudes and uses will have a profound influence on the actions of management agencies. Making the connection between attitudes, public uses, and changing social conditions will help managers respond to and anticipate the needs of local and regional residents. Ultimately this type of knowledge can help managers respond to challenges and opportunities at various geographic scales and for various user groups.

This assessment will provide a detailed description of the population dynamics in the region and selected areas such as INLAS. Ways to understand, articulate, and display the multiple and interrelated changes occurring within the region will be explored. Data from sources such as the U.S. Census and Internal Revenue Service will be used to develop graphical and interaction-oriented approaches to describe the population dynamics. Adopting this approach will allow for an analysis of the factors driving more localized changes as well as an examination of how local areas might influence and be influenced by regional population dynamics. The graphical approach will enhance our ability to engage in a broader dialogue regarding the nature of these changes.

Beyond a basic description, there is a need to address why the observed changes matter. Thus, a second focus will produce a series of propositions regarding how the changing character of the region's population may influence shifts in acceptability of forest management practices. Making this link between population dynamics, public uses, and attitudes will require the use of existing data as well as the possible collection of new information on resident attitudes toward natural resource management if time allows. This second product also will involve a focused examination of specific subregions within Oregon and Washington, including INLAS. The choice of communities will be made to highlight issues for areas that are currently experiencing rapid change along with those that have relatively slower rates of change.

---

[3] This work is being conducted by Theron Mi er and Steve McCoo at the University of Montana s Schoo of Forestry in conjunction with the author

Population change in rural areas has significant implications for the acceptability of various land management actions (e.g., treatment of fuels, use of fire, and management of wildlife). Where public lands are intermingled with private, rapidly developing lands, there are significant questions about how newly arriving individuals, with potentially different ties to public landscapes than long-term residents, will be attached to these landscapes, and how those attachments may affect acceptability of forest management.

In addition, population growth and redistribution have implications for demand of recreational opportunities provided on public lands. Because the in-migrating population may have characteristics different from existing residents, their patterns of participation in recreation may differ. As a result, the character and distribution of the supply of existing facilities and opportunities may no longer be adequate for the "new" population.

Beyond the benefits to individuals directly involved in management, this type of analysis could help provide an avenue for involvement of community leaders and concerned citizens. The process of understanding the many social changes to an area can facilitate both community learning and assist in efforts of problemsolving.

Component 3: Place–Based Analyses of Recreation Use

As described earlier, knowing the sites people use in forests is important for understanding the potential interactions between this use and other resource values and uses. In this project, we will focus on recreation as one example of human use taking place in the INLAS area.

Recreational uses often compete with timber, wildlife, fisheries, and other resource uses for the same sites (Clark 1988, Clark et al. 1984). An understanding of the relationships between recreation and other uses of forested lands is required for effective multi-resource management. Important questions needing answers include: Who are the visitors of specific areas? What are the activities in which they engage? When do they engage in these activities? Where do they engage in these activities? What site characteristics influence where they go? What are the effects on recreation in areas where other resource uses are managed and vice versa? How important are these effects from the perspective of the public and land managers? What concepts, frameworks, and management tools exist or might be developed to help mitigate adverse effects?

Knowing the importance forest visitors attach to particular features of recreational settings (called "site attributes") is the foundation of effective recreation management. Without information about these attributes, land managers cannot maintain or enhance desirable qualities, nor can they prevent or mitigate damage to recreational values as a result of other forest uses, such as timber management. There is a need for a better understanding of what attributes can be avoided and positive effects enhanced. Attributes constitute the features that define an area or site as a recreational resource. Knowing what these attributes are, their relative importance to recreationists participating in different activities or seeking different experiences, and the sensitivity of the attributes to change is essential input to integrated resource management.

Alterations in settings induced by nonrecreational resource uses can greatly change the type of recreational opportunities available. Conversely, maintaining the essential attributes of a particular recreational opportunity setting might represent a significant constraint on other uses. For example, a management objective to maintain semiprimitive or primitive recreation opportunities would limit the nature and extent of timber harvest activities appropriate in the area (Clark and Stankey 1979). Understanding these interdependencies is essential to the integration of different resource allocations and to minimizing conflict (Clark and Gibbons 1991, Clark and Stankey 1986).

We must understand the complex system of which recreation is a part. There remains, however, a lack of comprehensive knowledge and site-specific guidelines to facilitate effective integration of recreation and other resource uses at multiple temporal and spatial scales. Part of the problem is the limitation of knowledge about just where people go and what the characteristics are of those places. In this project, the author and colleagues developed and applied methods for several watersheds in eastern Washington that will be used to locate and characterize sites used by the public in parts of the INLAS area.

This assessment of places that people use will include:

• Locate specific places along formal and informal roads in several subareas of the INLAS project area where there is trace evidence of public use (including but not limited to recreation).

• Use a global positioning system to establish the location of sites identified.

• Complete a written description of the sites.

• Take photos that can be used to classify the site and its surroundings (at the microlevel and macrolevel).

• Describe and document the relationship between the sites identified and evidence of resource management activities.

• Create geographical information system data layers to allow analysis of the interrelationships between public use and other forest values and uses and forest management activities.

Knowledge of important recreation sites and their attributes will assist managers in evaluating the consequences of changes because of other resource uses on dispersed recreation opportunities (Brown et al. 1978, Clark and Stankey 1986). Such information will aid in developing strategies to prevent or mitigate undesirable impacts on biophysical resources while taking advantage of positive changes to provide a desired range of public benefits.

Expected Outcomes and Products

This work will provide three major types of products:

• Syntheses of available frameworks and concepts and how they might be used in the context of integrated research and development and management at multiple scales in areas such as INLAS.

• Empirical information about regional and local population migration and a framework to evaluate the potential effects of population changes on places people use and their acceptance of management practices.

• A description of specific places for parts of INLAS that are used by the public. This will be useful as a stand-alone product, but its best use will be in the context of an integrated approach to assessing the interactions between biophysical and social values and uses in areas such as INLAS.

It is yet to be determined how this information will be integrated with other biophysical information.

Users of Information

Both public and private resource policymakers and managers should find the information useful for designing, implementing, and evaluating options at multiple scales. The primary beneficiaries of this research effort will be natural resource managers of federal, state, and private lands. They will benefit from a clearer understanding of the dynamic populations and attitudes within the areas that they operate and the types of places that are important to existing and future populations. This will be particularly helpful for managers in areas currently experiencing rapid population changes and conflicts between human and other uses. Managers in other areas could use the results of this research to anticipate future changes.

The ultimate beneficiary of this information is the public who depends on the resource values and uses provided by areas such as those represented by INLAS.

Conclusions

Whether intended or not, almost all forest management activities affect public values and uses. The effects of management are not necessarily negative and largely depend on people's preferences and expectations. However, effective multiresource management demands an understanding of the interactions among public and other uses.

In addition, changes in human populations have significant implications for the use and management of diverse natural resources. It is not just how many people are leaving the area or moving in but what values and expectations they have for nearby as well as distant forests and rangelands.

Furthermore, it is critical to have detailed, place-based analysis of human and natural resource interactions. Information about public use—the where, who, when, why, and how—enables planning processes to consider human and natural resource interactions at multiple spatial and temporal scales.

From this brief overview, it seems evident that a holistic, systems perspective is needed to help integrate public uses such as recreation with other resources. The recreation resource, in particular, is unusual, compared to some resources, in that it is represented by the combination of all other physical and biological resources and how they are managed. The complex interrelationships among these resources have important implications for recreational opportunities and use (Clark et al. 1984).

The questions posed earlier can be resolved with a more holistic perspective that recognizes the nature of potential onsite interactions between public uses and other resources. Past management has focused primarily on public uses such as recreation apart from other uses. Expanding opportunities for the future and addressing the potential for onsite conflicts and ways to resolve them require an improved understanding of the complex system of which human concerns are an integral part. The overriding question is not whether human values and uses should be integrated with other resource uses, but where, when, and how such integration can be achieved.

It is critical that approaches developed to understand these interactions consider people and their uses at multiple scales. We must begin to make connections between biophysical and human systems, or we will continue to fall victim to extreme, polarized, solutions to resolving complex problems (Clark and Gibbons 1991).

Almost everything resource managers do, whether planned or not, will affect opportunities for the public. People react to this reality as they anticipate or discover undesirable changes in areas and at sites they value. Professionals must be sensitive to how what they do affects people and places people value. Failure to do so could easily lead to further polarization and loss of manager credibility as well as support for agency or landowner programs.

Unfortunately, there are few specific guidelines and little detailed information to facilitate such integration and few tested approaches for managing potentially incompatible uses at specific locations. There are, however, a variety of concepts and frameworks that can be used to address some of the questions listed earlier. These tools will provide aids to help managers, citizens, and scientists work through problemsolving for complex and controversial issues; rarely, however, will they provide definite answers.

Literature Cited

Allen, G.M.; Gould, E.M., Jr. 1986. Complexity, wickedness, and public forests. Journal of Forestry. 84(4): 20-23.

Bardwell, L. 1991. Problem-framing: a perspective on environmental problem-solving. Environmental Management. 15(5): 603-612.

Brown, P.J.; Driver, B.L.; McConnell, C. 1978. The opportunity spectrum concept and behavioral information in outdoor recreation resource supply inventories: background and application. In: Lund, G.H.; LaBau, V.J.; Ffolliott, P.F.; Robinson, D.W., tech. coords. Integrating inventories of renewable natural resources: Proceedings of the workshop. Gen. Tech. Rep. RM-55. Fort Collins, CO: U.S. Department of Agriculture, Forest Service, Rocky Mountain Forest and Range Experiment Station: 73-84.

Clark, R.N. 1987. Recreation management: a question of integration. Western Wildlands. 13(1): 20-23.

Clark, R.N. 1988. Enhancing recreation opportunities in silvicultural planning. In: Schmidt, W.C., comp. Proceedings: future forests of the mountain West: a stand culture symposium. Gen. Tech. Rep. INT-243. Ogden, UT: U.S. Department of Agriculture, Forest Service, Intermountain Forest and Range Experiment Station: 61-69.

Clark, R.N.; Downing, K.B. 1985. Why here and not there: the conditional nature of recreation choice. In: Stankey, G.H.; McCool, S.F., comps. Proceedings, symposium on recreation choice behavior. Gen. Tech. Rep. INT-GTR-184. Ogden, UT: U.S. Department of Agriculture, Forest Service, Intermountain Forest and Range Experiment Station: 61-70.

Clark, R.N.; Gibbons, D.R. 1991. Recreation. In: Meehan, W.R., ed. Influences of forest and rangeland on salmonid fishes and their habitats. Spec. Publ. 19. Bethesda, MD: American Fisheries Society: 459-481. Chapter 13.

Clark, R.N.; Koch, R.W.; Hogans, M.L. [et al.]. 1984. The value of roaded, multiple use areas as recreation sites in three national forests of the Pacific Northwest. Res. Pap. PNW-319. Portland, OR: U.S. Department of Agriculture, Forest Service, Pacific Northwest Forest and Range Experiment Station. 40 p.

Clark, R.N.; Kruger, L.E.; McCool, S.F.; Stankey, G.H. [In press]. Landscape perspectives. Res. Pap. Portland, OR: U.S. Department of Agriculture, Forest Service, Pacific Northwest Research Station.

Clark, R.N.; Stankey, G.H. 1979. The recreation opportunity spectrum: a framework for planning, management, and research. Gen. Tech. Rep. PNW-98. Portland, OR: U.S. Department of Agriculture, Forest Service, Pacific Northwest Forest and Range Experiment Station. 32 p.

Clark, R.N.; Stankey, G.H. 1986. Site attributes—a key to managing wilderness and dispersed recreation. In: Proceedings: national wilderness research conference. Gen. Tech. Rep. GTR-INT-212. Ogden, UT: U.S. Department of Agriculture, Forest Service, Intermountain Research Station: 509-515.

Clark, R.N.; Stankey, G.H.; Brown, P.J. [et al.] 1999. Toward an ecological approach: integrating social, economic, cultural, biological and physical considerations. In: Johnson, N.C.; Malk, A.J.; Sexton, W.T.; Szaro, R., eds. Ecological stewardship: a common reference for ecosystem management. Oxford, United Kingdom: Elsevier Science Ltd. 3: 297-318.

Downing, K.B.; Clark, R.N. 1979. Users' and managers' perceptions of dispersed recreation impacts: a focus on roaded forest lands. In: Ittner, R.; Potter, D.R.; Agee, J.K.; Anschell, S., eds. Recreational impact on wildlands: Proceedings of a conference. Portland, OR: U.S. Department of Agriculture, Forest Service, Pacific Northwest Region; U.S. Department of the Interior, National Park Service, Pacific Northwest Region: 18-23.

Jensen, M.E.; Bourgeron, P.S., eds. 2001. A guidebook for integrated ecological assessments. New York: Springer-Verlag, Inc. 536 p.

Kakoyannis, C.; Shindler, B.; Stankey, G.H. 2001. Understanding the social acceptability of natural resource decisionmaking processes by using a knowledge base modeling approach. Gen. Tech. Rep. PNW-GTR-518. Portland, OR: U.S. Department of Agriculture, Forest Service, Pacific Northwest Research Station. 40 p.

McCool, S.F.; Burchfield, J.A.; Allen, S.D. 1997. Social assessment of the basin. In: Quigley, T.M.; Arbelbide, S.J., tech. eds. An assessment of ecosystem components in the interior Columbia basin and portions of the Klamath and Great Basins. Gen. Tech. Rep. PNW-GTR-405. Portland, OR: U.S. Department of Agriculture, Forest Service, Pacific Northwest Research Station: 1873-2000. Chapter 7. Vol. 4. (Quigley, T.M., tech. ed.; Interior Columbia Basin Ecosystem Management Project: scientific assessment).

McCool, S.F.; Stankey, G.H.; Clark, R.N. 1985. Choosing recreation settings: processes, findings, and research directions. In: Stankey, G.H.; McCool, S.F., comps. Proceedings: symposium on recreation choice behavior. Gen. Tech. Rep. INT-GTR-184. Ogden, UT: U.S. Department of Agriculture, Forest Service, Intermountain Forest and Range Experiment Station: 1-8.

McGranahan, D.A. 1999. Natural amenities drive rural population change. Agric. Econ. Rep. 781. Washington, DC: U.S. Department of Agriculture, Food and Rural Economics Division, Economic Research Service. 24 p.

Senge, P.M. 1990. The fifth discipline: the art and practice of the learning organization. New York: Currency Doubleday. 423 p.

Shindler, B.; Brunson, M.; Stankey, G.H. 2002. Social acceptability of forest conditions and management practices: a problem analysis. Gen. Tech. Rep. PNW-GTR-537. Portland, OR: U.S. Department of Agriculture, Forest Service, Pacific Northwest Research Station. 68 p.

Socolow, R.H. 1976. Failures of discourse: obstacles to the integration of environmental values into natural resource policy. In: Tribe, L.H.; Schelling, C.S.; Voss, J., eds. When values conflict: essays on environmental analysis, discourse, and decision. Cambridge, MA: Ballinger Publication Co.: 1-33.

Stankey, G.H.; Clark, R.N. 1992. Social aspects of new perspectives in forestry: a problem analysis. The Pinchot Institute for Conservation Monograph Series. Milford, PA: Grey Towers Press. 33 p.

Stankey, G.H.; Clark, R.N.; Bliss, J. 2003. Fostering compatible forest resource management: the conditional nature of social acceptability. In: Monserud, R.A.; Haynes, R.W.; Johnson, A.C., eds. Compatible forest management. Dordrecht, The Netherlands: Kluwer Press: 453-480.

Stankey, G.H.; Cole, D.N.; Lucas, R.C. [et al.]. 1985. The limits of acceptable change (LAC) system for wilderness planning. Gen. Tech. Rep. INT-176. Ogden, UT: U.S. Department of Agriculture, Forest Service, Intermountain Forest and Range Experiment Station. 37 p.

Stankey, G.H.; McCool, S.F., comps. 1985. Proceedings: symposium on recreation choice behavior. Gen. Tech. Rep. INT-GTR-184. Ogden, UT: U.S. Department of Agriculture, Forest Service, Intermountain Forest and Range Experiment Station. 106 p.

Thomas, J.W., tech. ed. 1979. Wildlife habitats in managed forests: the Blue Mountains of Oregon and Washington. Agric. Handb. 533. Washington, DC: U.S. Department of Agriculture, Forest Service. 512 p.

Troy, L.R. 1998. Recent human migration to the interior Columbia basin and implications for natural resource management. Missoula, MT: University of Montana. 75 p. M.S. thesis.

Wondolleck, J.M. 1988. Public lands conflict and resolution: managing national forest disputes. New York: Plenum Press. 263 p.

Wondolleck, J.M.; Yaffee, S.L. 2000. Making collaboration work: lessons from innovation in natural resource management. Washington, DC: Island Press. 277 p.

Yankelovich, D. 1991. Coming to public judgment: making democracy work in a complex world. Syracuse, NY: Syracuse University Press. 290 p.

Yankelovich, D. 1999. The magic of dialogue: transforming conflict into cooperation. New York: Simon and Schuster. 236 p.

Chapter 12: Analysis and Modeling of Forest-Land Development at the Wildland/Urban Interface

Jeffrey D. Kline[1]

Abstract

Population growth and resulting land use changes are becoming increasingly important factors in forest management and fire planning as forests are converted to residential and other developed uses. This part of the Interior Northwest Landscape Analysis System (INLAS) project examines low-density residential and other development at the wildland/urban interface in the area surrounding the INLAS project area. The research contributes to an integrated analysis of fire risk by describing where humans are located on the forest landscape, how they are likely to manage the portion of the landscape they occupy, how the spatial distribution of humans will change in the future, and what their expectations will be regarding forest management and policy and fire planning.

Keywords: Wildland/urban interface, urbanization, land use change.

Overview

Increasingly important factors in forest management and fire planning are population growth and the impacts resulting land use changes can have on forests as they are converted to residential and other developed uses. In-migration of people to rural areas in the Pacific Northwest is resulting in increasing numbers of residences on forest landscapes. Forest-land conversion to developed uses essentially is a permanent change resulting in the interspersion of nonforest land uses with forest, and often fragmenting forest landscapes into smaller parcels of land. These processes can result in longer lasting ecological and economic impacts than forest cutting and fire, where regrowth and succession may overcome temporary loss of forest. Ecological impacts can include direct loss of habitat or changes in habitat quality. Economic impacts can include less intensive forest management for commercial timber resulting in reduced economic output on private lands. Analysis and modeling of existing and potential low-density residential and other development at the wildland/urban interface can anticipate where these

---

[1] **Jeffrey D. Kline** is a research forester U S Department of Agricu ture Forest Service Pacific Northwest Research Station Forestry Sciences Laboratory 3200 SW Jefferson Way Corva is OR 97331

changes are likely to occur in the future. Such research can contribute to an integrated analysis of fire risk by describing where humans are located on the forest landscape, how they are likely to manage the portion of the landscape they occupy, how the spatial distribution of humans will change in the future, and what their expectations will be regarding forest management and policy and fire planning.

A Brief Literature Review

What researchers and policymakers refer to as the wildland/urban interface is characterized by relatively low-density residential and other development on forest landscapes. Researchers and policymakers hypothesize that such development has the potential to increase the threat of wildfire associated with increased human habitation and activity in forests (Lorensen et al. 1993). Many forestry analysts also feel that increasing numbers of residences located in forested landscapes are leading to increasing costs owing to wildfire and overburdening firefighting resources that are redirected to save homes instead of containing fires (Milloy 2000). Along with the potential for increased wildfire threat and increased firefighting costs is the increased potential for significant loss of life and property. The 2001 fire season in the Pacific Northwest provided numerous examples of the particular challenges associated with fighting forest fires near homes (e.g., Cockle 2001, Larabee 2001, Quinn 2001).

In addition to these direct implications for fire planning, low-density residential and other development on forested landscapes can have fewer direct implications regarding forest management. For example, researchers believe that forest lands located within the wildland/urban interface become less productive as a result of their fragmentation into smaller and smaller management units, potentially diminishing the economies of scale in timber production (Row 1978). Forest tract size has been negatively correlated with the likelihood of commercial timber management (Thompson et al. 1981) and the propensity of forest owners to harvest timber (Cleaves and Bennett 1995). Lower harvest rates and less likelihood of commercial timber management also have been correlated with increasing population densities (Barlow et al. 1998, Wear et al. 1999).

As people migrate into forested areas, the characteristics and forest management objectives of newer more urban-minded forest-land owners also may change. It is believed that many nonindustrial private forest-land owners are motivated by amenity, recreation, and other nontimber objectives in addition to or in place of timber production objectives when making forest management decisions (Binkley 1981; Bowes et al. 1984; Dennis 1989, 1990; Englin and Klan 1990; Hyberg and Holthausen 1989; Kuuluvainen et al. 1996; Max and Lehman 1988; Newman and Wear 1993; Strang 1983; Swallow and Wear 1993). Such nontimber objectives have been shown to be important factors motivating nonindustrial private forest-land owners in the Pacific Northwest (Johnson et al. 1997; Kline et al. 2000a, 2000b). Smaller forest tract sizes and changing characteristics of forest-land owners can alter the manner in which private forest lands are managed and affect the potential range of management and policy options available to forest managers and policymakers regarding fire-risk reduction on private forest lands.

A potential secondary impact of development at the wildland/urban interface is overall changes in people's values and attitudes toward forestry. A growing number of social scientists believe that the Nation is experiencing rapid and significant changes in forest values (Bengston 1994) and attitudes concerning forest management (Davis et al. 1991, Schindler et al. 1993). Researchers observe that increasing migration of urbanites to rural areas is resulting in a shift in forest values and a push for forestry policies and practices that reflect changing forest values (Egan and Luloff 2000). Increasing development at the wildland/urban interface may be accompanied by a declining empathy toward timber industries and increasing demands for outdoor recreation and the protection of forest amenities and wildlife. Research suggests that these processes could be taking place in the Pacific Northwest (Kline and Armstrong 2001). Such changes could have implications regarding the political climate in which forest management and policy and fire planning decisions are made.

A common approach to multidisciplinary landscape-level analysis of socioeconomic and ecological processes has been to treat humans largely as exogenous to the forest landscape. Land use change analyses commonly have been used in multidisciplinary studies to delineate discrete forest and nonforest or forest and urban land use categories for integration with other landscape-level models describing socioeconomic and ecosystem processes and conditions (see, e.g., Bockstael 1996, Kline et al. 2001, Turner et al. 1996). Similar discrete treatments of land use can be found in Bradshaw and Muller (1998), Chomitz and Gray (1996), Helmer (2000), and Nelson and Hellerstein (1997). These models generally use spatially referenced land use data to estimate logit or probit regression models describing the timing and location of changes among discrete land use categories.

For many applications, a discrete treatment of land use may be appropriate when the processes under study are relatively insensitive to low levels of human habitation of land. However, in other applications, when socioeconomic and ecological processes may be sensitive to a range of human habitation, discrete land use categories may inadequately characterize the spatial and temporal interactions of humans as agents affecting the landscape-level processes under study. In the case of wildfire threat on forested landscapes, relatively low-density human habitation can be of particular interest. Wear and Bolstad (1998) offer an alternative to discrete land use change analysis by describing the "spatial diffusion" of human populations throughout a landscape. They use data describing building densities to identify explanatory variables useful in predicting building densities. Although Wear and Bolstad (1998) ultimately use their spatial diffusion model to project changes among discrete land use categories, Kline et al. (in press) show that their methods can be adapted to describe potential future building density scenarios that also can serve as inputs into landscape-level models.

Objectives

The objectives of the research are to (1) develop empirical spatial models of low-density residential and other development at the wildland/urban interface for select areas in eastern Oregon, (2) use the empirical models to describe likely future development scenarios based on projections of future population growth and in-migration, and (3) integrate potential future development scenarios with other INLAS submodels describing ecological conditions and processes and fire risk. The research is intended to provide information concerning (1) what socioeconomic and geographic factors have contributed to increased in-migration in eastern Oregon; (2) how these factors have influenced the spatial distribution of people; and (3) how institutional factors, such as land use zoning, have affected that spatial distribution.

Research Approach

Empirical models describing historical and future low-density residential and other development at the wildland/urban interface will be estimated for select areas in eastern Oregon. Model estimation will rely on building density data based on aerial photointerpretation similar to that described in Azuma et al. (1999) for western Oregon. The Oregon Department of Forestry currently is working to gather building density data for eastern Oregon. When available, these data will enable analysis and modeling of building density by using the methods of Wear and Bolstad (1998) and Kline et al. (in press). Empirical models will be estimated describing historical land use or building density changes as a function of socioeconomic and geographic variables. The empirical models will be used to project future building density scenarios based on projected changes in socioeconomic variables, such as population, included in the models. The projections will be used to create geographic information system maps (GIS) describing future building density scenarios, enabling projections to be integrated with other INLAS submodels describing ecological conditions and processes and wildfire threat.

The analytical method will closely follow methods used by Kline et al. (in press) to project potential future building density scenarios for western Oregon as part of the Coastal Landscape Analysis and Modeling Study (CLAMS) (Spies et al. 2002). In that analysis, a negative binomial model was estimated describing the spatial distribution and rate of change in historical building densities in western Oregon as a function of a gravity index of development pressure, existing building densities, slope, elevation, and existing land use zoning. A gravity index was used to describe the spatial proximity of land to existing cities of varying population sizes. The resulting empirical model was used to project pixel-level changes in building densities based on projected future population growth of cities included in the gravity index computation. The projected building density changes were applied to a 1995 building density map to describe the future spatial distributions of buildings for successive modeling periods (fig. 33). The building density maps are key inputs in other socioeconomic and ecological submodels comprising CLAMS.

If historical building density data are not available, analysis and modeling will be accomplished by using existing socioeconomic data available from the U.S. Bureau of the Census and other sources to develop empirical models of human migration (e.g., Amacher et al. 1998, McGranahan 1999, Swanson 1986). Analysis will focus on describing historical spatial variation in population densities and other socioeconomic variables, and in describing potential future changes in the spatial distributions of people across the INLAS study landscape. Landscape-level projections of future spatial distributions of people would be accomplished by simulating future forest-land development scenarios based on existing land use zoning maps and projections of future population (e.g., Bradshaw and Muller 1998, ECONorthwest 2000). Projections of future populations will be obtained from published U.S. Census figures or estimated from in-migration models. This alternative analysis would result in GIS maps describing future population density scenarios, enabling projections to be integrated with other INLAS submodels describing ecological conditions and processes and wildfire threat.

Products

Anticipated products include relatively fine-scale GIS maps of potential future low-density residential and other development at the wildland/urban interface for select regions of eastern Oregon, including the INLAS study area. The maps will be used both as stand-alone products and for integration with other INLAS submodels describing ecological conditions and processes and fire risk. For example, the maps will identify where forest land is most likely to be taken out of active management for timber production, enabling timber production submodels to account for a potentially diminishing forest-land base. The maps also will be used to identify locations within the INLAS study area where wildfire poses the greatest risk of significant loss of life and property, which may have implications for the types and locations of potential management prescriptions proposed and analyzed by INLAS researchers.

In addition to maps of potential low-density development will be descriptive analysis and projections regarding potential changes in the socioeconomic characteristics of the population of eastern Oregon, including the INLAS study area. Analysis will include discussion regarding the potential impacts of socioeconomic change on regional public

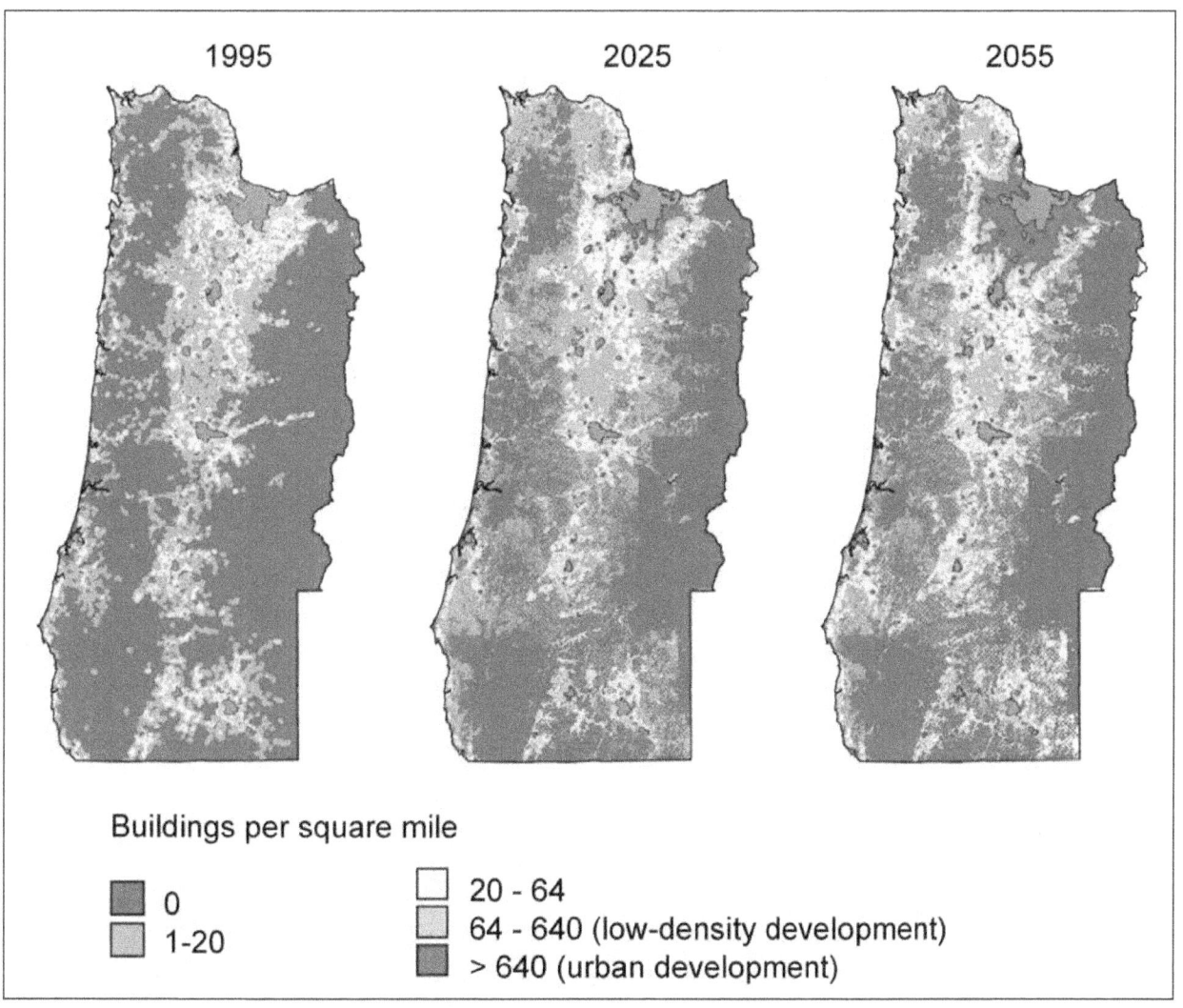

Figure 33   Base year and projected bui ding density categories in western Oregon created for the Coasta Landscape Ana ysis and
Mode ing Study Note: Based on negative binomia mode projections of bui ding density change app ied to 1995 base year map Existing
urban deve opment in 1995 base year shown in gray

demands regarding outdoor recreation and forest amenities, and public perceptions and
attitudes regarding forest management and policy and fire planning goals and strategies.
This analysis would be largely descriptive and contribute to providing the socioeconomic
context in which forest management and policy and fire planning will take place. Other
anticipated products include at least one technical journal article describing the analytical approach and one nontechnical report describing the analysis and its implications for
forest management and policy and fire planning.

Users

The users of the information produced by this research include national forest and land management agencies; state agencies; nonprofit organizations concerned with forests, fire, and land use change; and researchers seeking to integrate land use change information into landscape-level analyses of ecological conditions and processes. Geographic information system maps of potential future low-density residential and other development at the wildland/urban interface for select regions of eastern Oregon will serve as key inputs into other INLAS models of ecological conditions and processes.

Literature Cited

Amacher, G.S.; Cruz, W.; Grebner, D.; Hyde, W.F. 1998. Environmental motivations for migration: population pressure, poverty, and deforestation in the Philippines. Land Economics. 74(1): 92-101.

Azuma, D.L.; Birch, K.R.; DelZotto, P. [et al.]. 1999. Land use change on non-federal land in western Oregon, 1973-1994. Salem, OR: Oregon Department of Forestry. 55 p.

Barlow, S.A.; Munn, I.A.; Cleaves, D.A.; Evans, D.L. 1998. The effect of urban sprawl on timber harvesting. Journal of Forestry. 96(12): 10-14.

Bengston, D.N. 1994. Changing forest values and ecosystem management. Society and Natural Resources. 7: 515-533.

Binkley, C.S. 1981. Timber supply from private nonindustrial forests. Bull. 92. New Haven, CT: School of Forestry and Environmental Studies, Yale University. 97 p.

Bockstael, N.E. 1996. Modeling economics and ecology: the importance of a spatial perspective. American Journal of Agricultural Economics. 78: 1168-1180.

Bowes, M.D.; Krutilla, J.V.; Sherman, P.B. 1984. Forest management for increased timber and water yields. Water Resources Research. 20: 655-663.

Bradshaw, T.K.; Muller, B. 1998. Impacts of rapid urban growth on farmland conversion: application of new regional land use policy models and geographical information systems. Rural Sociology. 63: 1-25.

Chomitz, K.M.; Gray, D.A. 1996. Roads, land use, and deforestation: a spatial model applied to Belize. The World Bank Economic Review. 10: 487-512.

Cleaves, D.A.; Bennett, M. 1995. Timber harvesting by nonindustrial private forest landowners in western Oregon. Western Journal of Applied Forestry. 10(2): 66-71.

Cockle, R. 2001. Northeast Oregon town threatened. The Oregonian. August 17. http://www.oregonlive.com/news/oregonian/index.ssf?/xml/story.ssf/html_standard.xsl?/base/front_page/9980493443448189.xml. (10 September).

Davis, L.S.; Ruth, L.W.; Teeguarden, D.; Henly, R.K. 1991. Ballot box forestry. Journal of Forestry. 89(12): 10-18.

Dennis, D. 1989. An economic analysis of harvest behavior: integrating forest and ownership characteristics. Forest Science. 35: 1088-1104.

Dennis, D.F. 1990. A probit analysis of the harvest decision using pooled time-series and cross-sectional data. Journal of Environmental Economics and Management. 18: 176-187.

ECONorthwest. 2000. Research report 1: density, development patterns, and definition of alternatives. Prepared for Willamette Valley Alternative Futures, Eugene, OR. On file with: ECONorthwest, 99 West 10th, Suite 400, Eugene, OR 97401.

Egan, A.F.; Luloff, A.E. 2000. The exurbanization of America's forests: research in rural social science. Journal of Forestry. 98(3): 26-30.

Englin, J.E.; Klan, M.S. 1990. Optimal taxation: timber and externalities. Journal of Environmental Economics and Management. 18: 263-275.

Helmer, E.H. 2000. The landscape ecology of tropical secondary forest in montane Costa Rica. Ecosystems. 3: 98-114.

Hyberg, B.T.; Holthausen, D.M. 1989. The behavior of nonindustrial private forest land-owners. Canadian Journal of Forest Research. 19: 1014-1023.

Johnson, R.L.; Alig, R.J.; Moore, E.; Moulton, R.J. 1997. Nonindustrial private land-owners' view of regulation. Journal of Forestry. 59: 23-28.

Kline, J.D.; Alig, R.J.; Johnson, R.L. 2000a. Forest owner incentives to protect riparian habitat. Ecological Economics. 33(1): 29-43.

Kline, J.D.; Alig, R.J.; Johnson, R.L. 2000b. Fostering the production of nontimber services among forest owners with heterogeneous objectives. Forest Science. 46(2): 302-311.

Kline, J.D.; Armstrong, C. 2001. Autopsy of a forestry ballot initiative: characterizing voter support for Oregon's Measure 64. Journal of Forestry. 99(5): 20-27.

Kline, J.D.; Azuma, D.L.; Moses, A. [In press]. Modeling the spatially dynamic distribution of humans in the Oregon (USA) Coast Range. Landscape Ecology.

Kline, J.D.; Moses, A.; Alig, R.J. 2001. Integrating urbanization into landscape-level ecological assessments. Ecosystems. 4(1): 3-18.

Kuuluvainen, J.; Karppinen, H.; Ovaskainen, V. 1996. Landowner objectives and nonindustrial private timber supply. Forest Science. 42: 300-308.

Larabee, M. 2001. Fire brings urban peril into focus. The Oregonian. August 12. http://www.oregonlive.com/news/oregonian/index.ssf?/xml/story.ssf/html_standard.xsl?/base/front_page/9975309381909169.xml. (10 September).

Lorensen, T.; Birch, K.; Lettman, G. 1993. Wildfire prevention and control in areas of residential forest land development: an analysis of fire data. Tech. Bull. Salem, OR: Public Affairs Office, Oregon Department of Forestry. [Pages unknown].

Max, W.; Lehman, D.E. 1988. A behavioral model of timber supply. Journal of Environmental Economics and Management. 15: 71-86.

McGranahan, D.A. 1999. Natural amenities drive rural population change. Agric. Econ. Rep. 781. Washington, DC: U.S. Department of Agriculture, Economic Research Service. 24 p.

Milloy, R.E. 2000. Population trends heighten West's fire woes. New York Times. August 10: Sect. A: 10.

Nelson, G.C.; Hellerstein, D. 1997. Do roads cause deforestation? Using satellite images in econometric analysis of land use. American Journal of Agricultural Economics. 79: 80-88.

Newman, D.H.; Wear, D.N. 1993. Production economics of private forestry: a comparison of industrial and nonindustrial forest owners. American Journal of Agricultural Economics. 75: 674-684.

Quinn, B. 2001. Crews abandon 10 homes to Quartz Fire. The Oregonian. August 14. http://www.oregonlive.com/news/oregonian/index.ssf?/xml/story.ssf/html_standard.xsl?/base/front_page/99779015127150166.xml. (10 September).

Row, C. 1978. Economies of tract size in timber growing. Journal of Forestry. 78: 576-582.

Schindler, B.; List, P.; Steel, B.S. 1993. Managing federal forests: public attitudes in Oregon and nationwide. Journal of Forestry. 91(7): 36-42.

Spies, T.A.; Reeves, G.H.; Burnett, K.M. [et al.]. 2002. Assessing the ecological consequences of forest policies in a multi-ownership province in Oregon. In: Liu, J.; Taylor, W.W., eds. Integrating landscape ecology into natural resource management. New York: Cambridge University Press.

Strang, W.J. 1983. On the optimal forest harvesting decision. Economic Inquiry. 11: 576-583.

Swallow, S.K.; Wear, D.N. 1993. Spatial interactions in multiple-use forestry and substitution and wealth effects for the single stand. Journal of Environmental Economics and Management. 25: 103-120.

Swanson, L.L. 1986. What attracts new residents to nonmetro areas? Res. Rep. 56. Washington, DC: U.S. Department of Agriculture, Economic Research Service. 15 p.

Thompson, R.; Thompson, P.; Jones, J.G. 1981. Classifying nonindustrial private forest land by tract size. Journal of Forestry. 81: 288-291.

Turner, M.G.; Wear, D.N.; Flamm, R.O. 1996. Land ownership and land-cover change in the southern Appalachian Highlands and the Olympic Peninsula. Ecological Applications. 6: 1150-1172.

Wear, D.N.; Bolstad, P. 1998. Land-use changes in southern Appalachian landscapes: spatial analysis and forecast evaluation. Ecosystems. 1: 575-594.

Wear, D.N.; Liu, R.; Foreman, J.M.; Sheffield, R. 1999. The effects of population growth on timber management and inventories in Virginia. Forest Ecology and Management. 118(1-3): 107-115.

Chapter 13: Evaluating Forest Products as Part of Landscape Planning

R. James Barbour, Douglas Maguire, and Ryan Singleton[1]

Abstract

The probability that harvest activities will occur on any piece of ground is a function of the accessibility of the ground (both physically and administratively), the costs of implementing the treatment, and the value of the removed material. We describe the concept of combining these three attributes to develop a utilization index that can be used to display where on a landscape timber harvest might be most fruitfully used to alter stand structural conditions. Displaying the three component parts of this index allows managers to understand that a particular polygon on the landscape is either a good candidate for timber removal or not. At least in theory, these same techniques could be applied to the collection of any number of nontimber forest products.

Keywords: Timber management, harvesting, financial analysis, wood utilization.

Introduction

Outputs from the Interior Northwest Landscape Analysis System (INLAS) modeling framework (Barbour et al. Chapter 1) will help policymakers, managers, and the public understand the capacity of subbasin-sized landscapes (about 500,000 acres, or about 202 300 hectares) located in the interior Northwest to deliver ecological, social, and economic benefits including the potential to remove timber and nontimber forest products.[2]

[1] **R. James Barbour** is a research forest products technologist U S Department of Agriculture Forest Service Pacific Northwest Research Station Forestry Sciences Laboratory 620 SW Main Suite 400 Portland OR 97205 **Douglas Maguire** is an associate professor of silviculture and **Ryan Singleton** is a research forester Department of Forest Science Oregon State University Corvallis OR 97331

[2] Nontimber forest products (also referred to as special forest products) are defined as "species harvested from forests for other than timber commodities" (Vance et al 2001) They can include "nonwoody species such as mushrooms ferns and other understory plants; nonwoody parts of trees such as cones fruits bark foliage and sap; and woody material such as firewood poles and boughs" (von Hagen and Fight 1999)

The INLAS framework tracks the vegetation on individual landscape units (polygons) and projects the quality and abundance of various resources under different management policies while considering dynamic disturbance processes (Hemstrom et al. Chapter 2, Bettinger et al. Chapter 4).

The goal of the INLAS utilization analysis is to develop a simple metric that is useful for displaying the quality and abundance of timber and nontimber forest products under different policy goals. We call this metric the "utilization potential" and use it to integrate information about the economic costs of harvesting, the administrative and physical ease of accessing each polygon, and the types and values of materials removed. The utilization potential under alternative management scenarios depends on both the current stand conditions and the long-term stand growth responses to proposed silvicultural treatments. The utilization analysis will characterize the quality and quantity of current timber and nontimber forest products, and when possible also project their future quality and quantity in response to proposed treatments.

Research Objectives

Four questions make up the primary focus of the INLAS utilization analysis:

1. What is the product potential[3] for materials removed from each stand (polygon) under alternative management scenarios?

2. Will the various management scenarios require financial subsidies?

3. What is the accessibility of timber and nontimber forest products on each polygon?

4. What is the utilization potential[4] for each polygon?

We will address secondary questions indirectly through integration with the other discipline areas covered by the INLAS project. As the project develops, these questions may change in scope and complexity, but they will initially include:

1. What road network is necessary for utilization and what hazards (e.g., fires, sediment, resource damage) are associated with this network? (Links to vegetation, wildlife, and aquatics discipline areas).

2. How does active management affect the amount or duration of smoke associated with planned and unplanned fires? (Links to vegetation and disturbance discipline areas).

3. How does the collection of nontimber forest products contribute to the local economy? (Links to sociocultural and economics discipline areas).

4. How do various management scenarios influence the abundance and accessibility of nontimber forest products? (Links to vegetation and sociocultural discipline areas).

5. How do proposed treatments enhance or degrade production of nontimber forest products? (Links to vegetation and sociocultural discipline areas).

Research Approach

A key objective of the INLAS project is to use existing models as much as possible. The INLAS utilization module will use available models and methodology to evaluate (1) accessibility, (2) product potential, (3) financial return, and (4) utilization potential (composite of 1 through 3) for timber and nontimber forest products for each polygon on the

---

[3] The suitabi ity of harvested materia s for manufacturing a variety of timber and nontimber forest products

Uti ization combines product potentia accessibi ity and financia return

landscape. Models are available to describe the mechanics of timber harvest, the finances of harvesting and processing, the impacts of harvesting on other resources and ecological processes, wood utilization, and the subsequent economic impacts of wood processing industries. Comparable information does not currently exist for most nontimber forest products. This information gap leads to an apparent emphasis on timber over nontimber forest products in this section. Where possible we will incorporate available information on nontimber forest products into the INLAS framework. We hope to highlight those areas where additional research about nontimber forest products is needed and use our analysis of wood utilization to demonstrate how this information could be used for integrated landscape modeling.

Accessibility for Extraction of Forest Products

The potential economic value of all forest products is influenced by road access, the costs associated with harvesting, and transportation to markets. Geographical information system (GIS) layers are available with current road locations, polygon delineation, topographic features, and sensitive areas. We will define the physical accessibility of each polygon as the distance from the centroid of the polygon to the nearest road. Likewise, we will determine the haul distance from each polygon to one of three major exit points from the watershed. The physical access information will point out the need for new roads by indicating where the distance to the nearest road exceeds a predetermined threshold level. For nontimber forest products, travel times will include both the time required to drive to the closest access point for each polygon plus an estimate of the time required to walk from the closest road access to collection sites. Under some policy goals, administrative access to certain polygons is restricted or prohibited. In those cases we will reduce or eliminate accessibility to them accordingly.

We will compile information into an index and display it graphically as a set of maps that indicate access to both timber and nontimber resources. Prescription design and management scenarios can make use of this information, and the implications for utilization potential and product values can also be evaluated during allocation of treatments across the subbasin. Assigning specific polygons to classes of hauling/travel distances or administratively restricted access will provide a simple method to summarize the results of the GIS analysis.

Wood Utilization

Our analyses will include the expected performance of harvested materials in various primary-manufacturing applications. Projections of the volume and characteristics of wood removed under each management scenario will allow evaluation of alternative configurations of industrial facilities that might develop over the coming decades. The wood processing facilities that use materials from the Upper Grande Ronde basin, however, are likely to draw resources from a much broader geographic area, so it will not be possible to estimate the size of the industry that treatments might support.

Tree lists generated by the vegetation simulators (Hemstrom et al. Chapter 2, Bettinger et al. Chapter 4) will identify both the trees selected for removal and those slated for retention under each management scenario. We will use information on the residual stands to evaluate future timber volume and quality. For harvested material we will use existing methods to estimate the harvesting costs (Hartsough et al. 2001), and both the quantity (Wycoff et al. 1982) and characteristics (Barbour and Parry 2001, Barbour et al. 1997, Parry et al. 1996) of wood removed under different management alternatives. Surveys of delivered log prices (e.g., Log Lines 2003) to existing facilities will supply the initial input prices for financial analyses.

We will combine elements of existing models, e.g., FEEMA (Fight and Chmelik 1999), with new programming solutions and tree-level information from the vegetation simulators (Hemstrom et al. Chapter 2, Bettinger et al. Chapter 4) to develop estimates of both potential yields of and financial returns from various wood product options.

The system will pass tree lists from the vegetation simulators included in the INLAS framework to a tool for characterizing wood product potential and conducting financial analyses. Storage of results in a database will allow production of customized tabular outputs. Combining these results with GIS data on road systems and land allocation will result in maps illustrating where different types of wood material are located, the financial costs associated with removing it, and the biophysical or sociopolitical constraints on removing it (fig. 34).

Output tables will include information on the means and variability of initial and residual stand conditions, size and volume of merchantable and submerchantable trees removed during treatments, log diameter, species distribution, and financial return. The tremendous amount of data generated from each scenario evaluated by using the INLAS process makes the creation of a succinct set of tables essential. Final formats will reflect user needs, with one possible format shown in figure 35. This format was used for a recent analysis of current and projected future conditions in the state of Montana (Barbour et al., 2004).

A set of idealized maps (fig. 36) provides an example of spatially explicit graphical results for a hypothetical landscape with four polygons. These four simple maps provide estimates of (1) accessibility, (2) wood product potential, (3) financial return, and (4) utilization potential (an index arrived at by combining 1 through 3). Accessibility is a function of road density or road proximity, physical characteristics of the land, and land use designation. Wood product potential is derived from cut-tree lists and a set of rules describing the types of material that the local industry can process. Financial return is the difference between the estimated dollar costs of harvesting, hauling, handling, and processing the raw material and the selling price of the end products. The utilization potential is a composite measure calculated from the other three that provides a visual display of the current status of the landscape in terms of the potential for wood utilization.

In the example shown here, the northwest (upper left) polygon on this landscape has low accessibility, moderate wood product potential, and a low financial return. Perhaps it is a steep unroaded area where trees are of moderate size. Financial return is low because expensive logging systems—helicopters or long-span skyline systems—are required, and the material removed is not particularly valuable. As a result, the utilization potential of this polygon is low. Managers might want to consider strategies that would not require removal of wood from this polygon. The northeast polygon might represent a different flat part of the unroaded area where there are many large shade-tolerant trees that are slated for removal because of disease concerns or a desire to enhance regeneration of seral species. Even though this is an unroaded area, the trees are large enough to justify their removal with helicopters, which lowers financial return. As a result, the utilization potential for wood products is moderate. The southwest polygon is a flat roaded area with sensitive soils, where fuel reduction treatments are desired and trees are small. Financial return is moderate because the cost of removing trees is low, but soil mitigation adds to total harvesting costs. As a result, utilization potential is low. Finally, the southeast quadrant is a flat roaded area with no operational restrictions, so the harvesting

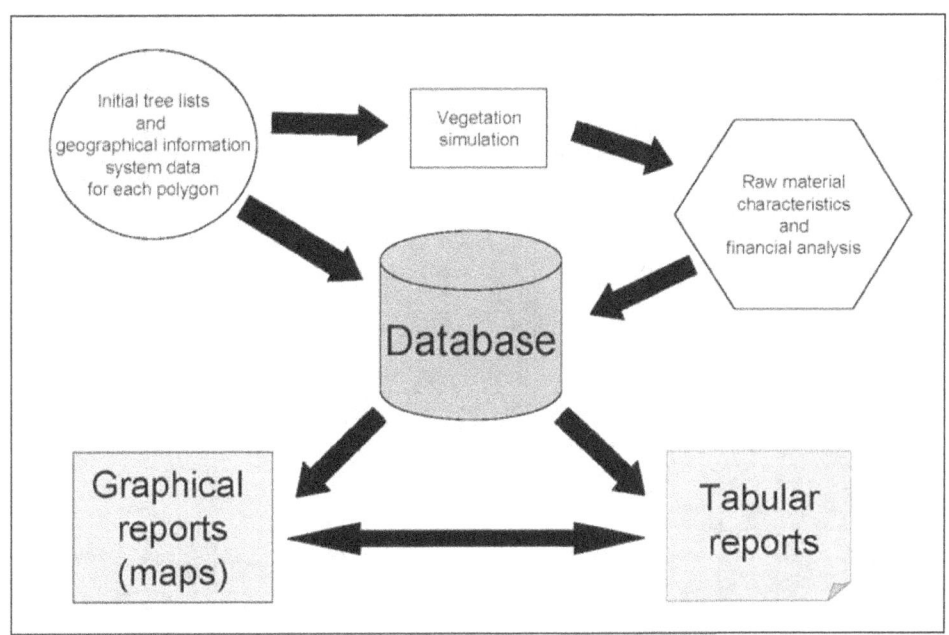

Figure 34   Steps in ana ytica process for the uti ization modu e (adapted from Christensen et a 2002
fig 1)

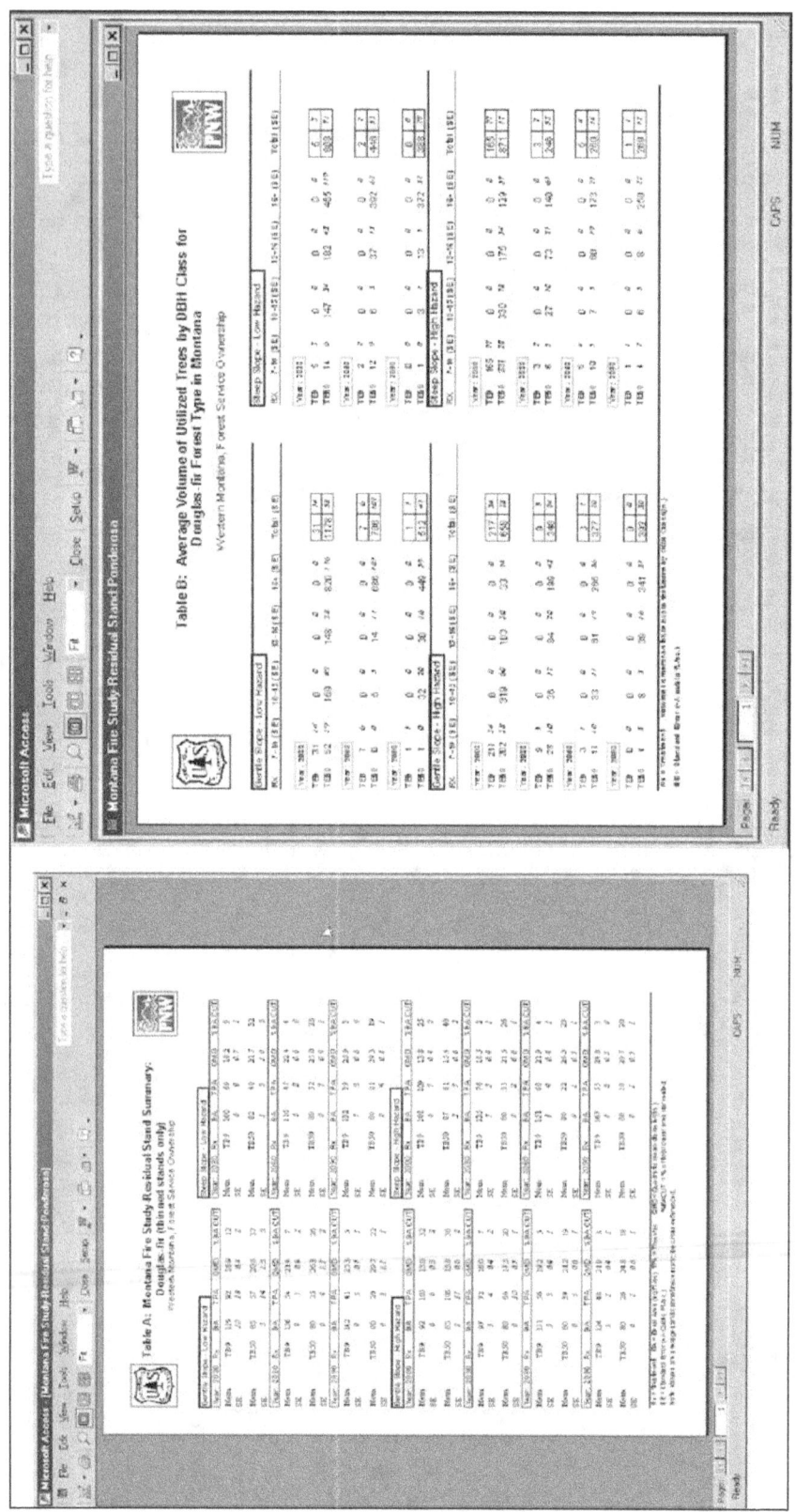

Figure 35—Potential formats for tabular reports (adapted from Christensen et al. 2002 figs. 2 and 3).

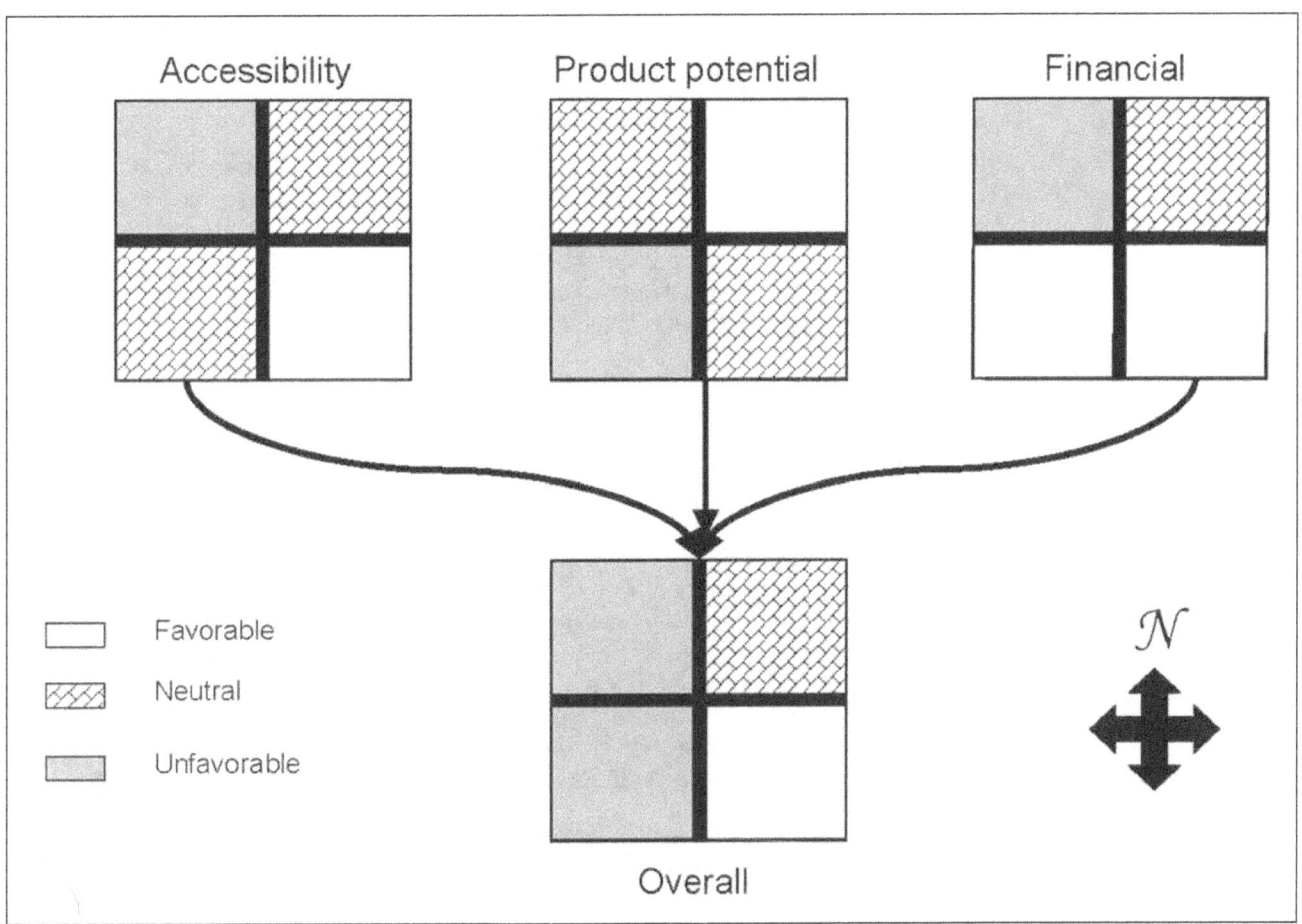

Figure 36 Example of geographic information system output for a highly simplified landscape with four polygons

costs are low; the trees are moderate in size, so the financial return is good. The utilization potential of this polygon is good. This might be the type of area where wood removals would prove most successful.

In practice, this system will account for many different constraints on operations, product characteristics, and land or stand conditions. At a glance it will provide an idea of the suitability of different parts of the landscape for treatments that involve removal of wood products at different points in time. It will also provide a visual method for diagnosing why particular polygons or groups of polygons are either desirable or undesirable in terms of wood removals. In many instances, such qualitative visual displays will produce sufficient detail. In others, they will help analysts identify places where quantitative information is needed. Tabular reports can then be used to provide that detail.

Utilization of Nontimber Forest Products

Current information on nontimber forest products is sparse. An initial task is to identify the set of potentially important nontimber forest products found in the Upper Grande Ronde watershed. Alternative products may be added or substituted as the project develops. The analyses will supply information on current demand for each of the targeted nontimber forest products. We also want to understand the contribution of different stand structures to providing a given quantity and quality of each nontimber forest product. The information will be summarized as the amount of material available by type, and where possible, its estimated economic value.

We will project nontimber forest product presence and abundance from known relations with stand structure and site or habitat type. Information to establish predictive models will be collected from the literature, and the models will be developed or refined from published and unpublished data that have not yet been incorporated into models. To the degree that existing information allows, the nontimber forest products module will provide tabular and graphical outputs similar to those for timber.

Products and Audience

The primary outputs from this analysis will be sets of tables and maps that are suitable for evaluating different management scenarios. Maps will graphically display the product potential, net financial return, relative accessibility, and overall utilization potential of timber and nontimber forest products for individual polygons or groups of polygons in a more qualitative fashion. Maps that illustrate outcomes will allow us to graphically display results more concisely, although less precisely, than the tabular format. These will be useful to groups who want a general picture of utilization potential and how it changes over time but do not need quantitative information. Often the same groups who are interested in tabular outputs will first look to maps to gain a general understanding of where the commodities they care about are most abundant. Some examples of these users are members of the public interested in utilization of wood, gathering of nontimber forest products, or forest conditions after treatments; policymakers who evaluate broad policy goals and want information on the materials generated by treatments or the costs of implementing treatments; and others interested in wood utilization or collection of nontimber forest products.

Tabular displays of data are intended to provide information to a variety of user groups who need quantitative information. These groups might include managers or planners who want information about wood or nontimber product outputs generated under different management scenarios; forest operators who bid on contracts to implement treatments; and wood processors or purchasers of nontimber forest products who need estimates of characteristics and volumes of materials available.

We anticipate that the nature of the outputs developed to describe utilization potential will evolve as we work with users and clients to implement the ideas presented in this paper. Our goal is to develop an easily understandable and useful method for evaluating the potential for use of timber and nontimber forest products that can be integrated with other resource outputs from subbasins in the interior Northwest, and to do that, collaboration with users is essential.

Literature Cited

Barbour, R.J.; Ager, A.A.; Hayes, J.L. 2004. A framework for the development and application of INLAS: the Interior Northwest Landscape Analysis System. In: Hayes, J.L.; Ager, A.A.; Barbour, R.J., tech. eds. Methods for integrated modeling of landscape change: Interior Northwest Landscape Analysis System. Gen. Tech. Rep. PNW-GTR-610. Portland, OR: U.S. Department of Agriculture, Forest Service, Pacific Northwest Research Station: 1-16. Chapter 1.

Barbour, R.J.; Fight, R.D.; Christensen, G.A.; Pinjuv, G.L.; Nagubadi, V. 2004. Thinning and prescribed fire and projected trends in wood product potential, financial return, and fire hazard in Montana. Gen. Tech. Rep. PNW-GTR-606. Portland, OR: U.S. Department of Agriculture, Forest Service, Pacific Northwest Research Station. 78 p.

Barbour, R.J.; Johnston, S.; Hayes, J.P.; Tucker, G.F. 1997. Simulated stand characteristics and wood product yields from Douglas-fir plantations managed for ecosystem objectives. Forest Ecology and Management. 91: 205-219.

Barbour, R.J.; Parry, D.L. 2001. Log and lumber grades as indicators of wood quality in 20- to 100-year-old Douglas-fir trees from thinned and unthinned stands. Gen. Tech. Rep. PNW-GTR-510. Portland, OR: U.S. Department of Agriculture, Forest Service, Pacific Northwest Research Station. 22 p.

Bettinger, P.; Graetz, D.; Ager, A.A.; Sessions, J. 2004. The SafeD forest landscape planning model. In: Hayes, J.L.; Ager, A.A.; Barbour, R.J., tech. eds. Methods for integrated modeling of landscape change: Interior Northwest Landscape Analysis System. Gen. Tech. Rep. PNW-GTR-610. Portland, OR: U.S. Department of Agriculture, Forest Service, Pacific Northwest Research Station: 41-63. Chapter 4.

Christensen, G.A.; Fight, R.D.; Barbour, R.J. 2002. Simulating fire hazard reduction, wood flow and economics of fuel treatments with FVS, FEEMA, and FIA data. In: Crookston, N.L.; Havies, R.N., comps. Second Forest Vegetation Simulator conference. Proc. RMRS-P-25. Ogden, UT: U.S. Department of Agriculture, Forest Service, Rocky Mountain Research Station: 91-103.

Fight, R.D.; Chmelik, J.T. 1999. Analysts guide to FEEMA for financial analysis of ecosystem management activities. Gen. Tech. Rep. FPL-GTR-111. Madison, WI: U.S Department of Agriculture, Forest Service, Forest Products Laboratory. 5 p.

Hartsough, B.R.; Zhang, X.; Fight, R.D. 2001. Harvesting cost model for small trees in natural stands in the interior Northwest. Forest Products Journal. 51(4): 54-61.

Hemstrom, M.; Ager, A.A.; Vavra, M. [et al.]. 2004. State and transition approach for integrating landscape models. In: Hayes, J.L.; Ager, A.A.; Barbour, R.J., tech. eds. Methods for integrated modeling of landscape change: Interior Northwest Landscape Analysis System. Gen. Tech. Rep. PNW-GTR-610. Portland, OR: U.S. Department of Agriculture, Forest Service, Pacific Northwest Research Station: 17-32. Chapter 2.

Log Lines. 2003. Monthly price reports. Mount Vernon, WA: Log Lines Price Reporting Service. 10 p.

Parry, D.L.; Filip, G.M.; Willits, S.A.; Parks, C.G. 1996. Lumber recovery and deterioration of beetle-killed Douglas-fir and grand fir in the Blue Mountains of eastern Oregon. Gen. Tech. Rep. PNW-GTR-376. Portland, OR: U.S. Department of Agriculture, Forest Service, Pacific Northwest Research Station. 24 p.

Vance, N.C.; Borsting, M.; Pilz, D.; Freed, J. 2001. Special forest products: species information guide for the Pacific Northwest. Gen. Tech. Rep. PNW-GTR-513. Portland, OR: U.S. Department of Agriculture, Forest Service, Pacific Northwest Research Station. 169 p.

von Hagen, B.; Fight, R.D. 1999. Opportunities for conservation-based development of nontimber forest products in the Pacific Northwest. Gen. Tech Rep. PNW-GTR-473. Portland, OR: U.S. Department of Agriculture, Forest Service, Pacific Northwest Research Station. 18 p.

Wycoff, W.R.; Crookston, N.L.; Stage, A.R. 1982. User's guide to the stand prognosis model. Gen. Tech. Rep. INT-133. Ogden, UT: U.S. Department of Agriculture, Forest Service, Intermountain Forest and Range Experiment Station. 112 p.

Chapter 14: Bibliography

Marti Aitken and Alan A. Ager[1]

Introduction

This chapter consists of a bibliography listing and index to recently published literature relating to the Interior Northwest Landscape Analysis System (INLAS) project area. The bibliography is intended to provide background information about the natural and socio-economic research that has been conducted in the project area. It is not a complete compendium of literature cited within the chapters of this general technical report.

The bibliography was developed by searching public and academic library databases in Oregon, Washington, and Idaho for literature specifically related to the INLAS study area. We also used DigiTop, the digital desktop library for the U.S. Department of Agriculture. The library emphasizes products focused on scientific research and provides access to databases, journals, newspapers, statistics, and other important digital information resources. The Thomson Institute for Scientific Information (ISI) Web of Knowledge was the primary platform used.

The INLAS study area is located in the Upper Grande Ronde watershed, in the Blue Mountains of northeast Oregon (fig. 37). The Upper Grande Ronde watershed is one of three hydrologic unit codes (HUC4) subwatersheds in the Grande Ronde basin and is approximately 178 000 ha. Because authors seldom reference the Upper Grande Ronde in their keywords, broader geographic references were used. These terms included Blue Mountains, Wallowa-Whitman National Forest, Umatilla National Forest, and Union County. Even broader-scale geographic references such as northeastern Oregon, or eastern Oregon were found to be too broad to be useful. Additional citation information was gathered through the Grande Ronde Model Watershed Program (GRMWP)

[1] **Marti Aitken** is a resource information manager and **Alan A. Ager** is an operations research ana yst U S Department of Agricu ture Forest Service Forestry and Range Sciences Laboratory 1401 Geke er Lane La Grande OR 97850

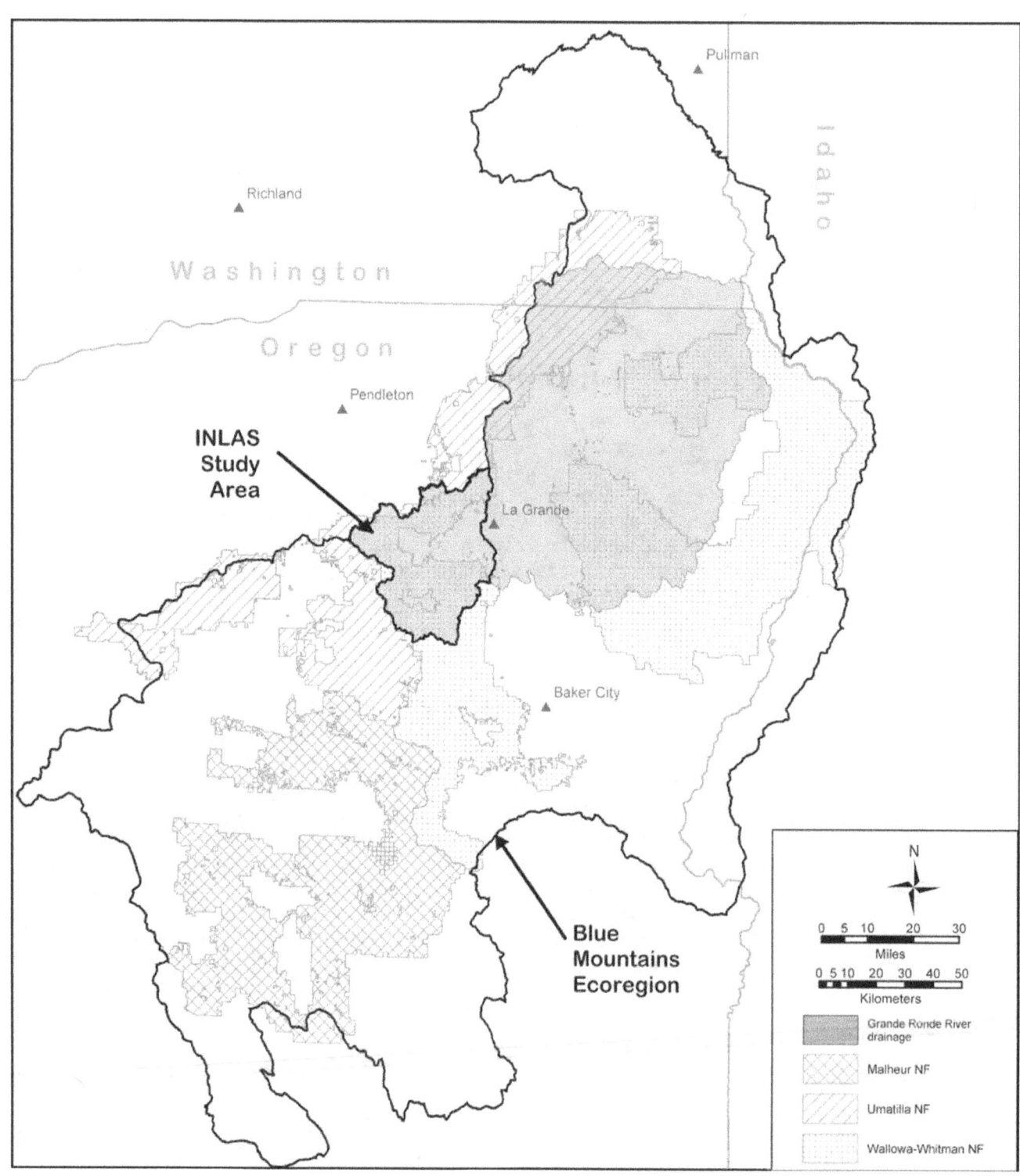

Figure 37 The INLAS study area in relation to the Grande Ronde watershed and the Blue Mountains

and from direct contact with local researchers and specialists. The GRMWP is composed of local representatives and agency personnel involved with the multiple uses of natural resources within the basin, and coordinates policy for the development, implementation, monitoring, and maintenance of the model watershed for the Grande Ronde River basin.

The complete search turned up more than 500 references. This bibliography contains the highlights of the search and consists of 358 citations dated from 1960 through April 2003. These citations cover a broad range of topics and have been grouped into the following 10 disciplines addressed in the INLAS project: aquatics, fire, grazing, herbivory, insects/disease, modeling, socioeconomics, utilization, vegetation, wildlife, and general. Citations addressing multiple disciplines (e.g., environmental impact analysis) can be found under the general grouping. Citations also have been grouped into three geographic categories: Upper Grande Ronde, Grande Ronde, and Blue Mountains. Geographic groupings are based on the best available information about the research locations. The intent was to reference as many citations as possible to the Upper Grande Ronde watershed. Citations that could not be georeferenced to the Upper Grande Ronde watershed were georeferenced either to the Grande Ronde watershed, or to the Blue Mountains, depending on the information available.

Publications include journal articles, government publications, reports, theses, and books. Although the study area includes the Starkey Experimental Forest and Range, we avoided duplicating references available through the Starkey Experimental Forest and Range Web site (http://www.fs.fed.us/pnw/starkey/publications/index.shtml). The Web site lists numerous publications related to ungulate behavior, habitat, and management. This bibliography also does not contain hydrologic and water quality references available through the Oregon Department of Water Resources Web site (http://www.wrd.state.or.us/surface_water/index.shtml) or the Oregon Department of Environmental Quality (http://www.deq.state.or.us/wq/TMDLs/TMDLs.htm).

Unfortunately, publications listed below are not on file or available for use at any central location. Libraries, especially those serving as federal depositories, are the first and best source for information. Listed theses and dissertations are available from the individual schools.

Citations are listed alphabetically by author, date, and title. The [brackets] around a date means the approximate year (exact date was not found on the publication).

Aquatics

Anderson et al. 1993
Bach 1995
Ballard 1998a
Ballard 1998b
Ballard 1999
Baxter 2002
Benner 1999
Beschta et al. 1991
Betts and Wisseman 1995
Bohle 1994
Bryant 1982
Bryce and Clarke 1996
Bryson 1993
Buckhouse and Gaither 1982
Bull and Carter 1996
Carlson 1989
Carmichael 1993
Carmichael and Boyce 1986
Chen 1996
Chen et al. 1998a
Chen et al. 1998b
Clifton et al. 1999
Cordova 1995
Corrarino and Brusven 1983
Diebel 1997
Dwire 2001
Ebersole 1994
Ebersole et al. 2002
Filip et al. 1989a
Fowler et al. 1979
Gill 1994
Helvey and Tiedemann 1978
Higgins et al. 1988
Higgins et al. 1989
Howell 2001
Huntington 1994
James 1984
Keefe et al. 1994
Keefe et al. 1995
Knight 1977
Lytjen 1998
Maloney et al. 1999
Marcot et al. 1994
McHugh 2003
McIntosh 1992
McIntosh 1995
McIntosh et al. 1994a
McIntosh et al. 1994b

McIntosh et al. 1995
McIver and Starr 2001
McLemore and Meehan 1988
Meays 2000
Mobrand et al. 1995
Moffat et al. 1990
Neitzel and Frest 1992
Noll et al. 1987
Northwest Power Planning Council 1990
Oregon Department of Fish and Wildlife [1988]
Oregon Department of Fish and Wildlife [1990]
Oregon Department of Fish and Wildlife [1993-1996]
Oregon Department of Fish and Wildlife [1994]
Oregon Department of Fish and Wildlife [1999]
Oregon Department of Transportation 1984
Parker et al. [1995]
Porath et al. 2002
Price 1998
Rieman et al. 2001
Robichaud and Brown 1999
Smith 1975a
Steel 1999
Tiedemann et al. 1988
Torgersen et al. 1999
U.S. Army Corps of Engineers 1999
U.S. Department of Agriculture, Forest Service 1992a
U.S. Department of Agriculture, Forest Service 1992b
U.S. Department of Agriculture, Forest Service 1994c
U.S. Department of Agriculture, Natural Resources Conservation Service and U.S.
  Department of Agriculture, Forest Service 1996
U.S. Department of Energy, Bonneville Power Administration 1997
U.S. Department of the Interior, Bureau of Land Management, Baker Resource Area
  Office 1993
U.S. Department of the Interior, Bureau of Reclamation, Pacific Northwest Region 1982
U.S. Department of the Interior, Geological Survey 1989
Van Cleve and Ting 1960
Walters et al. 1994
Watershed Sciences, LLC 2000
Wellman et al. 1993
Wells 1975
White et al. 1981
Widner 1991
Wissmar et al. 1994a
Wissmar et al. 1994b
Wondzell 2001

Fire and fuels

Agee 1994
Diaz-Avalos 1998
Diaz-Avalos et al. 2001

Filip and Yang-Erve 1997
Hall 1976
Hall 1977
Hall 1980
Heyerdahl 1997
Heyerdahl et al. 1996
Heyerdahl et al. 2001
Huff et al. 1995
Johnson [1998]
Langston 1995
Lehmkuhl et al. 1994
Maruka 1994
McIver and Starr 2000
McIver and Starr 2001
Mohr and Both 1996
Mutch et al. 1993
Olson 2000
Ottmar and Sandberg 2001
Petersen and Mohr 1984
Reed 1998
Robichaud and Brown 1999
Shindler and Reed 1996
Skovlin 1996
Skovlin and Thomas 1995
Thies and Niwa 2001
Tiedemann et al. 2000
Wickman 1992
Williamson 1999
Wissmar et al. 1994b

General

Anderson et al. 1993
Bauer 2000
Berggren 1983
Bormann et al. 1994
Clarke and Bryce 1997
Clarke et al. 1997
Everett 1994
Everett et al. 1994
Gast et al. 1991
Harvey et al. 1994
Jensen and Bourgeron 1994
Hessburg et al. 1994
Jaindl and Quigley 1996
Johnson et al. 1994
Keith 1991
Langston 1994
Langston 1995
Langston 2000
Marcot et al. 1994

Mutch et al. 1993
Oliver et al. 1994
Robbins and Wolf 1994
Starr et al. 2001
Tanaka et al. 1995
Thomas et al. 1976
U.S. Department of Agriculture, Forest Service 1992a
U.S. Department of Agriculture, Forest Service 1994b
U.S. Department of Agriculture, Forest Service 1998
U.S. Department of Agriculture, Forest Service 2002
U.S. Department of the Interior, Bureau of Land Management and U.S. Department of
  Agriculture, Forest Service 1990
Union Soil and Water Conservation District 1995
Whitney 1999
Williams 2000
Wissmar et al. 1994b

Grazing

Bryant 1982
Bull and Hayes 2000
Clark 1996
Cook et al. 1996
Edgerton and Smith 1971
Gebauer 1998
Gillen et al. 1985
Heyerdahl et al. 2001
Holechek et al. 1980
Holechek et al. 1981
Holechek et al. 1982a
Holechek et al. 1982b
Holechek et al. 1983
Holechek et al. 1987
Holechek and Vavra 1983
Irwin et al. 1994
Knight 1977
Maloney et al. 1999
McInnis et al. 1990
McIntosh et al. 1994a
McIntosh et al. 1994b
Moser and Witmer 2000
Porath et al. 2002
Quigley et al. 1991
Riggs et al. 2000
Roath and Krueger 1982
Sanderson et al. 1988
Sheehy 1987
Skovlin 1967
Skovlin et al. 1976
Sneva and Hyder 1962
Svejcar and Vavra 1985a

Svejcar and Vavra 1985b
Vavra and Phillips 1979
Vavra and Phillips 1980

Herbivory

Bryant 1993
Clark 1996
Cook et al. 1996
Gebauer 1998
Irwin et al. 1994
Moser and Witmer 2000
Parks et al. 1998
Riggs et al. 2000
Sheehy 1987
Skovlin 1967

Insects and disease

Aho 1974
Aho and Hadfield 1975
Beckwith and Stelzer 1979
Bull et al. 1992a
Bull et al. 1995
Delucchi 1976
Downing et al. 1977
Ferguson 1994
Filip et al. 1987
Filip et al. 1989b
Filip et al. 1989c
Filip et al. 1992
Filip et al. 1996
Filip and Parks 1987
Filip and Parks 1991
Filip and Yang-Erve 1997
Grimble and Beckwith 1992-1994
Grimble et al. 1993
Hayes and Daterman 2001
Hayes and Ragenovich 2001
Helvey and Tiedemann 1978
Hessburg et al. 1994
Kemp et al. 1986
LaBonte et al. 2001
Langston 1995
Lehmkuhl et al. 1994
Lundquist et al. 1996
Mason 1996
Mason and Paul 1988
Mason and Paul 1996
Mason and Wickman [1988]
McIver et al. 1997

Murphy and Croft 1990
Parks and Bull 1997
Parks and Flanagan 2001
Parks and Hoffman 1991
Parks et al. 1999
Parry et al. 1996
Powell 1994
Roush 1978
Ryan 1983
Ryan 1985
Ryan 1997
Swetnam et al. 1995
Thies 2001
Thies and Niwa 2001
Tiedemann et al. 2000
Torgersen 2001
Torgersen and Bull 1995
Wickman 1976
Wickman 1988
Wickman 1992
Wickman et al. 1980
Youngblood and Wickman 2002
Zack et al. 1979

Modeling

Baxter 1993
Bettinger et al. 1996a
Bettinger et al. 1996b
Chen 1996
Chen et al. 1998a
Chen et al. 1998b
Diaz-Avalos 1998
Diaz-Avalos et al. 2001
Hemstrom et al. 2002
Higgins et al. 1988
Hitchcock and Ager 1992
Kemp et al. 1986
Lundquist and Beatty 1999
Lundquist and Beatty 2002
McHugh 2003
McInnis et al. 1990
Sneva and Hyder 1962
Wells 1975
White et al. 1981

Social and economic

Applegate and O'Donnell 1994
Barklow 1987
Bormann et al. 1994
Braun 1991

Buan and Lewis 1991
Davis et al. 1991
Delucchi 1976
Downing et al. 1977
Duncan 1998
Ebert 1987
Evans 1991
Gildemeister 1998
Hall 1977
Hall and Bigler-Cole 2001
Haynes et al. 2001
Hermens and Turner 1985
Johnson [1997]
Keith 1991
Langston 1995
Langston 2000
Quigley 1992
Reed 1998
Shindler et al. [2002]
Shindler and Reed 1996
Starr and Quigley 1992
U.S. Department of the Interior, Bureau of Reclamation, Pacific Northwest Region 1982
Wells 1975
Williams 1976
Wissmar et al. 1994a
Womack 1982

Utilization

Aho 1974
Aho and Hadfield 1975
Bull and Carter 1996
Bull et al. 1997
Clausnitzer [1993]
Cochran and Barrett 1993
Cochran and Barrett 1995
Cochran and Dahms [1998]
Cochran and Seidel 1995
Coulter 1999
Filip et al. 1987
Filip et al. 1989c
Geist et al. 1989
Gill 1994
Haynes et al. 2001
Ince 1982
Klock and Lopushinsky 1980
Lennette 1999
Lundquist and Beatty 1999
Lundquist et al. 1996
McIntosh et al. 1994a
McIntosh et al. 1994b

McIver and Starr 2000
McIver and Starr 2001
Oester et al. 1995
Parry et al. 1996
Peterson and Hibbs 1989
Quigley 1992
Quigley et al. 2001
Reed 1998
Seidel 1982
Seidel and Head 1983
Shindler and Reed 1996
Skovlin et al. 1989
Tiedemann et al. 1988
Wickman 1978
Wickman 1986
Wickman et al. 1980
Williams 1988
Wilson et al. 2001
Wissmar et al. 1994a
Youngblood 2000

Vegetation

Beck 1996
Bohle 1994
Brady 2001
Brookshire 2000
Buckhouse and Gaither 1982
Bull et al. 2001b
Case 1995
Chen et al. 1998b
Clausnitzer 1979
Clausnitzer [1993]
Crowe and Clausnitzer 1997
Diaz-Avalos 1998
Diaz-Avalos et al. 2001
Dwire 2001
Ferguson 1994
Filip et al. 1989a
Filip and Yang-Erve 1997
Franklin and Dyrness 1973
Ganskopp 1978
Gebauer 1998
Hall 1973
Hall 1974
Hall 1976
Hall 1977
Hall 1980
Harrod 2001
Hemstrom 2001
Hemstrom et al. 2002

Hines 1998
Hines and Bradshaw 1997
Huntington 1994
Irwin et al. 1994
Johnson 1981
Johnson [1993]
Johnson [1998]
Johnson and Clausnitzer 1992
Lehmkuhl et al. 1994
Lennette 1999
Lundquist and Beatty 1999
Lundquist et al. 1996
Lytjen 1998
Mannan 1982
Maruka 1994
Moser and Witmer 2000
Oester et al. 1995
Olson 2000
Otting 1998
Parks et al. 1998
Parks and Schmitt 1997
Powell 1999
Reed 1998
Riegel 1989
Riggs et al. 2000
Shirley and Erickson 2001
Skovlin 1996
Skovlin et al. 1976
Skovlin and Thomas 1995
Smergut 1991
Tiedemann et al. 2000
Wissmar et al. 1994a
Wissmar et al. 1994b
Wood 1971
Youngblood 2001

Wildlife

Bolon 1994
Bryant 1993
Bull 1980
Bull 1984
Bull 1987
Bull 2000
Bull 2001
Bull [In press]
Bull and Anderson 1978
Bull and Beckwith 1993
Bull and Blumton 1997
Bull and Blumton 1999
Bull and Carter 1996

Bull and Collins 1993
Bull and Collins 1996
Bull and Hayes 2000
Bull and Hayes 2001
Bull and Hayes 2002
Bull and Heater 1995
Bull and Heater 2000
Bull and Heater 2001
Bull and Henjum 1990
Bull and Holthausen 1993
Bull et al. 1987
Bull et al. 1989
Bull et al. 1990
Bull et al. 1992a
Bull et al. 1992b
Bull et al. 1995
Bull et al. 1997
Bull et al. 2000
Bull et al. 2001a
Bull et al. 2001b
Bull and Meslow 1988
Bull and Shepherd 2003
Bull and Skovlin 1982
Bull and Wales 2001a
Bull and Wales 2001b
Cook et al. 1996
Cook et al. 1999
Ebert 1987
Edgerton and Smith 1971
Goggans 1985
Hitchcock and Ager 1992
Irwin et al. 1994
Korfhage et al. 1980
Leckenby 1984
Mannan 1982
Marcot et al. 1994
McCluskey 1976
Moore and Henny 1984
Moser and Witmer 2000
Nowak 1999
Noyes et al. 1996
Parks and Bull 1997
Parks et al. 1998
Parks et al. 1999
Pelren 1996
Pelren and Crawford 1999
Riggs et al. 2000
Sallabanks et al. 2002
Sheehy 1987
Sheehy and Slater 1998

Skovlin et al. 1989
Skovlin and Vavra 1979
Smith 1975a
Smith 1975b
Smith 1982
Snyder 2001
Thomas et al. 1976
Thomas et al. 1979
Thomas et al. 1986
Torgersen and Bull 1995
Wales 2001

Upper Grande Ronde

Anderson et al. 1993
Bach 1995
Ballard [1998a]
Bettinger et al. 1996b
Bohle 1994
Brookshire 2000
Bryce and Clarke 1996
Bull 1980
Bull 1984
Bull 1987
Bull 2000
Bull 2001
Bull [In press]
Bull and Anderson 1978
Bull and Beckwith 1993
Bull and Blumton 1997
Bull and Blumton 1999
Bull and Carter 1996
Bull and Collins 1993
Bull and Collins 1996
Bull and Hayes 2000
Bull and Hayes 2001
Bull and Hayes 2002
Bull and Heater 1995
Bull and Heater 2000
Bull and Heater 2001
Bull and Henjum 1990
Bull and Holthausen 1993
Bull and Meslow 1988
Bull et al. 1987
Bull et al. 1989
Bull et al. 1990
Bull et al. 1992a
Bull et al. 1992b
Bull et al. 1995
Bull et al. 1997
Bull et al. 2000

Bull et al. 2001b
Bull and Shepherd 2003
Bull and Skovlin 1982
Case 1995
Chen 1996
Chen et al. 1998a
Chen et al. 1998b
Clark 1996
Delucchi 1976
Dwire 2001
Edgerton and Smith 1971
Filip et al. 1987
Filip et al. 1989a
Filip et al. 1992
Filip and Parks 1987
Filip and Parks 1991
Ganskopp 1978
Gildemeister 1998
Gill 1994
Hemstrom et al. 2002
Hines 1998
Holechek et al. 1980
Holechek et al. 1981
Holechek et al. 1982a
Holechek et al. 1982b
Holechek et al. 1983
Holechek et al. 1987
Holechek and Vavra 1983
Knight 1977
Lytjen 1998
Mason and Paul 1988
Mason and Wickman [1988]
McHugh 2003
McIntosh 1992
McLemore and Meehan 1988
Otting 1998
Parks and Bull 1997
Parks et al. 1999
Parks and Schmitt 1997
Skovlin et al. 1976
Svejcar and Vavra 1985a
Swotnam et al. 1995
Torgersen and Bull 1995
U.S. Department of Agriculture, Forest Service 1992a
U.S. Department of Agriculture, Forest Service 1992b
U.S. Department of Agriculture, Forest Service 1994a
U.S. Department of Agriculture, Forest Service 1994b
U.S. Department of Agriculture, Forest Service 1994c
U.S. Department of Agriculture, Forest Service 1998
U.S. Department of Agriculture, Forest Service 2002

Union Soil and Water Conservation District 1999
Wickman 1976
Wickman 1978
Wickman 1986
Wickman 1988
Wickman et al. 1980
Youngblood 2000
Youngblood and Wickman 2002

Grande Ronde

Ballard 1998b
Ballard 1999
Bauer 2000
Baxter 2002
Beschta et al. 1991
Bryson 1993
Carmichael 1993
Carmichael and Boyce 1986
Cook et al. 1999
Corrarino and Brusven 1983
Diebel 1997
Duncan 1998
Filip et al. 1989b
Filip et al. 1989c
Hermens and Turner 1985
Hines and Bradshaw 1997
Huff et al. 1995
Huntington 1994
James 1984
Keefe et al. 1994
Keefe et al. 1995
Lennette 1999
Maruka 1994
McIntosh et al. 1994b
McIntosh et al. 1995
Mobrand et al. 1995
Neitzel and Frest 1992
Noll et al. 1987
Northwest Power Planning Council 1990
Oregon Department of Fish and Wildlife [1988]
Oregon Department of Fish and Wildlife [1990]
Oregon Department of Fish and Wildlife [1994]
Oregon Department of Fish and Wildlife [1999]
Oregon Department of Transportation 1984
Parker et al. [1995]
Ryan 1983
Ryan 1985
Ryan 1997
Sheehy and Slater 1998
Smergut 1991

Smith 1975a

Steel 1999

U.S. Army Corps of Engineers 1999

U.S. Department of Agriculture, Natural Resources Conservation Service and U.S.
    Department of Agriculture 1996

U.S. Department of Energy, Bonneville Power Administration 1997

U.S. Department of the Interior, Bureau of Land Management 1993

U.S. Department of the Interior, Bureau of Land Management and U.S. Department of
    Agriculture, Forest Service 1990

U.S. Department of the Interior, Geological Survey 1989

Union Soil and Water Conservation District 1995

Van Cleve and Ting 1960

Walters et al. 1994

Watershed Sciences, LLC 2000

Wells 1975

White et al. 1981

Whitney 1999

Wissmar et al. 1994a

Wissmar et al. 1994b

Blue Mountains

Agee 1994

Aho 1974

Aho and Hadfield 1975

Applegate and O'Donnell 1994

Barklow 1987

Baxter 1993

Beck 1996

Beckwith and Stelzer 1979

Benner 1999

Bettinger et al. 1996a

Betts and Wisseman 1995

Bolon 1994

Brady 2001

Braun 1991

Bryant 1982

Bryant 1993

Buan and Lewis 1991

Buckhouse and Gaither 1982

Bull et al. 2001a

Bull and Wales 2001a

Bull and Wales 2001b

Clarke and Bryce 1997

Clarke et al. 1997

Clausnitzer [1993]

Clausnitzer 1979

Clifton et al. 1999

Cochran and Barrett 1993

Cochran and Barrett 1995

Cochran and Dahms [1998]

Cochran and Seidel 1995
Cook et al. 1996
Cordova 1995
Coulter 1999
Crowe and Clausnitzer 1997
Diaz-Avalos 1998
Diaz-Avalos et al. 2001
Downing et al. 1977
Ebersole 1994
Ebersole et al. 2002
Ebert 1987
Evans 1991
Everett 1994
Everett et al. 1994
Ferguson 1994
Ferguson 2001
Filip et al. 1996
Filip and Yang-Erve 1997
Fowler et al. 1979
Franklin and Dyrness 1973
Gast et al. 1991
Gebauer 1998
Geist 1977
Geist et al. 1989
Geist and Strickler 1978
Gillen et al. 1985
Goggans 1985
Grimble and Beckwith 1992-1994
Grimble et al. 1993
Hall 1973
Hall 1974
Hall 1976
Hall 1977
Hall 1980
Hall and Bigler-Cole 2001
Harrod 2001
Harvey et al. 1994
Hayes and Daterman 2001
Hayes and Ragenovich 2001
Haynes et al. 2001
Helvey and Tiedemann 1978
Hemstrom 2001
Hessburg et al. 1994
Heyerdahl 1997
Heyerdahl et al. 1996
Heyerdahl et al. 2001
Higgins et al. 1988
Higgins et al. 1989
Hitchcock and Ager 1992
Howell 2001

Ince 1982
Irwin et al. 1994
Jaindl and Quigley 1996
Jensen and Bourgeron 1994
Johnson 1994
Johnson 1981
Johnson [1997]
Johnson [1998]
Johnson and Clausnitzer 1992
Johnson et al. 1994
Keith 1991
Klock and Lopushinsky 1980
Korfhage et al. 1980
Kreger and Roschke 1991
LaBonte et al. 2001
Langston 1994
Langston 1995
Langston 2000
Leckenby 1984
Lehmkuhl et al. 1994
Lundquist and Beatty 1999
Lundquist and Beatty 2002
Lundquist et al. 1996
Mannan 1982
Marcot et al. 1994
Mason 1996
Mason and Paul 1996
McInnis et al. 1990
McIver et al. 1997
McIver and Starr 2000
Mohr and Both 1996
Moore and Henny 1984
Moser and Witmer 2000
Murphy and Croft 1990
Mutch et al. 1993
Nowak 1999
Oester et al. 1995
Oliver et al. 1994
Olson 2000
Ottmar and Sandberg 2001
Parks and Hoffman 1991
Parks and Flanagan 2001
Parks et al. 1998
Parry et al. 1996
Pelren and Crawford 1999
Petersen and Mohr 1984
Peterson and Hibbs 1989
Porath et al. 2002
Powell 1994
Powell 1999

Price 1998
Quigley 1992
Quigley et al. 1991
Quigley et al. 2001
Reed 1998
Riegel 1989
Riggs et al. 2000
Roath and Krueger 1982
Robbins and Wolf 1994
Robichaud and Brown 1999
Sallabanks et al. 2002
Seidel 1982
Seidel and Head 1983
Sheehy 1987
Shindler and Reed 1996
Shirley and Erickson 2001
Skovlin 1967
Skovlin 1996
Skovlin and Thomas 1995
Skovlin and Vavra 1979
Skovlin et al. 1989
Smith 1975b
Smith 1982
Sneva and Hyder 1962
Starr and Quigley 1992
Starr et al. 2001
Svejcar and Vavra 1985b
Tanaka et al. 1995
Thies and Niwa 2001
Thies 2001
Thomas et al. 1976
Thomas et al. 1979
Thomas et al. 1986
Tiedemann et al. 1988
Tiedemann et al. 2000
Torgersen 2001
Trauba 1975
U.S. Department of Agriculture, Soil Conservation Service and Oregon State University
   Agricultural Experiment Station 1985
U.S. Department of the Interior, Bureau of Reclamation, Pacific Northwest Region 1982
U.S. Department of the Interior, Geological Survey 1996
Vavra and Phillips 1979
Vavra and Phillips 1980
Wales 2001
Wickman 1992
Widner 1991
Williams 1976
Williams 1988
Williams 2000
Williamson 1999

Wilson et al. 2001
Womack 1982
Wondzell 2001
Wood 1971
Youngblood 2001
Zack et al. 1979

Agee, J.K. 1994. Fire and weather disturbances in terrestrial ecosystems of the eastern Cascades. Gen. Tech. Rep. PNW-GTR-320. Portland, OR: U.S. Department of Agriculture, Forest Service, Pacific Northwest Research Station. 52 p. (Everett, R.L., assessment team leader, Eastside forest ecosystem health assessment; Hessburg, P.F., science team leader and tech. ed., Volume III: assessment).

Aho, P.E. 1974. Defect estimation for grand fir in the Blue Mountains of Oregon and Washington. Res. Pap. PNW-175. Portland, OR: U.S. Department of Agriculture, Forest Service, Pacific Northwest Forest and Range Experiment Station. 12 p.

Aho, P.E.; Hadfield, J.S. 1975. How to estimate defect in grand fir in the Blue Mountains of Oregon and Washington. Portland, OR: U.S. Department of Agriculture, Forest Service, Pacific Northwest Forest and Range Experiment Station. 10 p.

Anderson, J.W.; Beschta, R.L.; Boehne, P.L. [et al.]. 1993. A comprehensive approach to restoring habitat conditions needed to protect threatened salmon species in a severely degraded river—the Upper Grande Ronde River anadromous fish habitat protection, restoration and monitoring plan. In: Tellman, B.; Cortner, H.J.; Wallace, M.G. [et al.], tech. coords. Riparian management: common threads and shared interests. A western regional conference on river management strategies: Proceedings of a western regional conference on river management strategies. Gen. Tech. Rep. RM-226. Fort Collins, CO: U.S. Department of Agriculture, Forest Service, Rocky Mountain Forest and Range Experiment Station: 175-179.

Applegate, S.; O'Donnell, T., eds. 1994. Talking on paper: an anthology of Oregon letters and diaries. Corvallis, OR: Oregon State University Press. 324 p.

Bach, L. 1995. River basin assessment—Upper/Middle Grande Ronde River and Catherine Creek. Portland, OR: Oregon Department of Environmental Quality. [Pages unknown].

Ballard, T. [1998a]. 1994-1998 Grande Ronde River basin water quality monitoring report for the Upper Grande Ronde, Lower Grande Ronde, Wallowa and Imnaha sub-basins. Unpublished report. On file with: Grande Ronde Model Watershed, 10901 Island Avenue, La Grande, OR 97850.

Ballard, T. 1998b. Grande Ronde basin water quality monitoring report for six key subwatersheds. Portland, OR: U.S. Department of Energy, Bonneville Power Administration. Unpublished report. On file with: Grande Ronde Model Watershed, 10901 Island Avenue, La Grande, OR 97850.

Ballard, T. 1999. Grande Ronde River Basin, 1994-1998, water quality monitoring report. La Grande, OR: Union and Wallowa Soil and Water Conservation Districts and Grande Ronde Model Watershed Program. 211 p.

Barklow, I. 1987. From trails to rail: the post offices, stage stops, and wagon roads of Union County, Oregon. Enterprise, OR: Enchantments Publication of Oregon. 300 p.

Bauer, S.B. 2000. Grande Ronde River basin monitoring program review. Boise, ID: Pocket Water, Inc. Unpublished report. Submitted to Grande Ronde Basin Partnership. On file with: Grande Ronde Model Watershed, 10901 Island Ave., La Grande, OR 97850.

Baun, C.M.; Lewis, R. 1991. The first Oregonians: an illustrated collection of essays on traditional lifeways, federal-Indian relations, and the state's native people today. Portland, OR: Oregon Council for the Humanities. 128 p.

Baxter, C.V. 2002. Fish movement and assemblage dynamics in a Pacific Northwest riverscape. Corvallis, OR: Oregon State University. 174 p. Ph.D. dissertation.

Baxter, P.A. 1993. Utilizing GIS to analyze collections of the Eagle Cap Wilderness flora of northeastern Oregon. Pullman, WA: Washington State University. 60 p. M.S. thesis.

Beck, A.P. 1996. 4,400 years of vegetation change at Twin Lakes, Wallowa Mountains, northeastern Oregon. Pullman, WA: Washington State University. 51 p. M.A. thesis.

Beckwith, R.C.; Stelzer, M.J. 1979. The duration of cold storage and eclosion of the Douglas-fir tussock moth. Annals of the Entomological Society of America. 72(1): 158-161.

Benner, D.A. 1999. Evaporative heat loss of the upper Middle Fork of the John Day River, northeastern Oregon. Corvallis, OR: Oregon State University. 142 p. M.S. thesis.

Berggren, B.J. 1983. The minerology and morphology of loess derived soils along a traverse in northeastern Oregon. Corvallis, OR: Oregon State University. 147 p. M.S. thesis.

Beschta, R.L.; Platts, W.S.; Kauffman, J.B. [et al.]. 1991. Field review of fish habitat improvement projects in the Grande Ronde and John Day River basins in eastern Oregon. Portland, OR: U.S. Department of Energy, Bonneville Power Administration, Division of Fish and Wildlife. 53 p.

Bettinger, P.; Bradshaw, G.A.; Weaver, G.W. 1996a. Effects of geographic information system vector-raster-vector data conversion on landscape indices. Canadian Journal of Forest Research. 26(8): 1416-1425.

Bettinger, P.; Johnson, K.; Sessions, J. 1996b. Forest planning in an Oregon case study: defining the problem and attempting to meet goals with a spatial analysis technique. Environmental Management. 20(4): 565-577.

Betts, B.J.; Wisseman, R.W. 1995. Geographic range and habitat characteristics of the caddisfly *Cryptochia neosa*. Northwest Science. 69(1): 46-51.

Bohle, T.S. 1994. Stream temperatures, riparian vegetation, and channel morphology in the Upper Grande Ronde River watershed, Oregon. Corvallis, OR: Oregon State University. 116 p. M.S. thesis.

Bolon, N.A. 1994. Estimates of the values of elk in the Blue Mountains of Oregon and Washington. Gen. Tech. Rep. PNW-GTR-316. Portland, OR: U.S. Department of Agriculture, Forest Service, Pacific Northwest Research Station. 30 p.

Bormann, B.T.; Brookes, M.H.; Ford, E.D. [et al.]. 1994. Volume V: a framework for sustainable-ecosystem management. Gen. Tech. Rep. PNW-GTR-331. Portland, OR: U.S. Department of Agriculture, Forest Service, Pacific Northwest Research Station. 61 p. (Everett, R.L., assessment team leader, Eastside forest ecosystem health assessment).

Brady, T.J. 2001. The significance of population successional status to the evolution of seedling morphology in *Pinus contorta* var. *latifolia* (Pinaceae). Madroño. 48(3): 138-151.

Brookshire, E.N.J. 2000. Forests to floodplain meadows: detrital dynamics on two headwater streams. Corvallis, OR: Oregon State University. 112 p. M.S. thesis.

Bryant, L.D. 1982. Response of livestock to riparian zone exclusion. Journal of Range Management. 35(6): 780-785.

Bryant, L.D. 1993. Quality of bluebunch wheatgrass (*Agropyron spicatum*) as a winter range forage for Rocky Mountain elk (*Cervus elaphus nelsoni*) in the Blue Mountains of Oregon. Corvallis, OR: Oregon State University. 147 p. Ph.D. dissertation.

Bryce, S.A.; Clarke, S.E. 1996. Landscape-level ecological regions: linking state-level ecoregion frameworks with stream habitat classifications. Environmental Management. 20(3): 297-311 .

Bryson, D. 1993. Northeast Oregon hatchery Grande Ronde River management plan. Portland, OR: U.S. Department of Energy, Bonneville Power Administration; final report. [Pages unknown].

Buckhouse, J.C.; Gaither, R.E. 1982. Potential sediment production within vegetative communities in Oregon's Blue Mountains. Journal of Soil and Water Conservation. 37(2): 120-122.

Bull, E.L. 1980. Resource partitioning among woodpeckers in northeastern Oregon. Moscow, ID: University of Idaho. 109 p. Ph.D. dissertation.

Bull, E.L. 1984. Bird response to beetle-killed lodgepole pine. Murrelet. 64(3): 94-96.

Bull, E.L. 1987. Ecology of the pileated woodpecker in northeastern Oregon, USA. Journal of Wildlife Management. 51(2): 472-481.

Bull, E.L. 2000. Seasonal and sexual differences in American marten diet in northeastern Oregon. Northwest Science. 74(3): 186-191.

Bull, E.L. 2001. Survivorship of pileated woodpeckers in northeastern Oregon. Journal of Field Ornithology. 72(1): 131-135.

Bull, E.L. [In press]. Use of nest box use by Vaux's swifts. Journal of Field Ornithology.

Bull, E.L.; Akenson, J.J.; Henjum, M.G. 2000. Characteristics of black bear dens in trees and logs in northeastern Oregon. Northwestern Naturalist. 81: 148-153.

Bull, E.L.; Anderson, R.G. 1978. Notes on flammulated owls in northeastern Oregon. Murrelet. 59: 26-27.

Bull, E.L.; Aubry, K.B.; Wales, B.C. 2001a. Effects of disturbance on forest carnivores of conservation concern in eastern Oregon and Washington. Northwest Science. 75(Spec. issue): 180-184.

Bull, E.L.; Beckwith, R.C. 1993. Diet and foraging behavior of Vaux's swifts in northeastern Oregon. Condor. 95: 1016-1023.

Bull, E.L.; Blumton, A.K. 1997. Roosting behavior of postfledgling Vaux's swifts in northeastern Oregon. Journal of Field Ornithology. 8: 302-305.

Bull, E.L.; Blumton, A.K. 1999. Effect of fuels reduction on American martens and their prey. Res. Pap. PNW-RP-539. Portland, OR: U.S. Department of Agriculture, Forest Service, Pacific Northwest Research Station. 9 p.

Bull, E.L.; Carter, B.E. 1996. Tailed frogs: distribution, ecology, and association with timber harvest in northeastern Oregon. Res. Pap. PNW-RP-497. Portland, OR: U.S. Department of Agriculture, Forest Service, Pacific Northwest Research Station. 11 p.

Bull, E.L.; Collins, C.T. 1993. Nesting chronology, molt, and ectoparasites of Vaux's swifts in northeastern Oregon. Avocetta. 17: 203-207.

Bull, E.L.; Collins, C.T. 1996. Nest site fidelity, breeding age, and adult longevity in the Vaux's swift. North American Bird Bander. 21: 49-51.

Bull, E.L.; Hayes, M.P. 2000. Livestock effects on reproduction of the Columbia spotted frog. Journal of Range Management. 53(3): 291-294.

Bull, E.L.; Hayes, M.P. 2001. Post-breeding season movements of Columbia spotted frogs (*Rana luteiventris*) in northeastern Oregon. Western North American Naturalist. 6: 119-121.

Bull, E.L.; Hayes, M.P. 2002. Overwintering of Columbia spotted frogs in northeastern Oregon. Northwest Science. 76: 141-147.

Bull, E.L.; Heater, T.W. 1995. Intraspecific predation on American marten. Northwestern Naturalist. 76: 132-134.

Bull, E.L.; Heater, T.W. 2000. Resting and denning sites of American martens in northeastern Oregon. Northwest Science. 74(3): 179-185.

Bull, E.L.; Heater, T.W. 2001. Home range and dispersal of the American marten in northeastern Oregon. Northwestern Naturalist. 82: 7-11.

Bull, E.L.; Henjum, M.G. 1990. Ecology of the great gray owl. Gen. Tech. Rep. PNW-GTR-265. Portland, OR: U.S. Department of Agriculture, Forest Service, Pacific Northwest Research Station. 39 p.

Bull, E.L.; Hohmann, J.E.; Henjum, M.G. 1987. Northern pygmy-owl nests in northeastern Oregon. Journal of Raptor Research. 21(2): 77-78.

Bull, E.L.; Holthausen, R.S. 1993. Habitat use and management of pileated woodpeckers in northeastern Oregon. Journal of Wildlife Management. 57: 335-345.

Bull, E.L.; Holthausen, R.S.; Beckwith, R.C. 1992a. Arthropod diet of pileated woodpeckers in northeastern Oregon. Northwestern Naturalist. 73: 42-45.

Bull, E.L.; Holthausen, R.S.; Henjum, M.G. 1992b. Roost trees used by pileated woodpeckers in northeastern Oregon. Journal of Wildlife Management. 56: 786-793.

Bull, E.L.; Meslow, E.C. 1988. Breeding biology of the pileated woodpecker—management implications. Res. Note PNW-RN-474. Portland, OR: U.S. Department of Agriculture, Forest Service, Pacific Northwest Research Station. 8 p.

Bull, E.L.; Parks, C.G.; Torgersen, T.R. 1997. Trees and logs important to wildlife in the interior Columbia basin. Gen. Tech. Rep. PNW-GTR-391. Portland, OR: U.S. Department of Agriculture, Forest Service, Pacific Northwest Research Station. 55 p.

Bull, E.L.; Shepherd, J.F. 2003. Water temperature at oviposition sites of *Rana lueteiventris* in northeastern Oregon. Western North American Naturalist. 63(1): 108-113.

Bull, E.L.; Skovlin, J.M. 1982. Relationships between avifauna and streamside vegetation. Transactions of the 47th North American Wildlife and Natural Resources Conference: 496-506.

Bull, E.L.; Torgersen, T.R.; Blumton, A.K. [et al.]. 1995. Treatment of an old-growth stand and its effects on birds, ants, and large woody debris: a case study. Gen. Tech. Rep. PNW-GTR-353. Portland, OR: U.S. Department of Agriculture, Forest Service, Pacific Northwest Research Station. 12 p.

Bull, E.L.; Torgersen, T.R.; Wertz, T.L. 2001b. The importance of vegetation, insects, and neonate ungulates in black bear diet in northeast Oregon. Northwest Science. 75: 244-253.

Bull, E.L.; Wales, B.C. 2001a. Effects of disturbance on amphibians of conservation concern in eastern Oregon and Washington. Northwest Science. 75(Spec. issue): 174-179.

Bull, E.L.; Wales, B.C. 2001b. Effects of disturbance on birds of conservation concern in eastern Oregon and Washington. Northwest Science. 75(Spec. issue): 166-173.

Bull, E.L.; Wright, A.L.; Henjum, M.G. 1989. Nesting and diet of long-eared owls in conifer forests, Oregon. Condor. 91(4): 908-912.

Bull, E.L.; Wright, A.L.; Henjum, M.G. 1990. Nesting habitat of flammulated owls in Oregon. Journal of Raptor Research. 24: 52-55.

Carlson, J.Y. 1989. Effects of forest management on fish habitat and macroinvertebrates in northeast Oregon. Corvallis, OR: Oregon State University. 127 p. M.S. thesis.

Carmichael, R.W. 1993. Preliminary results of habitat patient-template analysis for Grande Ronde basin stocks of spring chinook. Tech. Memorandum. La Grande, OR: Oregon Department of Fish and Wildlife, Fish Research and Development. [Pages unknown].

Carmichael, R.W.; Boyce, R.R. 1986. U.S. v. Oregon, Grande Ronde River spring chinook production report. In: U.S. v. Oregon Subbasin Production Reports. Portland, OR: Oregon Department of Fish and Wildlife. [Irregular pagination].

Case, R.L. 1995. The ecology of riparian ecosystems of northeast Oregon: a shrub recovery at Meadow Creek and the structure and biomass of headwater Upper Grande Ronde ecosystems. Corvallis, OR: Oregon State University. 137 p. M.S. thesis.

Chen, Y.D. 1996. Hydrologic and water quality modeling for aquatic ecosystem protection and restoration in forest watersheds: a case study of stream temperature in the Upper Grande Ronde River, Oregon. Athens, GA: University of Georgia. 268 p. Ph.D. dissertation.

Chen, Y.D.; Carsel, R.F.; McCutcheon, S.C. [et al.]. 1998a. Stream temperature simulation of forested riparian areas: I. Watershed-scale model development. Journal of Environmental Engineering. 124(4): 304-315.

Chen, Y.D.; McCutcheon, S.C.; Norton, D.J. [et al.]. 1998b. Stream temperature simulation of forested riparian areas: II. Model application. Journal of Environmental Engineering. 124(4): 316-328.

Clark, P.E. 1996. Use of livestock to improve the quality of elk winter range forage in northeastern Oregon. Corvallis, OR: Oregon State University. 179 p. Ph.D. dissertation.

Clarke, S.E.; Bryce, S.A., eds. 1997. Hierarchical subdivisions of the Columbia Plateau and Blue Mountains ecoregions, Oregon, and Washington. Gen. Tech. Rep. PNW-GTR-395. Portland, OR: U.S. Department of Agriculture, Forest Service, Pacific Northwest Research Station. 114 p.

Clarke, S.E.; Garner, M.W.; McIntosh, B.A. [et al.]. 1997. Landscape-level ecoregions for seven contiguous watersheds, northeast Oregon and southeast Washington. In: Clarke, S.E.; Bryce, S.A., eds. Hierarchical subdivisions of the Columbia Plateau and Blue Mountains ecoregions, Oregon and Washington. Gen. Tech. Rep. PNW-GTR-395. Portland, OR: [U.S. Department of Agriculture], Forest Service, Pacific Northwest Research Station: 53-113.

Clausnitzer, R.R. 1979. Annual understory production as a function of overstory structure and successional status in the *Abies grandis/Pachistima myrsinites* habitat type in the Blue Mountains of southeastern Washington and northeastern Oregon. Pullman, WA: Washington State University. 58 p. M.S. thesis.

Clausnitzer, R.R. 1993. The grand fir series of northeastern Oregon and southeastern Washington [microform]: successional stages and management guide. R6-ECO-TP 050-93. Portland, OR: U.S. Department of Agriculture, Forest Service, Pacific Northwest Region, Wallowa-Whitman National Forest. 193 p.

Clifton, C.F.; Harris, R.M.; Fitzgerald, J.K. 1999. Flood effects and watershed response in the northern Blue Mountains, Oregon and Washington. In: Olsen, D.S.; Potyondy, J.P., eds. Wildland hydrology proceedings. Herdon, VA: American Water Resources Association: 175-182.

Cochran, P.H.; Barrett, J.W. 1993. Long-term response of planted ponderosa pine to thinning in Oregon's Blue Mountains. Western Journal of Applied Forestry. 8(4): 126-132.

Cochran, P.H.; Barrett, J.W. 1995. Growth and mortality of ponderosa pine poles thinned to various densities in the Blue Mountains of Oregon. Res. Pap. PNW-RP-483. Portland, OR: U.S. Department of Agriculture, Forest Service, Pacific Northwest Research Station. 27 p.

Cochran, P.H.; Dahms, W.G. [1998]. Lodgepole pine development after early spacing in the Blue Mountains of Oregon. Res. Pap. PNW-RP-503. [Portland, OR]: U.S. Departmont of Agriculture, Forest Service, Pacific Northwest Research Station. 24 p.

Cochran, P.H.; Seidel, K.W. 1995. Growth of western larch under controlled levels of stocking. In: Schmidt, W.C.; McDonald, K.J., comps. Ecology and management of *Larix* forests: a look ahead. Proceedings of an international symposium. Gen. Tech. Rep. INT-319. [Ogden, UT]: U.S. Department of Agriculture, Forest Service, Intermountain Research Station: 285-292.

Cook, J.G.; Irwin, L.L.; Bryant, L.D. [et al.]. 1999. Relations of forest cover and condition of elk: a test of the thermal cover hypothesis in summer and winter. Wildlife Monographs 141: 1-61.

Cook, J.G.; Riggs, R.A.; Tiedemann, A.R.; Irwin, L.L.; Bryant, L.D. 1996. Ungulate relationships on rangelands. In: Edge, W.D.; Olsen-Edge, S.L., eds. Proceedings of a symposium on sustaining rangeland ecosystems. [Corvallis, OR]: Oregon State University Extension Service: 155-159.

Cordova, J.J. 1995. Streamside forests, channel constraint, large woody debris characteristics, and pool morphology in low order streams, Blue Mountains, Oregon. Corvallis, OR: Oregon State University. 143 p. M.S. thesis.

Corrarino, C.A.; Brusven, M.A. 1983. The effects of reduced stream discharge on insect drift and stranding of insects. Freshwater Invertebrate Biology. 2(2): 88-98.

Coulter, E.D. 1999. Hungry Bob harvest production study: mechanical thinning for fuel reduction in the Blue Mountains of northeast Oregon. Corvallis, OR: Oregon State University. 96 p. M.S. thesis.

Crowe, E.A.; Clausnitzer, R.R. 1997. Mid-montane wetland plant associations of the Malheur, Umatilla, and Wallowa-Whitman National Forests. Tech. Pap. R6-NR-ECOL-TP-22-97. Portland, OR: U.S. Department of Agriculture, Forest Service, Pacific Northwest Region. 299 p.

Davis, L.S.; Ruth, L.W.; Teeguarden, D. [et al.]. 1991. Ballot box forestry. Journal of Forestry. 89(12): 10-18.

Delucchi, P.B. 1976. Effects of Douglas-fir tussock moth infestation on outdoor recreationists in the Blue Mountains, Oregon. Corvallis, OR: Oregon State University. 124 p. M.S. thesis.

Diaz-Avalos, C. 1998. Space-time analysis of forest fires. Seattle, WA: University of Washington. 120 p. Ph.D. dissertation.

Diaz-Avalos, C.; Peterson, D.L.; Alvarado, E. [et al.]. 2001. Space-time modelling of lightning-caused ignitions in the Blue Mountains, Oregon. Canadian Journal of Forest Research. 31(9): 1579-1593.

Diebel, K. 1997. Grande Ronde Basin Water Quality Monitoring: plans for six key subwatersheds. [La Grande, OR]. Unpublished document. On file with: Grande Ronde Model Watershed, 10901 Island Ave, La Grande, OR. Prepared for Union Soil and Water Conservation District, Wallowa Soil and Water Conservation District, and Grande Ronde Model Watershed Program. [Irregular pagination].

Downing, K.B.; Delucchi, P.B.; Williams, W.R. 1977. Impact of the Douglas-fir tussock moth on forest recreation in the Blue Mountains. Res. Pap. PNW-RP-224. Portland, OR: U.S. Department of Agriculture, Forest Service, Pacific Northwest Forest and Range Experiment Station. 14 p.

Duncan, A. 1998. History, science, the law, and watershed recovery in the Grande Ronde: a case study. ORESU-G-97-001. Corvallis, OR: Oregon Sea Grant. 82 p.

Dwire, K.A. 2001. Relations among hydrology, soils, and vegetation in riparian meadows: influence on organic matter distribution and storage. Corvallis, OR: Oregon State University. 168 p. Ph.D. dissertation.

Ebersole, J.L. 1994. Stream habitat classification and restoration in the Blue Mountains of northeast Oregon. Corvallis, OR: Oregon State University. 59 p. M.S. thesis.

Ebersole, J.L.; Liss, W.J.; Frissell, C.A. 2002. Heterogeneous thermal habitat for a stream fish assemblage. Ecological Society of America Annual Meeting Abstracts. 87: 120.

Ebert, K.M. 1987. The effects of wilderness recreation on avian species richness and distribution in the Eagle Cap Wilderness Area. Pullman, WA: Washington State University. 52 p. M.S. thesis.

Edgerton, P.J.; Smith, J.G. 1971. Seasonal forage use by deer and elk on the Starkey Experimental Forest and Range, Oregon. Res. Pap. PNW-112. Portland, OR: U.S. Department of Agriculture, Forest Service, Pacific Northwest Forest and Range Experiment Station. 12 p.

Evans, J.W. 1991. Powerful rockey: the Blue Mountains and the Oregon Trail, 1811-1883. La Grande, OR: Eastern Oregon State College and Pika Press. 374 p.

Everett, R.L., comp. 1994. Volume IV: restoration of stressed sites and processes. Gen. Tech. Rep. PNW-GTR-330. Portland, OR: U.S. Department of Agriculture, Forest Service, Pacific Northwest Research Station. 123 p. (Everett, R.L., assessment team leader, Eastside forest ecosystem health assessment; volume IV).

Everett, R.; Hessburg, P.; Jensen, M.; Bormann, B. 1994. Volume I: executive summary. Gen. Tech. Rep. PNW-GTR-317. Portland, OR: U.S. Department of Agriculture, Forest Service, Pacific Northwest Research Station. 61 p. (Everett, R.L., assessment team leader, Eastside forest ecosystem health assessment).

Ferguson, B.A. 1994. Fungal root pathogen interactions in a mixed conifer forest in the Blue Mountains of northeastern Oregon. Corvallis, OR: Oregon State University. 128 p. M.S. thesis.

Ferguson, S. 2001. Climatic variability in eastern Oregon and Washington. Northwest Science. 75(Spec. issue): 62-69.

Filip, G.M.; Bryant, L.D.; Parks, C.A. 1989a. Mass movement of river ice causes severe tree wounds along the Grande Ronde River in northeastern Oregon. Northwest Science. 63(5): 211-213.

Filip, G.M.; Christiansen, E.; Parks, C.A. 1989b. Secondary resin production increases with vigor of *Abies grandis* inoculated with *Trichosporium symbioticum* in northeastern Oregon. Res. Note PNW-RN-489. Portland, OR: U.S. Department of Agriculture, Forest Service, Pacific Northwest Research Station. 11 p.

Filip, G.M.; Colbert, J.J.; Parks, C.A. [et al.]. 1989c. Effects of thinning on volume growth of western larch infected with dwarf mistletoe in northeastern Oregon. Western Journal of Applied Forestry. 4(4): 143-144

Filip, G.M.; Parks, C.A. 1987. Simultaneous infestation by dwarf mistletoe and western spruce budworm decreases growth of Douglas-fir in the Blue Mountains of Oregon. Forest Science. 33(3): 767-773.

Filip, G.M.; Parks, C.A. 1991. First report of stem cankers caused by *Cytospora* species on *Alnus incana* in Oregon. Plant Disease. 75(12): 1286.

Filip, G.M.; Parks, C.A.; Seidel, K.W. [et al.]. 1987. Incidence of decay fungi in stumps of two thinned western larch stands in northeastern Oregon. Res. Note PNW-RN-468. Portland, OR: U.S. Department of Agriculture, Forest Service, Pacific Northwest Research Station. 5 p.

Filip, G.M.; Parks, C.A.; Starr, G.L. 1992. Incidence of wound-associated infection by *Cytospora* sp. in mountain alder, red-osier dogwood, and black hawthorn in Oregon. Northwest Science. 66(3): 194-198.

Filip, G.M.; Torgersen, T.R.; Parks, C.A. [et al.]. 1996. Insect and disease factors in the Blue Mountains. In: Jaindl, R.G.; Quigley, T.M., eds. Search for a solution: sustaining the land, people, and economy of the Blue Mountains. Washington, DC: American Forests: 169-202.

Filip, G.M.; Yang-Erve, L. 1997. Effects of prescribed burning on the viability of *Armillaria ostoyae* in mixed-conifer forest soils in the Blue Mountains of Oregon. Northwest Science. 71(2): 137-144.

Fowler, W.B.; Helvey, J.D.; Johnson, C. 1979. Baseline climatic and hydrologic relationships for the High Ridge evaluation area in the Blue Mountains of Oregon. Gen. Tech. Rep. PNW-GTR-91. Portland, OR: U.S. Department of Agriculture, Forest Service, Pacific Northwest Forest and Range Experiment Station. 17 p.

Franklin, J.F.; Dyrness, C.T. 1973. Natural vegetation in Oregon and Washington. Gen. Tech. Rep. PNW-8. Portland, OR: U.S. Department of Agriculture, Forest Service, Pacific Northwest Forest and Range Experiment Station. 417 p.

Ganskopp, D.C. 1978. Plant communities and habitat types of the Meadow Creek experimental watershed. Corvallis, OR: Oregon State University. 162 p. M.S. thesis.

Gast, W.R., Jr.; Scott, D.W.; Schmitt, D. [et al.]. 1991. Blue Mountains forest health report: new perspectives in forest health. [Portland, OR]: U.S. Department of Agriculture, Forest Service, Malheur, Umatilla, and Wallowa-Whitman National Forests. [Irregular pagination].

Gebauer, C.E. 1998 . Forest grazing and site quality: influences of cattle, big game and tree species on soil nutrients, soil compaction and vegetation of a seral forest in northeastern Oregon. Pullman, WA: Washington State University. 109 p. M.S. thesis.

Geist, J.M. 1977. Nitrogen response relationships of some volcanic ash soils. Soil Science Society of America. 41(5): 996-1000.

Geist, J.M.; Hazard, J.W.; Seidel, K.W. 1989. Assessing physical conditions of some Pacific Northwest volcanic ash soils after forest harvest. Soil Science Society of America. 53(3): 946-950.

Geist, J.M.; Strickler, G.S. 1978. Physical and chemical properties of some Blue Mountain soils in eastern Oregon. Res. Pap. PNW-236. Portland, OR: U.S. Department of Agriculture, Forest Service, Pacific Northwest Forest and Range Experiment Station. 19 p.

Gildemeister, J. 1998. Watershed history: Middle and Upper Grande Ronde River subbasins. La Grande, OR: [Publisher unknown]. [Irregular pagination].

Gill, R.E. 1994. Sediment delivery to headwater stream channels following road construction and timber harvest in the Blue Mountains, Oregon. Corvallis, OR: Oregon State University. 59 p. M.S. thesis.

Gillen, R.L.; Krueger, W.C.; Miller, R.F. 1985. Cattle use of riparian meadows in the Blue Mountains of northeastern Oregon. Journal of Range Management. 38(3): 205-209.

Goggans, R. 1985. Habitat use by flammulated owls in northeastern Oregon. Corvallis, OR: Oregon State University. 54 p. M.S. thesis.

Grimble, D.G.; Beckwith, R.C. 1992-1994. A survey of the Lepidoptera fauna from the Blue Mountains of eastern Oregon. Journal of Research on the Lepidoptera. 31(1-2): 83-102.

Grimble, D.G.; Beckwith, R.C.; Hammond, P.C. 1993. New Lepidoptera records for the Blue Mountains of eastern Oregon. Res. Pap. PNW-RP-469. Portland, OR: U.S. Department of Agriculture, Forest Service, Pacific Northwest Research Station. 6 p.

Hall, F.C. 1973. Plant communities of the Blue Mountains in eastern Oregon and southeastern Washington. R-6 Area Guide. [Portland, OR]: U.S. Department of Agriculture, Forest Service, Pacific Northwest Region. 62 p.

Hall, F.C. 1974. Key to environmental indicator plants of the Blue Mountains in eastern Oregon and southeastern Washington. R6 Area Guide 3-2. Portland, OR: U.S. Department of Agriculture, Forest Service, Pacific Northwest Region. 51 p.

Hall, F.C. 1976. Fire and vegetation in the Blue Mountains—implications for land managers. In: Komareck, E.V., ed. Tall Timbers Research Station. Proceedings of the 15th annual Tall Timbers fire ecology conference. Tallahassee, FL: Tall Timbers Research Station: 155-170.

Hall, F.C. 1977. Ecology of natural underburning in the Blue Mountains of Oregon. R6-Ecol. 79-001. Portland, OR: U.S. Department of Agriculture, Forest Service, Pacific Northwest Region. 11 p.

Hall, F.C. 1980. Fire history—Blue Mountains, Oregon. In: Stokes, M.A.; Dietrich, J.H., eds. Proceedings of fire history workshop. Fort Collins, CO: U.S. Department of Agriculture, Forest Service, Rocky Mountain Forest and Range Experiment Station: 75-81.

Hall, T.; Bigler-Cole, H. 2001. Sociocultural factors and forest health management. Northwest Science. 75(Spec. issue): 208-233.

Harrod, R.J. 2001. The effect of invasive and noxious plants on land management in eastern Oregon and Washington. Northwest Science. 75(Spec. issue): 85-90.

Harvey, A.E.; Geist, J.M.; McDonald, G.I. [et al.]. 1994. Biota and abiotic processes in eastside ecosystems: the effects of management on soil properties, processes, and productivity. Gen. Tech. Rep. PNW-GTR-323. Portland, OR: U.S. Department of Agriculture, Forest Service, Pacific Northwest Research Station. 71 p. (Everett, R.L., assessment team leader, Eastside forest ecosystem health assessment; Hessburg, P.F., science team leader and tech. ed., Volume III: assessment).

Hayes, J.L.; Daterman, G.E. 2001. Bark beetles in eastern Oregon and Washington. Northwest Science. 75(Spec. issue): 21-30.

Hayes, J.L.; Ragenovich, I. 2001. Non-native invasive forest insects of eastern Oregon and Washington. Northwest Science. 75(Spec. issue): 77-84.

Haynes, R.; Fight, R.; Lowell, E. [et al.]. 2001. Economic aspects of thinning and harvest for forest health improvement in eastern Oregon and Washington. Northwest Science. 75(Spec. issue): 199-207.

Helvey, J.D.; Tiedemann, A.R. 1978. Effects of defoliation by Douglas-fir tussock moth on timing and quantity of streamflow. Res. Note PNW-326. Portland, OR: U.S. Department of Agriculture, Forest Service, Pacific Northwest Forest and Range Experiment Station. 13 p.

Hemstrom, M. 2001. Vegetative patterns, disturbances, and forest health in eastern Oregon. Northwest Science. 75(Spec. issue): 91-109.

Hemstrom, M.; Smith, T.; Evans, T. [et al.]. 2002. Midscale analysis of streamside characteristics in the Upper Grande Ronde subbasin, northeastern Oregon. Res. Note PNW-RN-534. Portland, OR: U.S. Department of Agriculture, Forest Service, Pacific Northwest Research Station. 16 p.

Hermens, R.A.; Turner, J.E. 1985. La Grande, 1885-1985. La Grande, OR: Grande Ronde Publishing Co. 156 p.

Hessburg, P.F.; Mitchell, G.R.; Filip, G.M. 1994. Historical and current roles of insects and pathogens in eastern Oregon and Washington forested landscapes. Gen. Tech. Rep. PNW-GTR-327. Portland, OR: U.S. Department of Agriculture, Forest Service, Pacific Northwest Research Station. 72 p. (Everett, R.L., assessment team leader, Eastside forest ecosystem health assessment; Hessburg, P.F., science team leader and tech. ed., Volume III: assessment).

Heyerdahl, E.K. 1997. Spatial and temporal variation in historical fire regimes of the Blue Mountains, Oregon and Washington: the influence of climate. Seattle, WA: University of Washington. 224 p. Ph.D. dissertation.

Heyerdahl, E.K.; Agee, J.K.; Brubaker, L.B. 1996. Historical size and seasonality of low severity fires in the Blue Mountains, Oregon, from tree rings. Bulletin of the Ecological Society of America. 77(3 Suppl. Part 2): 195.

Heyerdahl, E.K.; Brubaker, L.B.; Agee, J.K. 2001. Spatial controls of historical fire regimes: a multiscale example from the interior West, USA. Ecology. 82(3): 660-678.

Higgins, D.A.; Maloney, S.B.; Tiedemann, A.R. [et al.]. 1988. Calibration of water-balance model for small watersheds in eastern Oregon. Water Resources Bulletin. 24(2): 347-360 .

Higgins, D.A.; Tiedemann, A.R.; Quigley, T.M. [et al.]. 1989. Streamflow characteristics of small watersheds in the Blue Mountains of Oregon. Water Resources Bulletin. 25(6): 1131-1149.

Hines, C.; Bradshaw, G.A. 1997. Landscape analysis of black cottonwood community dynamics, Grande Ronde River, Oregon, USA: assessing restoration potential and long-term viability. Bulletin of the Ecological Society of America. 78(4 Suppl): 109.

Hines, C.A. 1998. Evaluating the restoration potential of potential black cottonwood (*Populus trichocarpa*) from multiple scales of observation, Grande Ronde River basin, Oregon, USA. Corvallis, OR: Oregon State University. 149 p. M.S. thesis.

Hitchcock, M.; Ager, A. 1992. Microcomputer software for calculating an elk habitat effectiveness index on Blue Mountain winter range. Gen. Tech. Rep. PNW-GTR-301. Portland, OR: U.S. Department of Agriculture, Forest Service, Pacific Northwest Research Station. 13 p.

Holechek, J.; Vavra, M.; Skovlin, J. [et al.]. 1982a. Cattle diets in the Blue Mountains of Oregon, USA 1. Forests. Journal of Range Management. 35(2): 239-242.

Holechek, J.; Vavra, M.; Skovlin, J. [et al.]. 1982b. Cattle diets in the Blue Mountains of Oregon, USA 2. Grasslands. Journal of Range Management. 35(1): 109-112.

Holechek, J.L.; Berry, T.J.; Vavra, M. 1987. Grazing system influences on cattle performance on mountain range. Journal of Range Management. 40(1): 55-59.

Holechek, J.L.; Vavra, M. 1983. Fistula sample numbers required to determine cattle diets on forest and grassland ranges. Journal of Range Management. 36(3): 323-326.

Holechek, J.L.; Vavra, M.; Skovlin, J. 1980. Performance, diet and intake of yearling heifers under rest-rotation and season-long grazing systems. In: Society for Range Management 33rd annual meeting. [Place of publication unknown]: Society for Range Management: [Pages unknown].

Holechek, J.L.; Vavra, M.; Skovlin, J. 1981. Diet quality and performance of cattle on forest and grassland range. Journal of Animal Science. 53(2): 291-298.

Holechek, J.L.; Vavra, M.; Skovlin, J. 1983. Cattle diets and daily gains on a mountain riparian meadow in northeastern Oregon, USA. Journal of Range Management. 35(6): 745-757.

Howell, P.J. 2001. Effects of disturbance and management of forest health on fish and fish habitat in eastern Oregon and Washington. Northwest Science. 75(Spec. issue): 157-165.

Huff, M.H.; Ottmar, R.D.; Alvarado, E. [et al.]. 1995. Historical and current landscapes in eastern Oregon and Washington. Part II: Linking vegetation characteristics to potential fire behavior and related smoke production. Gen. Tech. Rep. PNW-GTR-355. Portland, OR: U.S. Department of Agriculture, Forest Service, Pacific Northwest Research Station. 43 p.

Huntington, C.W. 1994. Stream and riparian conditions in the Grande Ronde basin 1993. Canby, OR: Clearwater Biostudies, Inc. [Pages unknown]. Unpublished document. On file with: Grande Ronde Model Watershed, 10901 Island Ave., La Grande, OR 97850.

Ince, P.J. 1982. Economic perspective on harvesting and physical constraints on utilizing small, dead lodgepole pine. Forest Products Journal. 32(11/12): 61-66.

Irwin, L.L.; Cook, J.G.; Riggs, R.A.; Skovlin, J.M. 1994. Effects of long-term grazing by big game and livestock in the Blue Mountains forest ecosystems. Gen. Tech. Rep. PNW-GTR-325. Portland, OR: U.S. Department of Agriculture, Forest Service, Pacific Northwest Research Station. 49 p. (Everett, R.L., assessment team leader, Eastside forest ecosystem health assessment; Hessburg, P.F., science team leader and tech. ed., Volume III: assessment).

Jaindl, R.G.; Quigley, T.M., eds. 1996. Search for a solution: sustaining land, people, and the economy of the Blue Mountains. Washington, DC: American Forests. 316 p.

James, G. 1984. Grande Ronde River basin—recommended salmon and steelhead habitat improvement measures. Working Rep. [Place of publication unknown]: Confederated Tribes of the Umatilla Indian Reservation. 58 p. [plus appendices].

Jensen, M.E.; Bourgeron, P.S., tech. eds. 1994. Volume II: Ecosystem management: principles and applications. Gen. Tech. Rep. PNW-GTR-318. Portland, OR: U.S. Department of Agriculture, Forest Service, Pacific Northwest Research Station. 376 p. (Everett, R.L., assessment team leader, Eastside forest ecosystem health assessment).

Johnson, C.G., Jr. 1981. An interpretation of synecologic relationships in the Billy Meadows Area of the Wallowa-Whitman National Forest. Corvallis, OR: Oregon State University. 342 p. Ph.D. dissertation.

Johnson, C.G., Jr. 1994. Forest health in the Blue Mountains: a plant ecologist's perspective on ecosystem processes and biological diversity. Gen. Tech. Rep. PNW-GTR-339. Portland, OR: U.S. Department of Agriculture, Forest Service, Pacific Northwest Research Station. 23 p.

Johnson, C.G., Jr. [1998]. Vegetation response after wildfires in national forests of northeastern Oregon. Tech. Pap. R6-NR-ECOL-TP-06-98. [Portland, OR]: U.S. Department of Agriculture, Forest Service, Pacific Northwest Region. 157 p.

Johnson, C.G. Jr.; Clausnitzer, R.R. 1992. Plant associations of the Blue and Ochoco Mountains. Tech. Pap. R6-ERW-TP-036-92. [Portland, OR]: U.S. Department of Agriculture, Forest Service, Pacific Northwest Region, Wallowa-Whitman National Forest. 164 p.

Johnson, C.G. Jr.; Clausnitzer, R.R.; Mehringer, P.J.; Oliver, C.D. 1994. Biota and abiotic processes of eastside ecosystems: the effects of management on plant and community ecology, and on stand and landscape vegetation dynamics. Gen. Tech. Rep. PNW-GTR-322. Portland, OR: U.S. Department of Agriculture, Forest Service, Pacific Northwest Research Station. 66 p. (Everett, R.L., assessment team leader, Eastside forest ecosystem health assessment; Hessburg, P.F., science team leader and tech. ed., Volume III: assessment).

Johnson, L.C. [1997]. A brief history of Union County, Oregon. La Grande, OR: Grande Ronde Publishing Company. 76 p.

Keefe, M.; Anderson, D.J.; Carmichael, R.W. [et al.]. 1995. Early life history study of Grande Ronde River basin chinook salmon: annual progress report. Portland, OR: U.S. Department of Energy, Bonneville Power Administration. [Pages unknown].

Keefe, M.L.; Carmichael, R.W.; Jonasson, B.C. [et al.]. 1994. Fish research project Oregon: investigations into the life history of spring chinook salmon in the Grande Ronde River basin. La Grande, OR: Oregon Department of Fish and Wildlife. Annual report prepared for U.S. Department of Energy, Bonneville Power Administration, Environment, Fish and Wildlife; project number 92-026-01; contract 94BI33299. [Pages unknown]. On file with: Grande Ronde Model Watershed, 10901 Island Avenue, La Grande, OR 97850.

Keith, T. 1991. Restoring forest health in the Blue Mountains: a strategy and action plan for state and private lands. Salem, OR: Oregon Department of Forestry, Public Affairs Office. 7 p.

Kemp, W.P.; Dennis, B.; Beckwith, R.C. 1986. Stochastic phenology model for the western spruce budworm (Lepidoptera, Tortiricidae). Environmental Entomology. 15(3): 547-554.

Klock, G.O.; Lopushinsky, W. 1980. Soil water trends after clearcutting in the Blue Mountains of Oregon. Res. Note PNW-RN-361. Portland, OR: U.S. Department of Agriculture, Forest Service, Pacific Northwest Forest and Range Experiment Station. 8 p.

Knight, R.W. 1977. Streamside erosional response to animal grazing practices on Meadow Creek in northeastern Oregon. Corvallis, OR: Oregon State University. 68 p. M.S. thesis.

Korfhage, R.C.; Nelson, J.R.; Skovlin, J.M. 1980. Summer diets of Rocky Mountain elk in northeastern Oregon. Journal of Wildlife Management. 44(3): 746-750.

Kreger, A.E.; Roschke, D.J. 1991. Wallowa-Whitman National Forest soils database. Soil Survey Horizons. 32(4): 91-96.

LaBonte, J.R.; Scott, D.W.; McIver, J.D. [et al.]. 2001. Threatened, endangered, and sensitive insects in eastern Oregon and Washington forests and adjacent lands. Northwest Science. 75(Spec. issue): 185-198.

Langston, N. 1994. The general riot of the forest: landscape in the Blue Mountains. Seattle, WA: University of Washington. 324 p. Ph.D. dissertation.

Langston, N. 1995. Forest dreams, forest nightmares: the paradox of old growth in the inland West. Seattle, WA: University of Washington Press. 368 p.

Langston, N. 2000. When sound science is not enough: regulating the Blues. Journal of Forestry. 98(11): 31-35.

Leckenby, D.A. 1984. Elk use and availability of cover and forage habitat components in the Blue Mountains, northeast Oregon, 1976-1982. Wildlife Res. Rep. 14. Portland, OR: Oregon Department of Fish and Wildlife, Research and Development. 40 p.

Lehmkuhl, J.F.; Hessburg, P.F.; Everett, R.L. [et al.]. 1994. Historical and current forest landscapes of eastern Oregon and Washington. Part I: Vegetation pattern and insect and disease hazards. Gen. Tech. Rep. PNW-GTR-328. Portland, OR: U.S. Department of Agriculture, Forest Service, Pacific Northwest Research Station. 88 p. (Everett, R.L., assessment team leader, Eastside forest ecosystem health assessment; Hessburg, P.F., science team leader and tech. ed., Volume III: assessment).

Lennette, A.P. 1999. Twenty-five year response of *Larix occidentalis* stem forms to five stand density regimes in the Blue Mountains of eastern Oregon. Corvallis, OR: Oregon State University. 59 p. M.S. thesis.

Lundquist, J.E.; Beatty, J.S. 1999. A conceptual model for defining and assessing condition of forest stands. Environmental Management. 23(4): 519-525.

Lundquist, J.E.; Beatty, J.S. 2002. A method for characterizing and mimicking forest canopy gaps caused by different disturbances. Forest Science. 48(3): 582-594.

Lundquist, J.E.; King, R.M.; Beatty, J.S. 1996. Assessing the relative influence of disease in forest ecosystems in the Blue Mountains. Phytopathology. 86(11 Supplement): S38.

Lytjen, D.J. 1998. Ecology of woody riparian vegetation in tributaries of the Upper Grande Ronde River basin, Oregon. Corvallis, OR: Oregon State University. 76 p. M.S. thesis.

Maloney, S.B.; Tiedemann, A.R.; Higgins, D.A. [et al.]. 1999. Influence of stream characteristics and grazing intensity on stream temperatures in eastern Oregon. Gen. Tech. Rep. PNW-GTR-459. Portland, OR: U.S. Department of Agriculture, Forest Service, Pacific Northwest Research Station. 19 p.

Mannan, R.W. 1982. Bird populations and vegetation characteristics in managed and old-growth forests, northeastern Oregon. Corvallis, OR: Oregon State University. 67 p. Ph.D dissertation.

Marcot, B.G.; Wisdom, M.J.; Li, H.W.; Castillo, G.C. 1994. Managing for featured, threatened, endangered, and sensitive species and unique habitats for ecosystem sustainability. Gen. Tech. Rep. PNW-GTR-329. Portland, OR: U.S. Department of Agriculture, Forest Service, Pacific Northwest Research Station. 39 p. (Everett, R.L., assessment team leader, Eastside forest ecosystem health assessment; Hessburg, P.F., science team leader and tech. ed., Volume III: assessment).

Maruka, K.R. 1994. Fire history of *Pseudotsuga menziesii* and *Abies grandis* stands in the Blue Mountains of Oregon and Washington. Seattle, WA: University of Washington. 73 p. M.S. thesis.

Mason, R.R. 1996. Dynamic behavior of Douglas-fir tussock moth populations in the Pacific Northwest. Forest Science. 42(2): 182-191.

Mason, R.R.; Paul, H.G. 1988. Predation on larvae of Douglas-fir tussock moth, *Orgyia pseudotsugata* (Lepidoptera: Lymantriidae), by *Metaphidippus aeneolus* (Araneae: Salticidae). Pan-Pacific Entomologist. 64(3): 258-260.

Mason, R.R.; Paul, H.G. 1996. Case history of population change in a *Bacillus thuringiensis*-treated vs. an untreated outbreak of the western spruce budworm. Res. Note PNW-RN-521. Portland, OR: U.S. Department of Agriculture, Forest Service, Pacific Northwest Research Station. 11 p.

Mason, R.R.; Wickman, B.E. [1988]. The Douglas-fir tussock moth in the interior Pacific Northwest. In: Berryman, A.A., ed. Dynamics of forest insect populations: patterns, causes, implications. New York: Plenum Press: 179-209.

McCluskey, D.C. 1976. DDT and reproductive success of bluebirds and house wrens in northeastern Oregon. Corvallis, OR: Oregon State University. 44 p. M.S. thesis.

McHugh, P. 2003. A model-based approach to assessing the potential response of chinook salmon to habitat improvements. Logan, UT: Utah State University. 183 p. M.S. thesis.

McInnis, M.L.; Quigley, T.M.; Vavra, M. [et al.]. 1990. Predicting beef cattle stocking rates and live weight gains on eastern Oregon rangelands: description of a model. Simulation: 137-145.

McIntosh, B.A. 1992. Historical changes in anadromous fish habitats in the Upper Grande Ronde River, Oregon. Corvallis, OR: Oregon State University. 88 p. M.S. thesis.

McIntosh, B.A. 1995. Historical changes in stream habitats in the Columbia River basin. Corvallis, OR: Oregon State University. 175 p. Ph.D. dissertation.

McIntosh, B.A.; Price, D.M.; Torgersen, C.E. [et al.]. 1995. Distribution, habitat utilization, movement patterns, and the use of thermal refugia by spring chinook in the Grande Ronde, Imnaha, and John Day basins. Progress Rep. Project 93-700. Portland, OR: U.S. Department of Energy, Bonneville Power Administration. 16 p.

McIntosh, B.A.; Sedell, J.R.; Smith, J.E. [et al.]. 1994a. Historical changes in fish habitat for select river basins of eastern Oregon and Washington. Northwest Science. 68(Spec. issue): 36-53.

McIntosh, B.A.; Sedell, J.R.; Smith, J.E. [et al.]. 1994b. Management history of eastside ecosystems: changes in fish habitat over 50 years, 1935 to 1992. Gen. Tech. Rep. PNW-GTR-321. Portland, OR: U.S. Department of Agriculture, Forest Service, Pacific Northwest Research Station. 55 p. (Everett, R.L., assessment team leader, Eastside forest ecosystem health assessment; Hessburg, P.F., science team leader and tech. ed., Volume III: assessment).

McIver, J.D.; Starr, L. 2000. Environmental effects of postfire logging: literature review and annotated bibliography. Gen. Tech. Rep. PNW-GTR-486. Portland, OR: U.S. Department of Agriculture, Forest Service, Pacific Northwest Research Station. 72 p.

McIver, J.D.; Starr, L. 2001. A literature review on the environmental effects of postfire logging. Western Journal of Applied Forestry. 16(4): 159-168.

McIver, J.D.; Torgersen, T.R.; Cimon, N.J. 1997. A supercolony of the thatch ant *Formica obscuripes* Forel (Hymenoptera: Formicidae) from the Blue Mountains of Oregon. Northwest Science. 71(7): 18-29.

McLemore, C.E.; Meehan, W.R. 1988. Invertebrates of Meadow Creek, Union County, Oregon, and their use as food by trout. Res. Pap. PNW-RP-394. Portland, OR: U.S. Department of Agriculture, Forest Service, Pacific Northwest Research Station. 13 p.

Meays, C.L. 2000. Elevation, thermal environment, and stream temperatures on headwater streams in northeastern Oregon. Corvallis, OR: Oregon State University. 140 p. M.S. thesis.

Mobrand, L.; Lestell, L.; Gilbertson, L. [et al.]. 1995. Grande Ronde model watershed ecosystem diagnosis and treatment: template for planning status report for Grande Ronde Model Watershed project and progress report on the application of an ecosystem analysis method to the Grande Ronde watershed using spring chinook salmon as a diagnostic species. Portland, OR: U.S. Department of Energy, Bonneville Power Administration; final report; project 94-030. [Pages unknown]. On file with: Grande Ronde Model Watershed, 10901 Island Avenue, La Grande, OR 97850.

Moffat, R.; Wellman R.; Gordon, J. 1990. Statistical summaries of streamflow data in Oregon: monthly and annual streamflow, and flow-duration curves; open-file report 90-118. Portland, OR: U.S. Department of the Interior, Geological Survey. [Pages unknown]. Vol. 1.

Mohr, F.; Both, B. 1996. Confinement—a suppression response for the future? Fire Management Notes. 56(2): 17-22.

Moore, K.R.; Henny, C.J. 1984. Age-specific productivity and nest characteristics of Coopers hawks. Northwest Science. 58(4): 290-299.

Moser, B.W.; Witmer, G.W. 2000. The effects of elk and cattle foraging on the vegetation, birds, and small mammals of the Bridge Creek Wildlife Area, Oregon. International Biodeterioration and Biodegradation. 45(3-4): 151-157.

Murphy, C.F.; Croft, B.A. 1990. Forest ant composition and foraging following aerial spraying of carbaryl to suppress western spruce budworm. Canadian Entomologist. 122(7-8): 595-606.

Mutch, R.W.; Arno, S.F.; Brown, J.K. [et al.]. 1993. Forest health in the Blue Mountains: a management strategy for fire-adapted ecosystems. Gen. Tech. Rep. PNW-GTR-310. Portland, OR: U.S. Department of Agriculture, Forest Service, Pacific Northwest Research Station. 14 p.

Neitzel, D.A.; Frest, T.J. 1992. Survey of Columbia River basin streams for Columbia pebblesnail (*Fluminicola columbiana*) and shortface lanx (*Fisherola nuttalli*). Tech. Rep. PNL-8229. Richland, WA: Battelle Pacific Northwest Labs. 83 p.

Noll, W.; Williams, S.; Boyce, R. 1987. Grande Ronde River basin fish habitat improvement implementation plan. Portland, OR: Oregon Department of Fish and Wildlife. [Pages unknown].

Northwest Power Planning Council. 1990. Grande Ronde River subbasin salmon and steelhead production plan. Columbia basin system planning. Portland, OR: Northwest Power Planning Council, and the agencies and Indian tribes of the Columbia Basin Fish and Wildlife Authority. [Pages unknown].

Nowak, M.C. 1999. Predation rates and foraging ecology of adult female mountain lions in northeastern Oregon. Pullman, WA: Washington State University. 75 p. M.S. thesis.

Noyes, J.H.; Johnson, B.K.; Bryant, L.D. [et al.]. 1996. Effects of bull age on conception dates and pregnancy rates of cow elk. The Journal of Wildlife Management. 60(3): 508-517 .

Oester, P.T.; Emmingham, W.; Larson, P. [et al.]. 1995. Performance of ponderosa pine seedlings under four herbicide regimes in northeast Oregon. New Forests. 10(2): 123-131.

Oliver, C.D.; Irwin, L.L.; Knapp, W.H. 1994. Eastside forest management practices: historical overview, extent of their applications, and their effects on sustainability of ecosystems. Gen. Tech. Rep. PNW-GTR-324. Portland, OR: U.S. Department of Agriculture, Forest Service, Pacific Northwest Research Station. 73 p. (Everett, R.L., assessment team leader, Eastside forest ecosystem health assessment; Hessburg, P.F., science team leader and tech. ed., Volume III: assessment).

Olson, D.L. 2000. Fire in riparian zones: a comparison of historical fire occurrence in riparian and upslope forests in the Blue Mountains and southern Cascades of Oregon. Seattle, WA: University of Washington. 274 p. M.S. thesis.

Oregon Department of Fish and Wildlife. [1988]. Summer steelhead creel surveys in the Grande Ronde, Wallowa, and Imnaha Rivers for the 1987-88 run year; progress report. Portland, OR: Oregon Department of Fish and Wildlife, Fish Division. [Pages unknown].

Oregon Department of Fish and Wildlife. [1990]. Grande Ronde River subbasin: salmon and steelhead production plan. [Portland, OR]. 163 p.

Oregon Department of Fish and Wildlife. [1993-1996]. Residual hatchery steelhead: characteristics and potential interactions with spring chinook salmon in northeast Oregon; progress report. Portland, OR: [Pages unknown].

Oregon Department of Fish and Wildlife. [1994]. Smolt migration characteristics and mainstem Snake and Columbia River detection rates of Grande Ronde and Imnaha River naturally produced spring chinook salmon; progress report. Portland, OR: [Pages unknown].

Oregon Department of Fish and Wildlife. [1999]. Summer steelhead creel surveys in the Grande Ronde, Wallowa, and Imnaha Rivers for the 1998-99 run year; progress report. Portland, OR: Oregon Department of Fish and Wildlife, Fish Division. [Pages unknown].

Oregon Department of Transportation. 1984. Grande Ronde and Wallowa River scenic waterway study, Union and Wallowa Counties. [Place of publication unknown]: State Parks and Recreation Division, Scenic Waterways Program. [Pages unknown].

Otting, N.J. 1998. Ecological characteristics of montane floodplain plant communities in the Upper Grande Ronde basin, Oregon. Corvallis, OR: Oregon State University. 71 p. M.S. thesis.

Ottmar, R.D.; Sandberg, D.V. 2001. Wildland fire in eastern Oregon and Washington. Northwest Science. 75(Spec. issue): 46-54.

Parker, S.J.; Keefe, M.; Carmichael, R.W. [1995]. Natural escapement monitoring of spring chinook salmon in the Imnaha and Grande Ronde River basins; progress report. Portland, OR: Oregon Department of Fish and Wildlife. 15 p.

Parks, C.A.; Hoffman, J.T. 1991. Control of western dwarf mistletoe with the plant-growth regulator ethephon. Res. Note PNW-RN-506. Portland, OR: U.S. Department of Agriculture, Forest Service, Pacific Northwest Research Station. 4 p.

Parks, C.G.; Bednar, L.; Tiedemann, A.R. 1998. Browsing ungulates—an important consideration in dieback and mortality of Pacific yew (*Taxus brevifolia*) in a northeastern Oregon stand. Northwest Science. 72(3): 190-197.

Parks, C.G.; Bull, E.L. 1997. American marten use of rust and dwarf mistletoe brooms in northeastern Oregon. Western Journal of Applied Forestry. 12: 131-133.

Parks, C.G.; Bull, E.L.; Tinnin, R.O. [et al.]. 1999. Wildlife use of dwarf mistletoe brooms in Douglas-fir in northeastern Oregon. Western Journal of Applied Forestry. 14(2): 100-105.

Parks, C.G.; Flanagan, P.T. 2001. Dwarf mistletoes, rust disease, and stem decays in eastern Oregon and Washington. Northwest Science. 75(Spec. issue): 31-37.

Parks, C.G.; Schmitt, C.L. 1997. Wild edible mushrooms in the Blue Mountains: resource and issues. Gen. Tech. Rep. PNW-GTR-393. Portland, OR: U.S. Department of Agriculture, Forest Service, Pacific Northwest Research Station. 22 p.

Parry, D.L.; Filip, G.M.; Willits, S.A. [et al.]. 1996. Lumber recovery and deterioration of beetle-killed Douglas-fir and grand fir in the Blue Mountains of eastern Oregon. Gen. Tech. Rep. PNW-GTR-376. Portland, OR: U.S. Department of Agriculture, Forest Service, Pacific Northwest Research Station. 24 p.

Pelren, E.C. 1996. Blue grouse winter ecology in northeastern Oregon. Corvallis, OR: Oregon State University. 67 p. Ph.D. dissertation.

Pelren, E.C.; Crawford, J.A. 1999. Blue grouse nesting parameters and habitat associations in northeastern Oregon. Great Basin Naturalist. 59(4): 368-373.

Petersen, G.J.; Mohr, F.R. 1984. Underburning on white fir sites to induce natural regeneration and sanitation. Fire Management Notes. 45(2): 17-20.

Peterson, W.C.; Hibbs, D.E. 1989. Adjusting stand density management guides for sites with low stocking potential. Western Journal of Applied Forestry. 4(2): 62-65.

Porath, M.L.; Momont, P.A.; DelCurto, T. [et al.]. 2002. Offstream water and trace mineral salt as management strategies for improved cattle distribution. Journal of Animal Science. 80(2): 346-356.

Powell, D.C. 1994. Effects of the 1980s western spruce budworm outbreak on the Malheur National Forest in northeastern Oregon. Tech. Pap. R6-FI&D-TP-12-94. Portland, OR: U.S. Department of Agriculture, Forest Service, Pacific Northwest Region, Forest Insects and Diseases Group. 176 p.

Powell, D.C. 1999. Historical references about vegetation conditions: a bibliography with abstracts. Tech. Pap. F14-SO-TP-05-99. [Place of publication unknown]: U.S. Department of Agriculture, Forest Service, Pacific Northwest Region. 310 p.

Price, D.M. 1998. Multiscale habitat electivity and movement patterns by adult spring chinook salmon in seven river basins of northeast Oregon. Corvallis, OR: Oregon State University. 77 p. M.S. thesis.

Quigley, T.M. 1992. Forest health in the Blue Mountains: social and economic perspectives: science perspectives. Gen. Tech. Rep. PNW-GTR-296. Portland, OR: U.S. Department of Agriculture, Forest Service, Pacific Northwest Research Station. 9 p.

Quigley, T.M.; Hayes, J.L.; Starr, G.L. [et al.]. 2001. Improving forest health and productivity in eastern Oregon and Washington. Northwest Science. 75(Spec. issue): 234-251.

Quigley, T.M.; Tanaka, J.A.; Sanderson, H.R. [et al.]. 1991. Economically optimal private land grazing strategies for the Blue Mountains of eastern Oregon. Journal of Range Management. 44(1): 38-42.

Reed, M.A. 1998. On-site public evaluations on the use of prescribed fire and mechanical thinning. Corvallis, OR: Oregon State University. 102 p. M.S. thesis.

Riegel, G.M. 1989. Understory competition for resources in *Pinus ponderosa* forests of northeastern Oregon. Corvallis, OR: Oregon State University. 189 p. Ph.D. dissertation.

Rieman, B.; Peterson, J.T.; Clayton, J. [et al.]. 2001. Evaluations of potential effects of federal land management alternatives on trends of salmonids and their habitats in the interior Columbia River basin. Forest Ecology and Management. 153: 43-62.

Riggs, R.A.; Tiedemann, A.R.; Cook, J.G. [et al.]. 2000. Modification of mixed-conifer forests by ruminant herbivores in the Blue Mountains ecological provinces. Res. Pap. PNW-RP-527. Portland, OR: U.S. Department of Agriculture, Forest Service, Pacific Northwest Research Station. 77 p.

Roath, L.R.; Krueger, W.C. 1982. Cattle grazing and behavior on a forested range. Journal of Range Management. 33(3): 332-338.

Robbins, W.G.; Wolf, D.W. 1994. Landscape and the intermontane Northwest: an environment history. Gen. Tech. Rep. PNW-GTR-319. Portland, OR: U.S. Department of Agriculture, Forest Service, Pacific Northwest Research Station. 32 p. (Everett, R.L., assessment team leader, Eastside forest ecosystem health assessment; Hessburg, P.F., science team leader and tech. ed., Volume III: assessment).

Robichaud, P.R.; Brown, R.E. 1999. What happened after the smoke cleared: onsite erosion rates after a wildfire in eastern Oregon. Wildland Hydrology Proceedings: 419-426.

Roush, C.F. 1978. Nesting biologies and seasonal occurrence of yellowjackets in northeastern Oregon forests (Hymenoptera: Vespidae). Pullman, WA: Washington State University. 80 p. M.S. thesis.

Ryan, R.B. 1983. Population density and dynamics of the larch casebearer (Lepidoptera: Coleophoridae) in the Blue Mountains of Oregon and Washington before the build-up of exotic parasites. Canadian Entomologist. 115(19): 1095-1102.

Ryan, R.B. 1985. Relationship between parasitism of larch casebearer (Lepidoptera: Coleophoridae) and dead hosts in the Blue Mountains, 1973-1983. Canadian Entomologist. 117(8): 935-939.

Ryan, R.B. 1997. Before and after evaluation of biological control of the larch casebearer (Lepidoptera: Coleophoridae) in the Blue Mountains of Oregon and Washington 1972-1995. Environmental Entomology. 26(3): 703-715.

Sallabanks, R.; Riggs, R.A.; Cobb, L.E. 2002. Bird use of forest structural classes in grand fir forests of the Blue Mountains, Oregon. Forest Science. 48(2): 311-321.

Sanderson, H.R.; Quigley, T.M.; Spink, L.R. 1988. Defining, implementing and evaluating grazing management strategies. Journal of Soil and Water Conservation. 43(4): 345-348.

Seidel, K.W. 1982. Growth and yield of western larch: 15-year results of a levels-of-growing-stock study *Larix occidentalis*, Wallowa-Whitman National Forest, northeastern Oregon. Res. Note PNW-398. Portland, OR: U.S. Department of Agriculture, Forest Service, Pacific Northwest Forest and Range Experiment Station. 14 p.

Seidel, K.W.; Head, S.C. 1983. Regeneration in mixed-conifer partial cuttings in the Blue Mountains of Oregon and Washington. Res. Pap. PNW-310. Portland, OR: U.S. Department of Agriculture, Forest Service, Pacific Northwest Forest and Range Experiment Station. 14 p.

Sheehy, D.P. 1987. Grazing relationships of elk, deer, and cattle on seasonal rangelands in northeastern Oregon. Corvallis, OR: Oregon State University. 269 p. Ph.D. dissertation.

Sheehy, D.P.; Slater, R. 1998. Improvement of elk habitat in the North Grande Ronde Valley. Annual Report. [Place of publication unknown]: Eastern Oregon Agricultural Research Center. 125 p.

Shindler, B.A.; Brunson, M.; Stankey, G.H. 2002. Social acceptability of forest conditions and management practices: a problem analysis. Gen. Tech. Rep. PNW-GTR-537. Portland, OR: U.S. Department of Agriculture, Forest Service, Pacific Northwest Research Station. 68 p.

Shindler, B.A.; Reed, M. 1996. Forest management in the Blue Mountains: public perspectives on prescribed fire and mechanical thinning. Corvallis, OR: Oregon State University, Department of Forest Resources. 57 p.

Shirley, D.M.; Erickson, V. 2001. Aspen restoration in the Blue Mountains of northeast Oregon. In: Shepperd, W.D.; Binkley, D.; Bartos, D.L. [et al.], eds. Sustaining aspen in Western landscapes: symposium proceedings. Fort Collins, CO: U.S. Department of Agriculture, Forest Service, Rocky Mountain Research Station: 101-115.

Skovlin, J.M. 1967. Fluctuation in forage quality on summer range in the Blue Mountains. Res. Pap. PNW-44. Portland, OR: U.S. Department of Agriculture, Forest Service, Pacific Northwest Forest and Range Experiment Station. 20 p.

Skovlin, J.M. 1996. Interpreting landscape changes in the Blue Mountains of western North America through repeat photography. In: West, N.E., ed. Rangelands in a sustainable biosphere. Proceedings of the 5th international rangeland congress. Denver, CO: Society for Range Management: 521-522.

Skovlin, J.M.; Bryant, L.D.; Edgerton, P.J. 1989. Timber harvest affects elk distribution in the Blue Mountains of Oregon. Res. Pap. PNW-RP-415. Portland, OR: U.S. Department of Agriculture, Forest Service, Pacific Northwest Research Station. 10 p.

Skovlin, J.M.; Harris, R.W.; Strickler, G.S. [et al.]. 1976. Effects of cattle grazing methods on the ponderosa pine-bunchgrass range in the Pacific Northwest. Tech. Bull. 1531. [Place of publication unknown]: U.S. Department of Agriculture, Forest Service. 40 p.

Skovlin, J.M.; Thomas, J.W. 1995. Interpreting long-term trends in Blue Mountain ecosystems from repeat photography. Gen. Tech. Rep. PNW-GTR-315. Portland, OR: U.S. Department of Agriculture, Forest Service, Pacific Northwest Research Station. 102 p.

Skovlin, J.M.; Vavra, M. 1979. Winter diets of elk and deer in the Blue Mountains, Oregon. Res. Pap. PNW-260. Portland, OR: U.S. Department of Agriculture, Forest Service, Pacific Northwest Forest and Range Experiment Station. 21 p.

Smergut, T.A. 1991. *Cardaria draba* (L.) in the sagebrush ecosystem of northeastern Oregon. Corvallis, OR: Oregon State University. 42 p. M.S. thesis.

Smith, A.K. 1975a. Fish and wildlife resources of the Grande Ronde basin, Oregon, and their water requirements; federal aid to fish restoration project completion report. Portland, OR: Oregon Department of Fish and Wildlife. 51 p.

Smith, G.W. 1975b. An ecological study of the porcupine (*Erethizon dorsatum*) in the Umatilla National Forest, northeastern Oregon. Pullman, WA: Washington State University. 101 p. M.A. thesis.

Smith, G.W. 1982. Habitat use by porcupines in a ponderosa pine/Douglas-fir forest in northeastern Oregon. Northwest Science. 56(3): 236-240.

Sneva, F.A.; Hyder, D.N. 1962. Forecasting range herbage production in eastern Oregon. Station Bull. 588. Portland, OR: Oregon State University, Agricultural Experiment Station. 11 p.

Snyder, J.W. 2001. Restoration of Columbian sharp-tailed grouse into northeastern Oregon. Corvallis, OR: Oregon State University. 131 p. Ph.D. dissertation.

Starr, L.; Hayes, J.L.; Quigley, T.M. [et al.]. 2001. A framework for addressing forest health and productivity in eastern Oregon and Washington. Northwest Science. 75(Spec. issue): 1-10.

Starr, L.; Quigley, T.M., eds. 1992. Forest health in the Blue Mountains public forums, April-June 1991. B 62/2. Portland, OR: U.S. Department of Agriculture, Forest Service, Pacific Northwest Research Station, Blue Mountains Natural Resources Institute. 84 p.

Steel, E.A. 1999. In-stream factors affecting juvenile chinook salmon migration. Seattle, WA: University of Washington. 111 p. Ph.D. dissertation.

Svejcar, T.; Vavra, M. 1985a. Seasonal forage production and quality on four native and improved plant communities in eastern Oregon. Tech. Bull. 149. Corvallis, OR: Oregon State University, Agricultural Experiment Station. 24 p.

Svejcar, T.; Vavra, M. 1985b. The influence of several range improvements on estimated carrying capacity and potential beef production. Journal of Range Management. 38(5): 395-399.

Swetnam, T.W.; Wickman, B.E.; Paul, H.G. [et al.]. 1995. Historical patterns of western spruce budworm and Douglas-fir tussock moth outbreaks in the northern Blue Mountains, Oregon since A.D. 1700. Res. Pap. PNW-RP-484. Portland, OR: U.S. Department of Agriculture, Forest Service, Pacific Northwest Research Station. 27 p.

Tanaka, J.A.; Starr, L.; Quigley, T.M. 1995. Strategies and recommendations for addressing forest health issues in the Blue Mountains of Oregon and Washington. Gen. Tech. Rep. PNW-GTR-350. Portland, OR: U.S. Department of Agriculture, Forest Service, Pacific Northwest Research Station. 18 p.

Thies, W.G. 2001. Root diseases in eastern Oregon and Washington. Northwest Science. 75(Spec. issue): 38-45.

Thies, W.; Niwa, C. 2001. Interaction of various ecosystem components with prescribed fires in ponderosa pine stands in the southern Blue Mountains. Phytopathology. 91(6 Supplement): S155-S156.

Thomas, J.W., tech. ed. 1979. Wildlife habitats in managed forests: the Blue Mountains of Oregon and Washington. Handb. 553. Washington, DC: Wildlife Management Institute and U.S. Department of Agriculture, Forest Service. 512 p.

Thomas, J.W.; Leckenby, D.A.; Erickson, L.J. [et al.]. 1986. Wildlife habitat by design: national forests in the Blue Mountains of Oregon and Washington. In: Wildlife Management Institute, ed. Transactions of the 51st North American Wildlife and Natural Resources Conference. Washington, DC: Wildlife Management Institute: 203-214.

Thomas, J.W.; Miller, R.J.; Black, H. [et al.]. 1976. Guidelines for maintaining and enhancing wildlife habitat in forest management in the Blue Mountains of Oregon and Washington. In: Proceedings: Transactions of the 41st North American wildlife and natural resources conference. Washington, DC: Wildlife Management Institute: 452-476.

Tiedemann, A.R.; Klemmedson, J.O.; Bull, E.L. 2000. Solution of forest health problems with prescribed fire: Are forest productivity and wildlife at risk? Forest Ecology and Management. 127(1-3): 1-18.

Tiedemann, A.R.; Quigley, T.M.; Anderson, T.D. 1988. Effects of timber harvest on stream chemistry and dissolved nutrient losses in northeast Oregon. Forest Science. 34(2): 344-358.

Torgersen, C.E.; Price, D.M.; Li, H.W. [et al.]. 1999. Multiscale thermal refugia and stream habitat associates of chinook salmon in northeastern Oregon. Ecological Applications. 9(1): 301-319.

Torgersen, T.R. 2001. Defoliators in eastern Oregon and Washington. Northwest Science. 75(Spec. issue): 11-20.

Torgersen, T.R.; Bull, E.L. 1995. Down logs as habitat for forest dwelling ants—the primary prey of pileated woodpeckers in northeastern Oregon. Northwest Science. 69 (4): 294-303.

Trauba, W.C. 1975. Petrography of pre-tertiary rocks of the Blue Mountains, Umatilla County, northeast Oregon. Corvallis, OR: Oregon State University. 171 p. M.S. thesis.

U.S. Army Corps of Engineers. 1999. Grande Ronde River stream restoration, La Grande, Oregon: Grande Ronde Section 1135. Ecosystem restoration report and environmental assessment. La Grande, OR. [Pages unknown].

U.S. Department of Agriculture, Forest Service. 1992a. Monitoring strategy plan, appendix N- biological assessment. La Grande, OR: Wallowa-Whitman National Forest, La Grande Ranger District. [Pages unknown].

U.S. Department of Agriculture, Forest Service. 1992b. Upper Grande Ronde River anadromous fish habitat restoration and monitoring plan. Baker, OR: Wallowa-Whitman National Forest. [Pages unknown].

U.S. Department of Agriculture, Forest Service. 1994a. Biological assessment: Upper Grande Ronde River (section 7). [Place of publication unknown]: Wallowa-Whitman National Forest, La Grande Ranger District; Umatilla National Forest, North Fork John Day Ranger District; final report. [Irregular pagination].

U.S. Department of Agriculture, Forest Service. 1994b. Upper Grande Ronde watershed analysis report. La Grande, OR: Wallowa-Whitman National Forest. [Irregular pagination].

U.S. Department of Agriculture, Forest Service. 1994c. Upper Grande Ronde conservation strategy for endangered Snake River spring/summer chinook salmon. La Grande, OR: Wallowa-Whitman National Forest, La Grande Ranger District. [Irregular pagination].

U.S. Department of Agriculture, Forest Service. 1998. Beaver Creek watershed analysis. La Grande, OR: Wallowa-Whitman National Forest. [Irregular pagination].

U.S. Department of Agriculture, Forest Service. 2002. Meadow Creek watershed analysis. La Grande, OR: Wallowa-Whitman National Forest, La Grande Ranger District. [Irregular pagination].

U.S. Department of Agriculture, Natural Resources Conservation Service; U.S. Department of Agriculture, Forest Service. 1996. Grande Ronde cooperative river basin study for Union County. [La Grande, OR]. [Pages unknown]. Unpublished report. On file with: Grande Ronde Model Watershed, 10901 Island City Ave., La Grande, OR 97850.

U.S. Department of Agriculture, Soil Conservation Service; Oregon State University Agricultural Experiment Station. 1985. Soil survey of Union County area, Oregon. Washington, DC. 194 p.

U.S. Department of Energy, Bonneville Power Administration. 1997. Fish research project—Oregon investigations into the early life history of naturally produced spring chinook salmon in the Grande Ronde River basin: Bonneville Power Administration annual report 1996. [Place of publication unknown]: [Pages unknown].

U.S. Department of the Interior, Bureau of Land Management, Baker Resource Area Office. 1993. Wallowa and Grande Ronde Rivers: final management plan/environmental assessment. Washington, DC. [196 p.].

U.S. Department of the Interior, Bureau of Land Management; U.S. Department of Agriculture, Forest Service. 1990. Resource assessment: Grande Ronde River, National Wild and Scenic River. [Baker, OR]: BLM, Vale District and Wallowa-Whitman National Forest. 47 p.

U.S. Department of the Interior, Bureau of Reclamation. 1982. Baker project: Oregon, Baker and Union Counties. [Washington, DC]: [The Pacific Northwest Region]. 6 p.

U.S. Department of the Interior, Geological Survey. 1989. Water resources data, Oregon, water year 1988. Vol. 1. Eastern Oregon. [Place of publication unknown]. [Pages unknown].

U.S. Department of the Interior, Geological Survey. 1996. Geology of the Blue Mountains region of Oregon, Idaho, and Washington: petrology and tectonic evolution of pre-tertiary rocks of the Blue Mountains Region. [Place of publication unknown]. [Pages unknown].

Union Soil and Water Conservation District. 1995. Grande Ronde River basin study: abstracts. La Grande, OR. [Pages unknown].

Union Soil and Water Conservation District. 1999. Upper Grande Ronde River subbasin local agricultural water quality advisory committee—Upper Grande Ronde River subbasin agricultural water quality management area plan. La Grande, OR. [Pages unknown].

Van Cleve, R.; Ting, R. 1960. The condition of salmon stocks in the John Day, Umatilla, Walla Walla, Grande Ronde and Imnaha Rivers as reported by various fisheries agencies. Seattle, WA: University of Washington. 83 p.

Vavra, M.; Phillips, R.L. 1979. Diet quality and cattle performance on forested rangeland in northeastern Oregon. Proceedings, Western Section, American Society of Animal Science. 30: 170-173.

Vavra, M.; Phillips, R.L. 1980. Drought effects on cattle performance, diet quality and intake. Proceedings, Western Section, American Society of Animal Science. 31: 157-160 .

Wales, B.C. 2001. The management of insects, diseases, fire, and grazing and implications for terrestrial vertebrates using riparian habitats in eastern Oregon and Washington. Northwest Science. 75(Spec. issue): 119-127.

Walters, T.R.; Carmicheal, R.W.; Keefe, M. 1994. Smolt migration characteristics and mainstem Snake and Columbia River detection rates of PIT-tagged Grande Ronde and Imnaha River naturally produced spring chinook salmon: annual progress report. Portland, OR: Oregon Department of Fish and Wildlife. [Pages unknown].

Watershed Sciences, LLC. 2000. Remote sensing survey of the Grande Ronde River basin, thermal infrared and color videography; final report prepared for Oregon Department of Environmental Quality. Corvallis, OR. 49 p.

Wellman, R.E.; Gordon, J.M.; Moffat, R.L. 1993. Statistical summaries of streamflow data in Oregon: Vol. 2—Annual low and high flow, and instantaneous peak flow. Open File Report 93-63. Portland, OR: U.S. Department of the Interior, Geological Survey. [Pages unknown].

Wells, G.R. 1975. A sensitivity analysis of simulated river basin planning for capital budgeting decsions. Computer Operations and Research. 2(1): 49-54.

White, R.G.; Milligan, J.H.; Bingham, A.E. [et al.]. 1981. Effects of reduced stream discharge on fish and aquatic macroinvertebrate populations. OWRT B-045-IDA(1) 14-34-0001-8080. Springfield, VA: National Technical Information Service. 283 p.

Whitney, L. 1999. Grande Ronde Section 319 national monitoring program project, temperature monitoring summary report, 1993-1998. Portland, OR: Oregon Department of Environmental Quality. [Pages unknown].

Wickman, B.E. 1976 . Douglas-fir tussock moth egg hatch and larval development in relation to phenology of grand fir and Douglas-fir in northeastern Oregon. Res. Pap. PNW-206. Portland, OR: U.S. Department of Agriculture, Forest Service, Pacific Northwest Forest and Range Experiment Station. 13 p.

Wickman, B.E. 1978. Tree mortality and top kill related to defoliation by the Douglas-fir tussock moth in the Blue Mountains outbreak. Res. Pap. PNW-233. Portland, OR: U.S. Department of Agriculture, Forest Service, Pacific Northwest Forest and Range Experiment Station. 47 p.

Wickman, B.E. 1986. Radial growth of grand fir and Douglas-fir 10 years after defoliation by the Douglas-fir tussock moth in the Blue Mountain outbreak. Res. Pap. PNW-367. Portland, OR: U.S. Department of Agriculture, Forest Service, Pacific Northwest Research Station. 11 p.

Wickman, B.E. 1988. Seasonal variation of degree-day accumulation in relation to phenology of western spruce budworm, Douglas-fir tussock moth, and host trees in northeastern Oregon. Res. Note PNW-RN-482. Portland, OR: U.S. Department of Agriculture, Forest Service, Pacific Northwest Research Station. 11 p.

Wickman, B.E. 1992. Forest health in the Blue Mountains: the influence of insects and diseases. Forest health in the Blue Mountains: science perspectives. Gen. Tech. Rep. PNW-GTR-295. Portland, OR: U.S. Department of Agriculture, Forest Service, Pacific Northwest Research Station. 15 p. (Quigley, T.M., ed.; Forest health in the Blue Mountains: the influence of insects and disease).

Wickman, B.E.; Henshaw, D.L.; Gollob, S.K. 1980. Radial growth in grand fir and Douglas-fir related to defoliation by the Douglas-fir tussock moth in the Blue Mountains outbreak. Res. Pap. PNW-269. Portland, OR: U.S. Department of Agriculture, Forest Service, Pacific Northwest Forest and Range Experiment Station. 23 p.

Widner, G.L. 1991. Summer low flow characteristics of forest streams in northeast Oregon. Corvallis, OR: Oregon State University. 93 p. M.S. thesis.

Williams, J.D. 1988. Overland flow and sediment production potentials in logged and nonlogged sites of a ponderosa pine forest in northeastern Oregon. Corvallis, OR: Oregon State University. 108 p. M.S. thesis.

Williams, M. 2000. Putting 'flesh on the carbon-based bones' of forest history. In: Agnoletti, M.; Anderson, S., eds. Methods and approaches in forest history. Wallingford, United Kingdom: CABI Publishing: 35-46.

Williams, W.R. 1976. The economic impact of Douglas-fir tussock moth on private recreation businesses in northeastern Oregon. Corvallis, OR: Oregon State University. 73 p. M.S. thesis.

Williamson, N.M. 1999. Crown fuel characteristics, stand structure, and fire hazard in riparian forests of the Blue Mountains, Oregon. Seattle, WA: University of Washington. 98 p. M.S. thesis.

Wilson, D.; Maguire, D.; Ager, A. 2001. Effects of forest planning regulations on potential small diameter timber harvest from overstocked stands on the Umatillla National Forest. Misc. Rep. Pendleton, OR: U.S. Department of Agriculture, Forest Service, Umatilla National Forest. [Pages unknown].

Wissmar, R.C.; Smith, J.E.; McIntosh, B.A. [et al.]. 1994a. A history of resource use and disturbance in riverine basins of eastern Oregon and Washington (early 1800s-1900s). Northwest Science. 68(Spec. issue): 1-35.

Wissmar, R.C.; Smith, J.E.; McIntosh, B.A. [et al.]. 1994b. Ecological health of river basins in forested regions of eastern Washington and Oregon. Gen. Tech. Rep. PNW-GTR-326. [Portland, OR]: U.S. Department of Agriculture, Forest Service, Pacific Northwest Research Station. 65 p. (Everett, R.L., assessment team leader, Eastside forest ecosystem health assessment; Hessburg, P.F., science team leader and tech. ed., Volume III: assessment).

Womack, B. 1982. Prehistoric settlement patterns in the Crow and Elk Creek drainages Wallowa-Whitman National Forest, northeastern Oregon, USA. Northwest Anthropological Research Notes. 15(2): 220.

Wondzell, S. 2001. The influence of forest health and protection treatments on erosion and stream sedimentation in forested watersheds of eastern Oregon and Washington. Northwest Science. 75(Spec. issue): 128-140.

Wood, B.W. 1971. Response of Canada milkvetch (*Astragalus canadensis* var. *mortonii* (Nutt.) Wats.) to range and forest improvement practices in northeastern Oregon. Corvallis, OR: Oregon State University. 166 p. Ph.D. dissertation.

Youngblood, A. 2000. Damage to residual trees and advance regeneration from skyline and forwarder yarding in mixed-conifer stands of northeastern Oregon. Western Journal of Applied Forestry. 15(2): 101-107.

Youngblood, A. 2001. Old-growth forest structure in eastern Oregon and Washington. Northwest Science. 75(Spec. issue): 110-118.

Youngblood, A.; Wickman, B.E. 2002. The role of disturbance in creating dead wood: insect defoliation and tree mortality in northeastern Oregon. In: Laudenslayer, W.F., Jr.; Shea, P.J.; Valentine, B.E. [et al.], tech. coords. Proceedings of the symposium on the ecology and management of dead wood in Western forests. Gen. Tech. Rep. PSW-GTR-181. Albany, CA: U.S. Department of Agriculture, Forest Service, Pacific Southwest Research Station: 155-168.

Zack, R.S.; Davis, E.J.; Raffa, K. 1979. A new host record and notes on *Nosodendron californicum* Horn (Coleoptera: Nosodendridae). Coleopterists Bulletin. 33(1): 74.